# Lecture Notes in Computer Science        8890

*Commenced Publication in 1973*
Founding and Former Series Editors:
Gerhard Goos, Juris Hartmanis, and Jan van Leeuwen

T0213854

Adrian-Horia Dediu   Manuel Lozano
Carlos Martín-Vide (Eds.)

# Theory and Practice of Natural Computing

Third International Conference, TPNC 2014
Granada, Spain, December 9-11, 2014
Proceedings

 Springer

Volume Editors

Adrian-Horia Dediu
Rovira i Virgili University
Research Group on Mathematical Linguistics (GRLMC)
Av. Catalunya, 35
43002 Tarragona, Spain
E-mail: adrian.dediu@urv.cat

Manuel Lozano
University of Granada
School of Computer and Telecommunication Engineering
Department of Computer Science and Artificial Intelligence (DECSAI)
Periodista Daniel Saucedo Aranda, s/n
18071 Granada, Spain,
E-mail: lozano@decsai.ugr.es

Carlos Martín-Vide
Rovira i Virgili University
Research Group on Mathematical Linguistics (GRLMC)
Av. Catalunya, 35
43002 Tarragona, Spain
E-mail: carlos.martin@urv.cat

ISSN 0302-9743                                e-ISSN 1611-3349
ISBN 978-3-319-13748-3                        e-ISBN 978-3-319-13749-0
DOI 10.1007/978-3-319-13749-0
Springer Cham Heidelberg New York Dordrecht London

Library of Congress Control Number: 2014955447

LNCS Sublibrary: SL 1 – Theoretical Computer Science and General Issues

*Typesetting:* Camera-ready by author, data conversion by Scientific Publishing Services, Chennai, India

Printed on acid-free paper

Springer is part of Springer Science+Business Media (www.springer.com)

# Preface

This volume contains the papers presented at the Third International Conference on the Theory and Practice of Natural Computing (TPNC 2014), held in Granada, Spain, during December 9–11, 2014.

The scope of TPNC is rather broad, containing topics of either theoretical, experimental, or applied interest. The topics include but are not limited to:

- Nature-inspired models of computation
    - amorphous computing
    - cellular automata
    - chaos and dynamical systems-based computing
    - evolutionary computing
    - membrane computing
    - neural computing
    - optical computing
    - swarm intelligence

- Synthesizing nature by means of computation
    - artificial chemistry
    - artificial immune systems
    - artificial life

- Nature-inspired materials
    - computing with DNA
    - nanocomputing
    - physarum computing
    - quantum computing and quantum information
    - reaction-diffusion computing

- Information processing in nature
    - developmental systems
    - fractal geometry
    - gene assembly in unicellular organisms
    - rough/fuzzy computing in nature
    - synthetic biology
    - systems biology

- Applications of natural computing to algorithms, bioinformatics, control, cryptography, design, economics, graphics, hardware, learning, logistics, optimization, pattern recognition, programming, robotics, telecommunications etc.

There were 47 submissions. The committee decided to accept 22 papers, which represents an acceptance rate of 46.81%.

Part of the success in the management of the submissions and reviews is due to the excellent facilities provided by the EasyChair conference management system.

We would like to thank all invited speakers and authors for their contributions, the Program Committee and the external reviewers for their cooperation, the University of Granada for the excellent facilities put at our disposal, and Springer for its very professional publishing work.

September 2014

Adrian-Horia Dediu<br>
Manuel Lozano<br>
Carlos Martín-Vide

# Organization

TPNC 2014 was organized by the Soft Computing and Intelligent Information Systems – SCI²S group, from the University of Granada, and the Research Group on Mathematical Linguistics – GRLMC, from Rovira i Virgili University, Tarragona.

## Program Committee

| | |
|---|---|
| Hussein A. Abbass | University of New South Wales, Canberra, Australia |
| Uwe Aickelin | University of Nottingham, UK |
| Thomas Bäck | Leiden University, The Netherlands |
| Christian Blum | University of the Basque Country, San Sebastián, Spain |
| Jinde Cao | Southeast University, Nanjing, China |
| Vladimir Cherkassky | University of Minnesota at Minneapolis, USA |
| Sung-Bae Cho | Yonsei University, Seoul, South Korea |
| Andries P. Engelbrecht | University of Pretoria, South Africa |
| Terence C. Fogarty | London South Bank University, UK |
| Fernando Gomide | State University of Campinas, Brazil |
| Inman Harvey | University of Sussex, Brighton, UK |
| Francisco Herrera | University of Granada, Spain |
| Tzung-Pei Hong | National University of Kaohsiung, Taiwan |
| Thomas Jansen | Aberystwyth University, UK |
| Yaochu Jin | University of Surrey, Guildford, UK |
| Okyay Kaynak | Boğaziçi University, Istanbul, Turkey |
| Satoshi Kobayashi | University of Electro-Communications, Tokyo, Japan |
| Soo-Young Lee | Korea Advanced Institute of Science and Technology, Daejeon, South Korea |
| Derong Liu | University of Illinois at Chicago, USA |
| Manuel Lozano | University of Granada, Spain |
| Carlos Martín-Vide (Chair) | Rovira i Virgili University, Tarragona, Spain |
| Ujjwal Maulik | Jadavpur University, Kolkata, India |
| Risto Miikkulainen | University of Texas at Austin, USA |
| Frank Neumann | University of Adelaide, Australia |
| Leandro Nunes de Castro | Mackenzie University, São Paulo, Brazil |
| Erkki Oja | Aalto University, Finland |
| Lech Polkowski | Polish–Japanese Institute of Information Technology, Warsaw, Poland |
| Brian J. Ross | Brock University, St. Catharines, Canada |

| | |
|---|---|
| Marc Schoenauer | University of Paris Sud, Orsay, France |
| Biplab Kumar Sikdar | Bengal Engineering and Science University, Shibpur, India |
| Dipti Srinivasan | National University of Singapore, Singapore |
| Darko Stefanovic | University of New Mexico, Albuquerque, USA |
| Umberto Straccia | University of Pisa, Italy |
| Thomas Stützle | Université Libre de Bruxelles, Belgium |
| Ponnuthurai N. Suganthan | Nanyang Technological University, Singapore |
| Johan Suykens | KU Leuven, Belgium |
| El-Ghazali Talbi | University of Lille 1, France |
| Jon Timmis | University of York, UK |
| Fernando J. Von Zuben | State University of Campinas, Brazil |
| Michael N. Vrahatis | University of Patras, Greece |
| Xin Yao | University of Birmingham, UK |

## External Reviewers

Basu, Srinka
Das, Sukanta
Dediu, Adrian-Horia
Ghosh, Soumyabrata
Maiti, Nirmalya

Maji, Pradipta
Mo, Dandan
Seki, Shinnosuke
Tapia, Lydia
Williams, Lance

## Organizing Committee

Adrian-Horia Dediu, Tarragona
Carlos García-Martínez, Córdoba
Carlos Martín-Vide, Tarragona (Co-chair)
Manuel Lozano, Granada (Co-chair)
Francisco Javier Rodríguez, Granada
Florentina-Lilica Voicu, Tarragona

# Table of Contents

## Nature-Inspired Models of Computation

## Applications of Natural Computing I

# Nature-Inspired Computing Architectures

# Applications of Natural Computing II

# Information Processing in Nature

# Ultrametric Vs. Quantum Query Algorithms

Rūsiņš Freivalds

Institute of Mathematics and Computer Science, University of Latvia
Raiņa bulvāris 29, Riga, LV-1459, Latvia*
Rusins.Freivalds@mii.lu.lv

**Abstract.** Ultrametric algorithms are similar to probabilistic algorithms but they describe the degree of indeterminism by $p$-adic numbers instead of real numbers. This paper introduces the notion of ultrametric query algorithms and shows an example of advantages of ultrametric query algorithms over deterministic, probabilistic and quantum query algorithms.

**Keywords:** Nature-inspired models of computation, ultrametric algorithms, probabilistic algorithms, quantum algorithms.

## 1 Introduction

Let $f : \{0,1\}^n \to \{0,1\}$ be a Boolean function. A query algorithm is an algorithm for computing $f(x_1, \ldots, x_n)$ that accesses $x_1, \ldots, x_n$ by asking questions about the values of $x_i$. The complexity of a query algorithm is the maximum number of questions that it asks. The query complexity of a function $f$ is the minimum complexity of a query algorithm correctly computing $f$. The theory of computation studies various models of computation: deterministic, non-deterministic, and probabilistic and quantum (see [27,1,9,10,11,12,13,14] on traditional models of computation and [24,3,21,7] on quantum computation). Similarly, there are query algorithms of all those types.

Deterministic, nondeterministic, probabilistic and quantum query algorithms are widely considered in literature (e.g., see survey [6]). We introduce a new type of query algorithms, namely, ultrametric query algorithms. All ultrametric algorithms and particularly ultrametric query algorithms rather closely follow the example of the corresponding probabilistic and quantum algorithms.

A quantum computation with $t$ queries is just a sequence of unitary transformations

$$U_0 \to O \to U_1 \to O \to \ldots \to U_{t-1} \to O \to U_t.$$

The $U_j$'s can be arbitrary unitary transformations that do not depend on the input bits $x_1, \ldots, x_n$. The $O$'s are query (oracle) transformations which depend on $x_1, \ldots, x_n$. To define $O$, we represent basis states as $\mid i, z >$ where i consists of $\lceil \log(N+1) \rceil$ bits and $z$ consists of all other bits. Then, $O_x$ maps $\mid 0, z >$ to itself and $\mid i, z >$ to $(-1)^{x_i} \mid i, z >$ for $i \in \{1, \ldots, n\}$ (i.e., we change phase depending on $x_i$, unless $i = 0$ in which case we do nothing). The computation starts with

---

* The research was supported by Project 271/2012 from the Latvian Council of Science.

A.-H. Dediu et al. (Eds.): TPNC 2014, LNCS 8890, pp. 1–10, 2014.

a state $\mid 0 >$. Then, we apply $U_0, O_x, \ldots, O_x, U_t$ and measure the final state. The result of the computation is the rightmost bit of the state obtained by the measurement.

The quantum computation computes $f$ exactly if, for every $x = (x_1, \ldots, x_n)$, the rightmost bit of $U_T O_x \ldots O_x U_0 \mid 0 >$ equals $f(x_1, \ldots, x_n)$ with certainty.

The quantum computation computes $f$ with bounded error if, for every $x = (x_1, \ldots, x_n)$, the probability that the rightmost bit of $U_T O_x \ldots O_x U_0 \mid 0 >$ equals $f(x_1, \ldots, x_n)$ is at least $1 - \epsilon$ for some fixed . $\epsilon < \frac{1}{2}$.

## 2   Ultrametric Algorithms

A new type of indeterministic algorithms called *ultrametric* algorithms was introduced in [15]. An extensive research on ultrametric algorithms of various kinds has been performed by several authors (cf. [4,16,23,29]). So, ultrametric algorithms is a very new concept and their potential still has to be explored. This is the first paper showing a problem where ultrametric algorithms have advantages over quantum algorithms.

Ultrametric algorithms are very similar to probabilistic algorithms but while probabilistic algorithms use *real* numbers $r$ with $0 \leq r \leq 1$ as parameters, ultrametric algorithms use *p-adic* numbers as parameters. The usage of $p$-adic numbers as *amplitudes* and the ability to perform *measurements* to transform amplitudes into real numbers are inspired by quantum computations and allow for algorithms not possible in classical computations. Slightly simplifying the description of the definitions, one can say that ultrametric algorithms are the same as probabilistic algorithms, only the *interpretation* of the probabilities is *different*.

The choice of $p$-adic numbers instead of real numbers is not quite arbitrary. Ostrowski [26] proved that any non-trivial absolute value on the rational numbers $\mathbb{Q}$ is equivalent to either the usual real absolute value or a $p$-adic absolute value. This result shows that using $p$-adic numbers was not merely one of many possibilities to generalize the definition of deterministic algorithms but rather the only remaining possibility not yet explored.

The notion of $p$-adic numbers is widely used in science. String theory [28], chemistry [22] and molecular biology [8,19] have introduced $p$-adic numbers to describe measures of indeterminism. Indeed, research on indeterminism in nature has a long history. Pascal and Fermat believed that every event of indeterminism can be described by a real number between 0 and 1 called *probability*. Quantum physics introduced a description in terms of complex numbers called *amplitude of probabilities* and later in terms of probabilistic combinations of amplitudes most conveniently described by *density matrices*. Using $p$-adic numbers to describe indeterminism allows to explore some aspects of indeterminism but, of course, does not exhaust all the aspects of it.

There are many distinct $p$-adic absolute values corresponding to the many prime numbers $p$. These absolute values are traditionally called *ultrametric*. Absolute values are needed to consider *distances* among objects. We are used to rational and irrational numbers as measures for distances, and there is a psychological difficulty to imagine that something else can be used instead of rational and irrational numbers, respectively. However, there is an important feature that distinguishes $p$-adic numbers from real numbers. Real numbers (both rational and irrational) are linearly ordered, while $p$-adic numbers *cannot* be linearly ordered. This is why *valuations* and *norms* of $p$-adic numbers are considered.

The situation is similar in Quantum Computation (see [24]). Quantum amplitudes are complex numbers which also cannot be linearly ordered. The counterpart of valuation for quantum algorithms is *measurement* translating a complex number $a + bi$ into a real number $a^2 + b^2$. Norms of $p$-adic numbers are rational numbers. We continue with a short description of $p$-adic numbers.

## 3  p-adic Numbers and p-ultrametric Algorithms

Let $p$ be an arbitrary prime number. A number $a \in \mathbb{N}$ with $0 \leq a \leq p - 1$ is called a *p-adic digit*. A *p-adic integer* is by definition a sequence $(a_i)_{i \in \mathbb{N}}$ of $p$-adic digits. We write this conventionally as $\cdots a_i \cdots a_2 a_1 a_0$, i.e., the $a_i$ are written from left to right.

If $n$ is a natural number, and $n = \overline{a_{k-1} a_{k-2} \cdots a_1 a_0}$ is its $p$-adic representation, i.e., $n = \sum_{i=0}^{k-1} a_i p^i$, where each $a_i$ is a $p$-adic digit, then we identify $n$ with the $p$-adic integer $(a_i)$, where $a_i = 0$ for all $i \geq k$. This means that the natural numbers can be identified with the $p$-adic integers $(a_i)_{i \in \mathbb{N}}$ for which all but finitely many digits are 0. In particular, the number 0 is the $p$-adic integer all of whose digits are 0, and 1 is the $p$-adic integer all of whose digits are 0 except the right-most digit $a_0$ which is 1.

To obtain $p$-adic representations of all rational numbers, $\frac{1}{p}$ is represented as $\cdots 00.1$, the number $\frac{1}{p^2}$ as $\cdots 00.01$, and so on. For any $p$-adic number it is allowed to have infinitely many (!) digits to the left of the "$p$-adic" point but only a finite number of digits to the right of it.

However, $p$-adic numbers are not merely a generalization of rational numbers. They are related to the notion of *absolute value* of numbers. If $X$ is a nonempty set, a distance, or metric, on $X$ is a function $d$ from $X \times X$ to the nonnegative real numbers such that for all $(x, y) \in X \times X$ the following conditions are satisfied.

(1) $d(x, y) \geq 0$, and $d(x, y) = 0$ if and only if $x = y$,
(2) $d(x, y) = d(y, x)$,
(3) $d(x, y) \leq d(x, z) + d(z, y)$ for all $z \in X$.

A set $X$ together with a metric $d$ is called a *metric space*. The same set $X$ can give rise to many different metric spaces. If $X$ is a linear space over the real numbers then the *norm* of an element $x \in X$ is its distance from 0, i.e., for all $x, y \in X$ and $\alpha$ any real number we have:

(1) $\|x\| \geq 0$, and $\|x\| = 0$ if and only if $x = 0$,
(2) $\|\alpha \cdot y\| = |\alpha| \cdot \|y\|$,
(3) $\|x + y\| \leq \|x\| + \|y\|$.

Note that every norm induces a metric $d$, i.e., $d(x, y) = \|x - y\|$. A well-known example is the metric over $\mathbb{Q}$ induced by the ordinary absolute value. However, there are other norms as well. A norm is called *ultrametric* if Requirement (3) can be replaced by the stronger statement: $\|x + y\| \leq \max\{\|x\|, \|y\|\}$. Otherwise, the norm is called *Archimedean*.

**Definition 1.** *Let $p \in \{2, 3, 5, 7, 11, 13, \ldots\}$ be any prime number. For any nonzero integer $a$, let the $p$-adic ordinal (or valuation) of $a$, denoted $\text{ord}_p\, a$, be the highest power of $p$ which divides $a$, i.e., the greatest number $m \in \mathbb{N}$ such that $a \equiv 0 \pmod{p^m}$. For any rational number $x = a/b$ we define $\text{ord}_p\, x =_{df} \text{ord}_p\, a - \text{ord}_p\, b$. Additionally, $\text{ord}_p\, x =_{df} \infty$ if and only if $x = 0$.*

For example, let $x = 63/550 = 2^{-1} \cdot 3^2 \cdot 5^{-2} \cdot 7^1 \cdot 11^{-1}$. Thus, we have

$$\text{ord}_2\, x = -1 \qquad \text{ord}_7\, x = +1$$
$$\text{ord}_3\, x = +2 \qquad \text{ord}_{11}\, x = -1$$
$$\text{ord}_5\, x = -2 \qquad \text{ord}_p\, x = 0 \quad \text{for every prime } p \notin \{2, 3, 5, 7, 11\}\,.$$

**Definition 2.** *Let $p \in \{2, 3, 5, 7, 11, 13, \ldots\}$ be any prime number. For any rational number $x$, we define its $p$-norm as $p^{-\text{ord}_p\, x}$, and we set $\|0\|_p =_{df} 0$.*

For example, with $x = 63/550 = 2^{-1}3^2 5^{-2}7^1 11^{-1}$ we obtain:

$$\|x\|_2 = 2 \qquad \|x\|_7 = 1/7$$
$$\|x\|_3 = 1/9 \qquad \|x\|_{11} = 11$$
$$\|x\|_5 = 25 \qquad \|x\|_p = 1 \quad \text{for every prime } p \notin \{2, 3, 5, 7, 11\}\,.$$

Rational numbers are $p$-adic integers for all prime numbers $p$. Since the definitions given above are all we need, we finish our exposition of $p$-adic numbers here. For a more detailed description of $p$-adic numbers we refer to [17,20].

We continue with *ultrametric algorithms*. In the following, $p$ always denotes a prime number. Ultrametric algorithms are described by finite directed acyclic graphs (abbr. DAG), where exactly one node is marked as root. As usual, the root does not have any incoming edge. Furthermore, every node having outdegree zero is said to be a *leaf*. The leaves are the output nodes of the DAG.

Let $v$ be a node in such a graph. Then each outgoing edge is labeled by a $p$-adic number which we call *amplitude*. We require that the sum of all amplitudes that correspond to $v$ is 1. In order to determine the *total amplitude* along a computation path, we need the following definition.

**Definition 3.** *The total amplitude of the root is defined to be 1. Furthermore, let $v$ be a node at depth $d$ in the DAG, let $\alpha$ be its total amplitude, and let $\beta_1, \beta_2, \cdots, \beta_k$ be the amplitudes corresponding to the outgoing edges $e_1, \ldots, e_k$ of $v$. Let $v_1, \ldots, v_k$ be the nodes where the edges $e_1, \ldots, e_k$ point to. Then the total amplitude of $v_\ell$, $\ell \in \{1, \ldots, k\}$, is defined as follows.*

(1) *If the indegree of $v_\ell$ is one, then its total amplitude is $\alpha\beta_\ell$.*

(2) *If the indegree of $v_\ell$ is bigger than one, i.e., if two or more computation paths are joined, say $m$ paths, then let $\alpha, \gamma_2, \ldots, \gamma_m$ be the corresponding total amplitudes of the predecessors of $v_\ell$ and let $\beta_\ell, \delta_2, \ldots, \delta_m$ be the amplitudes of the incoming edges The total amplitude of the node $v_\ell$ is then defined to be $\alpha\beta_\ell + \gamma_2\delta_2 + \cdots + \delta_m\gamma_m$.*

Note that the total amplitude is a $p$-adic integer.

It remains to define what is meant by saying that a $p$-ultrametric algorithm produces a result with a certain probability. This is specified by performing a so-called *measurement* at the leaves of the corresponding DAG. Here by measurement we mean that we transform the total amplitude $\beta$ of each leaf to $\|\beta\|_p$. We refer to $\|\beta\|_p$ as the $p$-*probability* of the corresponding computation path.

**Definition 4.** *We say that a $p$-ultrametric algorithm produces a result $m$ with a probability $q$ if the sum of the $p$-probabilities of all leaves which correctly produce the result $m$ is no less than $q$.*

**Comment.** Just as in Quantum Computation, there is something counterintuitive in ultrametric algorithms. The notion of probability which is the result of measurement not always correspond to our expectations. It was not easy to accept that L. Grover's algorithm [18] does not read all the input on any computation path. There is a similar situation in ultrametric query algorithms. It is more easy to accept the definition of ultrametric query algorithms in the case when there is only one accepting state in the algorithm. The 3-ultrametric query algorithm in Theorem 16 has only one accepting state.

## 4   Kushilevitz's Function

Kushilevitz exhibited a function $f$ that provides the largest gap in the exponent of a polynomial in $deg(f)$ that gives an upper bound on $bs(f)$. Never published by Kushilevitz, the function appears in footnote 1 of the Nisan-Wigderson paper [25].

Kushilevitz's function $h$ of 6 Boolean variables is defined as follows:
$h(z_1, \ldots, z_6) = \Sigma_i z_i - \Sigma_{i \neq j} z_i z_j + z_1 z_3 z_4 + z_1 z_2 z_5 + z_1 z_4 z_5 + z_2 z_3 z_4 + z_2 z_3 z_5 + z_1 z_2 z_6 + z_1 z_3 z_6 + z_2 z_4 z_6 + z_3 z_5 z_6 + z_4 z_5 z_6$.

To explore properties of the Kushilevitz's function we introduce 10 auxiliary sets of variables.

$$
\begin{array}{l|l}
S_1 = \{z_1, z_3, z_4\} & T_1 = \{z_2, z_5, z_6\} \\
S_2 = \{z_1, z_2, z_5\} & T_2 = \{z_3, z_4, z_6\} \\
S_3 = \{z_1, z_4, z_5\} & T_3 = \{z_2, z_3, z_6\} \\
S_4 = \{z_2, z_3, z_4\} & T_4 = \{z_1, z_5, z_6\} \\
S_5 = \{z_2, z_3, z_5\} & T_5 = \{z_1, z_4, z_6\} \\
S_6 = \{z_1, z_2, z_6\} & T_6 = \{z_3, z_4, z_5\} \\
S_7 = \{z_1, z_3, z_6\} & T_7 = \{z_2, z_4, z_5\} \\
S_8 = \{z_2, z_4, z_6\} & T_8 = \{z_1, z_3, z_5\} \\
S_9 = \{z_3, z_5, z_6\} & T_9 = \{z_1, z_2, z_4\} \\
S_{10} = \{z_4, z_5, z_6\} & T_{10} = \{z_1, z_2, z_3\}
\end{array}
$$

By $S$ we denote the class $(S_1, \ldots, S_{10})$ and by $T$ we denote the class $(T_1, \ldots, T_{10})$.

**Lemma 5.** *For every $i \in \{1, \ldots, 6\}$, the union $S_i \cup T_i$ equals $\{1, \ldots, 6\}$.*

**Lemma 6.** *For every $i \in \{1, \ldots, 6\}$, the variable $z_i$ is a member of exactly 5 sets in $S$ and a member of exactly 5 sets in $T$.*

**Lemma 7.** *For every $i \in \{1, \ldots, 6\}$, the variable $z_i$ has an empty intersection with exactly 5 sets in $S$ and with exactly 5 sets in $T$.*

**Lemma 8.** *For every pair $(i, j)$ such that $i \neq j$ and $i \in \{1, \ldots, 6\}, j \in \{1, \ldots, 6\}$, the pair of variables $(z_i, z_j)$ is a member of exactly 2 sets in $S$ and a member of exactly 2 sets in $T$.*

**Lemma 9.** *For every pair $(i, j)$ such that $i \neq j$ and $i \in \{1, \ldots, 6\}, j \in \{1, \ldots, 6\}$, the pair of variables $(z_i, z_j)$ has an empty intersection with exactly 2 sets in $S$ and with exactly 2 sets in $T$.*

**Lemma 10.** *For every triple $(i, j, k)$ of pairwise distinct elements of $\{1, \ldots, 6\}$, the triple of variables $(z_i, z_j, z_k)$ coincides either with some set $S_i \in S$ or with some set $T_j$.*

**Lemma 11.** *No triple $(i, j, k)$ of pairwise distinct elements of $\{1, \ldots, 6\}$ is such that the triple of variables $(z_i, z_j, z_k)$ is a member of both $S$ and $T$.*

**Lemma 12.** *For every quadruple $(i, j, k, l)$ of pairwise distinct elements of $\{1, \ldots, 6\}$, the quadruple of variables $(z_i, z_j, z_k, z_l)$ contains exactly 2 sets $S_i \in S$ and exactly 2 sets $T_i \in T$.*

**Proof.** Immediately from Lemma 8. □

**Lemma 13.** *For every quintuple $(i, j, k, l, m)$ of pairwise distinct elements of $\{1, \ldots, 6\}$, the quintuple of variables $(z_i, z_j, z_k, z_l, z_m)$ contains exactly 5 sets $S_i \in S$ and exactly 5 sets $T_i \in T$.*

**Proof.** Immediately from Lemma 6. □

**Lemma 14.** *1) If $\Sigma_i z_i = 0$ then $h(z_1, \ldots, z_6) = 0$.*
*2) If $\Sigma_i z_i = 1$ then $h(z_1, \ldots, z_6) = 1$,*
*3) If $\Sigma_i z_i = 2$ then $h(z_1, \ldots, z_6) = 1$,*
*4) If $\Sigma_i z_i = 4$ then $h(z_1, \ldots, z_6) = 0$,*
*5) If $\Sigma_i z_i = 5$ then $h(z_1, \ldots, z_6) = 0$,*
*6) If $\Sigma_i z_i = 6$ then $h(z_1, \ldots, z_6) = 1$,*
*7) If $\Sigma_i z_i = 3$ and there exist 3 pairwise distinct $(j, k, l)$ such that $(z_j = z_k = z_l = 1)$ and $(z_j, z_k, z_l) \in S$ then $h(z_1, \ldots, z_6) = 1$,*
*8) If $\Sigma_i z_i = 3$ and there exist 3 pairwise distinct $(j, k, l)$ such that $(z_j = z_k = z_l = 1)$ and $(z_j, z_k, z_l) \in T$ then $h(z_1, \ldots, z_6) = 0$.*

**Proof.** If $\Sigma_i z_i = 0$ then all monomials in the definition of $h(z_1, \ldots, z_6)$ equal zero. If $\Sigma_i z_i = 1$ then $\Sigma_i z_i = 1$ but all the other monomials in the definition of $h(z_1, \ldots, z_6)$ equal zero. If $\Sigma_i z_i = 2$ then $h(z_1, \ldots, z_6) = \Sigma_i z_i - \Sigma_{i \neq j} z_i z_j = 2 - 1$. If $\Sigma_i z_i = 3$ and $(z_j, z_k, z_l) \in S$ then $h(z_1, \ldots, z_6) = \Sigma_i z_i - \Sigma_{i \neq j} z_i z_j = 3 - 3 + 1$. If $\Sigma_i z_i = 3$ and $(z_j, z_k, z_l) \in T$ then $h(z_1, \ldots, z_6) = \Sigma_i z_i - \Sigma_{i \neq j} z_i z_j = 3 - 3 + 0$. If $\Sigma_i z_i = 4$ then, by Lemma 12, $h(z_1, \ldots, z_6) = \Sigma_i z_i - \Sigma_{i \neq j} z_i z_j = 4 - 6 + 2$. If $\Sigma_i z_i = 5$ then, by Lemma 13, $h(z_1, \ldots, z_6) = \Sigma_i z_i - \Sigma_{i \neq j} z_i z_j = 5 - 10 + 5$. If $\Sigma_i z_i = 6$ then $h(z_1, \ldots, z_6) = \Sigma_i z_i - \Sigma_{i \neq j} z_i z_j = 6 - 15 + 10$.         □

By $\alpha(z_1, \ldots, z_6)$ we denote the cardinality of those $S_i = (z_j, z_k, z_l)$ such that $z_j = z_k = z_l = 1$. By $\beta(z_1, \ldots, z_6)$ we denote the cardinality of those $S_i = (z_j, z_k, z_l)$ such that $z_j = z_k = z_l = 0$.

**Lemma 15.** *1) For arbitrary 6-tuple $(z_1, \ldots, z_6) \in \{0, 1\}^6$, $h(z_1, \ldots, z_6) = 1$ iff $\alpha(z_1, \ldots, z_6) - \beta(z_1, \ldots, z_6)$ is congruent to 1 modulo 3.*
*2) For arbitrary 6-tuple $(z_1, \ldots, z_6) \in \{0, 1\}^6$, $h(z_1, \ldots, z_6) = 0$ iff $\alpha(z_1, \ldots, z_6) - \beta(z_1, \ldots, z_6)$ is congruent to 2 modulo 3.*

**Proof.** If $\Sigma_i z_i = 0$ then $\alpha(z_1, \ldots, z_6) - \beta(z_1, \ldots, z_6) = 0 - 10 \equiv 2(\mod 3)$. If $\Sigma_i z_i = 1$ then, by Lemma 7, $\alpha(z_1, \ldots, z_6) - \beta(z_1, \ldots, z_6) = 0 - 5 \equiv 1(\mod 3)$. If $\Sigma_i z_i = 2$ then, by Lemma 9, $\alpha(z_1, \ldots, z_6) - \beta(z_1, \ldots, z_6) = 0 - 2 \equiv 1(\mod 3)$. If $\Sigma_i z_i = 3$ and there exist 3 pairwise distinct $(j, k, l)$ such that $(z_j = z_k = z_l = 1)$ and $(z_j, z_k, z_l) \in S$ then, by Lemmas 10 and 11, $\alpha(z_1, \ldots, z_6) - \beta(z_1, \ldots, z_6) = 1 - 0 \equiv 1(\mod 3)$. If $\Sigma_i z_i = 3$ and there exist 3 pairwise distinct $(j, k, l)$ such that $(z_j = z_k = z_l = 1)$ and $(z_j, z_k, z_l) \in T$ then, by Lemmas 10 and 11, $\alpha(z_1, \ldots, z_6) - \beta(z_1, \ldots, z_6) = 0 - 1 \equiv 2(\mod 3)$. If $\Sigma_i z_i = 4$ then, by Lemma 12, $\alpha(z_1, \ldots, z_6) - \beta(z_1, \ldots, z_6) = 2 - 0 \equiv 2(\mod 3)$. If $\Sigma_i z_i = 5$ then, by Lemma 13, $\alpha(z_1, \ldots, z_6) - \beta(z_1, \ldots, z_6) = 5 - 0 \equiv 2(\mod 3)$. If $\Sigma_i z_i = 5$ then $\alpha(z_1, \ldots, z_6) - \beta(z_1, \ldots, z_6) = 10 - 0 \equiv 1(\mod 3)$. These results correspond to Lemma 14.         □

**Theorem 16.** *There exists a 3-ultrametric query algorithm computing the Kushilevitz's function using 3 queries.*

**Proof.** The desired algorithm branches its computation path into 31 branches at the root. We assign to each starting edge of the computation path the amplitude $\frac{1}{61}$.

The first 10 branches (labeled with numbers $1, \ldots, 10$) correspond to exactly one set $S_i$.

Let $S_i$ consist of elements $z_j, z_k, z_l$. Then the algorithm queries $z_j, z_k, z_l$. If all the queried values equal 1 then the algorithm goes to the state $q_3$. If all the queried values equal 0 then the algorithm goes to the state $q_3$ but multiplies the amplitude to $(-1)$. (For the proof it is important that for every 3-adic number $a$ the norm $\|-a\| = \|a\|$.) If the queried values are not all equal then the algorithm goes to the state $q_4$.

The next 10 branches (labeled with numbers $11, \ldots, 20$) also correspond to exactly one set $S_i$. Let $S_i$ consist of elements $z_j, z_k, z_l$. Then the algorithm queries

$z_j, z_k, z_l$. If all the queried values equal 1 then the algorithm goes to the state $q_5$. If all the queried values equal 0 then the algorithm goes to the state $q_3$. If the queried values are not all equal then the algorithm goes to the state $q_4$ but multiplies the amplitude to $(-1)$.

11 branches (labeled with numbers $21, \ldots, 31$) ask no query and the algorithm goes to the state $q_3$.

In result of this computation the amplitude $A_3$ of the states $q_3$ has become

$$A_3 = \frac{1}{31}(11 + \alpha(z_1, \ldots, z_6) - \beta(z_1, \ldots, z_6)),$$

The 3-ultrametric query algorithm performs measurement of the state $q_3$. The amplitude $A_3$ is transformed into a rational number $\|A_3\|$. As it was noted in Section 3, 3-adic notation for the number 31 is $\ldots 000112$ and 3-adic notation for the number $\frac{1}{31}$ is $\ldots 0212111221021$. Hence, for every 3-adic integer $\gamma$, $\|\gamma\| = \|\frac{1}{31}\gamma\|$.

By Lemma 15, $\|11 + \alpha(z_1, \ldots, z_6) - \beta(z_1, \ldots, z_6)\| = 1$ if $h(z_1, \ldots, z_6) = 1$ and $\|11 + \alpha(z_1, \ldots, z_6) - \beta(z_1, \ldots, z_6)\| = \frac{1}{3}$ if $h(z_1, \ldots, z_6) = 0$. □

## 5   Conclusions

Theorem 16 shows that there exists a bounded error 3-ultrametric query algorithm for the Kushilevitz's function whose complexity is much smaller than complexity of any *known* deterministic, nondeterministic, probabilistic and quantum query algorithm for this function. Moreover, Lemma 15 heavily exploits advantages of ultrametric algorithms, and this invites to conjecture that Kushilevitz's function is specific for advantages of ultrametric algorithms.

More difficult problem is to compare theorem 16 with the provable lower bounds of complexity. It is known that deterministic and nondeterministic query complexity of the Kushilevitz's function is 6. There exists an exact quantum query algorithm for the Kushilevitz's function with complexity 5 (see paper [5]) but nobody can prove that exact quantum query complexity for this function exceeds 3. There is an indirect proof of this conjecture.

Iterated functions are defined as follows.

Define a sequence $h_1, h_2, \ldots$ with $h_d$ being a function of $6^d$ variables by: $h_1 = h$, $h_{d+1} = h(h_d(x_1, \ldots, x_{6d}), h_d(x_{6d+1}, \ldots, x_{2 \cdot 6d})), h_d(x_{2 \cdot 6d+1}, \ldots, x_{3 \cdot 6d}),$ $h_d(x_{2 \cdot 6d+1}, \ldots, x_{3 \cdot 6d}), h_d(x_{3 \cdot 6d+1}, \ldots, x_{4 \cdot 6d}), h_d(x_{4 \cdot 6d+1}, \ldots, x_{5 \cdot 6d}),$ $h_d(x_{5 \cdot 6d+1}, \ldots, x_{6 \cdot 6d}))$

A. Ambainis proved in [2] that even bounded error query complexity for the iterated Kushilevitz's function exceeds $\Omega((\frac{\sqrt{39}}{2})^d) = \Omega((3.12\ldots)^d)$. Had this proof been valid for $d = 1$, we would have that error bounded quantum query complexity for Kushilevitz's function exceeds 3. Unfortunately, Ambainis proof works for *large* values of $d$.

# References

1. Ablayev, F.M., Freivalds, R.: Why sometimes probabilistic algorithms can be more effective. In: Wiedermann, J., Gruska, J., Rovan, B. (eds.) MFCS 1986. LNCS, vol. 233, pp. 1–14. Springer, Heidelberg (1986)
2. Ambainis, A.: Polynomial degree vs. quantum query complexity. Journal of Computer and System Sciences 72(2), 220–238 (2006)
3. Ambainis, A., Freivalds, R.: 1-way quantum finite automata: strengths, weaknesses and generalizations. In: Proc. IEEE FOCS 1998, pp. 332–341 (1998)
4. Balodis, K., Beriņa, A., Cīpola, K., Dimitrijevs, M., Iraids, J., Jēriņš, K., Kacs, V., Kalājs, J., Krišlauks, R., Lukstiņš, K., Raumanis, R., Scegulnaja, I., Somova, N., Vanaga, A., Freivalds, R.: On the state complexity of ultrametric finite automata. In: Proceedings of SOFSEM, vol. 2, pp. 1–9 (2013)
5. Bērziņa, A., Freivalds, R.: On quantum query complexity of kushilevitz function. In: Proceedings of Baltic DB&IS 2004, vol. 2, pp. 57–65 (2004)
6. Buhrman, H., Wolf, R.D.: Complexity measures and decision tree complexity: a survey. Theoretical Computer Science 288(1), 21–43 (2002)
7. Moore, C., Quantum, J.C.: automata and quantum grammars. Theoretical Computer Science 237(1-2), 275–306 (2000)
8. Dragovich, B., Dragovich, A.: A p-adic model of dna sequence and genetic code. p-Adic Numbers, Ultrametric Analysis, and Applications 1(1), 34–41 (2009)
9. Freivalds, R.: Recognition of languages with high probability on different classes of automata. Doklady Akademii Nauk SSSR 239(1), 60–62 (1978)
10. Freivalds, R.: Projections of languages recognizable by probabilistic and alternating finite multi-tape automata. Information Processing Letters 13(4-5), 195–198 (1981)
11. Freivalds, R.: On the growth of the number of states in result of the determinization of probabilistic finite automata. Avtomatika i Vichislitel'naya Tekhnika (3), 39–42 (1982)
12. Freivalds, R.: Complexity of probabilistic versus deterministic automata. In: Barzdins, J., Bjorner, D. (eds.) Baltic Computer Science. LNCS, vol. 502, pp. 565–613. Springer, Heidelberg (1991)
13. Freivalds, R.: Languages recognizable by quantum finite automata. In: Farré, J., Litovsky, I., Schmitz, S. (eds.) CIAA 2005. LNCS, vol. 3845, pp. 1–14. Springer, Heidelberg (2006)
14. Freivalds, R.: Non-constructive methods for finite probabilistic automata. International Journal of Foundations of Computer Science 19, 565–580 (2008)
15. Freivalds, R.: Ultrametric finite automata and turing machines. In: Béal, M.-P., Carton, O. (eds.) DLT 2013. LNCS, vol. 7907, pp. 1–11. Springer, Heidelberg (2013)
16. Freivalds, R., Zeugmann, T.: Active learning of recursive functions by ultrametric algorithms. In: Geffert, V., Preneel, B., Rovan, B., Štuller, J., Tjoa, A.M. (eds.) SOFSEM 2014. LNCS, vol. 8327, pp. 246–257. Springer, Heidelberg (2014)
17. Gouvea, F.Q.: p-adic numbers: An introduction, universitext (1983)
18. Grover, L.K.: A fast quantum mechanical algorithm for database search. In: Proceedings of the 28th ACM Symposium on Theory of Computing, pp. 212–219 (1996)
19. Khrennikov, A.Y.: Non-Archimedean Analysis: Quantum Paradoxes, Dynamical Systems and Biological Models. Kluwer Academic Publishers (1997)
20. Koblitz, N.: P-adic Numbers, p-adic Analysis, and Zeta-Functions, 2nd edn. Graduate Texts in Mathematics, vol. 58. Springer (1984)
21. Kondacs, A., Watrous, J.: On the power of quantum finite state automata. In: Proc. IEEE FOCS 1997, pp. 66–75 (1997)

22. Kozyrev, S.V.: Ultrametric analysis and interbasin kinetics. In: Proc. of the 2nd International Conference on p-Adic Mathematical Physics, vol. 826, pp. 121–128. American Institute Conference Proceedings (2006)

23. Krišlauks, R., Rukšāne, I., Balodis, K., Kucevalovs, I., Freivalds, R., Agele, I.N.: Ultrametric turing machines with limited reversal complexity. In: Proceedings of SOFSEM, vol. 2, pp. 87–94 (2013)

24. Nielsen, M.A., Chuang, I.L.: Quantum computation and quantum information. Cambridge University Press (2000)

25. Nisan, N., Wigderson, A.: On rank vs. communication complexity. Combinatorica 15(4), 557–565 (1995)

26. Ostrowski, A.: Über einige Lösungen der Funktionalgleichung $\varphi(x)\varphi(y) = \varphi(xy)$. Acta Mathematica 41(1), 271–284 (1916)

27. Papadimitriou, C.H.: Computational complexity. John Wiley and Sons Ltd, Chichester (2003)

28. Vladimirov, V.S., Volovich, I.V., Zelenov, E.I.: p-Adic Analysis and Mathematical Physics. World Scientific, Singapore (1995)

29. Zariņa, S., Freivalds, R.: Visualisation and and ultrametric analysis of koch fractals. In: Proc. 16th Japan Conference on Discrete and Computational Geometry and Graphs, pp. 84–85. Tokyo (2013)

# Cellular Programming

Peter Niebert and Mathieu Caralp

Aix Marseille Université*, CNRS, LIF UMR 7279, 13288, Marseille, France
{peter.niebert,mathieu.caralp}@univ-amu.fr

**Abstract.** We present a design approach for "smart surfaces" inspired by cellular automata. The aim is to construct and to program *scalable distributed realtime* interactive systems composed of inexpensive microcontrollers to build surfaces that interact physically with their environment. Our work is both pragmatic and integrated: it covers the entire chain from hardware considerations, a programming model based on a networked *locally synchronous virtual machine*, dedicated programming language features, a distributed embedded implementation and an integrated programming environment with a simulator implementation of the locally synchronous virtual machine.

The platform which we have developed allows for arbitrary distributed algorithms to be implemented, including those that cannot perform scalably in realtime. We argue for a pragmatic coexistence of certain non-realtime algorithms together with "cellular" algorithms that operate much like cellular automata.

Our "case study" is an application of this approach for modular interactive lighting systems.

## 1 Introduction

Cellular automata have many virtues which make them a popular formalism in various scientific disciplines [13]. The key aspect of cellular automata is the local and simple nature of the computation that leads to a complex global behaviour. They are often used for modeling and simulation of complex systems. On the other hand, cellular automata are also popular for their mathematical esthetics, notably for visually observable computation.

Simulation of cellular automata has the advantage of being highly parallelizable and thus quite compatible with current trends in computing architectures.

However, we believe that cellular automata are also a very useful paradigm for the design of scalable distributed, embedded realtime computation with applications in ubiquitous or pervasive computing [9] such as smart surfaces and materials. Such devices combine physically coupled sensors and actuators by a network of microcontrollers. The presence of microcontrollers turns the entire surface or material into a computing device that interacts physically with its environment.

* This work was supported in part by the ANR project MACARON. Special thanks to the sponsors of the LED's CHAT exhibition, notably the region Provence Alpes Côte d'Azur, Marseille Provence 2013 and Lumicom.

A.-H. Dediu et al. (Eds.): TPNC 2014, LNCS 8890, pp. 11–22, 2014.
© Springer International Publishing Switzerland 2014

The natural physical architecture for such systems are modules with sensors and actuators that are linked among each other for communication and for energy distribution. The communication links will be for the major part local between neighbouring modules, for a minor part connected to other computing devices or networks or the internet. The function of the device is to react to stimuli from the sensors by control of the actuators. One architectural choice for the control of such a system is to use the network of microcontrollers for information collection (from the sensors, mergecast) and command distribution (broadcast), but this choice misses a major technological promise, scalability. Indeed, if the computation itself is performed by the microcontrollers, then we might hope that an extension of the surface by additional modules adds the computational resources necessary for its operation: local computing power (additional microcontrollers) and bandwidth (for local communication). The second promise of decentralized control is low latency, since the path from the stimulus to the actuators is short.

**Fig. 1.** A visitor sending coloured waves through the LED's CHAT installation

In this article, we describe a concrete engineering approach in this direction of decentralized control which is inspired by cellular automata and which we call "cellular programming". It is the result of an adventure that initially aimed to visually simulate cellular automata on LED modules as an exercice for computer science students in designing embedded software. As we went along, the aim shifted to the design of an environment for building scalable modular, interactive embedded systems, together with a dedicated programming language, an integrated development environment and a distributed embedded runtime system. As an application, the event "Marseille Provence, European Capital of Culture 2013" allowed us to build a prototype using 500 triangular modules with more than 15000 LEDs and 2000 sensors and to expose an interactive installation to the public.

The aim of the article is to cover an integrated view of our work, including, beyond hardware design and distributed embedded software, an abstraction layer, the *locally synchronous virtual machine*, allowing for simulation of cellular programs, as well as programming language considerations and to put "cellular algorithms" into a distributed programming perspective.

*Related work.* Closest in spirit to our work, but with a different emphasis, is the rich body of work on sensor networks[7]. The latter have in common with our setting the need of operating on primitive microcontrollers, but the main emphasis in that domain is a low energy profile for autonomous, often battery powered microcontrollers. Rather than "smart surfaces", sensor networks are more related to "smart dust" as concept in ubiquitous computing.

The computational constraints of sensor networks have given rise to works on lightweight runtime environments, notably TinyOS [12] and its derivatives. The notion of coroutines, which we use in our programming concept, has also come up in this context under the name of "protothreads" [3], which allow to program pseudo parallel programs without a scheduler. However, the temporal behaviour of protothreads is not semantically linked between modules but restricted to local use.

Certain works in sensor networks also mention cellular automata or local algorithms, e.g. [2].

As to wired systems, cellular automata show up in certain studies of "smart surfaces", e.g. [10]. However, we are not aware of a general programming oriented approach as we have presented in this work.

Networks of microprocessors have been considered as scalable computing platform for several decades, a recent attempt is presented in [1]. Our approach in contrast is not about scalable computation but about scalable interaction of the smart surface with it's environment. The design goals, in particular concerning performance considerations, are quite opposed in both cases. E.g. recent trends in manufacturing [8] may allow in the future to integrate big numbers of extremely low power and low performance microcontrollers to constitute active materials, which call for programming approaches as the one we present here.

**The article is structured as follows.** In Section 2, we introduce a programming model for the locally synchronous virtual machine. In Section 3, we present a lightweight dedicated programming language for this programming model. In Section 4, we discuss with examples the notion of « cellular algorithms » allowing to understand in which sense the distributed algorithms are scalable. We conclude in Section 5 with some remarks on the actual implementation in our demonstrator.

## 2  Cellular Programming Model

*Modules and Topology.* We consider systems composed of modules in a topological neighbourhood relationship. E.g. squares in a matrix with up to four neighbours each, or hexagones with up to six neighbours. Unlike cellular automata such as Conway's game of life, we limit the neighbourhood relation on common edges of the modules, not common vertices. The topology need not necessarily be flat, e.g. triangles may be grouped together to build complex threedimensional surfaces. We suppose physical links between modules sharing an edge, which allow the modules to communicate. Each module is equipped with sensors, actuators and communication channels.

From now on, we consider the modules to be the "cells" of a system and we describe the execution model with the double inspiration of cellular automata and synchronous programming [6].

We consider that each cell has a state composed of variable values, where we distinguish five kinds of variables in three groups.

**Output variables :** Variables controlling the *actuators*, or the "visible" part of the cell state ; variables for "publishing" part of a state to the neighbours.
**Input variables :** Sensor values; variables for "observing" the published states of the neighbours.
**Internal variables :** all other explicit or hidden variables (e.g. stack ... ).

In pure cellular automata, there would be no sensor variables and we just suppose the possibility of integrating the neighbouring states into the rules and we would suppose that the state of a cell is fully visible. Thus, there would be no distinction between internal variables and published or visible variables. The pragmatic reason for the distinction here is the fact that storage (state) and computation (complex rules) are generally much more abundantly available than communication bandwidth.

*Locally synchronous virtual machine.* A very important aspect of our approach is that it allows to implement faithfully a globally synchronous semantics in an asynchronous setting. Based on the three groups of variables present in each module, we propose the following execution model of a *locally synchronous virtual machine* in each *round* :

1. Wait for all neighbors to finish previous the round.
2. Update input variables :
   a) Read sensors.
   b) Copy output variables of modules to input variables of all neighbours. On a physical system, this requires communication between modules.
3. Compute new values for internal variables and output variables for the next round.

We observe the following consequences :

- If a module is executing round $n$ then its neighbors have finished round $n-1$.
- The order of execution of the computation in each module has no consequence on the local variables.

We suppose that the computation in (3) is deterministic, i.e. based on the same state of input variables and internal variables, the resulting values of internal variables and output variables will always be the same. However, the sensor readings may be subject to non-determinism or probabilistic distribution, which might carry through to the behavior of the module.

As a result, we can define global states as snapshots combining the local states of modules after executing the same number of rounds. We can faithfully simulate this semantics by pretending that all modules execute synchronously in parallel even though, in a real time setting, distant modules may be executing different rounds at the same (global) time. Neighboring modules will in contrast always expose combined state coherent with a globally synchronous semantics.

**Inherent latency.** Similar to cellular automata, there is an inherent latency to this execution model. At any round, a bit of information will only pass across one edge in the network topology and hence, the minimal latency of information flow for modules at distance $n$ is $n$ rounds.

## 3   A Dedicated Programming Language

The semantic model of the previous section basically is a synchronous system with rounds for local computation and a delay of one round for copying of variables from a module to a neighbour. We present a simple programming language which is designed to be quickly adopted by anyone with a minimal programming experience with little syntax and semantic concepts to learn. For example, as in *Processing* (popular in digital arts), essential system resources and functionalities should be accessible without syntactic overhead.

Given the synchronous execution model, a synchronous language [6] could be an option for writing applications, but the first author's teaching experience suggested that the « good old coroutine » is much easier to adopt for casual developpers. We thus propose an integration of dedicated primitives for coroutines into a C like language.

### 3.1   Synchronous Programming with Coroutines

Coroutines are an old, maybe the first concept of concurrency in programming and are generally seen as a lightweight version of threads. A coroutine is a function with a special construct for returning from a call, often called yield, or just return. However, when calling a coroutine two times, the second call will pick up the computation *after* the return of the first call. This implies that the values of the variables of the coroutine must be retained between successive calls.

In our framework, coroutines can be declared such that the call is implicit, once per round. Since each such coroutine will be called once per round, a yield or return call means a change of round or a delay of one round period. Syntactically, we write the pseudo instruction "`sleep n;`", where n is an expression for the number of rounds to wait.

A simple illustration is to have two LEDs blink at different rates. Here, we suppose a fixed round duration of 10ms. In this example, LED 0 blinks with a period of 1s (100 times 10ms) and LED 1 blinks with a period of 260ms. As can be seen, the structuring of the code into several coroutines allows for asynchronous behaviour in a synchronous setting.

```
coroutine blink0 {
   while(1){
       led[0] = white; sleep 50; led[0] = black; sleep 50;
   }
}

coroutine blink1 {
   while(1) {
       led[1] = green; sleep 13; led[1] = black; sleep 13;
   }
}
```

It has to be underlined that the "sleeping interval" starts based on the current execution round, not on an occurrence time of the last instruction. Coroutines written in this way provide an easy access to synchronous pseudo-parallelism within a module and between modules.

In the case of several coroutines, the execution order or call order may have an influence on the result of the computation, when referring to shared variables. In order to obtain a deterministic semantics, the call order is determined, here by the alphabetical order of the name of the coroutine.

### 3.2   Synchronous Communication with Shared Variables

As mentioned in Section 2, the communication between modules is based on input and output variables. In the API, these variables are simply called in and out, where both are arrays indexed by the direction of the communication, where the base type (elements of these arrays) represents the amount of information that can be shared each round. Typically, in and out are thus two dimensional arrays where the first dimension concerns the direction of communication and the second dimension gives access to multiple scalar bits of information passed at each round.

It is important to note the one round delay between the assignment of a value to out[i] and the availability of the same value in in[j] in the corresponding neighbouring module. As an example on the use of these variables, consider a distributed simulation of a cellular automaton. This simulation can really take place within a coroutine of the following structure.

```
coroutine cellular {
   //... initialisation code for setup of local variables

   while(1) {
       // assign "out" with information shared about local state
       sleep 1; // receive copy of neighbour's shared state in "i"
```

```
    // compute new local state based on "in" and old local state
  }
}
```

As can be seen, the `sleep` statement structures the cyclic operation into two phases, before and after emission. It is interesting to note that a change of perspective takes place between these two phases, since the first phase is done from the point of view of the sender and the second phase from the point of view of the receiver.

As another example, let us consider "migration" of an "agent", i.e. an activity that can move from one module to another. We implement such movement with a coroutine that is present on all modules, but with a difference in perspective. Variables in and out are used to signal migration from one module to another.

```
coroutine agent {
  bool present;

  // initialize "present" so that it represents the presence
  // of the agent on the current module.
  while(1){
    // set "out" to tell neighbours no agent is coming (default)
    if(present) {
        bool migrate;
        int target;
        // do locally, what the agent has to do, in particular
        // set "migrate" and "target" if the agent has to move

        if(migrate){
          // update "out[target]" to announce coming agent
          present = false; // note that agent is leaving
        }
    }
    sleep 1; // pass information
    if(!present){
        // check "in" to see if agent is coming in
        // and update "present"
    }
  }
}
```

Again, this example shows how the "sleep" statement means a change of perspective/location within the same coroutine. Before the sleep, we have the perspective of the agent, after the sleep, we take the perspective of a potential module receiving the agent. Note also the lightweight nature of this kind of migration requiring a single persistent bit per module and a single bit of communication bandwidth per link and per round.

# 4    Cellular and non Cellular Algorithms

We believe that the actual interest in applying a cellular paradigm to modular systems as described in this work is scalability, i.e. that the design holds for arbitrarily or at least very large collections of modules and that locally, the performance of the modules executing their "cellular" task is not influenced by the size of the installation. Since the system interacts with the physical world, its response must be real time. There are indeed reasons to hope for such scalability, since with each added module we also add local computational power and bandwidth.

However, not all distributed algorithms (see e.g. [11] for an introduction) are scalable in this way. We call an algorithm *cellular*[1] iff its execution time in number of rounds, bandwidth, memory requirements as well as computational requirements are constant, independent of the dimension of the network. We claim that this definition reflects "scalable, distributed realtime" performance.

The basic execution model of the locally synchronous virtual machine is that of one round. The bandwidth per round is bounded by the type of the communication variables in and out. The memory resources are verifiably limited by allowing only static (compile time) allocation. The computing power can practically only be verified at runtime in simulation.

As a result, the locally synchronous virtual machine allows in principle only the execution of cellular algorithms in an even stricter sense, one round algorithms with bounded bandwidth and computational resources. But using coroutines, it is possible to specify multi-round algorithms, e.g. including various sleep statements at different points in the algorithm. Syntactically, arbitrary synchronous distributed algorithms can be coded in the formalism.

In practice, there are good reasons to allow the coexistence of cellular and non-cellular algorithms (in different coroutines). Examples of highly useful non-cellular algorithms include diameter measurement (at least twice the diameter number of rounds), broadcast (diameter number of rounds for propagation plus number of rounds for information passing depending on the bandwidth), firmware update (broadcast), 2D map computation, etc. In the following, we present two interesting applications of cellular algorithms.

## 4.1    Distributed Signal Processing

We suppose that each module carries sensors, depending on the application. The fusion of sensor values in a bounded perimeter allows observations not possible with individual sensors.

E.g. in the case of our interactive light animation, we used infrared flash lights as a "pointing device". The flash lights through a cone of light that is observed

---

[1] A related theoretical notion in distributed algorithms used to state impossibility results is that of a "local algorithm", which must terminate in a bounded number of rounds independent of the network size. Local algorithms may use arbitrary bandwidth and computing resources, though.

by individual sensors, but with an intensity that varies with the distance of the flash light as well as with the distance from the central axis of the light cone. By combining the observations of several sensors, we can estimate the position of the axis of the light cone. In practice, this approach allows to observe gestures with a precision far beyond the sensor density.

The implementation is based on a cellular algorithm that routes sensor values in a bounded perimeter to each module. The routing takes a number of rounds equivalent to the topological distance of the modules integrated into the observation. The latency of the availability of sensor values depends on this distance.

Depending on the setting, the routing scheme itself may have to be calculated in advance with a non-cellular algorithm, but this algorithm has to execute only when changes in the topology take place.

## 4.2 Distributed Simulation

We believe that the initial motivation of distributed simulation of cellular automata is close to the "typical application", but the notion of "cellular automaton" has to be taken widely to see the potential. In each round, each module simulates its cell or sub cells and communicates the state of the subcells required for the computation to the neighbours.

What are the limitations? In principle, it would seem that generations cannot be computed faster than rounds, but things are a bit more complicated.

Consider for instance a distributed simulation of Conway's Game of Life on squared modules, where each module covers $n \times n$ cells and is connected to four neighbouring modules. In a naïve implementation, we will communicate to each direct neighbour the values of the cells on the edge in one round, and the corners will have to be passed on to the diagonal neighbours in a second round. So only after two rounds, the information is ready for the computation of the next generation, hence the fastest distributed simulation speed would be one generation every two rounds. However, if we communicate more than the edge at each round, for instance the three cells around each corner, then the diagonal module, which receives the values of these cells two rounds later can compute the value of the corner of the previous round and can thus immediately compute the next generation. Thus, one generation can be computed every round. If even more cells are communicated, several generations can be computed each round. Of course, when integrating perturbations, e.g. as a consequence of sensor observations, it still takes the distance number of rounds before the observation can be taken into account. But the consequence is sensor latency, not limited simulation speed.

Another example is finite element simulation, a commonly used approximative simulation approach for continuous processes, e.g. fluid dynamics. To avoid misunderstandings, the aim of a distributed finite element simulation in our context is not efficient simulation, but rather a low latency link between the sensors, the actuators and the simulated process. A simulated continuous medium mapped on our modules is subdivided into cells, a bounded number of cells per module. We can use continuous (floating point) variables and fixed step numerical integration to simulate (pseudo-)physical processes on these cells, where the values of a cell after an integration step depend only on values in a bounded environment before the step. In short, this simulation is a cellular automaton. Again, for the distributed simulation we communicate the values of the bordering cells to the neighbours. If we intend real time simulation of (pseudo-)physical processes, then the step width is linked to the duration of a round, but the accuracy of the simulation depends on the density of cells as well as on the step width. Increasing the number of cells on a module implies increasing the number of values to communicate to the neighbours and more computation. Likewise, decreasing the step width for higher accuracy implies more computation and more communication. Since microcontrollers are often not equipped with floating point units, the computation is as likely a limiting factor for spatial and temporal resolution as is the communication.

## 5  Implementation, "LED's CHAT"

### 5.1  Hardware

We implemented the above concepts as an ambitious prototype which was exposed at the "LED's CHAT" exhibition. The modules (shaped as equilateral triangles) carry LEDs as actuators and Infrared sensors (for interaction), as well as connecting cables for communication and power distribution. A microcontroller is used to implement all the tasks of a module (reading sensors, controlling LED's communicating with neighbors).

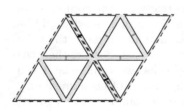 From a computational perspective, a sufficiently powerful single processor can obviously simulate several cells of a cellular automaton or several less powerful "submodules". The converse is also true to some extent: several modules can cooperate to perform certain collective tasks in parallel, thus combining their computing and communication resources. This observation suggests to design the surfaces of the modules in such a manner as to be compatible with a subdivision into submodules in a way that preserves the communication infrastructure. E.g., for triangular modules communicating on edges, a subdivision of triangles into four subtriangles implies two triangles on each edge and an interiour triangle.

For this case, the communication channels on an edge between two modules will have to be shared for the communication of the two pairs of submodules, whereas the communication within the module is simulated by software. On the other hand, grouping modules together to constitute supermodules introduces latency into the communication: the information received via a module on the edge is not immediately available to all the modules in the supermodule but may need time for propagation.

These observations imply pragmatic trade-offs in terms of production cost as well as energy usage when deciding on the granularity of the design. It also means that a purist "cellular automaton" approach to the design of such systems will be suboptimal, at least with off the shelf components. In the case of the triangular LED's CHAT modules, we opted for a subdivision into 25 cells with RGB LED's in the center[2] controlled by a 32bit Micro-controller running at 80MHz and disposing of 128kB or RAM. However, in a previous prototype, we used an 8bit Microcontroller running at 20MHz and only 4kB of RAM for controlling 6 RGB LEDs. This illustrates how little resources can suffice in principle for each module.

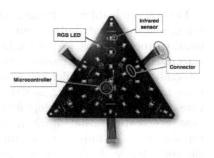

In future applications, trends in manufacturing [8] may open the path to networks of tiny modules with each significantly reduced resources directly integrated into "smart surfaces".

## 5.2   Software

In Section 2, we have indicated the semantics of a locally synchronous virtual machine which executes synchronous distributed programs in rounds. Here, we briefly discuss implementation issues concerning an actual distributed implementation of the virtual machine to be executed on embedded modules.

The design goal of the embedded implementation of the virtual machine is to execute it on primitive microcontrollers with as little as 4kB RAM.

Each microcontroller has to cope with four essential tasks, reading sensors, manipulating actuators, participating in the communication framework and executing application code. A crucial possibility is to dispatch an application across the network by a distributed bootloader. This is achieved by a non-cellular distributed algorithm which however can still be coded within the same framework.

The heart of the implementation is the communication framework. Its task is to synchronize the microcontrollers and to copy variables between neighbouring vertices, as well as certain administrative tasks, such as distributed reset etc.

It turns out that a key issue in the communication framework is synchronization between modules, a problem related to the much researched topic of clock synchronization. However, for the locally synchronous virtual machine, it is sufficient to closely synchronize neighbouring modules (and to less synchronize more distant modules), an objective introduced as *gradient synchronization* in [5]. In [4], an algorithm using an external clock source like GPS for a subset of nodes is proposed, that matches closely our setting. In a concrete implementation of the locally synchronous virtual machine, the synchronization of neighbours is implicitly necessary in every round.

---

[2] The picky reader will actually identify 31 LEDs, 6 additional LEDs are placed at the corners between triangles).

Beyond embedded software, the development of distributed applications requires tool support. We have built an *integrated development environment* with integrated editor, compiler and visual real time simulator/debugger, as well as features helping for the development of robust applications that work in various topologies. It is important to underline 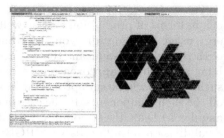 the consistency of synchronous simulation (with a multi threaded simulator executing the synchronous semantics) and asynchronous physical execution.

# References

1. Ackley, D.H., Cannon, D.C., Williams, L.R.: A movable architecture for robust spatial computing. The Computer Journal (2012)
2. Choudhury, S.: Cellular automaton based algorithms for wireless sensor networks. Ph.D. thesis, Queen's University, Kingston, Ontario, Canada (2012)
3. Dunkels, A., Schmidt, O., Voigt, T., Ali, M.: Protothreads: Simplifying event-driven programming of memory-constrained embedded systems. In: Proceedings of the 4th International Conference on Embedded Networked Sensor Systems, SenSys 2006, pp. 29–42. ACM, New York (2006)
4. Fan, R.: Lower Bounds in Distributed Computing. Ph.D. thesis, Massachusetts Institute of Technology (2008)
5. Fan, R., Lynch, N.: Gradient clock synchronization. Distributed Computing 18(4), 255–266 (2006)
6. Halbwachs, N.: Synchronous Programming of Reactive Systems. The Springer International Series in Engineering and Computer Science. Springer (1992)
7. Iyengar, S.S., Brooks, R.R. (eds.): Sensor Networking and Applications. Chapman and Hall/CRC (2012)
8. Leenen, M.A., Arning, V., Thiem, H., Steiger, J., Anselmann, R.: Printable electronics: flexibility for the future. Physica Status Solidi (a) 206(4), 588–597 (2009)
9. Obaidat, M., Denko, M., Woungang, I.: Pervasive Computing and Networking. Wiley (2011)
10. Pérez, G.B.: S.N.A.K.E.: A dynamically reconfigurable artificial sensate skin. Master of science in media arts and sciences, Massachusetts Institute of Technology (2006)
11. Tel, G.: Introduction to Distributed Algorithms. Cambridge University Press (2000)
12. TinyOS web page, http://www.tinyos.net
13. Wolfram, S.: A new kind of science. General science, Wolfram Media (2002)

# Multi-Noisy-objective Optimization Based on Prediction of Worst-Case Performance

Kiyoharu Tagawa[1] and Shoichi Harada[2]

[1] School of Science and Engineering, Kinki University
Higashi-Osaka 577-8502, Japan
tagawa@info.kindai.ac.jp
[2] Graduate School of Science and Engineering Research, Kinki University
Higashi-Osaka 577-8502, Japan

**Abstract.** This paper proposes a new approach to cope with multi-objective optimization problems in presence of noise. In the first place, since considering the worst-case performance is important in many real-world optimization problems, a solution is evaluated based on the upper bounds of respective noisy objective functions predicted statistically by multiple sampling. Secondary, a rational way to decide the maximum sample size for the solution is shown. Thirdly, to allocate the computing budget of a proposed evolutionary algorithm only to promising solutions, two pruning techniques are contrived to judge hopeless solutions only by a few sampling and skip the evaluation of the upper bounds for them.

**Keywords:** evolutionary computing, multi-objective optimization.

## 1   Introduction

Many real-world Multi-objective Optimization Problems (MOPs) have more than one objective function contaminated by noise. The presence of noise leads to different results for repeated evaluations of the same solution. Therefore, for solving Multi-Noisy-objective Optimization Problems (MNOPs), various Multi-Objective Evolutionary Algorithms (MOEAs) have also been reported. The goal of those MOEAs is to produce a set of distributed solutions that are not only of high quality, but also robust. However, there are many possible notations of robustness. Even among them, the worst-case performance is important in particular if the decision maker is very risk averse, or if the stakes are high.

This paper thinks about a new class of MNOPs in which the predicted upper bounds of respective noisy objective functions are minimized simultaneously. The predicted upper bounds of noisy objective functions provide a proper criterion to measure the worst-case performance. However, the multiple sampling of every solution to predict the upper bounds statistically is still expensive. Therefore, a novel MOEA based on Differential Evolution (DE) [1] is proposed for solving the new class of MNOPs effectively. In order to examine as many solutions as possible within a limited number of function evaluations, the proposed MOEA uses two pruning techniques, which are called U-cut and C-cut respectively, to judge hopeless solutions only by a few sampling and skip their evaluations.

A.-H. Dediu et al. (Eds.): TPNC 2014, LNCS 8890, pp. 23–34, 2014.
© Springer International Publishing Switzerland 2014

## 2    Related Work on Multi-Noisy-objective Optimization

To date, a number of methods including various MOEAs have been reported to solve MNOPs [2]. As stated above, the goal of those methods is to produce a set of distributed solutions that are not only of high quality, but also robust. There are many possible notations of robustness, including a good expected performance, a good worst-case performance, a low variability in performance, or a large range of disturbance still leading to acceptable performance [3].

In order to evaluate the good expected performance for a solution, averaging over multiple samples is a most fundamental approach. That is because it is applicable even if the properties of uncertainties are completely unknown [4,5]. On the other hand, some assumptions on the probability distribution of objective function values are often introduced into the problem formulation, namely, a normal distribution with constant variance [6,7,8], a normal distribution with variable variance [9,10], a uniform distribution [11], and so on. Thereby, statistical approaches such as Probabilistic dominance [6] can be used to compare two uncertain solutions. Incidentally, for the case that the objective functions are distributed normally with a constant variance, learning algorithms have also been reported to estimate the constant variance during the optimization [7].

In order to evaluate the worst-case performance for a solution, the concept of min-max robustness is introduced into the problem formulation. Thereby, the worst value of each objective function is found by the multiple sampling of the same solution [12]. Another interpretation of the uncertainty in MOPs is based on scenarios instead of noise. The objective function values for a given solution depend on scenarios. A set of objective function values for all possible scenarios is considered. Then the worst-case performance for the solution is obtained as a set of non-dominated objective function values by solving an inversed MOP [13,14]. The objective function values of a solution for all possible scenarios can be also depicted as a polygon in the objective space. Therefore, the worst-case performance of the solution is represented deterministically as a set of extremal points of the polygon. For finding those extremal points one by one, a single objective optimization algorithm is used repeatedly [15].

It can be seen that the previous work that addresses the worst-case performance in MNOPs is relatively limited. Moreover, to the best of our knowledge, the statistical approach based on the predicted upper bounds of noisy objective functions has not yet been reported. Because it is impossible to find the worst value of a stochastic objective function in a finite number of samples, we think that the statistical approach proposed in this paper is practically useful.

## 3    Problem Formulation

### 3.1    Noisy-objective and Prediction Interval

Let $x = (x_1, \cdots, x_j, \cdots, x_D)$ denote a vector of decision variables $x_j \in \Re$ that can be changed by an algorithm. The decision vector $x \in \Re^D$ is often referred to as a solution. An objective vector $f(x) = (f_1(x), \cdots, f_m(x), \cdots, f_M(x))$

depending on a solution $x \in \Re^D$ is composed of $M$ ($M \geq 2$) objective functions $f_m(x) \in \Re$, $m \in \mathcal{I}_M = \{1, \cdots, M\}$. The objective vector $f(x)$ is minimized in MOPs. Now, we assume that each objective function $f_m(x)$ is contaminated with noise in MNOPs. Therefore, every time a solution $x \in \Re^D$ is evaluated, a different objective vector may be returned. Let $f_m^n(x) \in \Re$, $n \in \mathcal{I}_N = \{1, \cdots, N\}$ be observed values of $f_m(x)$, which are distributed normally as

$$f_m^n(x) \sim \mathcal{N}(\mu_m(x), \ \sigma_m(x)^2) = \mathcal{N}(f_m(x), \ \sigma_m(x)^2), \tag{1}$$

where the mean $\mu_m(x) = f_m(x)$, $m \in \mathcal{I}_M$ and the variance $\sigma_m(x)^2$, $m \in \mathcal{I}_M$ are mutually independent functions that depend on the solution $x \in \Re^D$.

Because the mean $\mu_m(x)$ and the variance $\sigma_m(x)^2$ in (1) are usually unknown, we have to estimate those values, respectively, by the sample mean and the unbiased variance. From a sample set $\{f_m^1(x), \cdots, f_m^n(x), \cdots, f_m^N(x)\}$ of an objective function $f_m(x)$ for $x \in \Re^D$, the sample mean is calculated as

$$\overline{f}_m(x) = \frac{1}{N} \sum_{n=1}^{N} f_m^n(x). \tag{2}$$

The unbiased variance is also calculated from the sample set and (2) as

$$s_m(x)^2 = \frac{1}{N-1} \sum_{n=1}^{N} (f_m^n(x) - \overline{f}_m(x))^2. \tag{3}$$

By using $\overline{f}_m(x)$ and $s_m(x)^2$ instead of $\mu_m(x)$ and $\sigma_m(x)^2$ respectively, the normal distribution in (1) is approximated by Student's t-distribution. We have already obtained the sample set $\{f_m^n(x) \in \Re \mid n \in \mathcal{I}_N\}$ of size $N$. Let $f_m^{N+1}(x)$ be the $(N+1)$-th sample, or the future observation of $f_m(x)$. Then the following statistic yields Student's t-distribution with $N-1$ degrees of freedom [16]:

$$\frac{f_m^{N+1}(x) - \overline{f}_m(x)}{s_m(x)\sqrt{1+\dfrac{1}{N}}} \sim \mathcal{T}(N-1). \tag{4}$$

Let $\alpha$ ($0 < \alpha \leq 0.05$) be a significance level. The one-side prediction interval in which the future observation $f_m^{N+1}(x)$ will fall is derived from (4) as

$$-\infty < f_m^{N+1}(x) \leq \overline{f}_m(x) + t(N-1, \alpha)\, s_m(x)\sqrt{1+\frac{1}{N}} = f_m^U(x), \tag{5}$$

where $t(N-1, \alpha)$ is the $\alpha$-quantile of Student's t-distribution with $N-1$ degrees of freedom. The upper bound of the prediction interval is denoted by $f_m^U(x)$.

The probability of the future observation $f_m^{N+1}(x)$ of the noisy objective function $f_m(x)$ falling in the prediction interval shown in (5) is

$$\mathcal{P}(f_m^{N+1}(x) \leq f_m^U(x)) = 1 - \alpha. \tag{6}$$

On the other hand, the probability that the future observation $f_m^{N+1}(x)$ doesn't fall in the prediction interval in (5) is very small such as

$$\mathcal{P}(f_m^U(x) \leq f_m^{N+1}(x)) = \alpha. \tag{7}$$

## 3.2 Multi-Noisy-objective Optimization Problem

Let $\{\boldsymbol{f}^n(\boldsymbol{x}) = (f_1^n(\boldsymbol{x}), \cdots, f_m^n(\boldsymbol{x}), \cdots f_M^n(\boldsymbol{x})) \mid n \in \mathcal{I}_N\}$ be a sample set of an objective vector $\boldsymbol{f}(\boldsymbol{x}) \in \Re^M$ depending on a solution $\boldsymbol{x} \in \Re^D$. From (2), (3), (5), and the sample set $\{\boldsymbol{f}^n(\boldsymbol{x}) \in \Re^M \mid n \in \mathcal{I}_N\}$ of size $N$, we can predict the upper bound $\boldsymbol{f}^U(\boldsymbol{x}) \in \Re^M$ of the future observation $\boldsymbol{f}^{N+1}(\boldsymbol{x}) \in \Re^M$. We also suppose that each of decision variables $x_j \in \Re$, $j \in \mathcal{I}_D = \{1, \cdots, D\}$ is limited to the range between the lower $x_j^L$ and the upper $x_j^U$ bounds. Thereby, a Multi-Noisy-objective Optimization Problem (MNOP) is formulated as

$$\begin{bmatrix} \text{minimize} & \boldsymbol{f}^U(\boldsymbol{x}) = (f_1^U(\boldsymbol{x}), \cdots, f_m^U(\boldsymbol{x}), \cdots, f_M^U(\boldsymbol{x})), \\ \text{subject to} & \boldsymbol{x} = (x_1, \cdots, x_j, \cdots, x_D) \in \boldsymbol{X}, \end{bmatrix} \quad (8)$$

where $\boldsymbol{X} = \{\boldsymbol{x} \in \Re^D \mid \forall j \in \mathcal{I}_D : x_j^L \leq x_j \leq x_j^U\}$ is called the decision space. Furthermore, $\boldsymbol{F} = \{\boldsymbol{f}^U(\boldsymbol{x}) \in \Re^M \mid \boldsymbol{x} \in \boldsymbol{X}\}$ is called the objective space. In order to simplify the notation in this paper, we will sometimes use an objective vector $\boldsymbol{f}^U(\boldsymbol{x}) \in \boldsymbol{F}$ to represent a corresponding solution $\boldsymbol{x} \in \boldsymbol{X}$, and vice versa.

**Definition 1.** *A vector* $\boldsymbol{v} = (v_1, \cdots, v_m, \cdots, v_M) \in \Re^M$ *is said to dominate the other* $\boldsymbol{v}' \in \Re^M$ *and denoted as* $\boldsymbol{v} \succ \boldsymbol{v}'$, *if the following condition is true:*

$$(\forall m \in \mathcal{I}_M : v_m \leq v_m') \wedge (\exists n \in \mathcal{I}_M : v_n < v_n'). \quad (9)$$

**Definition 2.** *A vector* $\boldsymbol{v} = (v_1, \cdots, v_M) \in \Re^M$ *is said to weakly dominate the other* $\boldsymbol{v}' \in \Re^M$ *and denoted as* $\boldsymbol{v} \succeq \boldsymbol{v}'$, *if the following condition is true:*

$$\forall m \in \mathcal{I}_M : v_m \leq v_m'. \quad (10)$$

From (6), the probability of $\boldsymbol{f}^{N+1}(\boldsymbol{x})$ weakly dominating $\boldsymbol{f}^U(\boldsymbol{x})$ is

$$\mathcal{P}(\boldsymbol{f}^{N+1}(\boldsymbol{x}) \succeq \boldsymbol{f}^U(\boldsymbol{x})) = \prod_{m=1}^M \mathcal{P}(f_m^{N+1}(\boldsymbol{x}) \leq f_m^U(\boldsymbol{x})) = (1 - \alpha)^M. \quad (11)$$

From (7), the probability of $\boldsymbol{f}^U(\boldsymbol{x})$ weakly dominating $\boldsymbol{f}^{N+1}(\boldsymbol{x})$ is

$$\mathcal{P}(\boldsymbol{f}^U(\boldsymbol{x}) \succeq \boldsymbol{f}^{N+1}(\boldsymbol{x})) = \prod_{m=1}^M \mathcal{P}(f_m^U(\boldsymbol{x}) \leq f_m^{N+1}(\boldsymbol{x})) = \alpha^M. \quad (12)$$

## 3.3 Selection of Sample Size

For calculating an objective vector $\boldsymbol{f}^U(\boldsymbol{x})$ in (8), a solution $\boldsymbol{x} \in X$ needs to be evaluated $N$ times. Sampling size selection is actually a burden to balance the quality of the objective vector $\boldsymbol{f}^U(\boldsymbol{x})$ with the computational overhead.

We employ a rational way to determine an appropriate sample size $N$ from the accuracy of the unbiased variance $s_m(\boldsymbol{x})^2$ in (3). The both-side confidence interval of the variance $\sigma_m(\boldsymbol{x})^2$ appeared in (1) is given as follows [16]:

$$\frac{N-1}{\chi^2(N-1, \alpha/2)} s_m(\boldsymbol{x})^2 \leq \sigma_m(\boldsymbol{x})^2 \leq \frac{N-1}{\chi^2(N-1, 1-\alpha/2)} s_m(\boldsymbol{x})^2, \quad (13)$$

where $\chi^2(N-1, \alpha/2)$ and $\chi^2(N-1, 1-\alpha/2)$ are the $\alpha/2$-quantile and the $(1-\alpha/2)$-quantile of the $\chi^2$-distribution with $N-1$ degrees of freedom.

Let $\delta$ $(\delta > 1)$ be a tolerance for the ratio of the upper bound to the lower bound of the confidence interval in (13). Thereby, the ratio is limited as

$$\frac{\chi^2(N-1, \alpha/2)}{\chi^2(N-1, 1-\alpha/2)} \leq \delta. \tag{14}$$

From the condition in (14) and the Fisher's approximation of $\chi^2$-distribution [17], we decide a sample size $N$ for a given tolerance $\delta$ $(\delta > 1)$ as follows:

$$N \geq \frac{1}{2}\left(\frac{(1+\sqrt{\delta})\,z_{\alpha/2}}{\sqrt{\delta}-1}\right)^2 + \frac{3}{2}, \tag{15}$$

where $z_{\alpha/2}$ is the $\alpha/2$-quantile of the standard normal distribution: $\mathcal{N}(0, 1)$. The sample size $N$ increases quickly as we attempt to reduce the tolerance $\delta$.

## 4 Differential Evolution for MNOP

If we calculate the objective vector $\boldsymbol{f}^U(\boldsymbol{x})$ in (8) from the sample set of size $N$ for every examined solution $\boldsymbol{x} \in \boldsymbol{X}$, we can apply conventional MOEAs, such as NSGA-II [18] and DEMO [19], to MNOP without modification. In order to cope with MNOP, we select DEMO as the basic MOEA for its simplicity in coding, fewer control parameters, good accuracy, and fast speed convergence [5].

Algorithm 1 provides the pseudo-code of DEMO applied to MNOP. First of all, an initial population $\boldsymbol{P} \subset \boldsymbol{X}$ of size $N_P$ is generated randomly. Thereafter, the objective vector $\boldsymbol{f}^U(\boldsymbol{x}_i)$ is evaluated for each $\boldsymbol{x}_i \in \boldsymbol{P}$ from a sample set $\{\boldsymbol{f}^n(\boldsymbol{x}_i) \mid n \in \mathcal{I}_N\}$ of size $N$. Every solution $\boldsymbol{x}_i \in \boldsymbol{P}$, $i = 1, \cdots, N_P$ is chosen to be the target vector $\boldsymbol{x}_i$ in turn. By using a basic strategy named "DE/rand/1/exp" [1], a new trial vector $\boldsymbol{u} \in \boldsymbol{X}$ is generated from the target vector $\boldsymbol{x}_i \in \boldsymbol{P}$ and other solutions selected randomly in $\boldsymbol{P}$ at the 7th line.

The search efficiency of DE depends on the control parameters, namely the scale factor $S_F$ and the crossover rate $C_R$, which are used in the strategy. Thus, we introduce a self-adapting mechanism of them [20] into DEMO. A different set of parameter values $S_{F,i}$ and $C_{R,i}$ are assigned to each $\boldsymbol{x}_i \in \boldsymbol{P}$, $i = 1, \cdots, N_P$. The strategy generates $\boldsymbol{u}$ from $\boldsymbol{x}_i \in \boldsymbol{P}$ by using $S_F$ and $C_R$ decided as

$$S_F = \begin{cases} 0.1 + \text{rand}_1[0, 1]\,0.9, & \text{if rand}_2[0, 1] < 0.1, \\ S_{F,i}, & \text{otherwise}, \end{cases} \tag{16}$$

$$C_R = \begin{cases} \text{rand}_3[0, 1], & \text{if rand}_4[0, 1] < 0.1, \\ C_{R,i}, & \text{otherwise}, \end{cases} \tag{17}$$

where $\text{rand}_k[0, 1] \in [0, 1]$ denotes a uniformly distributed random number.

The objective vector $\boldsymbol{f}^U(\boldsymbol{u})$ is evaluated for the trial vector $\boldsymbol{u}$ from a sample set $\{\boldsymbol{f}^n(\boldsymbol{u}) \mid n \in \mathcal{I}_N\}$ of size $N$ at the 8th line. In lines 9-15, the trial vector $\boldsymbol{u}$

**Algorithm 1.** DEMO APPLIED TO MNOP

1: $\boldsymbol{P} := \text{GENERATE\_INITIAL\_POPULATION}(N_P)$;
2: **for** $i := 1$ to $N_P$ **do**
3:     $\boldsymbol{f}^U(\boldsymbol{x}_i) := \text{PREDICT\_UPPER\_BOUND}(\boldsymbol{f}^n(\boldsymbol{x}_i),\ n \in \mathcal{I}_N)$;
4: **end for**
5: **repeat**
6:     **for** $i := 1$ to $N_P$ **do**
7:         $\boldsymbol{u} := \text{STRATEGY}(\boldsymbol{x}_i \in \boldsymbol{P})$;   /* Generate a new trial vector $\boldsymbol{u} \in \boldsymbol{X}$ */
8:         $\boldsymbol{f}^U(\boldsymbol{u}) := \text{PREDICT\_UPPER\_BOUND}(\boldsymbol{f}^n(\boldsymbol{u}),\ n \in \mathcal{I}_N)$;
9:         **if** $\boldsymbol{f}^U(\boldsymbol{u}) \succeq \boldsymbol{f}^U(\boldsymbol{x}_i)$ **then**
10:             $\boldsymbol{x}_i := \boldsymbol{u}$;   /* Replace $\boldsymbol{x}_i \in \boldsymbol{P}$ by $\boldsymbol{u}$. */
11:         **else**
12:             **if** $\boldsymbol{f}^U(\boldsymbol{x}_i) \not\succ \boldsymbol{f}^U(\boldsymbol{u})$ **then**
13:                 $\boldsymbol{P} := \boldsymbol{P} \cup \{\boldsymbol{u}\}$;   /* Add $\boldsymbol{u}$ to $\boldsymbol{P}$. Thus, $|\boldsymbol{P}| > N_P$ holds. */
14:             **end if**
15:         **end if**
16:     **end for**
17:     $\boldsymbol{P} := \text{TRUNCATION\_METHOD\#1}(\boldsymbol{P}, N_P)$;   /* $|\boldsymbol{P}| = N_P$ holds. */
18: **until** a termination condition is satisfied;
19: Output the non-dominated solution set $\check{\boldsymbol{P}} \subseteq \boldsymbol{P}$;

is compared to the target vector $\boldsymbol{x}_i \in \boldsymbol{P}$. If $\boldsymbol{f}^U(\boldsymbol{u})$ weakly dominates $\boldsymbol{f}^U(\boldsymbol{x}_i)$, $\boldsymbol{u}$ replaces $\boldsymbol{x}_i$. However, when they are non-dominated each other, $\boldsymbol{u}$ is added to $\boldsymbol{P}$. Otherwise, $\boldsymbol{u}$ is discarded. As a result, if $\boldsymbol{u}$ survives, the control parameters $S_F$ and $C_R$ used for $\boldsymbol{u}$ are assigned to the new solution $\boldsymbol{u} \in \boldsymbol{P}$. The number of solutions in $\boldsymbol{P}$ becomes $N_P \leq |\boldsymbol{P}| \leq 2\,N_P$ at the 17th line. In order to return the population size to $N_P$, the following truncation method is applied to $\boldsymbol{P}$.

   [**truncation method #1**]

**Step 1** Decide the non-domination rank [18] for each solution $\boldsymbol{x}_i \in \boldsymbol{P}$ and then select $N_P$ solutions from $\boldsymbol{P}$ in the ascending order on the rank.
**Step 2** If some solutions need to be selected from $\boldsymbol{P}_r \subseteq \boldsymbol{P}$ with the same rank, evaluate $\epsilon$-DOM criterion [21] for $\boldsymbol{x}_i \in \boldsymbol{P}_r$. Thereafter, select the necessary number of solutions from $\boldsymbol{P}_r$ in the descending order on the criterion.

   For sorting non-dominated solutions, some secondary criteria that can replace the crowding-distance [18] have been reported. From the result of comparative study, $\epsilon$-DOM was the best in the average among examined secondary criteria [21]. Therefore, $\epsilon$-DOM is adopted in Step 2 of the truncation method #1.

## 5   Proposed Approach to MNOP

Multiple sampling of every examined solution is very expensive in most of real-world optimization problems. To allocate the computing budget of DEMO only to promising solutions of MNOP, we propose two novel pruning techniques of hopeless solutions, which are called U-cut and C-cut respectively. First of all, we restrict the value of each $f_m^U(\boldsymbol{x})$ in (8) to be less than $\gamma_m \in \Re$ because

1. in real-world applications, every solution has to meet absolute standards,
2. a part of the Pareto-front is usually sufficient for decision making,
3. expensive evaluation may be omitted for unacceptable solutions.

Let $\boldsymbol{\gamma} = \{\gamma_1, \cdots, \gamma_M\} \in \Re^M$ be a cutoff point specified by the designer. A Multi-Noisy-Hard-objective Optimization Problem (MNHOP) is formulated as

$$\left[\begin{array}{l} \text{minimize} \quad \boldsymbol{f}^U(\boldsymbol{x}) = (f_1^U(\boldsymbol{x}), \cdots, f_m^U(\boldsymbol{x}), \cdots, f_M^U(\boldsymbol{x})), \\ \text{subject to} \ (\boldsymbol{x} \in \boldsymbol{X}) \wedge (\boldsymbol{f}^U(\boldsymbol{x}) \succeq \boldsymbol{\gamma}), \end{array}\right. \tag{18}$$

where a solution $\boldsymbol{x} \in \boldsymbol{X}$ is feasible if the solution satisfies all constraints. The feasible space $\boldsymbol{G} \subseteq \boldsymbol{F}$ is defined as $\boldsymbol{G} = \{\boldsymbol{f}^U(\boldsymbol{x}) \in \boldsymbol{F} \mid \forall m \in \mathcal{I}_M : f_m^U(\boldsymbol{x}) \leq \gamma_m\}$.

---

**Algorithm 2.** DEUC APPLIED TO MNHOP

---

1: $\boldsymbol{P} := \text{GENERATE\_INITIAL\_POPULATION}(N_P)$;
2: **for** $i := 1$ to $N_P$ **do**
3:     **if** $\forall n \in \mathcal{I}_N : \boldsymbol{f}^n(\boldsymbol{x}_i) \succeq \boldsymbol{\gamma}$ **then**
4:         $\boldsymbol{g}(\boldsymbol{x}_i) := (\boldsymbol{f}^U(\boldsymbol{x}_i) := \text{PREDICT\_UPPER\_BOUND}(\boldsymbol{f}^n(\boldsymbol{x}_i), \ n \in \mathcal{I}_N))$;
5:     **else**
6:         $\boldsymbol{g}(\boldsymbol{x}_i) := \boldsymbol{f}^{\hat{n}}(\boldsymbol{x}_i)$;  /* $\exists \hat{n} \in \mathcal{I}_N : \boldsymbol{f}^{\hat{n}}(\boldsymbol{x}_i) \not\succeq \boldsymbol{\gamma}$ */
7:     **end if**
8: **end for**
9: **repeat**
10:     **for** $i := 1$ to $N_P$ **do**
11:         $\boldsymbol{u} := \text{STRATEGY}(\boldsymbol{x}_i \in \boldsymbol{P})$;  /* Generate a new trial vector $\boldsymbol{u} \in \boldsymbol{X}$ */
12:         **if** $\forall n \in \mathcal{I}_N : (\boldsymbol{g}(\boldsymbol{x}_i) \not\succ \boldsymbol{f}^n(\boldsymbol{u})) \wedge (\boldsymbol{f}^n(\boldsymbol{u}) \succeq \boldsymbol{\gamma})$ **then**
13:             $\boldsymbol{g}(\boldsymbol{u}) := (\boldsymbol{f}^U(\boldsymbol{u}) := \text{PREDICT\_UPPER\_BOUND}(\boldsymbol{f}^n(\boldsymbol{u}), \ n \in \mathcal{I}_N))$;
14:         **else**
15:             $\boldsymbol{g}(\boldsymbol{u}) := \boldsymbol{f}^{\hat{n}}(\boldsymbol{u})$;  /* $\exists \hat{n} \in \mathcal{I}_N : (\boldsymbol{g}(\boldsymbol{x}_i) \succ \boldsymbol{f}^{\hat{n}}(\boldsymbol{u})) \vee (\boldsymbol{f}^{\hat{n}}(\boldsymbol{u}) \not\succeq \boldsymbol{\gamma})$ */
16:         **end if**
17:         **if** $\boldsymbol{g}(\boldsymbol{u}) \succeq \boldsymbol{g}(\boldsymbol{x}_i)$ **then**
18:             $\boldsymbol{x}_i := \boldsymbol{u}$;  /* Replace $\boldsymbol{x}_i \in \boldsymbol{P}$ by $\boldsymbol{u}$. */
19:         **else**
20:             **if** $\boldsymbol{g}(\boldsymbol{x}_i) \not\succ \boldsymbol{g}(\boldsymbol{u})$ **then**
21:                 $\boldsymbol{P} := \boldsymbol{P} \cup \{\boldsymbol{u}\}$;  /* Add $\boldsymbol{u}$ to $\boldsymbol{P}$. Thus, $|\boldsymbol{P}| > N_P$ holds. */
22:             **end if**
23:         **end if**
24:     **end for**
25:     $\boldsymbol{P} := \text{TRUNCATION\_METHOD\#2}(\boldsymbol{P}, N_P, \eta)$;  /* $|\boldsymbol{P}| = N_P$ holds. */
26: **until** a termination condition is satisfied;
27: Output the non-dominated feasible solution set $\check{\boldsymbol{Q}} \subseteq \boldsymbol{Q} \subseteq \boldsymbol{P}$;

---

Differential Evolution with U-cut & C-cut (DEUC) is an extended DEMO and applied to MNHOP in (18) instead of MNOP in (8). Algorithm 2 provides the pseudo-code of DEUC. The proposed DEUC evaluates solutions $\boldsymbol{x}_i \in \boldsymbol{P}$ by the fitness vectors $\boldsymbol{g}(\boldsymbol{x}_i) \in \Re^M$ instead of the objective vectors $\boldsymbol{f}^U(\boldsymbol{x}_i) \in \Re^M$. The fitness vectors are initialized for $\boldsymbol{x}_i \in \boldsymbol{P}$, $i = 1, \cdots, N_P$ in lines 2-8 as

$$g(\boldsymbol{x}_i) = \begin{cases} \boldsymbol{f}^U(\boldsymbol{x}_i) = (f_1^U(\boldsymbol{x}_i), \cdots, f_M^U(\boldsymbol{x}_i)), \text{ if } \forall n \in \mathcal{I}_N : \boldsymbol{f}^n(\boldsymbol{x}_i) \succeq \boldsymbol{\gamma}, \\ \boldsymbol{f}^{\hat{n}}(\boldsymbol{x}_i) = (f_1^{\hat{n}}(\boldsymbol{x}_i), \cdots, f_M^{\hat{n}}(\boldsymbol{x}_i)), \text{ otherwise,} \end{cases} \qquad (19)$$

where $(\forall n \in \{1, \cdots, \hat{n} - 1\} \subset \mathcal{I}_N : \boldsymbol{f}^n(\boldsymbol{x}_i) \succeq \boldsymbol{\gamma}) \wedge (\boldsymbol{f}^{\hat{n}}(\boldsymbol{x}_i) \nsucceq \boldsymbol{\gamma})$ holds.

DEUP generates the trial vector $\boldsymbol{u} \in \boldsymbol{X}$ at the 11th line in the same way with DEMO in Algorithm 1. The fitness vector $g(\boldsymbol{u})$ of $\boldsymbol{u}$ is evaluated in lines 12-16. From (11), if $g(\boldsymbol{x}_i)$ dominates $\boldsymbol{f}^{\hat{n}}(\boldsymbol{u})$, $g(\boldsymbol{x}_i)$ also dominates $\boldsymbol{f}^U(\boldsymbol{u})$ in short odds. Therefore, the U-cut based on the upper bounds of objective functions skips additional sampling of $\boldsymbol{u}$ and set $\boldsymbol{f}^{\hat{n}}(\boldsymbol{u})$ to $g(\boldsymbol{u})$. On the other hand, if $\boldsymbol{f}^{\hat{n}}(\boldsymbol{u})$ doesn't dominate $\boldsymbol{\gamma} \in \Re^M$, $\boldsymbol{u}$ is probably infeasible. Therefore, the C-cut based on the cut -off point also skips additional sampling of $\boldsymbol{u}$ and set $\boldsymbol{f}^{\hat{n}}(\boldsymbol{u})$ to $g(\boldsymbol{u})$. The objective vector $\boldsymbol{f}^U(\boldsymbol{u})$ is evaluated and substituted for $g(\boldsymbol{u})$ at the 13th line only if $\boldsymbol{u}$ is feasible and $g(\boldsymbol{x}_i)$ doesn't dominate every $\boldsymbol{f}^n(\boldsymbol{u})$, $n \in \mathcal{I}_N$.

The trial vector $\boldsymbol{u}$ is compared to the target vector $\boldsymbol{x}_i \in \boldsymbol{P}$ in lines 17-23 based on their fitness vectors. The feasibility of solutions doesn't need to be considered in the comparison between $\boldsymbol{u}$ and $\boldsymbol{x}_i \in \boldsymbol{P}$, because it is proven that feasible solutions $\boldsymbol{f}^U(\boldsymbol{x}) \in \boldsymbol{G}$ are not dominated by any infeasible ones [22]:

$$\boldsymbol{f}^U(\boldsymbol{x}) \in \boldsymbol{F} \wedge \boldsymbol{f}^U(\boldsymbol{x}') \in \boldsymbol{G} \wedge \boldsymbol{f}^U(\boldsymbol{x}) \succeq \boldsymbol{f}^U(\boldsymbol{x}') \Rightarrow \boldsymbol{f}^U(\boldsymbol{x}) \in \boldsymbol{G}. \qquad (20)$$

In order to return the population size to $N_P$ at the 25th line, the following truncation method #2 is applied to $\boldsymbol{P}$. The truncation method #2 was proposed for multi-hard-objective optimization problems in our previous paper [22]. Hard-objective differs from constrained objective because the former has no conflict with its constraint. If an objective function $f_m^U(\boldsymbol{x})$ is minimized in MNHOP, its constraint $f_m^U(\boldsymbol{x}) \le \gamma_m$ will be satisfied sooner or later. Let $\boldsymbol{Q} \subseteq \boldsymbol{P}$ be a set of feasible solutions defined as $\boldsymbol{Q} = \{\boldsymbol{x}_i \in \boldsymbol{P} \mid \boldsymbol{f}^U(\boldsymbol{x}_i) \in \boldsymbol{G}\}$. Feasible solutions $\boldsymbol{x}_i \in \boldsymbol{Q}$ have priority over infeasible ones in $\boldsymbol{P}$. For sorting infeasible solutions, alternative schemes are chosen by a control parameter $\eta$ $(0 \le \eta \le 1)$.

[truncation method #2]

**Step 1** If $|\boldsymbol{Q}| \ge N_P$ then apply truncation method #1 to $\boldsymbol{Q} \subseteq \boldsymbol{P}$.

**Step 2** If $|\boldsymbol{Q}| < N_P$ then select all feasible solutions $\boldsymbol{x}_i \in \boldsymbol{Q}$. Thereafter, the shortage is selected from the set of infeasible solutions $\boldsymbol{Q}^c = \boldsymbol{P} \setminus \boldsymbol{Q}$ as

**Step 2.1** If $|\boldsymbol{Q}| \le \eta N_P$ then apply truncation method #1 to $\boldsymbol{Q}^c \subseteq \boldsymbol{P}$.

**Step 2.2** Otherwise, select the necessary number of solutions $\boldsymbol{x}_i \in \boldsymbol{Q}^c \subseteq \boldsymbol{P}$ in the ascending order on the violation distance $d(\boldsymbol{x}_i) \in \Re$ defined as

$$d(\boldsymbol{x}_i) = \sum_{m=1}^{M} \max\{0, (g_m(\boldsymbol{x}_i) - \gamma_m)\}. \qquad (21)$$

# 6   Numerical Experiments

## 6.1   Experimental Setup

In most real-world MNOPs, the higher objective function values are usually expected to have more errors than lower ones [10]. Therefore, by using a deterministic function $f_m(\boldsymbol{x}) \in \Re$, the noisy objective function is defined as

**Table 1.** Number of obtained solutions

(a) DEMO applied to MNOP

| $M$ | 2 | 4 | 6 | 8 |
|---|---|---|---|---|
| DTLZ1 | 85.7 | 99.9 | 100.0 | 100.0 |
| DTLZ2 | 98.3 | 100.0 | 100.0 | 100.0 |
| DTLZ3 | 98.7 | 100.0 | 100.0 | 100.0 |
| DTLZ4 | 98.5 | 100.0 | 100.0 | 100.0 |
| DTLZ5 | 98.3 | 100.0 | 100.0 | 100.0 |
| DTLZ6 | 79.7 | 100.0 | 100.0 | 100.0 |

(b) DEUC applied to MNHOP

| $M$ | 2 | 4 | 6 | 8 |
|---|---|---|---|---|
| DTLZ1 | 92.0 | 100.0 | 100.0 | 76.6 |
| DTLZ2 | 99.0 | 100.0 | 100.0 | 100.0 |
| DTLZ3 | 99.4 | 100.0 | 100.0 | 63.3 |
| DTLZ4 | 98.7 | 100.0 | 100.0 | 100.0 |
| DTLZ5 | 99.0 | 100.0 | 100.0 | 100.0 |
| DTLZ6 | 95.1 | 100.0 | 100.0 | 100.0 |

**Table 2.** Comparison of DEMO and DEPC by Wilcoxon test

(a) Convergence (CM)

| $M$ | 2 | 4 | 6 | 8 |
|---|---|---|---|---|
| DTLZ1 | △ | △ | △ | △ |
| DTLZ2 | — | △ | △ | △ |
| DTLZ3 | △ | △ | △ | △ |
| DTLZ4 | ▲ | △ | △ | △ |
| DTLZ5 | — | △ | ▲ | △ |
| DTLZ6 | △ | △ | △ | △ |

(b) Diversity (MS)

| $M$ | 2 | 4 | 6 | 8 |
|---|---|---|---|---|
| DTLZ1 | ▽ | ▽ | ▽ | ▽ |
| DTLZ2 | — | ▽ | ▽ | ▽ |
| DTLZ3 | ▽ | ▽ | ▽ | ▽ |
| DTLZ4 | — | ▽ | ▽ | — |
| DTLZ5 | — | ▽ | ▽ | ▽ |
| DTLZ6 | ▽ | ▽ | ▽ | ▽ |

(c) Hypervolume (Hv)

| $M$ | 2 | 4 | 6 | 8 |
|---|---|---|---|---|
| DTLZ1 | △ | △ | △ | △ |
| DTLZ2 | — | — | — | — |
| DTLZ3 | △ | △ | △ | △ |
| DTLZ4 | — | — | — | — |
| DTLZ5 | — | △ | — | — |
| DTLZ6 | △ | △ | △ | △ |

$$f_m^n(\boldsymbol{x}) = f_m(\boldsymbol{x}) + \lambda_m\, f_m(\boldsymbol{x})\, \varepsilon_m^a + \kappa_m\, \varepsilon_m^b, \tag{22}$$

where $\varepsilon_m^a \sim \mathcal{N}(0,\ 1)$, $\varepsilon_m^b \sim \mathcal{N}(0,\ 1)$, $\lambda_m > 0$, and $\kappa_m > 0$.

According to a model of noise [10], the noise in (22) is also composed of two components: variable one $\lambda_m\, f_m(\boldsymbol{x})$ and constant one $\kappa_m$. From the reproductive property of the normal distribution [16], $f_m^n(\boldsymbol{x})$ is distributed normally as

$$f_m^n(\boldsymbol{x}) \sim \mathcal{N}(f_m(\boldsymbol{x}),\ \sigma_m(\boldsymbol{x})^2) = \mathcal{N}(f_m(\boldsymbol{x}),\ \lambda_m^2\, f_m(\boldsymbol{x})^2 + \kappa_m^2). \tag{23}$$

The scalable test MOPs [23] with $M$ objectives are employed for providing $f_m(\boldsymbol{x})$ in (22) with $\lambda_m = 0.01$ and $\kappa_m = 0.05$, $m \in \mathcal{I}_M$. From (15), the minimum sample size $N = 40$ is calculated for $\alpha = 0.05$ and $\delta = 2.5$. DEMO is applied to each instance of MNOP in (8) 30 times. The population size is chosen as $N_P = 100$. As the termination condition, the total number of function evaluations is limited to $8 \times 10^5$. Similarly, DEUC is applied to each instance of MNHOP in (18), where a cutoff point $\boldsymbol{\gamma} \in \Re^M$ is given for all cases as $\gamma_m = 2.0$, $m \in \mathcal{I}_M$. A recommended value $\eta = 0.2$ [22] is used for the truncation method #2.

## 6.2   Results and Discussion

Table 1 compares the average numbers of solutions obtained by DEMO and DEUC. Because the solutions obtained by DEUC have to be feasible, DEUC finds fewer solutions than DEMO in two cases: DTLZ1 and DTLZ3 ($M = 8$).

To evaluate the solutions in Table 1, we use three metrics: 1) Convergence Measure (CM) of the original test MOPs [23], 2) Maximum Spread (MS) [24], and 3) Hypervolume (Hv). MS is a metric to evaluate the diversity of solutions. Hv is a comprehensive metric evaluating both convergence and diversity.

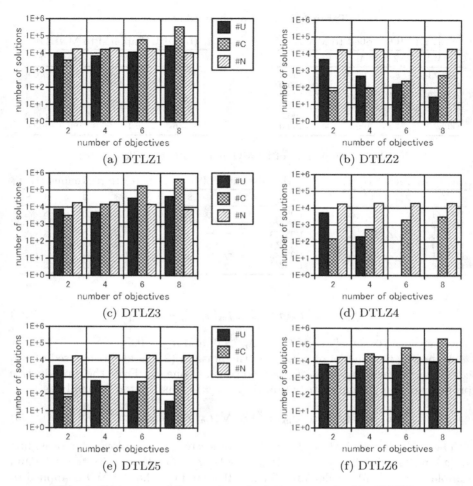

**Fig. 1.** Histogram of the number of solutions examined by DEUC

Table 2 compares DEUC with DEMO by using Wilcoxon test about CM, MS, and Hv: $\triangle$ ($\triangledown$) means that DEUC is significantly better (worse) than DEMO with risk 1[%]; $\blacktriangle$ ($\blacktriangledown$) means that DEUC is better (worse) than DEMO with risk 5[%]; and "—" means that there is no significant difference between DEUC and DEMO. From Table 2, DEUC is not defeated by DEMO in CM for all cases. On the other hand, DEUC can't beat DEMO in MS. Comparing to DEMO in Hv, DEUC is not defeated for all cases and significantly better for many cases.

From Table 2(c), DEMO is competitive with DEUC in DTLZ2 and DTLZ4. However, DEUC defeats DEMO in DTLZ1, DTLZ3, and DTLZ6. Fig. 1 shows the histogram of the number of solutions examined by DEUC in each problem. Category #N in Fig. 1 denotes the number of solutions evaluated $N = 40$ times. Categories #U and #C denote the numbers of solutions evaluated less than $N = 40$ times due to U-cut and C-cut respectively, where DEUC applies U-cut to each solution before C-cut. Because DEMO evaluates every solution $N = 40$ times, the number of examined solutions is always $(8 \times 10^5)/40 = 2 \times 10^4$. Contrarily, DEUC examines more solutions than DEMO as shown in Fig. 1.

From Fig. 1, both U-cut and C-cut work effectively in DTLZ1, DTLZ3, and DTLZ6. Especially, C-cut becomes more effective as the number of objective functions increases. Because a lot of hopeless solutions are evaluated only a few times due to U-cut and C-cut, the total numbers of solutions examined by DEUC become very large in those problems. On the other hand, neither U-cut nor C-cut is effective for the other problems. Especially, U-put doesn't work when the number of objective functions is large. Consequently, the total numbers of examined solutions don't increase so much in DTLZ2, DTLZ4, and DTLZ5.

## 7 Conclusion

It is important to consider the worst-case performance for real-world MNOPs. Therefore, we have predicted statistically the upper bounds of noisy objective functions from a finite number of samples. In order to omit useless multiple sampling, we have also proposed an extended DEMO named DEUC that uses two pruning techniques of hopeless solutions. DEUC was not defeated by DEMO in all test problems. Besides, DEUC outperformed DEMO in many test problems. Even though DEUC requires a new control parameter, namely the cutoff point, an appropriate cutoff point can be decided easily for real-world MNOPs from specifications or an existing solution. Actually, a sufficient improvement over an existing solution should be acceptable in real-world applications.

Future work will include an in-depth evaluation of the proposed DEUP on a broad range of practical MNHOPs with various cutoff points. Furthermore, handling non-Gaussian noise efficiently remains as an active area of research.

**Acknowledgment.** This work was supported by a grant from Japan Society for the Promotion of Science (JSPS) (Project No. 24560503).

## References

1. Price, K.V., Storn, R.M., Lampinen, J.A.: Differential Evolution - A Practical Approach to Global Optimization. Springer (2005)
2. Jin, Y., Branke, J.: Evolutionary optimization in uncertain environments - a survey. IEEE Trans. on Evolutionary Computation 9(3), 303–317 (2005)
3. Gunawan, S., Azarm, S.: Multi-objective robust optimization using a sensitivity region concept. Structural and Multidisciplinary Optimization 29(1), 50–60 (2005)
4. Voß, T., Trautmann, H., Igel, C.: New uncertainty handling strategies in multi-objective evolutionary optimization. In: Schaefer, R., Cotta, C., Kołodziej, J., Rudolph, G. (eds.) PPSN XI. LNCS, vol. 6239, pp. 260–269. Springer, Heidelberg (2010)
5. Rakshit, P., Konar, A., Das, S., Jain, L.C., Nagar, A.K.: Uncertainty management in differential evolution induced multiobjective optimization in presence of measurement noise. IEEE Trans. on Systems, Man, and Cybernetics: Systems 44(7), 922–937 (2013)

6. Hughes, E.J.: Evolutionary multi-objective ranking with uncertainty and noise. In: Zitzler, E., Deb, K., Thiele, L., Coello Coello, C.A., Corne, D.W. (eds.) EMO 2001. LNCS, vol. 1993, pp. 329–342. Springer, Heidelberg (2001)
7. Fieldsend, J.E., Everson, R.M.: Multi-objective optimization in the presence of uncertainty. In: Proc. IEEE CEC 2005, pp. 243–250 (2005)
8. Shim, V.A., Tan, K.C., Chia, J.Y., Mamun, A.A.: Multi-objective optimization with estimation of distribution algorithm in a noisy environment. Evolutionary Computation 21(1), 149–177 (2013)
9. Bui, L.T., Abbass, H.A., Essam, D.: Localization for solving noisy multi-objective optimization problems. Evolutionary Computation 17(3), 379–409 (2009)
10. Eskandari, H., Geiger, C.D.: Evolutionary multiobjective optimization in noisy problem environments. Journal of Heuristics 15(6), 559–595 (2009)
11. Teich, J.: Pareto-front exploration with uncertain objectives. In: Zitzler, E., Deb, K., Thiele, L., Coello Coello, C.A., Corne, D.W. (eds.) EMO 2001. LNCS, vol. 1993, pp. 314–328. Springer, Heidelberg (2001)
12. Kuroiwa, D., Lee, G.M.: On robust multiobjective optimization. Vietnam Journal of Mathematics 40(2&3), 305–317 (2012)
13. Avigad, G., Branke, J.: Embedded evolutionary multi-objective optimization for worst case robustness. In: Proc. GECCO 2008, pp. 617–624 (2008)
14. Branke, J., Avigad, G., Moshaiov, A.: Multi-objective worst case optimization by means of evolutionary algorithms. Working Paper, Coventry UK: WBS, University of Warwick (2013), http://wrap.warwick.ac.uk/55724
15. Ehrgott, M., Ide, J., Schöbel, A.: Minmax robustness for multi-objective optimization problems. European Journal of Operation Research (2014), http://dx.doi.org/10.1016/j.ejor.2014.03.013
16. Wackerly, D.D., Mendenhall, W., Scheaffer, R.L.: Mathematical Statistics with Applications, 7th edn. Thomson Learning, Inc. (2008)
17. Fisher, R.A.: On the interpretation of $\chi^2$ from contingency tables, and calculation of $\mathcal{P}$. Journal of the Royal Statistical Society 85(1), 87–94 (1922)
18. Deb, K., Pratap, A., Agarwal, S., Meyarivan, T.: A fast and elitist multiobjective genetic algorithm: NSGA-II. IEEE Trans. on Evolutionary Computation 6(2), 182–197 (2002)
19. Robič, T., Filipič, B.: DEMO: Differential evolution for multiobjective optimization. In: Coello Coello, C.A., Hernández Aguirre, A., Zitzler, E. (eds.) EMO 2005. LNCS, vol. 3410, pp. 520–533. Springer, Heidelberg (2005)
20. Brest, J., Greiner, S., Bošković, B., Merink, M., Žumer, V.: Self-adapting control parameters in differential evolution: a comparative study on numerical benchmark problems. IEEE Trans. on Evolutionary Computation 10(6), 646–657 (2006)
21. Köppen, M., Yoshida, K.: Substitute distance assignments in NSGA-II for handling many-objective optimization problems. In: Obayashi, S., Deb, K., Poloni, C., Hiroyasu, T., Murata, T. (eds.) EMO 2007. LNCS, vol. 4403, pp. 727–741. Springer, Heidelberg (2007)
22. Tagawa, K., Imamura, A.: Many-hard-objective optimization using differential evolution based on two-stage constraint-handling. In: Proc. GECCO 2013, pp. 671–678 (2013)
23. Deb, K., Thiele, L., Laumanns, M., Zitzler, E.: Scalable test problems for evolutionary multi-objective optimization. TIK-Technical Report, 112, 1–27 (2001)
24. Zitzler, E.: Evolutionary Algorithms for Multiobjective Optimization: Methods and Applications, PhD thesis, Swiss Federal Institute of Technology, Zurich (1999)

# Generalization in Maze Navigation Using Grammatical Evolution and Novelty Search

Paulo Urbano[1,*], Enrique Naredo[2], and Leonardo Trujillo[2]

[1] LabMAg, Universidade de Lisboa, 1749-016 Lisbon, Portugal
pub@di.fc.ul.pt
[2] Tree-Lab, Instituto Tecnológico de Tijuana, Calz. del Tecnológico S/N,
Tomás Aquino, 22414 Tijuana, Baja California, México
enriquenaredo@gmail.com, leonardo.trujillo@tectijuana.edu.mx

**Abstract.** Recent research on evolutionary algorithms has begun to focus on the issue of generalization. While most works emphasize the evolution of high quality solutions for particular problem instances, others are addressing the issue of evolving solutions that can generalize in different scenarios, which is also the focus of the present paper. In particular, this paper compares fitness-based search, Novelty Search (NS), and random search in a set of generalization oriented experiments in a maze navigation problem using Grammatical Evolution (GE), a variant of Genetic Programming. Experimental results suggest that NS outperforms the other search methods in terms of evolving general navigation behaviors that are able to cope with different initial conditions within a static deceptive maze.

**Keywords:** Novelty Search, Grammatical Evolution, Genetic Programming.

## 1 Introduction

Genetic Programming (GP) is a machine learning approach for the discovery of computer programs through an evolutionary search process. An important evaluation criteria for artificial learning systems, and for GP in particular, is their ability to find high quality solutions. However, generalization is also crucial, and several works have been devoted to this issue [2,7,6]. A general solution is one that is able to have a high performance on cases used for learning, and also on newer unseen cases. For example, in maze navigation, an artificial agent must find its way through the maze, from the start to a target point. An evolved control program may be successful in solving a particular navigation task, able to reach the target starting from a fixed point within the maze, but unable to solve the task when we change some aspect of the problem such as the initial conditions or environmental structure. In this scenario, the learned program is considered to be overfitted to the particular scenario used for learning. Ideally we would like to evolve programs that exhibit general navigation behaviors; i. e., performs well within a wide range of previously unseen maze scenarios.

---

* Corresponding author.

A.-H. Dediu et al. (Eds.): TPNC 2014, LNCS 8890, pp. 35–46, 2014.

Some maze navigation tasks are used as deceptive benchmark problems for traditional Evolutionary Algorithms (EA). The wall configurations of mazes may create occlusions and *cul-de-sacs*, complicating the navigation task. Suppose that fitness is proportional to the Euclidean distance of a robot to the target. Then, when the walls of the mazes are obstacles that block the direct path to the target, the fitness gradient does not lead towards a feasible direction, thus deceiving the evolutionary search process, towards a local optima.

Therefore, to solve a deceptive maze navigation task, the search process must diverge from areas of high fitness and explore areas of low fitness. The problem with fitness-based EA is that, by following the gradient of the fitness function, it will not reward low fitness individuals, thus failing to reach the target. In EA literature, the main methods for avoiding local optima have focused on the promotion of genomic diversity [15,1]. Recently, rewarding diversity in the space of behaviors has received growing attention [12]. In general, all diversity-preserving algorithms take fitness into account, but Novelty Search (NS), a recent divergent evolutionary technique, takes a more unique step.

NS ignores the fitness function explicitly, relying only on behavioral diversity as the sole criteria for selection and reproduction. Therefore, instead of guiding the search for the *fittest* individual, NS guides the search for the most novel individual, replacing fitness measure by a novelty score taken from the individuals' behavior description. NS explores the behavioral space without any goal, besides generating novelty, ultimately an individual with the desired behavior may be found. NS has been successfully applied in several deceptive problems in neuro-evolution [5,10], and in GP [9,14,13] in some cases outperforming fitness-based EA.

However, most of the research on NS has ignored the issue of generalization. The motivation of the current paper is to study the capabilities of NS regarding generalization using maze navigation and Grammatical Evolution (GE) [16]. We use a fixed maze and a fixed target point for training, and we vary the starting point and orientation during testing. The goal is to test how general are the behaviors when they are evolved using only a single training instance, and also if different initial conditions have implications on the generalization of the solutions. We also used a bigger training set composed of several initial conditions, with the goal of evolving behaviors that are able to solve the maze task for every training case. The generalization abilities of the best evolved behaviors are also evaluated in the same test set. The performance of NS on the train and test set is compared against fitness based and random search. Our hypothesis is that an heterogeneous training set might originate a second level of deception to traditional fitness-based evolution. Some instances of the training set will be easier to solve than others and fitness-based evolution might tend to reward individuals fitted to the easiest training scenarios, failing to generalize. We also hypothesize that NS might play a significant role in the evolution of general maze navigation agents, preventing evolution to get trapped in local optima.

**Fig. 1.** Example of a GE genotype-phenotype mapping, where the binary genotype is translated into an integer string used to select production rules from a grammar. The derivation sequence of the program is shown on the right. All codons were used but wrapping was unnecessary.

## 2  Grammatical Evolution

Grammatical Evolution (GE) is an evolutionary algorithm that can evolve computer programs in an arbitrary language [16] defined by a Backus-Naur Form (BNF) grammar. Programs are indirectly represented by variable length binary genomes, and are built in a development process. The genome linear representation allows the application of genetic operators such as crossover and mutation in a typical genetic algorithm manner, unlike in the standard tree-based GP approach. Beginning with the start symbol of the grammar, a genotypephenotype mapping is employed such that each individual's binary genome, contains in its codons (typically groups of 8 bits) the information to select and apply the grammar production rules and generate a program.

Production rules for each non-terminal will be indexed starting from 0. In order to select a production rule for the left-most non-terminal of the developing program, from left to right the next codon value on the genome is read and interpreted using the following formula: $I = c\%r$, where $c$ represents the current codon value, % represents the modulus operator, and $r$ is the number of production rules for the left-most non-terminal. The correspondent production in the $I$-th index will be used to replace the left-most non-terminal. If, while reading codons, the algorithm reaches the end of the genome, a wrapping operator is invoked and it starts reading again from the beginning of the genome. The process stops when all of the non-terminal symbols have been replaced, resulting in a valid program. In the wrapping process, if an individual fails with this condition after a maximum of wraps, then it is considered an invalid individual, and is given the lowest score. The mapping process is illustrated with an example in Figure 1, where we use a Grammar for describing maze navigation programs written in Netlogo [19].

## 3  Novelty Search

Implementing Novelty Search [8] requires little change to any evolutionary algorithm aside from replacing the fitness function with a domain dependent novelty metric. The novelty metric measures how different an individual is from other individuals with respect to behavior. In NS, there is a constant evolutionary pressure towards behavioral innovation. The behavior of each individual is normally characterized bey a vector of real numbers that capture behavior information along the whole evaluation or which is just sampled at some particular instants. The novelty of an individual is measured with respect to the behaviors of the current population and of a sample of predecessor individuals, stored in an archive. The archive is initially empty, and new behaviors are added to it if they are significantly different from the ones already there, i.e., if their novelty is above a dynamically computed threshold.

The novelty metric characterises how far the new individual is from the rest of the population and its predecessors in behavior space, based on the sparseness at the respective point in the behavior space. A simple measure of sparseness at a point is the average distance to the $k$-nearest neighbours at that point, where $k$ is a constant empirically determined. Intuitively, if the average distance to a given point's nearest neighbours is large then it is in a sparse area; it is in a dense region if the average distance is small. The sparseness at each point is given by Equation 1, where $\mu_i$ is the $i$th-nearest neighbour of $x$ with respect to the behavior distance metric $dist$, which typically is the Euclidean distance between domain-dependent behavior characterisation vectors.

$$\rho(x) = \frac{1}{k} \sum_{i=1}^{k} dist(x, \mu_i) \, . \tag{1}$$

Candidates from more sparse regions of this behavioral search space then receive higher novelty scores, thus guiding the search towards what is new, with no other explicit objective.

## 4  Related Work

With the exception of [2,11], as far as we know, the research on NS has mostly ignored the issue of generalization in robotic domains. For example, Lehman and Stanley in neuro-evolution [9], Lehman and Stanley in GP [10], as well as Loukas and Georgiou in GE [4], have made experiments using a variety of mazes with different levels of deception, but the evolved behaviors were specific for each maze configuration and initial conditions. It was not tested if the evolved behaviors were able to generalize to different starting and target points or to different mazes. Velez and Clune in [18] transferred maze navigation robots evolved with NS to new scenarios. Their experiments in neuro-evolution have confirmed that agents using NS do learn exploration skills. The transferred robots did in fact perform much better than randomly generated agents but did not outperform transferred robots evolved by a standard fitness-based EA. In [9], using standard GP, and in [17], using Grammatical Evolution, NS was applied successfully to the Santa Fe Trail Problem (SFT), a known deceptive problem in GP, but their goal was finding individuals able to perform well in that trail. Kushchu [7]

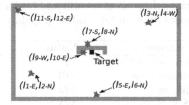 

**Fig. 2.** The Medium Maze is a rectangle of $38 \times 22$ tiles. Left figure shows the target represented by a black square, and the 12 training instances labelled from $I_1$ to $I_{12}$. On each location there are 2 instances with different orientations. The initial orientations are labeled by: N=North, E=East, S=South, W=West. The right figure shows the 100 initial conditions used for testing, randomly generated.

has identified the SFT problem as an example of evolution of brittle solutions in fitness-based GP. His experimental results showed that most of the time, a successful ant won't perform well on some variations of the same trail. Kushchu in [7] proposed to train an ant on a set composed of variations of the SFT, sharing similar characteristics and tested the learned behaviors on a different set of similar trails. He was able to successfully evolve general trail following ant behaviors for a class of trails similar in difficulty to the SFT. Doucette and Heywood [2] have empirically evaluated the impact of NS on generalization performance for the SFT, using SFT as a single set and a test set of similar trails. They evaluated a cross-section of combined novelty and fitness, and fitness only function, and no method was to produce successful individuals in both the SFT and the trails from the set. However, results showed that the classical fitness-based GP provided best train and test performances, but programs evolved by NS alone had more generalization abilities, i.e., lower differences between train and test performance. In contrast, in two other experiments [9,17] NS outperformed fitness-search in the SFT.

## 5   Maze Navigation Experiments

Given the static maze shown in Figure 2, similar to the Medium Maze of [9], an agent controlled by a GE program must navigate from a specific starting point and orientation to a target point using a limit number of moves. The chosen maze has some potential for deception as the target is behind an inner wall blocking direct paths. The agent may sense the wall in the square in front, in the square on the right and on the left. It has 3 possible actions each one consuming one move: it may move forward one square if is there is no wall in front, it may turn right or left, rotating 90 degrees, clockwise or counter clockwise, respectively.

The grammar that defines the space of possible programs is given in Figure 1, the one we used to illustrate genotype to phenotype mapping in GE. We used 3 sensor boolean functions (wall-ahead?, wall-left? and wall-right?), and three actions (move, turn-left and turn-right). The program will be repeatedly

**Table 1.** Parameters used for both experimental setups. Codons-min and Codons-max are the minimal and maximal number of codons in the initial random population.

| Parameter | Value | Parameter | Value |
|-----------|-------|-----------|-------|
| Codon-size | 8 | Generational | YES |
| Codons-min | 15 | Mutation prob | 0.01 |
| Codons-max | 25 | Elitism | 10% |
| Number of runs | 100 | NS archive | NO |
| Wraps | 10 | Crossover | codon-crossover |
| Number of individuals | 250 | NS $k-$neighbors | 3 |
| Crossover prob. | 0.9 | Maximum of moves | 100, 500 |
| | | Selection | Roulette Wheel |

executed until the agent hits the target or reaches the maximum number of moves. The agent succeeds if it hits the target square within the fixed limit of moves.

We compared novelty, fitness and random-based search in a series of generalization experiments. We want to assess how general the evolved behaviors are using only a single training instance. We have tried out different starting conditions, i.e., different single instance training sets. We have chosen 12 initial conditions for training the agent shown in the picture on the left side of Figure 2. Training instances were chosen to be heterogeneous in terms of the level of deception and difficulty imposed by the navigation task. Some starting points will be more or less blocked by walls, may be more or less distant to the target point, adjacent to the wall with the target or near the external wall, far from the target, others will be in the empty space, distant from both walls. For each initial condition, we have evaluated, in a series of runs, the performance of the best program from each run on an independent test set of initial conditions, not used for learning. For testing, we used the 100 initial positions and orientations presented on the right of Figure 2, that were randomly generated but correspond to a wide range of initial conditions. We also used a training set composed with all of the 12 initial conditions, and evaluate the generalization abilities in the same test set with 100 instances. Our objective is to evolve behaviors that are successful for all 12 initial conditions and evaluate their generalization abilities.

All experiments mentioned in this study are performed using the jGE library [3], which is a Java implementation of GE, and jGE Netlogo [4], which is a Netlogo extension of the jGE library. The Netlogo program was extended with an implementation of NS. The phenotype is a NetLogo program and the space of possible programs is given by the BNF-grammar showed on Figure 1. The experiments were repeated 100 times with a population of 250 individuals for 50 generations. The parameters used are presented in Table 1.

Fitness-based search needs a measure of performance to evaluate individuals, thus fitness is computed by $1/(1 + \text{dist}(p, q))$, where $p$ is the final position, and $q$ the maze target. In the case of a training data with 12 instances, each agent is evaluated 12 times and the final fitness is the average score across all the evaluations. Similarly, the fitness on the test set will be the average fitness across all 100 evaluations.

NS needs a behavior descriptor, so we used same descriptor from [10], which is the final position of the robot after hitting the target point or exhausting the maximal number of moves. By ignoring the details of the trajectories, NS will rewards agents that end in zones where nobody or less agents have ended before. In the case of a training set with 12 instances, the agent is evaluated 12 times, for every instance of the training set, and its final behavior descriptor is composed by the 12 ending points, which are concatenated in a vector to obtain a single descriptor. For an invalid individual, a value of 0 is given for both fitness and novelty. In the NS extension of GE, the novelty score of an individual will be the average behavior distance towards the behaviors of its $k$-nearest valid neighbours. After some preliminary exploration, we set to 3 the number of neighbours used to compute novelty score and we did not use an archive as in [8] since in our experiments it did not help to improve the performance.

## 6   Results

We begin by presenting and discussing results gathered from experiments where the agents are limited to 100 moves following [9].

### 6.1   Results and Analysis for a Maximal of 100 Moves

The results have been separated into training and testing performance. Considering the best programs from each run, we measured the percentage of hits and the average fitness in the train and test sets. Results are illustrated in Table 3 for each training set composed of a single instance comparing all three methods. Although NS did not obtain a 100% percentage of hits for every instance, it had the best performance, followed by fitness-based search, and finally random search. As random search has attained almost maximal performance with the following set of initial instances: $\{I_5, I_6, I_7, I_8, I_9, I_{10}\}$, we may conclude that they define easy navigation tasks. The best behaviors evolved by the three methods performed poorly on the test set: Not a single behavior was able to hit the target for every testing instance and the average fitness scores were low and very similar for all three methods. The results obtained with experiments with a training set composed with the 12 instances presented in Table 2, show that none of the methods were able to evolve behaviors that hit the target for all 12 training instances, exhibiting also a very poor performance on the test set. Our explanation about the poor training performance of both fitness-based search and NS on on the 12 instances experiments, is that a maximum number of 100 movements, following [9], imposes a heavy constraint inhibiting maze exploration and thwarting the evolution of general maze navigation behaviors. Hence, we have repeated the experiments fixing a new limit for the number of moves: 500, which increases *time* for maze exploration.

### 6.2   Results and Analysis for a Maximal of 500 Moves

The results regarding training sets with a single instance are presented in Table 3. These results are better for novelty and fitness-based search when compared with

**Table 2.** Table of results from the training set composed with the 12 instances. L-100 and L-500 stands for the limit of moves. NS-K3 stands for Novelty Search with the $k$-neighbour parameter set to 3. Fit stands for the average fitness score of the best program from each run, and Hits for the average number of best programs that hit the target.

|  |  | Training | | Testing | |
|---|---|---|---|---|---|
|  |  | Hits | Fit | Hits | Fit |
| **L-100** | NS-K3 | 0% | 0.46 | 0% | 0.14 |
|  | Fitness | 0% | 0.40 | 0% | 0.13 |
|  | Random | 0% | 0.39 | 0% | 0.12 |
| **L-500** | NS-K3 | 61% | 0.93 | 41% | 0.89 |
|  | Fitness | 22% | 0.63 | 13% | 0.47 |
|  | Random | 1% | 0.40 | 0% | 0.16 |

experiments with the number of moves limited to 100. On the other hand, the differences for random search are not so relevant: It was still able to get a 100% of successful solutions for some of the initial conditions, and a very low hit percentage and average fitness for the most difficult cases, similar to the experiment with a limit of 100 moves. NS outperforms fitness-based and random search in terms of training performance, having a 100% of hits for every training instance, and a higher average fitness. Fitness-based against random search shows better results for some of the instances, while for the instances $I_5, I_7$ it shows lower performance than random search. However, instances $\{I_1, I_2, I_3, I_4, I_{11}, I_{12}\}$ introduce more difficulty for the methods tested. Those points, when used as single training sets will generate behaviors with higher generalization abilities than other instances. In contrast the easiest starting conditions resulted in behaviors with the lowest generalization abilities. All three methods were still unable to evolve general behaviors after being trained with a single instance. Nevertheless, NS showed the best performance against fitness and random-based search, and the best test performance was 13% for $I_{12}$.

Results obtained from experiments with a training set of 12 instances are presented in Table 2. In this experiment, NS had the best performance again in terms of training and testing, 61% of the runs generate a program which hit the target from every initial condition in the training set, while 41% of the runs perform successfully in the test set. Fitness-based search had 22% of hits in the training set, and 13 exhibit general navigation skills which are able to cope with every initial condition in the test set. In terms of average fitness scores, fitness-based search, was clearly outperformed by NS: a difference of 0.3 in the training set and 0.43 in the test set. In a training set composed of instances that correspond to tasks with different levels of difficulty and deception, it will be easy to find individuals that solve the less difficult cases and it will harder to solve instances defining more deceptive tasks, creating local optima for fitness-based search.

Furthermore, one interesting observation regarding both limits of moves: $L -$ 100 and $L - 500$, is that the orientations in some of the initial conditions are

```
move move turn-left
ifelse wall-left?
[tu rn-left]
[move move ifelse wall-ahead?
 [ turn-right move move ]
 [ move turn-right] ]
```
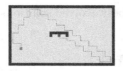  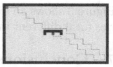

**Fig. 3.** Left figure shows an example of an evolved program able to solve the maze for every test instance, exhibiting general navigation. Figures at the right show the trajectory when using this program for initial conditions: $I_1, I_7, I_{11}$, respectively.

**Table 3.** Table of results from each of the twelve instances, where the sub-index stands for the number of the training instance. L-100, and L-500 stands for the limit of moves. NS-K3 stands for Novelty Search with the $k$-neighbour parameter set to 3. Fit stands for the average fitness score, and Hits for the percent of best individuals which reach the target.

| Instance | Method | L-100 Train Hits | Fit | L-100 Test Hits | Fit | L-500 Train Hits | Fit | L-500 Test Hits | Fit |
|---|---|---|---|---|---|---|---|---|---|
| $I_1$ | NS-K3 | 100% | 1.000 | 0% | 0.110 | 100% | 1.00 | 3% | 0.263 |
| | Fitness | 94% | 0.950 | 0% | 0.112 | 94% | 0.74 | 3% | 0.286 |
| | Random | 19% | 0.330 | 0% | 0.111 | 34% | 0.44 | 1% | 0.149 |
| $I_2$ | NS-K3 | 100% | 1.000 | 0% | 0.133 | 100% | 1.00 | 6% | 0.365 |
| | Fitness | 73% | 0.796 | 0% | 0.126 | 69% | 0.95 | 2% | 0.201 |
| | Random | 10% | 0.233 | 0% | 0.102 | 14% | 0.28 | 2% | 0.159 |
| $I_3$ | NS-K3 | 77% | 0.864 | 0% | 0.166 | 100% | 1.00 | 12% | 0.476 |
| | Fitness | 7% | 0.295 | 0% | 0.166 | 62% | 0.69 | 1% | 0.328 |
| | Random | 0% | 0.129 | 0% | 0.115 | 8% | 0.20 | 0% | 0.145 |
| $I_4$ | NS-K3 | 92% | 0.949 | 0% | 0.141 | 100% | 1.00 | 8% | 0.455 |
| | Fitness | 22% | 0.430 | 0% | 0.124 | 68% | 1.00 | 3% | 0.665 |
| | Random | 0% | 0.149 | 0% | 0.124 | 10% | 0.22 | 1% | 0.165 |
| $I_5$ | NS-K3 | 100% | 1.000 | 0% | 0.079 | 100% | 1.00 | 0% | 0.091 |
| | Fitness | 96% | 0.980 | 0% | 0.073 | 95% | 0.98 | 0% | 0.072 |
| | Random | 100% | 1.000 | 0% | 0.074 | 100% | 1.00 | 0% | 0.083 |
| $I_6$ | NS-K3 | 100% | 1.000 | 0% | 0.010 | 100% | 1.00 | 4% | 0.168 |
| | Fitness | 86% | 0.930 | 0% | 0.081 | 90% | 0.95 | 2% | 0.107 |
| | Random | 83% | 0.915 | 0% | 0.089 | 86% | 0.93 | 0% | 0.106 |
| $I_7$ | NS-K3 | 100% | 1.000 | 0% | 0.120 | 100% | 1.00 | 0% | 0.124 |
| | Fitness | 100% | 1.000 | 0% | 0.117 | 99% | 0.99 | 0% | 0.125 |
| | Random | 100% | 1.000 | 0% | 0.118 | 100% | 1.00 | 0% | 0.120 |
| $I_8$ | NS-K3 | 100% | 1.000 | 0% | 0.114 | 100% | 1.00 | 0% | 0.121 |
| | Fitness | 100% | 1.000 | 0% | 0.113 | 100% | 1.00 | 0% | 0.120 |
| | Random | 100% | 1.000 | 0% | 0.113 | 100% | 1.00 | 0% | 0.115 |
| $I_9$ | NS-K3 | 100% | 1.000 | 0% | 0.098 | 100% | 1.00 | 0% | 0.095 |
| | Fitness | 100% | 1.000 | 0% | 0.099 | 100% | 1.00 | 0% | 0.096 |
| | Random | 100% | 1.000 | 0% | 0.097 | 100% | 1.00 | 0% | 0.095 |
| $I_{10}$ | NS-K3 | 100% | 1.000 | 0% | 0.082 | 100% | 1.00 | 0% | 0.081 |
| | Fitness | 100% | 1.000 | 0% | 0.083 | 100% | 1.00 | 0% | 0.081 |
| | Random | 100% | 1.000 | 0% | 0.082 | 100% | 1.00 | 0% | 0.084 |
| $I_{11}$ | NS-K3 | 60% | 0.741 | 0% | 0.160 | 100% | 1.00 | 11% | 0.538 |
| | Fitness | 8% | 0.264 | 0% | 0.128 | 57% | 0.64 | 6% | 0.387 |
| | Random | 0% | 0.139 | 0% | 0.111 | 7% | 0.19 | 2% | 0.173 |
| $I_{12}$ | NS-K3 | 68% | 0.793 | 0% | 0.163 | 100% | 1.00 | 13% | 0.627 |
| | Fitness | 7% | 0.274 | 0% | 0.116 | 59% | 0.67 | 2% | 0.422 |
| | Random | 1% | 0.140 | 0% | 0.114 | 6% | 0.19 | 2% | 0.174 |

in fact relevant in the training set as well as in the test set, since they impact on the overall generalization performance. We can see in Table 3 differences in train and test performance between some pairs of instances: I1 and I2, I3 and I4.

Figure 3 shows an example of one of the best evolved solutions, and the trajectories for 3 different initial conditions.

## 7   Conclusions and Future Work

This work presents the first application of NS with GE to study their generalization abilities on a maze navigation task. An agent controlled by a GE program must navigate in a maze from a specific starting point and orientation to a target point using a limit number of moves. We have compared novelty, fitness and random based evolution using GE in a series of generalization experiments. We have used a fixed maze a fixed target and varied the agent initial position and orientation. The goal is to evolve behaviors that are able to hit the target starting from any point and facing any direction. In this work, we consider 12 different initial conditions for the agent, where some positions are easier or less deceptive than others. First, we start by using just one instance at a time, then we use all 12 instances as training set, and the evolved programs were tested on a set of 100 random instances. Furthermore, we use two different moves limit: 100 and 500. The experiments with a limitation of 100 moves showed that it was not possible to evolve programs with general navigational abilities. The performances exhibited by the best programs evolved by the three methods were very similar and very poor in the test set. The three methods were also unable to evolve a single program able to hit the target for every starting condition in the training set composed with the 12 instances. Anyhow, NS exhibited the best performance, followed by fitness based search. Regarding evolution using single instances training sets, NS outperformed fitness based search and also random search for the more deceptive cases, as it was expected, since it does not follow the gradient of the fitness function, but all showed similar results in the easier cases. Anyhow, all successful behaviors for single training instances were too overfitted and failed in the test set.

When we increase the limit of moves to 500, allowing more time for exploration, every method is still unable to evolve general navigation abilities for the single instance training sets, composed with the easier starting conditions. In contrast, all three methods were able to evolve programs with general navigation abilities, able to solve the maze task for every condition in the test set, using single instance training sets that impose more difficulty and deception. This happened not so frequently but more frequently with NS than with the other two methods. Therefore, instances that appear to impose a higher difficulty in the navigation task, when used alone in the training set, seem to induce better general navigation skills using all three methods. But, if we use a more numerous training set, using the 12 training instances all together, random based search was unable to find general behaviors that solve the maze task for every instance of the training set and the same happened in the test set. NS had the best performance both in the training set (12 instances) and in the test set evolving more frequently general navigation programs. Fitness based search seems to be overfitting to some of the instances of the training set, the easiest ones, which is enough to achieve a higher score, creating a local optima.

NS in these experiments exhibits a substantial improvement in the evolution of general maze navigation agents, avoiding the deception involved in the maze task, preventing evolution from being trapped in local optima. This research work presents a window of opportunity for generalization research, for instance, instead of having fixed targets we may perform generalization experiments where we vary both the initial conditions and the target of maze tasks. Additionally, we may try to transfer agents evolved with NS to new mazes to test if the skills acquired in a particular environment generalize to unseen environments. Finally, in a general way, one further work will be trying to understand what must be the right ingredients to get the right training set in order to evolve successfully general behaviors.

**Acknowledgments.** The authors acknowledge the following projects. First author is supported by FCT project EXPL/EEI-SII/1861/2013. Second author is supported by CONACYT (México) scholarship No. 232288. Third author is supported by CONACYT (México) Basic Science Research Project No. 178323, DGEST (México) Research Projects No.5149.13-P, also by TIJ-ING-2012-110, and by FP7-Marie Curie-IRSES 2013 project ACoBSEC funded by the European Comission.

# References

1. Burke, E.K., Gustafson, S., Kendall, G., Krasnogor, N.: Is Increased Diversity in Genetic Programming Beneficial? An Analysis of Lineage Selection. Ph.D. thesis, University of Nottingham, UK (February 2004)
2. Doucette, J., Heywood, M.: Novelty-based fitness: An evaluation under the santa fe trail. Genetic Programming, 50–61 (2010)
3. Georgiou, L., Teahan, W.J.: jge - a java implementation of grammatical evolution. In: 10th WSEAS International Conference on Systems, Athens, Greece, pp. 534–869 (2006)
4. Georgiou, L., Teahan, W.J.: Grammatical evolution and the santa fe trail problem. In: International Conference on Evolutionary Computation (ICEC), pp. 10–19. SciTePress, Valencia (2010)
5. Gomes, J.C., Urbano, P., Christensen, A.L.: Evolution of swarm robotics systems with novelty search. CoRR abs/1304.3362 (2013)
6. Gonçalves, I., Silva, S.: Experiments on controlling overfitting in genetic programming. In: 15th Portuguese Conference on Artificial Intelligence (EPIA 2011) (2011)
7. Kushchu, I.: Genetic programming and evolutionary generalization. IEEE Transactions on Evolutionary Computation 6(5), 431–442 (2002)
8. Lehman, J., Stanley, K.: Exploiting open-endedness to solve problems through the search for novelty. In: Bullock, S., Noble, J., Watson, R., Bedau, M.A. (eds.) Artificial Life XI: Proceedings of the Eleventh International Conference on the Simulation and Synthesis of Living Systems, pp. 329–336. MIT Press, Cambridge (2008)
9. Lehman, J., Stanley, K.O.: Efficiently evolving programs through the search for novelty. In: Pelikan, M., Branke, J. (eds.) GECCO, pp. 837–844. ACM (2010)

10. Lehman, J., Stanley, K.O.: Abandoning objectives: Evolution through the search for novelty alone. Evolutionary Computation 19(2), 189–223 (2011)
11. Li, J., Storie, J., Clune, J.: Encouraging creative thinking in robots improves their ability to solve challenging problems. In: Proceedings of the 2014 Conference on Genetic and Evolutionary Computation, GECCO 2014, pp. 193–200. ACM (2014)
12. Mouret, J.B., Doncieux, S.: Encouraging behavioral diversity in evolutionary robotics: An empirical study. Evolutionary Computation 20(1), 91–133 (2012)
13. Naredo, E., Trujillo, L.: Searching for novel clustering programs. In: GECCO, pp. 1093–1100 (2013)
14. Naredo, E., Trujillo, L., Martínez, Y.: Searching for novel classifiers. In: Krawiec, K., Moraglio, A., Hu, T., Etaner-Uyar, A.Ş., Hu, B. (eds.) EuroGP 2013. LNCS, vol. 7831, pp. 145–156. Springer, Heidelberg (2013)
15. Nicoară, E.S.: Mechanisms to avoid the premature convergence of genetic algorithms. Petroleum - Gas University of Ploiesti Bulletin, Mathematics LXI(1) (2009)
16. O'Neill, M., Ryan, C.: Grammatical evolution. IEEE Trans. Evolutionary Computation 5(4), 349–358 (2001)
17. Urbano, P., Loukas, G.: Improving grammatical evolution in santa fe trail using novelty search. In: Advances in Artificial Life, ECAL, pp. 917–924 (2013)
18. Velez, R., Clune, J.: Novelty search creates robots with general skills for exploration. In: Proceedings of the 2014 Conference on Genetic and Evolutionary Computation, GECCO 2014, pp. 737–744. ACM (2014)
19. Wilensky, U.: Netlogo, Evanston, IL: Center for Connected Learning and Computer-Based Modeling (1999), http://ccl.northwestern.edu/netlogo

# Comparing the Optimization Behaviour
# of Heuristics with Topology Based Visualization

Simon Bin[1], Sebastian Volke[2], Gerik Scheuermann[2], and Martin Middendorf[1]

[1] Parallel Computing and Complex Systems Group, Institute of Computer Science,
University of Leipzig, Germany
{sbin,middendorf}@informatik.uni-leipzig.de
[2] Image and Signal Processing Group, Institute of Computer Science,
University of Leipzig, Germany
{volke,scheuermann}@informatik.uni-leipzig.de

**Abstract.** In this paper we propose some changes and extensions of the visualization approach that is used in the visualization tool dPSO-Vis. It is shown also how corresponding visualizations can help for the analysis of fitness landscapes of combinatorial optimization problems and for understanding and comparing the optimization behaviour of heuristics. As an example we use a small instance of the Travelling Salesperson Problem (TSP) and the three heuristics Greedy, Random greedy, and Simulated Annealing.

**Keywords:** visualization, fitness landscape, combinatorial optimization problem, barrier landscape, heuristic, optimization behaviour.

## 1 Introduction

In this paper we show how visualization can be helpful for comparing and understanding the optimization behaviour of (meta)heuristics for combinatorial optimization problems. In particular, we propose some changes and extensions of the visualization approach that is used in the recent visualization tool dPSO-Vis ([11]). A one-dimensional landscape is used for the visualization of the topology of the search space and of the search process of the meta-heuristic. We concentrate here on the visualization of small problem instances for which it is possible to generate all solutions and to determine their fitness values. We also shortly discuss how the concepts that are introduced in this paper could be applied to larger problem instances. The Travelling Salesperson Problem (TSP) is used as the example optimization problem and the heuristics Greedy, Random greedy, and Simulated Annealing are the example metaheuristics.

It is assumed here that an optimization problem is given as a finite set of solutions $X$ together with an objective function $f : X \to \mathbb{R}$ that assigns each solution its fitness. The optimization problem is then to find a solution with minimum objective value, i.e. with highest fitness. Instead of a minimization problem, a maximization problem could also be considered. In addition it is assumed that a neighbourhood relation $N \subset X \times X$ is given on the set of

A.-H. Dediu et al. (Eds.): TPNC 2014, LNCS 8890, pp. 47–58, 2014.
© Springer International Publishing Switzerland 2014

solutions. Here we assume that $N$ is symmetric, i.e. $(x, y) \in N$ iff $(y, x) \in N$. Let $N(x) = \{y \in X \mid (x, y) \in N\}$ be the neighbours of $x$. Then $(X, N)$ is the neighbourhood graph and $(X, N, f)$ is called fitness landscape. In this paper we assume that $(X, N)$ is connected. The neighbourhood relation should reflect the process used by the heuristic to create new solutions from a given solution as described in the following. Given a solution $x \in X$ the heuristic can create a new solution $y$ from $x$ only when $(x, y) \in N$. Alternatively, when the heuristic is allowed to perform several steps for creating a new solution, it can create $y$ from $x$ only when there exists solutions $x = x_1, x_2, \ldots, x_k = y$ such that $(x_i, x_{i+1}) \in N$ for $i \in \{1, 2, \ldots, k - 1\}$. In some cases the neighbourhood graph might reflect not all possible transitions but only the transitions that occur with a certain likelihood. The details of which solutions are actually created and from which starting solutions depend on the particular heuristic.

The basic concept for the one-dimensional landscape that is used here for the visualization stems from Volke et al. [11]. Their approach has been implemented in the visualization tool dPSO-Vis. More details are described in Section 2. It was also shown by Volke et al. in [10] how dPSO-Vis can be used to compare the optimization behaviour of two discrete Particle Swarm Optimization algorithms (PSO) for solving the RNA folding problem. We do not give an overview on other visualization methods here but point the reader to [9].

The changes and extensions that are introduced here to the visualization concept of dPSO-Vis are explained in Section 2. The used heuristics and the test instances are described in Section 3. Results are shown in Section 4. The paper ends with conclusions in Section 5.

## 2   Visualization Method

The visualization of dPSO-Vis [11] is based on the barrier tree data structure which has been proposed by Flamm et al. [1] to represent the topology of a fitness landscape $(X, N, f)$. The barrier tree can be used to partition the nodes of $(X, N)$ into so called basins and to associate every barrier tree arc with one basin ([11]). In the following this is explained in more detail.

The barrier tree is a directed tree $B$ where each node $v$ of $B$ has a height $h(v) \in \mathbb{R}$. For a node $v$ in $B$ let $B_v$ be the subtree of $B$ with node $v$. Let $(X, N)_\eta$ be the subgraph of $(X, N)$ that is generated by all nodes $x \in X$ with $f(x) \leq \eta$, Similarly, let $(X, N)_{<\eta}$ be the subgraph of $(X, N)$ that is generated by all nodes $x \in X$ with $f(x) < \eta$. In the barrier tree $B$ each leaf represents a local minimum of $(X, N, f)$, i.e. a node $x \in X$ such $f(x) \leq f(y)$ for all $y \in N(x)$. If there exists a set of local minima that are connected in the subgraph of $(X, N)$ that is generated by the local minima, all nodes in the set are represented by the same single leaf in $B$. Each subtree of $B$ with root $v$ and height $h(v)$ corresponds to a connected component $C$ of $(X, N)_{h(v)}$ such that this component is not connected in $(X, N)_{<h(v)}$, i.e. $C_{<\eta}$ is not connected. $C$ is the component of $(X, N)_{h(v)}$ that contains the local minima which are represented by the leaves of $B_v$. The height $h(v)$ is called the barrier between the components of $C_{<\eta}$. Thus, an inner node

$v$ of the barrier tree represents all nodes $x \in C$ with $h(x) = h(v)$. Some of these nodes represent a barrier between the different parts of the fitness landscape that correspond to the child nodes of $v$. An edge $(u, v)$ of the barrier tree $B$ corresponds to all nodes $x$ of $(X, N)$ for which it holds: i) $x \notin (X, N)_{<h(u)}$ and ii) $x \in (X, N)_{<h(v)}$ and $x$ is connected to a leaf of $B_v$. This set of nodes is called basin. As a consequence, the subtree $B_v$ represents all nodes in $(X, N)_{h(v)}$ which are connected to a local minimum that corresponds to a leaf in $B_v$.

Volke et al. [11] proposed to add a node $v$, that corresponds to the global maximum of $(X, N, f)$, to the nodes of the barrier tree $B$. Also, an edge is inserted from the (original) root of the barrier tree to $v$. Then, every edge of the barrier tree represents a subset of the nodes of $(X, N)$ with an objective value that lies in a certain interval of $\mathbb{R}$. Also, all nodes of $(X, N)$ are represented by $B$ and the edges of $B$ partition the nodes of $(X, N)$ into basins. It should be noted that the barrier tree can be computed with a flooding algorithm [1]. This algorithm can be easily extended to also compute the partitioning of the solution space ([11]).

In dPSO-Vis a 2D landscape profile called barrier landscape is computed that is topologically equivalent to $(X, N, f)$ and therefore has the same barrier tree (details see [11]). The form of the 2D landscape is a height graph over a 1D line which contains a valley for every leaf node of the barrier tree and nested valleys for every subtree of it. If two subtrees are joined by an inner node, there is a corresponding mountain pass within the landscape profile that joins the corresponding valleys. Each edge $(u, v)$ of the barrier tree corresponds to the right slope and the left slope of the corresponding valley. The middle part of the valley corresponds to the subtree $B_u$. This construction leads to a roughly symmetric impression of the barrier landscape with high slopes at both sides and the lowest part in the middle.

In this paper we use an asymmetric visualization of the barrier landscape where all nodes of $(X, N)$ that correspond to a single edge of the barrier tree are drawn as a single slope which increases from left to right (examples are shown in figures 2 and 4). Moreover, for each inner node $v$ of $B$ and each edge $(u, v)$ we add a line that connects the highest node of $(X, N)$ which is represented by $(u, v)$ to the leftmost node that is represented by $v$. We call these lines barrier lines. Recall that several nodes of $(X, N)$ with the same height might be represented by $v$. Some additional changes with respect to the barrier landscape in dPSO-Vis are: i) All local minimum nodes are marked in the barrier landscape (if several connected minimum nodes exist, only the leftmost is marked), ii) all leftmost nodes that are represented by inner nodes of the barrier tree are marked, and iii) for each node the height of its lowest neighbour in $(X, N)$ is shown below it.

In order to visualize the behaviour of a heuristic we mark the solutions that are the result of a run of the heuristic. Since for several runs of a heuristic a solution might have been found several times, the size of the marking is proportional to how often the solution has been found. It should be noted that the type of the used markings and their colour can by easily changed for the visualization.

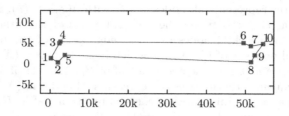

**Fig. 1.** The TSP test instance

## 3   Heuristic Algorithms and Test Instance

As a test optimization problem we use the well known Travelling Salesperson Problem (TSP). Given is a set of $n$ cities and an $n \times n$ distance matrix $D = |d(i,j)|_{i,j \in \{1,\ldots,n\}}$ where $d(i,j)$ is the distance from city $i$ to city $j$. Here we consider symmetric TSP instances only, i.e. $d(i,j) = d(j,i)$ for $i,j \in \{1,2,\ldots,n\}$. The problem then is to find a shortest round tour that contains each city exactly once, i.e. to find a permutation $\pi$ of $1,2,\ldots,n$ such that $d(\pi(n), \pi(1)) + \sum_{i=1}^{n} d(\pi(i), \pi(i+1))$ is minimal. Note, that every cyclic shift of a permutation $\pi$ and the corresponding inverse permutations lead to the same round tour and therefore to the same solution. Thus, the set $X$ of solutions can be described by choosing one representative from each equivalence class of solutions, e.g. as the set of all permutations $\pi$ of $\{1,2,\ldots,n\}$ with $\pi(1) = 1$ and $\pi(2) \leq \lfloor n/2 \rfloor + 1$.

The neighbourhood relations that we consider here as examples are the swap neighbourhood and the width restricted interchange neighbourhood. In the swap neighbourhood two permutations $\pi$, $\pi'$ are neighboured if one of the following conditions hold: i) $i \in \{1,2,\ldots,n-1\}$ such that $\pi(i) = \pi'(i+1)$, $\pi(i+1) = \pi'(i)$ and $\pi(j) = \pi'(j)$ for all $j \in \{1,2,\ldots,n\} - \{i, i+1\}$, or ii) $\pi(n) = \pi'(1)$, $\pi(1) = \pi'(n)$ and $\pi(j) = \pi'(j)$ for all $j \in \{2,3,\ldots,n-1\}$. In the interchange neighbourhood two permutations $\pi$, $\pi'$ a neighboured if one of the following conditions hold: if there exists $i,j \in \{1,2,\ldots,n\}$ such that $\pi(i) = \pi'(j)$, $\pi(j) = \pi'(i)$ and $\pi(h) = \pi'(h)$ for all $h \in \{1,2,\ldots,n\} - \{i,j\}$. The $k$-width restricted interchange neighbourhood has the additional restriction that $|i - j| \leq k$ must hold. Note, that there exists many other (and for heuristics often better) neighbourhoods that are used for solving the TSP problem.

As a test instance we have chosen a 10 city TSP instance that consists of 2 clusters of 5 cities each. The instance is shown in Figure 1. The distances between the cities are the Euclidean distances.

In order to demonstrate how the visualization can be used to compare the optimization behaviour of heuristics we have chosen the following three example heuristics: Random start greedy, Randomized greedy, and Simulated Annealing.

Greedy starts with a uniform randomly chosen permutation $\pi \in X$. Then it chooses the best permutation $\pi' \in N(\pi)$, i.e. the permutation $\pi'$ with minimum

**Algorithm 1.** Simulated Annealing algorithm

1: $T \leftarrow 1$ probability to accept a worse solution
2: $s \leftarrow x$ where $x \in X$ is chosen randomly
3: $accept \leftarrow true$
4: **while** accept=true **do**
5:      $accept \leftarrow false$
6:      **while** $accept = false$ **and** $\exists$ untested neighbour in $N(s)$ **do**
7:          randomly choose untested neighbour $x \in N(s)$
8:          **if** $f(x) < f(s)$ **or** $r < T$ where $r$ is uniform randomly
            chosen in $[1,0]$ **then**
9:              $s \leftarrow x$
10:              $accept \leftarrow true$
11:          **end if**
12:      **end while**
13:      $T \leftarrow (1 - \rho)T$
14: **end while**
15: return the best found solution

value $f(\pi')$. If there exists more than one such permutation one of them is chosen randomly. If $f(\pi') < f(\pi)$ then the last step is executed again (with $\pi'$ instead of $\pi$). Otherwise, the algorithm stops.

Randomized greedy works similar as Greedy but with the difference that it chooses a random solution (instead of the best solution) from all solutions $\pi' \in N(\pi)$ for which $f(\pi') < f(\pi)$ holds if such a solution exists. Otherwise, the algorithm stops.

The third heuristic is a simple standard Simulated Annealing algorithm. A pseudo-code can be found in Algorithm 1. For the tests the value $\rho = 0.05$ has been used for the parameter of changing the temperature.

# 4    Results

In this section we show what the proposed visualization method can tell us about the fitness landscape of a problem instance, the neighbourhood relation, the optimization behaviour of the heuristics and the connections between these three aspects. If not mentioned otherwise, all results use the swap neighbourhood.

## 4.1    Fitness Landscape

A visualization of the whole fitness landscape of the test instance is shown in Figure 2. The figure shows that the landscape consists of 5 plateaus with a steep descent between two neighboured plateaus. The fitness differences between the solutions within each plateau are smaller than the fitness differences between two plateaus. An exception is the third (numbered from left to right) plateau in the middle where several very narrow valleys exist that have solutions with a fitness that is in the range of fitness of the second plateau. A detailed view

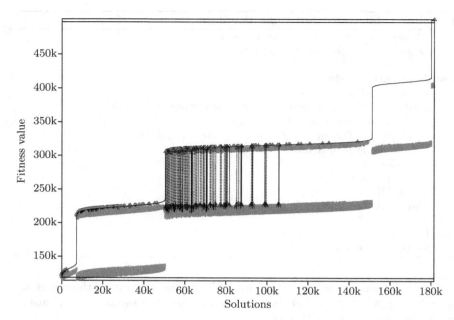

**Fig. 2.** Visualization of the fitness landscape of the TSP test instance: fitness of all solutions, local minima (red filled triangles), representatives for barriers (explained in the text) (blue triangles), quality of best neighbours (grey crosses).

of these valleys can be seen in Figure 3. The figure shows that only very few solutions are part of each valley. Figure 2 shows also that the plateau with the best (worst) solutions is very small and contains only about 2% of the solutions. The middle plateau, in contrast, contains more than half of the solutions.

Another interesting fact that can be seen from the visualization is, that the two worst plateaus do not contain any local minimum. For heuristic algorithms which consider the whole neighbourhood of a solution this means that there is no danger to get stuck at the very bad solutions of plateaus 4 and 5. The other three plateaus contain many local minima and most of them lay in the better (left) part of each plateau. The fitness of all these local minima is not much better than their neighbours in the plateau (with the exception of the already mentioned steep valleys that occur in the left part of middle plateau).

It can be seen that many solutions that lay within one of the plateaus 2-5 have a best neighbour which has a much better quality than the node itself. These neighbours lay in the plateau that is the next to the left. This shows that heuristics which evaluate the whole neighbourhood of a solution have good chances for a fast improvement, i.e. to jump directly from one plateau to the next better plateau.

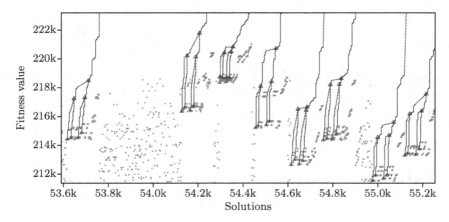

**Fig. 3.** Detailed view of some deep valleys of the middle plateau; local minima (red filled triangles), representatives for barriers (explained in the text) (blue triangles), quality of best neighbours (grey crosses), barrier lines (dotted lines).

A detailed view of the left part of the first plateau, i.e. the best part of the fitness landscape, is shown in Figure 4 (top). The many local minima in that plateau show that it might easily happen for a heuristic to get stuck in one of these local minima.

For the example test instance it was shown that the visualization of its fitness landscape reveals several interesting properties. Also, the extent of the properties is immediate from the visualization. However, it could not be estimated from simply looking at the problem instance alone. The visualization also leads directly to conclusions about the presumed optimization behaviour of heuristics in the respective part of the landscape. A closer look at the problem instance then gives us explanations for some of the properties. For example, the reason why there are five plateaus is the following. The problem instance consists of two clusters of five cities each. Each solution has 2, 4, 6, 8 or 10 edges that contain one city from each cluster. Obviously, the smaller the number of such edges is the better is a solution. Thus, the 5 plateaus correspond to these five classes of solutions. The middle plateau contains most of the solutions, because — as a short combinatorial calculation shows — the number of solutions with 6 edges between the clusters is much larger than the number of solutions with fewer or more such edges.

## 4.2   Neighbourhood Relation

The lower part of Figure 4 shows the same part of the fitness landscape for different neighbourhoods. Clearly, the quality of the solutions is independent of the neighbourhood. What changes is the number and the location of local

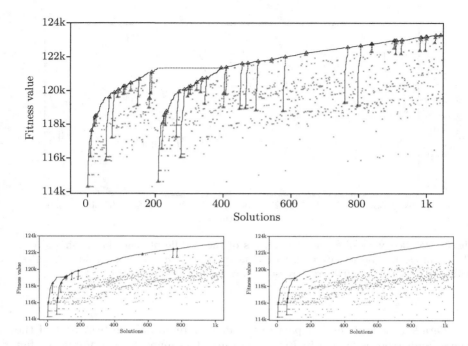

**Fig. 4.** Detailed view of the left (best) part of the fitness landscape; local minima (red filled triangles), representatives for barriers (explained in the text) (blue triangles), quality of best neighbours (grey crosses), barrier lines (dotted lines). Swap neighbourhood (top), 2-restricted interchange neighbourhood (bottom left) and 3-restricted interchange neighbourhood (bottom right).

minima. It can be seen clearly that the landscape with the (width restricted) interchange neighbourhood is simpler and has less local minima than the landscape with the swap neighbourhood. Moreover, the landscape with the 3-width restricted interchange neighbourhood is simpler than the landscape with the 2-width restricted interchange neighbourhood. The reason is that a solution has more neighbours in the 2-width restricted interchange neighbourhood than in the swap neighbourhood and it has more neighbours in the 3-width restricted interchange neighbourhood than in the 2-width restricted interchange neighbourhood. It may also be noted, that the 1-width restricted interchange neighbourhood is equal to the swap neighbourhood.

For a heuristic this means that the problem becomes simpler and the danger to get stuck in a local minimum is smaller with the 2- or 3-width restricted interchange neighbourhood than with the swap neighbourhood. This is at the expense of a growing neighbourhood. It should be mentioned that we do not argue here, that such observations are new. The point is, that the proposed visualization shows such effects of different neighbourhoods very clearly and also the strength of this effect is easily visible for the user.

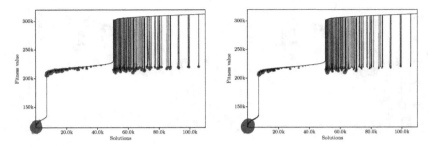

**Fig. 5.** Solutions of the heuristics Greedy (left) and Simulated Annealing (right), 10000 runs of each; shown is the left half of the fitness landscape; red bright dots = found local minima, blue dark dots = found non local minima.

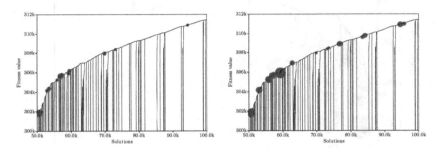

**Fig. 6.** Solutions found by heuristics Greedy (left) and Random greedy (right), 10000 runs of each; shown is the left upper part of plateau 3; red bright dots = found local minima.

## 4.3   Optimization Behaviour

The optimization behaviour of the heuristics Greedy and Simulated Annealing can be seen in Figure 5. In each figure the results of 10000 runs of the corresponding heuristic are shown. It can be seen that both heuristics often find solutions that lay within the best plateau. However, many solutions lay also in the left part of plateau 2 and also in the deep valleys of plateau 3. It can be seen that Simulated Annealing works on average slightly better than Greedy because more solutions of the former lay within plateau 1. Also the solutions of Simulated Annealing within plateau 2 lay more in the better (left) part. The visualization also shows that some solutions of Greedy lay also outside of the deep valleys on plateau 3. Since this cannot be seen in the print version of Figure 5 a detailed version of that part is shown in Figure 6. This figure shows also that Random greedy has more solutions than Greedy in this not so good part of the fitness landscape. In principle, this could have been expected. However, the visualization shows this effect quantitatively.

A detailed view of the best (left) part of plateau 1 is shown in Figure 7. All local minima have been found by at least one of the 10000 runs of each heuristic.

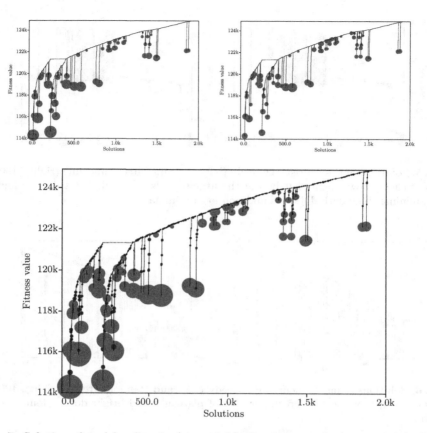

**Fig. 7.** Solutions found by Greedy (upper left), Random greedy (upper right), Simulated Annealing (bottom), 10000 runs of each; shown is the left (best) part of the fitness landscape; red bright dots = found local minima, blue dark dots = found non local minima.

It can be seen that Simulated Annealing found the best solutions more often than the other heuristics. Greedy found the best solutions slightly more often than Random greedy. By definition of the heuristics, all solutions of Greedy and Random greedy are local minima. This is different for Simulated Annealing: most but not all of the solutions that have been found in the best part of the fitness landscape are local minima. The reason is that Simulated Annealing might end in the basin of attraction of a local minimum which is worse than the best solution that was found during the run. The visualization shows that nearly every of the solutions in the best part of the front was the best solution in at least one of the 10000 runs of Simulated Annealing. As a consequence it might be reasonable to improve Simulated Annealing by performing one run of Greedy on the best solution found by Simulated Annealing. Of course this makes the algorithm slightly slower. The user can see from the visualization that this would improve a significant part of the good solutions that have been found.

As a final note, we want to mention that the proposed visualization method can not be directly used for large problem instances, for the simple reason that there exists too many solutions. However similar ideas can be applied to a sample of the set of all solutions. It will be interesting, to develop proper sampling techniques on which such a visualization can be based. For the case of RNA folding landscapes, which were the original motivation to introduce the barrier tree data, this has been done very recently in [5].

# 5  Conclusions

Some extensions of the visualization approach that is used by the visualization tool dPSO-Vis ([11]) have been proposed. Examples are: i) barrier lines are introduced that connect a valley of the landscape with a barrier, ii) local minimum nodes can be marked in the barrier landscape, and iii) the fitness of best neighbour nodes are shown. Also, for a visualization of the optimization behaviour of heuristics the solutions that it has found in one or more runs can be marked. The size of such a mark is proportional to how often the corresponding solution has been found. For the example of a small instance of the Travelling Salesperson Problem (TSP) and the three heuristics Greedy, Random greedy, and Simulated Annealing, it was shown how the introduced visualization method can help for the analysis of the fitness landscapes and for understanding the optimization behaviour of the heuristics. Clearly, some of the conclusions that were drawn from the visualization could also, at least in principle, be found by other methods. However, it was argued that the proposed visualization can easily give an approximate quantitative and detailed insight which is often difficult to get by other methods.

The proposed visualization method can be applied in principle to any combinatorial optimization problem. The only requirement is that a neighbourhood relation between solutions can be defined that is used by the heuristics to create new solutions. Future work is to extend the proposed visualization methods to sampled solution sets in order to be able to apply it to larger problem instances.

**Acknowledgement.** This work has been supported by the European Social Fund (ESF) and the Free State of Saxony (ESF App.No. 100098248 and App.No. 100098251).

# References

1. Flamm, C., Hofacker, I.L., Stadler, P.F., Wolfinger, M.T.: Barrier Trees of Degenerate Landscapes. Z. Phys. Chem. 216, 1–19 (2002)
2. Halim, S., Yap, R.H.C.: Designing and Tuning SLS Through Animation and Graphics: An Extended Walk-Through. In: Stützle, T., Birattari, M., Hoos, H.H. (eds.) SLS 2007. LNCS, vol. 4638, pp. 16–30. Springer, Heidelberg (2007)

3. Halim, S., Yap, R.H.C., Lau, H.C.: Viz: A Visual Analysis Suite for Explaining Local Search Behavior. In: Proc. 19th Annual ACM Symposium on User Interface Software and Technology (UIST 2006), pp. 57–66 (2006)
4. Halim, S., Yap, R.H.C., Lau, H.C.: Search Trajectory Visualization for Analysing Trajectory-Based Meta-Heuristic Search Algorithm. In: Proc. European Conference on Artificial Intelligence, pp. 703–704 (2006)
5. Kuchařík, M., Hofacker, I., Stadler, P.F., Qin, J.: Basin Hopping Graph: a computational framework to characterize RNA folding landscapes. Bioinformatics 30(14), 2009–2017 (2014)
6. Oesterling, P., Heine, C., Jänicke, H., Scheuermann, G., Heyer, G.: Visualization of high-dimensional point clouds using their density distribution's topology. IEEE Transactions on Visualization and Computer Graphics 17(11), 1547–1559 (2011)
7. Pérez, J., Mexicano-Santoyo, A., Santaolaya, R., Alvarado, I.L., Hidalgo, M.A., De la Rosa, R.: A visual tool for analyzing the behavior of metaheuristic algorithms. International Journal of Combinatorial Optimization Problems and Informatics 3(2), 31–43 (2012)
8. Pérez, J., Mexicano-Santoyo, A., Santaolaya, R., Alvarado, I.L., Hidalgo, M.A., De la Rosa, R.: A Graphical Visualization Tool for Analyzing the Behavior of Meta-heuristic Algorithms. International Journal of Emerging Technology and Advanced Engineering 3(4), 32–36 (2013)
9. Richter, H., Engelbrecht, A. (eds.): Recent Advances in the Theory and Application of Fitness Landscapes. Springer Series Emergence, Complexity and Computation, vol. 6, pp. 487–507 (2014)
10. Volke, S., Bin, S., Zeckzer, D., Middendorf, M., Scheuermann, G.: Visual Analysis of Discrete Particle Swarm Optimization using Fitness Landscapes. In: Richter, H., Engelbrecht, A. (eds.) Recent Advances in the Theory and Application of Fitness Landscapes. Series Emergence, Complexity and Computation, vol. 6, pp. 487–507. Springer (2014)
11. Volke, S., Middendorf, M., Hlawitschka, M., Kasten, J., Zeckzer, D., Scheuermann, G.: dPSO-Vis: Topological Visualization of Discrete Particle Swarm Optimization. Computer Graphics Forum 32(3), 351–360 (2013)

# Parameterized Message-Passing Metaheuristic Schemes on a Heterogeneous Computing System

José-Matías Cutillas-Lozano and Domingo Giménez

Departamento de Informática y Sistemas, University of Murcia
30071 Murcia, Spain
{josematias.cutillas,domingo}@um.es
http://dis.um.es

**Abstract.** This paper focuses on the development of message-passing parameterized schemes of metaheuristics in a heterogeneous cluster. An island model implemented with the master-slave scheme is used. Previous parameterized schemes are extended with new metaheuristic-parallelism parameters representing the migration frequency, the size of the migration and the number of processes. An optimization Problem of Electricity Consumption in the Exploitation of Wells is used as test case. The best experimental results are obtained in terms of speed-up and quality of the solution by mapping a number of processes close to the value of the population size, and considering the relative speeds of the components of the heterogeneous system.

**Keywords:** Parameterized metaheuristic schemes, Parallel metaheuristics, Message-passing metaheuristic schemes, Heterogeneous computing.

## 1   Introduction

The use of a unified parameterized scheme for metaheuristics facilitates the development of metaheuristics and their application [3,6]. Although the metaheuristic scheme has proved efficient, its use for solving large problem instances greatly increases the execution time. The application of high performance computing strategies to metaheuristics is an interesting option for reducing the execution time. There is a large number of parallel strategies that can be applied to different metaheuristics in parallel environments of different characteristics [2,9,12].

This work studies the development of message-passing parameterized metaheuristics and their optimization for heterogeneous clusters. A basic parameterized metaheuristic scheme is expanded with new metaheuristic-parallelism parameters, which control the intensity and frequency of information exchange between processes. The island model is used for the message-passing scheme [8,10,11], with the master-slave paradigm [1,4].

A Problem of Electricity Consumption in Exploitation of Wells (PECEW) is used as test case [7]. The same methodology could be applied to other problems simply adapting the basic functions and parameters of the metaheuristic scheme to each particular case [3]. The message-passing parameterized metaheuristic

A.-H. Dediu et al. (Eds.): TPNC 2014, LNCS 8890, pp. 59–70, 2014.

scheme allows us to speed-up the execution of the algorithm, and the best results in terms of speed-up and quality of the solution are obtained through a processes to processors mapping based on the relative speed of the computational components in the system.

The rest of the paper is organized as follows. Section 2 summarizes the ideas of parameterized metaheuristic schemes. A message-passing scheme is discused in Section 3. Section 4 briefly describes the problem PECEW used as test case and shows the experimental results of the application of the message-passing scheme with several mapping techniques for hetereogeneous systems. Section 5 concludes the paper and offers some future research lines.

## 2    A Parameterized Scheme of Metaheuristics

A parameterized metaheuristic scheme is presented in [3]. The scheme (Algorithm 1) considers a set of basic functions whose instantiation, by selecting the appropriate values of the metaheuristic parameters, $ParamMet = \{ParamIni, ParamEnd, ParamSel, ParamCom, ParamImp, ParamInc\}$, determines the particular metaheuristic. The arguments S, SS, SS1, and SS2 correspond to the sets of solutions that the method manipulates in successive iterations. The same scheme represents several metaheuristics and allows reuse of the functions and variables.

---

**Algorithm 1.** Parameterized metaheuristic scheme

---
```
Initialize(S,ParamIni)
while (not EndCondition(S,ParamEnd)) do
   SS=Select(S,ParamSel)
   SS1=Combine(SS,ParamCom)
   SS2=Improve(SS1,ParamImp)
   S=Include(SS2,ParamInc)
end while
```
---

The meaning and number of the parameters depend on the basic metaheuristics considered and on the implementation of the basic functions. The basic metaheuristics used in our work are Greedy Randomized Adaptive Search Procedure (GRASP), Genetic Algorithms (GA), Scatter Search (SS) and Tabu Search (TS). The basic functions and the meaning of the parameters in the parameterized scheme are briefly commented on. A more complete description of the parameters and the implementation of the basic functions, together with their application to different optimization problems can be found in [3,5,6].

- **Initialize**: Elements are randomly generated to form an initial set with $INEIni$ elements. A subset with $FNEIni$ elements is selected for the iterations. In some metaheuristics, some initial elements are improved by using, for example, a local search or a greedy approach. A parameter $PEIIni$ indicates the percentage of elements to be improved, and the improvement may be more or less intense, which is represented by an intensification parameter, $IIEIni$. The parameter $STMIni$ is used to set the extension of Tabu short-term memory in the improvement.

- **EndCondition:** One end condition common to the different metaheuristics consists of a maximum number of iterations ($MNIEnd$) or a maximum number of iterations without improving the best solution ($NIREnd$).
- **Select:** Two sets are established, one with the best elements and one with the worst, according to the objective function. The number of best elements is $NBESel$ and of worst elements $NWESel$.
- **Combine:** The total number of elements to be obtained by combination is $2(NBBCom + NBWCom + NWWCom)$, where the parameters represent the number of combinations of the best with the best elements, the number of the best with the worst and the number of the worst with the worst.
- **Improve:** As in the improvement in the initialization, $PEIImp$, $IIEImp$ and $SMIImp$ represent the percentage of elements to be improved, the intensification of the improvement and the short-term memory in the improvement of the elements generated in the combination; and $PEDImp$, $IDEImp$ and $SMDImp$ represent the corresponding values in a diversification, which is equivalent to the mutation in the GA.
- **Include:** The $NBEInc$ best elements are maintained in the reference set, and the other $FNEIni - NBEInc$ are selected from the remaining elements, with some selection criteria; for example, randomly or according to some distance function. $LTMInc$ is a Tabu parameter (long-term memory) used for tracking the most frequently explored individuals.

There is a set with 20 metaheuristic parameters with which it is possible to experiment to hybridize, mix and adapt the metaheuristics to the target problem. The basic metaheuristics can be implemented in different ways, and more metaheuristics can be incorporated into the scheme, so having a different number of parameters with different meanings, but the methodology for the use of the parameterized scheme and for the development of parameterized parallel schemes is common to different implementations and can be extended to other types of parameterized algorithmic schemes.

## 3    A Parameterized Message-passing Metaheuristic Scheme

The development of message-passing parameterized schemes is analyzed with MPI implementations, because distributed memory systems comprising multi-core nodes can solve larger problems in shorter execution time. An island model is used, with division of the population in different subsets assigned to $p$ processes, with identifiers from 0 to $p - 1$, where the process $P_0$ acts as master in the communications, and the remaining processes are the slaves.

The parameterized scheme in Algorithm 1 is extended to obtain a parameterized message-passing scheme (Algorithm 2) with the introduction of a new function (migration) and new metaheuristic-parallelism parameters, which comprise the number of processes $(p)$, the number of generations between migrations $(NGMPar)$ and the volume of data transferred $(NEMPar)$. A homogeneous data partition is considered, with assignation of the same number of elements to each process. So, subsets $S_i$ are processed in parallel by processes $P_i$, with $|S_i| = \frac{|S|}{p}$, and $S = S_0 \cup ... \cup S_{p-1}$. Each process is initialized with $\frac{INEIni}{p}$ elements. Then, the metaheuristic scheme of Algorithm 3 is applied sequentially to each subset over a number of iterations. The sizes of the other sets in each process are also divided by the number of processes: $\frac{FNEIni}{p}$, $\frac{NBESel}{p}$, $\frac{NWESel}{p}$, $\frac{NBBCom}{p}$, $\frac{NBWCom}{p}$, $\frac{NWWCom}{p}$ and $\frac{NBEInc}{p}$. The end condition is established now with the number of evolution-migrations, $\frac{MNIEnd}{NGMPar}$. The master informs the slaves when the end condition is accomplished.

---

**Algorithm 2.** Parameterized message-passing metaheuristic scheme. Island Model($S$,ParamMet,ParamPar).

---
1: IN PARALLEL in each process $P_i$ $(i = 0, ..., p - 1)$ DO
2:   Initialize($S_i$,ParamIni)
3:   while (not EndCondition(ParamEnd,NGMPar)) do
4:     Sequential_Metaheuristic_Scheme($S_i$,NGMPar)
5:     Immigrate($S_i$,$S_0$,NEMPar)
6:     In $P_0$ Integrate Subpopulations($S_0$)
7:     Emigrate($S_0$,$S_i$,NEMPar)
8:   end while
9: END PARALLEL
10: Solution: best $s_k \in S_0$

---

**Algorithm 3.** Sequential Metaheuristic Scheme($S_i$,ParamMet,NGMPar).

---
  while (not EndCondition(NGMPar)) do
    $SS_i$=Select($S_i$,ParamSel)
    $SS1_i$=Combine($SS_i$,ParamCom)
    $SS2_i$=Improve($SS1_i$,ParamImp)
    $S_i$=Include($SS2_i$,ParamInc)
  end while

---

The set of metaheuristic parameters is completed with the three new metaheuristic-parallelism parameters, $ParamPar = \{p, NGMPar, NEMPar\}$. The influence of these parameters on the fitness and the execution time is analyzed in the computational results section. There are many possibilities for the implementation of the new function (migration), but our initial goal is to analyze the advantages of using a parameterized message-passing metaheuristic scheme and to adapt it to a heterogeneous cluster. So, we use a simple migration scheme, with immigrations from the slaves to the master (line 5 of Algorithm 2) and emigrations from the master to the slaves (line 7), and with the same number of elements in the immigration and the emigration ($NEMPar$). No exchange of elements among slaves is considered, allowing only the combination of the best elements from each subset (and subsequent improvements and diversifications) in the master process (line 6). The percentage of migrating elements of each subset should not be very high in order to enhance only the migration of the best elements of each subset and reduce the execution time while maintaining a certain amount of native elements in each subset. Besides, high values could produce an increment in the cost of the communications. The number of generations between migrations ($NGMPar$) also affects the goodness of the solution and the execution time. High values mean less information exchange between processes, and possibly worse final solutions or more iterations to converge, but at the same time they reduce the number of communications and the execution time per iteration.

## 4    Computational Results

A problem of electricity consumption in exploitation of wells [7] is used as test case to evaluate the message-passing parameterized scheme. We consider a water system consisting of a series of pumps ($B$) of known power, located in wells, that draw water flows along a daily time range $R$. The total flow is the sum of the flows contributed by each well. The pumps may be running or idle at any given time. The pumps operate electrically and the electricity has a daily cost which should be minimized. The objective function is:

$$\textbf{Minimize} \quad C_e = \sum_{i=1}^{R} \sum_{j=1}^{B} T_i P_j N_i x_{ij} \tag{1}$$

where $C_e$ represents the cost of the electricity consumed by the combination of pumps selected in a day; $T_i$ is the cost of the electricity in the range $i$; $P_j$ is the electric power consumed by the pump $j$; $N_i$ is the number of hours of pump operation in the time slot $i$; and $x_{ij}$ represents a binary element of a matrix with values 1 or 0 for pump on or off. Using the notation of evolutionary algorithms, an individual or element is represented by the binary matrix, $x$, of size $B \times R$, which encodes the set of pumps distributed in different time slots. The set of individuals constitutes a population.

The results below are obtained when applying the metaheuristic scheme on a heterogeneous cluster to different instances of the problem. The experiments were carried out using the metaheuristic combinations in table 1 and varying the number of processes and mappings to the computational nodes. Metaheuristic parameters in table 1 were chosen because they form a metaheuristic set with different population sizes (populations of 50, 100 and 200 individuals) with reasonable parameters for distributed-memory parallelism ($NGMPar$ equal to 10, and values of $NEMPar$ of 10, 15 or 20). Furthermore, the number of iterations was fixed to 100, which allows easy comparison of the execution times between subpopulations of different sizes and is sufficiently high to get good fitness results. We are interested in reducing the execution time and in obtaining good quality solutions; so the inverse of the product of the fitness and the execution time is used as a common indicator. High values are desired for this indicator.

Experiments have been carried out in a heterogeneous cluster with four nodes:

- *Saturno* is a NUMA system with 4 Intel hexa-core NEHALEM-EX EC E7530 nodes (24 cores), 1.87 GHz, 32 GB of shared-memory.
- *Marte* and *Mercurio* are AMD Phenom II X6 1075T (hexa-core), 3 GHz, 15 GB (Marte) and 8 GB (Mercurio), each with private L1 and L2 caches of 64 KB and 512 KB, and L3 of 6 MB shared by all the cores.
- *Luna* is an Intel Core 2 Quad Q6600, 2.4 GHz, 4 GB.

**Table 1.** Values of the metaheuristic parameters used in the experiments

|     | INEIni | FNEIni | PEIIni | IIEIni | STMIni | NGMPar | NEMPar | NBESel | NWESel | NBBCom |
| --- | --- | --- | --- | --- | --- | --- | --- | --- | --- | --- |
| m1 | 50 | 50 | 100 | 15 | 4 | 10 | 10 | 25 | 25 | 45 |
| m2 | 100 | 100 | 100 | 15 | 8 | 10 | 15 | 50 | 50 | 90 |
| m3 | 200 | 200 | 100 | 15 | 12 | 10 | 20 | 100 | 100 | 10 |

|     | NBWCom | NWWCom | PEIImp | IIEImp | SMIImp | PEDImp | IDEImp | SMDImp | NBEInc | LTMInc |
| --- | --- | --- | --- | --- | --- | --- | --- | --- | --- | --- |
| m1 | 50 | 45 | 100 | 5 | 4 | 10 | 5 | 4 | 25 | 4 |
| m2 | 100 | 90 | 100 | 5 | 8 | 10 | 5 | 8 | 50 | 8 |
| m3 | 200 | 180 | 100 | 5 | 12 | 10 | 5 | 12 | 100 | 12 |

A homogeneous assignation of data to the processes in the message-passing scheme is considered, and satisfactory mappings of the processes to the nodes in the heterogeneous system should be obtained. There are many options for homogeneous data assignation to heterogeneous processors. Two types of basic criteria for mapping have been followed: one based on the number of cores in each system and the other based on the relative speed of the nodes. The assignation based on relative speed is more natural, but preliminary results also advised following a criterion based on the number of processors on each node, which is simpler and in some cases gives satisfactory results when there is not a big difference in the relative speed of the cores in the different nodes. Table 2 shows the number of processes assigned to each node in the system, for different assignation criteria:

- *Non Oversubscribed Cores (NOC)*: The number of processes assigned to a node coincides with the number of cores in the node (column *NOC* in the table).
- *Non Balanced Oversubscription (NBO)*: A number of processes ($p$) proportional to the number of cores is assigned to each node, with the total number of processes equal to $FNEIni$. For example, if we consider the node *Saturno*,

$$p_{sat} = \left\lfloor \frac{FNEIni}{numCores_{total}} \right\rfloor \cdot numCores_{sat} + \left\lceil DIF \cdot \frac{numCores_{sat}}{numCores_{total}} \right\rceil \quad (2)$$

**Table 2.** Number of processes launched for the three metaheuristic combinations in table 1 applied to PECEW 50-6 in the heterogeneous system *Saturno*(sat) + *Marte*(mar) + *Mercurio*(mer) + *Luna*(lun), with the mapping techniques: *Non Oversubscribed Cores (NOC)*, *Non Balanced Oversubscription (NBO)*, *Fully Balanced Oversubscription (FBO)*, and *yFBO*.

| | | NOC | NBO | FBO | 0.2·FBO | 0.4·FBO | 0.6·FBO | 0.8·FBO |
|---|---|---|---|---|---|---|---|---|
| m1 | sat | 24 | 30 | 31 | 6 | 12 | 19 | 25 |
| | mar | 6 | 8 | 7 | 1 | 3 | 4 | 6 |
| | mer | 6 | 7 | 7 | 1 | 3 | 4 | 6 |
| | lun | 4 | 5 | 5 | 1 | 2 | 3 | 4 |
| | total | 40 | 50 | 50 | 9 | 20 | 30 | 41 |
| m2 | sat | 24 | 60 | 62 | 12 | 25 | 37 | 50 |
| | mar | 6 | 15 | 14 | 3 | 6 | 9 | 11 |
| | mer | 6 | 15 | 14 | 3 | 6 | 8 | 11 |
| | lun | 4 | 10 | 10 | 2 | 4 | 6 | 8 |
| | total | 40 | 100 | 100 | 20 | 39 | 60 | 80 |
| m3 | sat | 24 | 120 | 122 | 24 | 49 | 73 | 98 |
| | mar | 6 | 30 | 28 | 6 | 11 | 17 | 22 |
| | mer | 6 | 30 | 28 | 6 | 11 | 17 | 22 |
| | lun | 4 | 20 | 22 | 4 | 9 | 13 | 17 |
| | total | 40 | 200 | 200 | 40 | 80 | 120 | 159 |

with $numCores_{total} = 40$ for our heterogeneous cluster, $numCores_{sat} = 24$ for *Saturno*, $DIF = FNEIni - numCores_{total} \cdot \left\lfloor \frac{FNEIni}{numCores_{total}} \right\rfloor$ is the remainder of the quotient $\frac{FNEIni}{numCores_{total}}$, and $\left[ DIF \cdot \frac{numCores_{sat}}{numCores_{total}} \right]$ represents the rounding to the nearest integer, which is $\left\lfloor DIF \cdot \frac{numCores_{sat}}{numCores_{total}} \right\rfloor$ and $\left\lceil DIF \cdot \frac{numCores_{sat}}{numCores_{total}} \right\rceil$ for the slowest and fastest nodes, respectively. So, for $FNEIni = 100$ (m2 in table 1), $p_{sat} = 60$. In the same way, we can calculate $p_{mar}$ (with $numCores_{mar} = 6$ for *Marte*), $p_{mer}$ (with $numCores_{mer} = 6$ for *Mercurio*) and $p_{lun}$ (with $numCores_{lun} = 4$ for *Luna*), resulting in $p_{mar} = p_{mer} = 15$ and $p_{lun} = 10$.

- *Fully Balanced Oversubscription (FBO)*: A total number of processes equal to *FNEIni* are executed, but in this case the computational load is distributed proportionally to the relative speeds of the nodes. If we have *FNEIni* individuals, the number of processes assigned to each node, $p_x$ (with $x = sat, mar, mer, lun$), is obtained with the equations:

$$
\begin{aligned}
p_{mar} &= p_{sat} \cdot \frac{v_{mar}}{v_{sat}} \\
p_{mer} &= p_{sat} \cdot \frac{v_{mer}}{v_{sat}} \\
p_{lun} &= p_{sat} \cdot \frac{v_{lun}}{v_{sat}} \\
p_{sat} &+ p_{mar} + p_{mer} + p_{lun} = FNEIni
\end{aligned}
\tag{3}
$$

where $v_x = \frac{numCores_x}{t_{secuen,x}}$ represents the relative speed of the sequential metaheuristic algorithm in each node, and $numCores_x$ and $t_{secuen,x}$ are the number of cores and the sequential execution time of the algorithm in the node $x$. For example, considering the relative speeds $v_{sat} = 1.000$, $v_{mar} = 0.236$,

$v_{mer} = 0.224$ and $v_{lun} = 0.177$, and value of $FNEIni = 50$ (m1 in table 1), the values of the number of processes are $p_{sat} = 31$, $p_{mar} = p_{mer} = 7$ and $p_{lun} = 5$, where each variable obtained is rounded to the nearest integer.

– $yFBO$: To reduce the overhead that a large number of processes produces, the number of processes assigned to each node should be proportional to the speed of the nodes but with the number of processes scaled with a value $y$ (values considered in the experiments were $y = 0.1, 0.2, \ldots, 0.9$). So, $p_x(yFBO) = y \cdot p_x(FBO)$ (where $x = sat, mar, mer, lun$). For example, for a number of processes in *Saturno* according to the configuration $FBO$, $p_{sat}(FBO) = 31$, and for $y = 0.5$ a value of $p_{sat}(0.5FBO) = 16$ (rounded to the nearest integer) is obtained.

In the first two configurations the number of processes in each node is proportional to the number of cores. The third configuration is proportional to the relative speeds of the nodes, which are calculated from the sequential execution time of an execution of the algorithm in each node. In the cluster we are using, the differences in computing capacity of the cores in the different nodes for the problem we are working with are not big, which makes the assignations based on the number of cores (column $NBO$) or on their relative speed (column $FBO$) very similar, and so similar speed-ups are obtained.

The figures and tables below represent the mean values of ten observations for each variable measured. Figure 1 (a) shows the speed-ups achieved when applying the three metaheuristics in table 1 to PECEW, for the three basic configurations of heterogeneous processes of table 2 (columns 1 to 3), and figure 1 (b) compares the speed-ups obtained when varying the number of processes of $FBO$ (configurations $yFBO$) by multiplying it by several reduction factors (0.1 to 0.9). The configurations $NBO$ and $FBO$ yield, on average, the same speed-up (52), which is the highest obtained. Fitness values have also been considered. Figure 2 shows the corresponding fitness values for the speed-ups in figure 1. We can see that the quality of the solution found does not vary too much with the processes mapping (a), although a variation of fitness with the total number of processes launched is observed for the $FBO$ configuration (b). In general, there is a minimum value for the fitness corresponding to a value of $y$ close or below 0.5 in $yFBO$. This can be seen in m2 and m3 specially. This minimum can be explained considering that the $FBO$ configuration implies to launch a number of processes equal to the total number of individuals in the population $FNEIni$. A decrease in the fitness could be expected when increasing the number of processes (islands) because it enables a greater exchange of information between subpopulations (values of $y$ between 0.1 and 0.5 in $yFBO$), however, when reaching a greater number of islands than a half of the total population to be distributed, the effect begins to be otherwise, that is, each island would be formed by a single individual with the possibility of diversity decreased (this can be seen from $y$ greater than 0.5 with some fluctuations). So, the best fitnesses are obtained with medium-low values of $y$ (close or below 0.5) in $yFBO$, but at the expense of low speed-ups.

To take into consideration both the execution time ($t$) and the fitness ($f$), we consider a Common Indicator $CI = \frac{10^6}{f \cdot t}$. High values are desirable, but it could

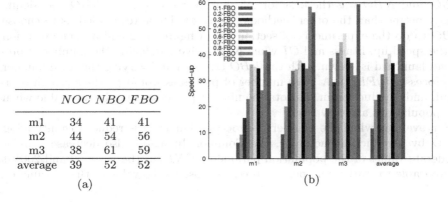

|         | NOC | NBO | FBO |
|---------|-----|-----|-----|
| m1      | 34  | 41  | 41  |
| m2      | 44  | 54  | 56  |
| m3      | 38  | 61  | 59  |
| average | 39  | 52  | 52  |

(a)                                                 (b)

**Fig. 1.** Speed-up achieved: (a) with the three basic configurations of heterogeneous processes of table 2 and the three metaheuristics considered and (b) when varying the number of processes of $FBO$ on multiplying it by several reduction factors (0.1 to 0.9).

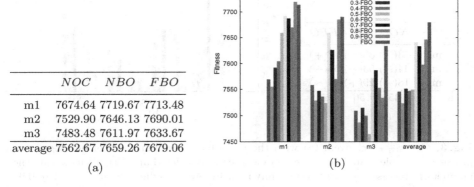

|         | NOC     | NBO     | FBO     |
|---------|---------|---------|---------|
| m1      | 7674.64 | 7719.67 | 7713.48 |
| m2      | 7529.90 | 7646.13 | 7690.01 |
| m3      | 7483.48 | 7611.97 | 7633.67 |
| average | 7562.67 | 7659.26 | 7679.06 |

(a)                                                 (b)

**Fig. 2.** Fitness obtained: (a) with the three basic configurations of heterogeneous processes of table 2 and the three metaheuristics considered and (b) when varying the number of processes of $FBO$ on multiplying it by several reduction factors (0.1 to 0.9).

be modified to give more importance to time or fitness, or bi-objective optimization could be considered. The values for different processes configurations and metaheuristics are shown in figure 3. The Kruskal-Wallis test revealed statistical differences in the $CI$ means for the three metaheuristic configurations applied. A deeper analysis of the groups of processes configurations for each metaheuristic was made. The Wilcoxon rank sum test with continuity correction was applied at a significance level $\alpha = 0.05$. The algorithm performing best (higher values of $CI$) for a particular data set is indicated by a symbol +. Algorithms against which it is statistically superior are indicated with a −, and ∼ represents that there was no difference in the means. For m1 and m2 the best configuration was

$FBO$, and $NBO$ was the best for m3. Furthermore, for m2, $FBO$ was significantly better than the other methods (figure 4). These results led us to choose $FBO$ to do the experiments of section (b) of figures 1, 2 and 3. The evolution of the speed-up, fitness and $CI$ when progressively reducing the number of processes launched is shown, with the $FBO$ criterion and varying the total number of processes ($yFBO$). A large number of processes would produce a high overhead, and a reduction in the total number of processes may be advisable when the populations are very large.

On average, when the number of processes launched is reduced (multiplying $FBO$ by a reduction factor $y$), the Common Indicator also decreases, so for moderate values of the population parameter $FNEIni$ (between 50 and 200) it is advisable to start a number of processes close to the value of this parameter,

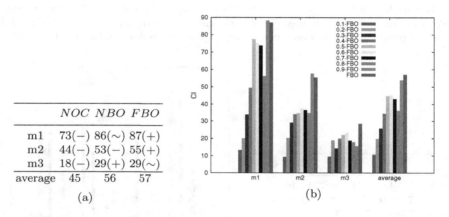

|     | NOC | NBO | FBO |
|-----|-----|-----|-----|
| m1 | 73($-$) | 86($\sim$) | 87($+$) |
| m2 | 44($-$) | 53($-$) | 55($+$) |
| m3 | 18($-$) | 29($+$) | 29($\sim$) |
| average | 45 | 56 | 57 |

(a)

(b)

**Fig. 3.** $CI = \frac{10^6}{f \cdot t}$ achieved: (a) with the three basic configurations of heterogeneous processes of table 2 and the three metaheuristics considered and (b) when varying the number of processes of $FBO$ on multiplying it by several reduction factors (0.1 to 0.9).

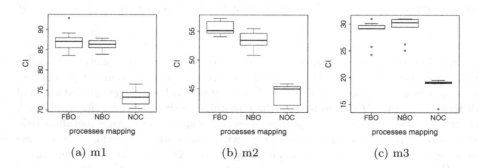

(a) m1          (b) m2          (c) m3

**Fig. 4.** Statistical summary of $CI = \frac{10^6}{f \cdot t}$, for the three basic configurations of heterogeneous processes in table 2 and the three metaheuristics considered.

using a mapping based on the relative speeds of the nodes ($FBO$), but if the fitness is the key factor, the balanced distribution with a medium number of processes ($y = 0.4$ or $0.5$) is preferred.

# 5    Conclusions and Future Work

This work studies the adaptation of a parameterized message-passing meta-heuristic scheme for computation in heterogeneous clusters. Three metaheuristic-parallelism parameters ($NEMPar$, $NGMPar$ and $p$) appear in the message-passing scheme, which follows an island model implemented with the master-slave paradigm. The parameters allow us to control the intensity and frequency of information exchange between processes and the volume of data transferred. A problem of optimization of electricity consumption in wells exploitation was used as test case. For this problem and in the heterogeneous cluster used for the experiments, the best results in terms of speed-up and quality of the solution are obtained through a processes to heterogeneous processors mapping based on relative speeds of the nodes in the cluster. Furthermore, for moderate population sizes, it is better to use a total number of processes close to the size of the population.

As part of our future work, the application of the message-passing scheme to get parallel hyperheuristics is being analyzed, and the design of message-passing schemes with heterogeneous distribution of data and a number of processes equal to the number of cores is also being considered. To fully exploit the computational systems in a cluster, possibly with GPUs in each node, a multicore+GPU version of the scheme should be developed and integrated with the message-passing version. We are also working on modeling the execution time as a function of the metaheuristic and parallelism parameters, which could facilitate the inclusion of autotuning in the message-passing scheme. The problem of deciding the best processes-to-processors distribution could be tackled as a bi-objective problem, and hyperheuristics to approach this problem could be developed on top of parameterized bi-objective metaheuristics.

**Acknowledgements.** This work was supported by the Spanish MINECO, as well as European Commission FEDER funds, under grant TIN2012-38341-C04-03.

# References

1. Aida, K., Natsume, W., Futakata, Y.: Distributed computing with hierarchical master-worker paradigm for parallel branch and bound algorithm. In: Proceedings of the 3rd IEEE/ACM International Symposium on Cluster Computing and the Grid (CCGrid 2003), pp. 156–163 (2003)
2. Alba, E.: Parallel Metaheuristics: A New Class of Algorithms. Wiley-Interscience (2005)

3. Almeida, F., Giménez, D., López-Espín, J.-J., Pérez-Pérez, M.: Parameterised schemes of metaheuristics: basic ideas and applications with Genetic algorithms, Scatter Search and GRASP. IEEE Transactions on Systems, Man and Cybernetics, Part A: Systems and Humans 43(3), 570–586 (2013)
4. Bendjoudi, A., Melab, N., Talbi, E.-G.: An adaptive hierarchical master-worker (AHMW) framework for grids - application to B&B algorithms. J. Parallel Distrib. Comput. 72(2), 120–131 (2012)
5. Cutillas-Lozano, J.-M., Giménez, D.: Determination of the kinetic constants of a chemical reaction in heterogeneous phase using parameterized metaheuristics. In: ICCS (2013)
6. Cutillas-Lozano, J.-M., Giménez, D.: Optimizing shared-memory hyperheuristics on top of parameterized metaheuristics. In: ICCS (2014)
7. Cutillas-Lozano, L.-G.: Metaheurística aplicada a la optimización de los criterios de producción de aguas subterráneas. Sondea Project (in Spanish). Final-studies dissertation, University of Alicante (2012)
8. Van Luong, T., Melab, N., Talbi, E.-G.: GPU-based island model for evolutionary algorithms. In: GECCO, pp. 1089–1096 (2010)
9. Luque, G., Alba, E.: Parallel Genetic Algorithms: Theory and Real World Applications. Springer (2011)
10. Mezmaz, M.-S., Kessaci, Y., Choon Lee, Y., Melab, N., Talbi, E.-G., Zomaya, A.Y., Tuyttens, D.: A parallel island-based hybrid genetic algorithm for precedence-constrained applications to minimize energy consumption and makespan. In: GRID, pp. 274–281 (2010)
11. Mezmaz, M.-S., Melab, N., Talbi, E.-G.: Using the multi-start and island models for parallel multi-objective optimization on the computational grid. In: e-Science, pp. 112 (2006)
12. Talbi, E.-G.: Metaheuristics - From Design to Implementation. Wiley (2009)

# Modeling Fluid Flow Induced by *C. elegans* Swimming at Low Reynolds Number

Jonathan Gutierrez[1], Megan Sorenson[2], and Eva Strawbridge[3]

[1] St. Mary's University, San Antonio, TX 78228, USA
[2] Concordia University Irvine, Irvine, CA 92612, USA
[3] James Madison University, Harrisonburg, Virginia 22807, USA
strawbem@jmu.edu

**Abstract.** *C. elegans* have been extensively researched regarding locomotion. However, most mathematical studies have focused on body dynamics rather than the fluid. As the nematodes undulate in a sinusoidal
fashion, they cause fluid movement that has been studied experimentally
but not modeled computationally on this scale. Utilizing the Navier-
Stokes equation, regularized stokeslets, and the method of images, we
computed the dynamics of the surrounding fluid. Our results strikingly
matched experimental outcomes in various ways, including the distance
particles travelled in one period of undulation, as well as qualitatively
and quantitatively matching velocity fields. We then implemented this
method using video data of swimming *C. elegans* and successfully repro-
duced the fluid dynamics. This is a novel application of the method of
regularized stokeslets that combines theory and experiment. We expect
this approach to provide insight in generating hypotheses and informing
experimental design.

**Keywords:** Applications of computing, computing with biology, *C. elegans*, low Reynolds number, regularized stokeslets, swimming.

## 1 Introduction

The past decade has evinced significant research into the locomotion of microorganisms, in particular that of the nematode *Caenorhabditis elegans* both theoretical and experimental [16,15,17,2,3,11,14]. However, while there have been a
number of experimental investigations into the induced fluid movement of bacterial flagella or carpets [10,7], artificial helices [18], and nematodes [16], to the
authors' knowledge, there has been little theoretical investigations into the induced fluid flows, particularly at the intermediate scale of *C. elegans*, a 1mm
long, unsegmented round worm.

Fluid movement is potentially important for a number of reasons including
mixing of either passive or active chemicals in the fluid [10,7,5], transport of
nonzero volume particles [5], and swarm interactions of large numbers of organisms [9] all at low Reynolds number where viscosity, rather than inertia,
dominates. In a viscosity dominated regime, where forcing is proportional to

A.-H. Dediu et al. (Eds.): TPNC 2014, LNCS 8890, pp. 71–82, 2014.

velocity rather than acceleration, mixing and flows are often counter intuitive due the reversibility. That is, any action which causes a flow in the fluid, if reversed *not necessarily at the same velocity* will effectively undo any flow, mixing, or propulsion. To overcome this reversibility and achieve forward locomotion, microorganisms utilize asymmetric motions such as corkscrewing of a helical flagella as with the bacteria *E. coli* or longitudinally asymmetric undulation as with *C. elegans*. In all of these cases, the organisms interact with the fluid which then interacts with either dissolved chemical species, suspended nonzero volume particles, or with other microorganisms to produce non-intuitive global behavior or results which are more than simply the sum of the individual motions of each swimmer separately.

Here we investigate these fluid motions first for an isolated swimmer in order to validate our computational model for the fluid and transport dynamics against experimental data in [16]. We use the method of regularized stokeslets in order to first model the induced fluid velocities of an artificial numerical swimmer and finally to extract fluid velocities from physical video data of a nematode swimming in a salt water solution. Even without fine tuning physical parameters, our model is able to reproduce experimental results including the appropriate decay of velocity magnitudes away from the forcing (i.e. organism) as well as qualitatively and quantitatively matching extremely well with PIV (particle image velocometry) measurements from [16] of the surrounding velocity fields.

By tracking particles or chemicals species in the fluid surrounding the multiple *C. elegans*, it may be possible to study mixing and chemical interactions theoretically. From this information, we hope to eventually inform experimental design and construct hypotheses which may be tested in the lab. The methods used here can also be adapted to computationally study the fluid flows induced by large numbers of swimming nematodes. Moreover, with some modifications to the computational swimmers it is also possible to further analyze organism-organism interactions in non-dilute populations in order to study the fluid dynamics contributions to swarm behavior.

## 2    Materials and Methods

The organism of study here is the nematode *C. elegans*, which are $1.06 \pm 0.06$ mm long and 80 $\mu$m in diameter [16]. Their wavelike movement has an average amplitude of 0.25 mm and a frequency of 2 Hz [16,2], meaning that a full beating cycle is completed in 0.5 seconds. The average forward swimming speed has been found to be $0.36 \pm 0.06$ mm/s by [16] and to be 0.12 mm/s at James Madison University's Wiggling Organism Research and Modeling (WORM) lab (the discrepancy here is likely due to the age, adult and L4 respectively, and size of the worms used in the respective experiments). The worms were analyzed swimming in M9, a salt water solution composed of $Na_2HPO_4 \cdot 7H_2O$, $KH_2PO_4$, NaCl, and $NH_4Cl$, between two slides separated by 0.15 mm coverslip spacers. The viscosity of M9 was measured in the WORM lab to be 1.596 cP at 20°C using a Brookfield DV-III LV Rheometer.

The induced fluid motion due to swimming *C. elegans* was studied using an in-house microscope designed based on the MRC Worm-Tracker microscope and implementing the Worm-Tracker software along with a strobing light source. Videos were taken at 10 and 15 frames per second of wild-type (N2) nematodes. The worms were maintained on agar plates using the standard OP50 *E. coli* strain at 20° C. These videos were processed and the centerlines extracted using Matlab©.

# 3   The Navier-Stokes Equation

The dynamics of incompressible Newtonian fluids are given by the Navier-Stokes equations,

$$- \nabla p + \mu \Delta u = \rho \left( \frac{\partial u}{\partial t} + u \cdot \nabla u \right) - f \ , \tag{1}$$

$$\nabla \cdot u = 0 \ , \tag{2}$$

where $-\nabla p$ is the pressure gradient, $\mu$ the dynamic viscosity, $\nabla = \left( \frac{\partial}{\partial x}, \frac{\partial}{\partial y}, \frac{\partial}{\partial z} \right)$ is the gradient operator, $\Delta = \frac{\partial^2}{\partial x^2} + \frac{\partial^2}{\partial y^2} + \frac{\partial^2}{\partial z^2}$ is the three dimensional Laplacian operator, $u$ the flow velocity, $\rho$ the fluid density. Finally, $-f$ represents external forces due to, for example, a body moving in the fluid. We will use the method of regularized stokeslets (described later in the text) to determine an appropriate representation for $f$. Equation (2) represents the incompressibility condition. Because all solutions of interest here are aqueous and water is incompressible this condition plus and appropriate representation of $f$, closes the system of equations above.

It is worth noting that the terms of the Navier-Stokes equation yield the individual forces in the system where $\mu \Delta u$ is the viscous force and $\rho \left( \frac{\partial u}{\partial t} + u \cdot \nabla u \right)$, the only component which is nonlinear in velocity, corresponds to the inertial forces. In the next section we will argue that for the regime of interest, the nonlinear inertial terms may be neglected, reducing the system to a linear one and enabling the use of regularized stokes ets and the method of images.

## 3.1   Nondimensionalization

We have previously referred to *C. elegans* as a low Reynolds number swimmer, meaning that we expect this to be a viscosity dominated regime. The Reynolds number is effectively the ratio of the size of inertial to viscous forces. If this ratio is small, viscosity dominates; if it is large, inertia dominates; and if it is approximately 1, then both should remain important. Inertia works to keep an object going at a constant velocity while viscosity is the resistance of the fluid to flow [13]. At this point it is salient to note that 1mm, while small, is not microscopic and can be seen with the naked eye. Additionally, the viscosity of M9 is only about 1.5 times that of water, which is most certainly not a viscous fluid. Therefore it is imperative to determine the Reynolds number for these experiments.

For the nondimensionalization of the Navier-Stokes equation, the unknowns are separated into two components, units and scalars, allowing units to be removed in order to compare the relative importance of inertial and viscous forces. We use p = $P_0\hat{p}$, x = $L\hat{x}$, y = $L\hat{y}$, z = $L\hat{z}$, t = $T\hat{t}$, and $\boldsymbol{u} = \frac{L}{T}\hat{u}$, where the hats indicate the nondimensional variables. Here $\frac{L}{T}\hat{u}$ is the natural component for velocity. Additionally, we chose the units of pressure to be $\frac{\mu}{T}$. Utilizing these substitutions and with some simplification (1) becomes

$$-\hat{\nabla}\hat{p} + \hat{\Delta}\hat{u} = \boxed{\frac{\rho L^2}{T\mu}} \left( \frac{\partial \hat{u}}{\partial \hat{t}} + (\hat{u} \cdot \hat{\nabla}\hat{u}) \right) \ , \tag{3}$$

where the highlighted term is the Reynolds number.

By rewriting $V = \frac{L}{T}$ and $\eta = \frac{\mu}{\rho}$, the Reynolds number becomes $\frac{LV}{\eta}$, where L and V represent a characteristic length and velocity of the system respectively and $\eta$ represents dynamic viscosity. Using the appropriate parameters for *C. elegans* we find $\frac{LV}{\eta} = \frac{(1\text{mm})(0.12\frac{\text{mm}}{\text{s}})}{1.596\text{cP}} = 0.075$, which is much less than one. The inertial terms can be dropped, simplifying (1) to a linear system which is called the Stokes equation. The Stokes equation always possesses a unique solution and moreover, linearity allows the calculation of the velocity due to different forces to be summed separately rather than solved simultaneously.

## 3.2   Regularized Stokeslets

As previously indicated, modeling the fluid flow induced by the locomotion of swimming nematodes is appropriate using the forced Stokes equation which is given by

$$-\nabla p + \mu \Delta \boldsymbol{u} = -\boldsymbol{f}, \tag{4}$$

where $p$ and $\boldsymbol{u}$ are the nondimensionalized pressure and velocity respectively after dropping the hat notation, and $\boldsymbol{f}$ is the nondimensional external forcing acting on the fluid. When $\boldsymbol{f}$ represents a point force we have $\boldsymbol{f} = \boldsymbol{g}\delta(\boldsymbol{X})$ where $\delta$ is the Dirac delta function and $\boldsymbol{X} = \boldsymbol{x} - \boldsymbol{x}_0$ is the vector difference between a position $\boldsymbol{x}$ and the location of the point force at $\boldsymbol{x}_0$. Here the position of the point forces lie along the body of the swimmer. For the delta function point force (4) has an exact solution which is given by the stokeslet. While this solution is exact at all locations away from the object, it is singular at the location $\boldsymbol{x}_0$. Numerically this presents a problem when the point forces are distributed along a curve in three-dimensions as is desired in this case when modeling a slender body because the velocity field becomes infinite on the filament itself [4,6].

To resolve the numerical issues due to this singularity, rather than using delta functions the forcing is chosen to be represented by smooth but localized force which is defined everywhere, $\boldsymbol{f} = \boldsymbol{g}\phi_\epsilon(\boldsymbol{X})$. Generally this smooth, radially symmetric function, $\phi_\epsilon$, is referred to as a "blob" function and is required to decay sufficiently fast. That is, we shall require $\int_0^\infty r^2 \phi_\epsilon(r)dr = \frac{1}{4\pi}$. The parameter $\epsilon$

controls where the majority of the force is concentrated and is generally chosen to represent a physical quantity such as the radius of the filamentary object, here the radius of the worm, $40\mu$m. With the forcing given by this smooth function, (4) has an exact solution given by the regularized stokeslet [5]. A typical blob function is of the form $\phi_\epsilon(r) = \frac{15\epsilon^4}{8\pi(r^2+\epsilon^2)^{7/2}}$. Then the corresponding biharmonic function to this regularized stokeslet is given by $\Delta^2 B_\epsilon(r) = \phi_\epsilon(r)$ so the regularized stokeslet is then

$$\frac{1}{8\pi} S_\epsilon\left(\boldsymbol{X}\right) = \left(-\frac{B''_\epsilon(r)}{r} - B''_\epsilon(r)\right) \boldsymbol{I} + \left(\frac{rB''(r) - B'_\epsilon(r)}{r^3}\right) \boldsymbol{X}\boldsymbol{X}. \qquad (5)$$

## 3.3  Method of Images

Because all experimental data to which these computations will be compared have walls, we implemented a version of the regularized stokeslet which also contains solutions using the method of images. The method of images is a common mathematical approach to enforce wall boundary conditions in one direction for linear partial differential equations, as in this case with a floor. In essence, to ensure zero flow through the wall due to a force in the fluid, an imaginary force is added which mirrors the real force on the other side of the wall. These two forces then effectively "cancel" each other out. This procedure is technically more complicated for the regularized stokeslet and requires the additional use of a doublet and potential dipole at the mirror image point as well but has been previously obtained by [1] and is implemented here. A complete treatment of the method of images for regularized stokeslets is beyond the scope of this paper but can be found in compete detail in [1].

## 4  The Model Nematode

Our initial investigations implemented a computationally artificial model of *C. elegans* given by

$$x = [2\pi ks + \iota\omega t]/L_{arc} , \qquad (6)$$

$$y = \left[A\sin\left(\frac{2\pi s}{\lambda} + \omega t\right)e^{\alpha s}\right]/L_{arc} . \qquad (7)$$

The parameters $Ae^{\alpha s}$ control the maximum amplitude. The value of $A$ is chosen based on $\alpha$, which controls the decay of amplitude through the worm from head to tail. However, it should be noted that A is not a direct reflection of the maximum amplitude. The parameter $\lambda$ is the wave length, $s$ is the parameterization variable, and $\omega$ is the oscillation frequency. *C. elegans'* forward displacement is not equal to $\omega$, so a slip parameter $\iota$ was introduced. To account for the length, 1 mm, of the worm, we normalize by the arc length $L_{arc}$ of the function at each time.

To use the method of regularized stokeslets, we implemented a blob parameter of $d = 40$ $\mu$m equally spaced along the nematode so that there were $\lfloor 1/2d \rfloor$

(13 in this case) blobs. Adjacent forces positioned too far apart would result in our worm having holes, allowing fluid flow through the centerline. Conversely, the blobs cannot be too close together because overlapping blobs would create a total force much greater than the actual force induced by the worm [5].

## 5   Results

### 5.1   Velocity Field

Using regularized stokeslets, the method of images, and knowing the position and velocity of the blob forces, the forcing on, and therefore velocity of the fluid can be computed exactly at any point in time and space. *That is, this is a grid free method.* This allows us to compute the velocity vector field around the worm as is shown in Fig. 1a. Here we can see that the velocity vectors (which are denoted as lines with circles at the heads) are largest near the body as predicted, particularly around areas of greater body displacement as was observed in the experiments of [16,8]. Additionally, circular trajectories rotating in alternating directions are observed. These circular regions remain near the body, opposed to traveling out into the fluid, a characteristic of low Reynolds number swimmers' fluid dynamics [16].

Figure 1b shows a color map of the velocity magnitude in a grid surrounding the nematode as was produced from the experimental data of [16]. Larger velocities are seen near the areas of greater body displacement and circular flow regions remain present. Once again, the theoretical nematode is consistent with the experimental results. When similar parameters as those shown in the figures of [16] were implemented, the maximum magnitudes were within approximately 10 $\mu$ m/s. Additionally, we found that the magnitudes of the velocities vary significantly with fluctuation in the nematode length, frequency, and wavelength.

### 5.2   Velocity Magnitude and Distance from the Wall

We computed the normalized average velocity magnitude as a function of the the normalized distance $r/L$ from the worm (here L = 1mm) averaged over the length of the worm and one full beat period. Because the bulk fluid flow is zero, we expect the velocity to decay to zero as our observations move away from the worm. Figure 2a depicts the calculation scheme and Fig. 2b indicates the theoretically predicted exponential decay rate, $e^{-2\pi r/\lambda}$, as the solid blue line [12]. This method is consistent with the computations of [5] and the experimental observations of [18] with rotating metal helices.

The experimental techniques of [16] specifically measured the velocity magnitudes of the nematodes at 300 $\mu$m (roughly $7d$, where $d$ is the nematode radius) from the bottom wall of the fluid containing cell. Our numerical method enables us to examine the effect of distance from the wall and its impact on the fluid behavior. We computed the velocity magnitudes as a function of distance from the nematode's maximum amplitude (as shown in Fig. 2a) for heights ranging

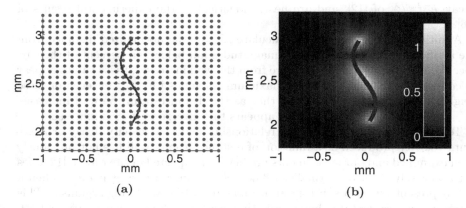

**Fig. 1.** (a) The velocity vector field shows the direction of fluid surrounding the worm and a rough magnitude of each vector. The circles indicate position at which the velocity vectors were calculated. (b) The grayscale bar indicates the magnitude of the velocity vector.

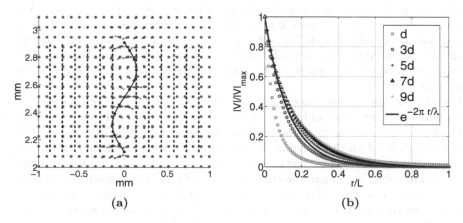

**Fig. 2.** (a) Along each of the dashed vertical lines we computed the normalized flow velocity magnitudes at a distance, r, away from our model worm ($L = 1$ mm). The circles indicate position at which the velocity vectors were calculated. (b) Velocity magnitudes are observed as the distance from the nematode increases. The decaying velocities at different heights away from the wall are then plotted. The solid line shows the predicted outcome from [12]

from $d$ to $10d$ above the bottom wall. When the distance is roughly 300 $\mu$m, the numerical results (Fig. 2b labeled in black) lie just above the the predicted decay, $e^{-2\pi r/\lambda}$, of [12], and are nearly identical to the experimental results of [16].

Additionally, we were able to calculate $X_{thres}$, the normalized distance from the artificial worm where velocity magnitudes fall below ten percent of their respective maximums. As the distance from the wall increases, these values appear to converge to 0.5039. When the maximum velocities $|V|_{max}$ for each of these heights were calculated, we found that as the distance from the wall increases, $|V|_{max}$ increases as well and also appears to converge to 0.7853 mm/sec.

To the authors' knowledge, the relationship between velocity decay or maximum velocity produced as a function of distance from a wall has not previously been examined and our experiments predict that expected decay rate of [12] does not accurately describe normalized fluid velocity magnitudes generated when a wall is present but at a substantial distance from the swimming organism. This represents a very testable hypothesis that we hope to investigate further both numerically and experimentally.

## 5.3   Particle Tracking

Fluid particles located in the plane of the worm's motion were tracked and these particle paths are shown in Fig. 3. The circular flow patterns are again evident and the particles are seen to have moved the greatest distance near the regions of greatest body displacement, indicating that these circular regions are characteristic of streamlines, not simple vector fields at a snapshot in time. We wanted to ensure that our particle movement was an accurate representation of the actual change in position. To test this, we tracked particles directly on the worm. If computed exactly, particle on the body will remain on the nematode for all time. However, we expect to observe first order error in the time evolution of particle location.

Because the integration scheme used is first order in time, as the time step $dt$ is decreased, the error should decrease proportionally. To check our numerical method we computed the euclidian distance between the actual location of fluid particles initialized on the worm itself, and the point where it should have been positioned on the worm. This distance is recorded in Table 1. At T = 0.1 (roughly the end time used for the particle tracking in Fig. 3) and 0.5 seconds (a full beat cycle), we see from this table that we do in fact have first order convergence. However, as the end time is increased, the method for tracking particles does not continue to show the appropriate relationship. The increased error is likely caused by the method of evenly distributing the blob forces on the sinusoidal curve as a function of time. However, our model works well for all periods of time for which experimental data exists with which to compare.

Particles paths were also plotted where color corresponds to a total distance traveled (Fig. 4). From this figure we see that the maximum distance a fluid particle traveled is approximately 50 $\mu$m. This is strikingly consistent with the experimental data from [16] which was produced using PIV and suspended florescent particles. We found that the distance each particle traveled was effected greatly by the physical parameters such as the length of the nematode, beat frequency, and wave length, indicating that further investigation into this is needed in order to determine upper bounds for mixing, and compare with real experimental situations.

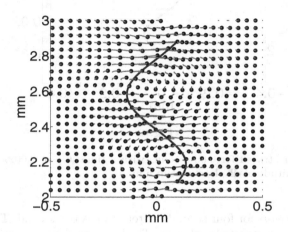

**Fig. 3.** Particles are tracked for 0.125 seconds with a dt of 0.001 as the worm swims through the fluid where the particles themselves are plotted as dots at the ending time

**Table 1.** The relationship between time step size and error decrease is the correct proportion for T = 0.1 and T = 0.5 seconds

(a) Total Time = 0.1

| dt | distance | $\frac{dd_{n+1}}{dd_n}$ |
|---|---|---|
| 0.1 | 0.0071 | - |
| 0.05 | 0.0035 | 2.0014 |
| 0.025 | 0.0018 | 2.0018 |
| 0.0125 | 0.0009 | 2.0030 |
| 0.00625 | 0.0004 | 2.0057 |

(b) Total Time = 0.5

| dt | distance | $\frac{dd_{n+1}}{dd_n}$ |
|---|---|---|
| 0.1 | 0.0070 | - |
| 0.05 | 0.0035 | 2.0193 |
| 0.025 | 0.0017 | 2.0371 |
| 0.0125 | 0.0008 | 2.0757 |
| 0.00625 | 0.0004 | 2.1631 |

# 6   From Theory to Experiment

After validating our computational model with the numerical artificial swimmer, we extended this work to experimental data obtained in our own lab. Videos were

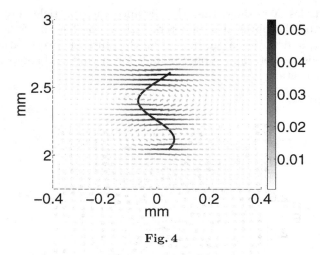

**Fig. 4**

**Fig. 5.** Particles are traced for 0.06 seconds with a time step of 0.002. The color bar indicates the magnitude of displacement in mm.

taken of L4 *C. elegans* for four seconds at ten frames per second. The centerline of these worms was extracted and normalized into mm, as seen in Fig. 6a. The worm centerlines were then divided up into the 13 blob forces used to create the velocity field around the nematode. Two consecutive frames were plotted, and the velocities were calculated by tracking the distance each blob traveled and dividing this the change in time between frames. Figure 6b depicts the worm's initial position plotted with a dashed line and the final position plotted as a solid line. Three regions of higher velocity magnitude are present, along with the circular motion of the velocity vectors, once again consistent with the results found by [16]. While the velocity magnitudes obtained here are slightly larger than those found by [16], we believe this is due the significant variation of movements between worms as well as over time. This parameter dependence is a subject of future study.

# 7   Conclusion

We implemented an algorithm that utilizes regularized stokeslets and the method of images to track the fluid dynamics around a swimming *C. elegans* at low Reynolds number. Results were obtained using both a computationally artificial worm and experimentally obtained video data to study the fluid dynamics associated with nematode locomotion. Particles carried by the fluid were tracked numerically, reproducing experimental outcomes with respect to particle displacement. The velocity fields as well as the velocity magnitudes as a function of lateral distance from the worm also match both qualitatively and quantitatively with the experiments of [16] and the theoretical predictions of [12]. Moreover, by

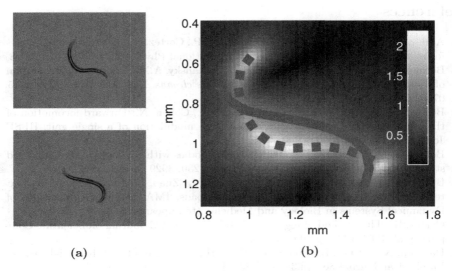

(a)                                    (b)

**Fig. 6.** (a) *C. elegans* photographs with extracted centerline gathered in our lab. (b) The color velocity field based on *C. elegans* movement as the worm moves from the dashed line to the solid line over 0.1 seconds. The grayscale color bar indicates magnitude of the velocity vectors in mm/s.

computationally studying the impact of experimentally relevant boundaries (i.e. the bottom of the fluid chamber), we can predict this decay rate as a function of distance from this wall.

In future work we hope to extend this research to study the precise relationship between flow features and the physical and locomotive parameters of real nematodes (e.g. body length, wave length, longitudinal asymmetry, wave speed, etc.) as well as to include multiple swimmers in order to analyze fluid dynamics contributions of swarm behavior through organism-organism interaction in non-dilute environments. In order to study complex patterns and behaviors associated with dense or non dilute populations of swimmers (i.e. potential swarms) in fluids, a clear understanding of the dynamic role of the *fluid* in this behavior and communication between organisms is needed. Additionally, this method can be used to track particles or chemical species in fluids to further investigate microscopic mixing as well as the chemical processes aided by active flow. This is particularly applicable to the construction of microfluidic devices and mixing using bacterial carpets [10].

**Acknowledgements.** This research was partially funded by NSF grant number 1004516, and James Madison University Mathematics and Statistic Department provided funding for the WORM lab. Charles Wolgemuth and Karin Leiderman contributed the original centerline and regularized stokeslets programs respectively.

# References

1. Ainley, J.S., Durkin, S., Embid, R., Boindala, P., Cortez, R.: The method of images for regularized stokeslets. Journal of Computational Physics 227, 4600–4616 (2008)
2. Berman, R.S., Kenneth, O., Sznitman, J., Leshansky, A.M.: Undulatory locomotion of finite filaments: lessons from *Caenorhabditis elegans*. New Journal of Physics 15, 075022 (2013)
3. Berri, S., Boyle, J.H., Tassieri, M., Hope, I.A., Cohen, N.: Forward locomotion of the nematode *C. elegans* is achieved through modulation of a single gait. HFSP Journal 3, 186–193 (2009)
4. Bouzarth, E., Minion, M.: Modeling slender bodies with the method of regularized stokeslets. Journal of Computational Physics 230, 3929–3947 (2011)
5. Buchman, A.L., Fauci, L.J., Strawbridge, E.M., Zhao, L.: Flow included by bacterial carpets and transport of microscale loads. IMA Volume: Applications of Dynamical Systems in Biology and Medicine (to appear, 2014)
6. Cortez, R.: The method of regularized stokeslets. SIAM Journal on Scientific Computing 23, 1204–1225 (2001)
7. Darnton, N., Turner, L., Breuer, K., Berg, H.: Moving fluid with bacterial carpets. Biophysical Journal 86, 1863–1870 (2004)
8. Gray, J., Lissmann, H.W.: The locomotion of nematodes. Journal of Experimental Biology 41, 135 (1964)
9. Ishikawa, T., Pedley, T.J.: Coherent structures in mololayers of swimming particles. Physical Review Letters 100, 088103 (2008)
10. Kim, M., Breuer, K.: Use of bacterial carpets to enhance mixing in microfluidic systems. Journal of Fluids Engineering 46, 139 (2007)
11. Korta, J., Clark, D.A., Gabel, C.V., Mahadevan, L., Samuel, A.D.T.: Mechanosensation and mechanical load modulate the locomotory gait of swimming *C. elegans*. The Journal of Experimental Biology 210, 2382–2389 (2007)
12. Lighthill, J.: Flagellar hydrodynamics. SIAM Reviews 18, 161 (1976)
13. Purcell, E.M.: Life at low reynolds number. American Journal of Physics 45, 3 (1977)
14. Shen, X.N., Arratia, P.E.: Undulatory swimming in viscoelastic fluids. Physical Review Letters 106, 208101 (2011)
15. Sznitman, J., Prashant, K., Purohit, P., Lamitina, T., Arratia, P.E.: Material properties of *Caenorhabditis elegans* swimming at low reynolds number. Biophysical Journal 98, 617–626 (2010)
16. Sznitman, J., Shen, X., Sznitman, R., Arratia, P.E.: Propulsive force measurements and flow behavior of undulatory swimmers at low reynolds number. Physics of Fluids 22, 121901 (2010)
17. Sznitman, R., Gupta, M., Hager, G.D., Arratia, P.E., Sznitman, J.: Multi-environment model estimation for motility analysis of Caenorhabditis elegans. PLoS One 5, e11631 (2010)
18. Zhong, S., Moored, K.W., Pinedo, V., Garcia-Gonzalez, J., Smits, A.J.: The flow field and axial thrust generated by a rotating rigid helix at low reynolds number. Experimental Thermal and Fluid Science 46, 1–7 (2013)

# Detecting Symmetry in Cellular Automata Generated Patterns Using Swarm Intelligence

Mohammad Ali Javaheri Javid, Mohammad Majid al-Rifaie,
and Robert Zimmer

Department of Computing
Goldsmiths, University of London
London SE14 6NW, UK
{m.javaheri,m.majid,r.zimmer}@gold.ac.uk

**Abstract.** Since the introduction of cellular automata in the late 1940's they have been used to address various types of problems in computer science and other multidisciplinary fields. Their generative capabilities have been used for simulating and modelling various natural, physical and chemical phenomena. Besides these applications, the lattice grid of cellular automata has been providing a by-product interface to generate graphical patterns for digital art creation. One important aspect of cellular automata is symmetry, detecting of which is often a difficult task and computationally expensive. In this paper a swarm intelligence algorithm – Stochastic Diffusion Search – is proposed as a tool to identify axes of symmetry in the cellular automata generated patterns.

**Keywords:** Cellular automata, swarm intelligence, symmetry, aesthetics.

## 1 Introduction

Creating aesthetically pleasing images has been investigated by many researches in the context of evolutionary computing, including the Bimorphs of Dawkins [9], Mutator of Latham [30], and Virtual Creatures of Sims [29]. Although some impressive results have been achieved, there still remain problems with the aesthetic selection. According to [18], first, the subjective comparison process, even for a small number of phenotypes, is slow and forms a bottleneck in the evolutionary process. Human users would take hours to evaluate many successive generations that in an automated system could be performed in a matter of seconds. Secondly, genotype-phenotype mappings are often not linear or uniform. That is, a minor change in genotype may produce a radical change in phenotype. Such non-uniformities are particularly common in tree or graph based genotype representations such as in evolutionary programming, where changes to nodes can have a radical effect on the resultant phenotype. In this study we approach the problem in the framework of dynamical systems and define a criterion for aesthetic selection in terms of its association with symmetry. The association of aesthetics and symmetry has been investigated from different points of view.

A.-H. Dediu et al. (Eds.): TPNC 2014, LNCS 8890, pp. 83–94, 2014.
© Springer International Publishing Switzerland 2014

In this work, a brief account on cellular automata is presented, followed by a section on symmetry and its significance in aesthetics. Then a swarm intelligence algorithm – Stochastic Diffusion Search – is explained, highlighting its main features. Afterwards, the application of the algorithm in detecting symmetry along various axes of symmetry is detailed, illustrating the performance of the method proposed.

## 2   Cellular Automata

**Definition 1:** *A Cellular Automaton (CA) is a lattice of regularly arranged homogeneous finite state automaton as unit cells in Euclidean space.* It can be represented as a quadruple of $A = \{ S, N, d, f \}$ where:

1. $S$ is a finite set of integer numbers as *states,*
2. $N$ is a finite set of integer numbers as *neighbourhood,*
3. $d$ is a finite set of integer numbers as the *dimension* of the space,
4. $f : S^n \mapsto S$ is the *transition function.*

In a *discrete two-dimensional (d = 2) finite lattice* with a *periodic boundary* the state of each cell (automaton) at time ($t$) is determined by the states of immediate surrounding neighbourhood cells at time $t - 1$.

The 9-cell mapping is also known as a *Moor* neighbourhood and a mapping that satisfies the following condition is called a *quiescent state* ($S = 0$).

$$f(0, 0, 0, 0, 0, 0, 0, 0, 0) = 0 \tag{1}$$

The behaviour of CA at a certain point of time emergences from a *synchronous* iterative application of transition function (local rule) over the initial configuration at time $t_0$. There are some distinctive characteristics in CA which can make them particularly attractive to digital artists and suitable for image and pattern generation purposes (each automaton acting as picture element). Furthermore, the significance of CA for computer art comes from the fact that simple rules can generate observationally unpredictable complex behaviours and there is a vast universe of behaviours which can be explored. Generally the behaviour of a particular cellular automaton is constrained by its initial configuration, transaction function and number of states. A two-dimensional multi-state cellular automaton with periodic boundary provides an endless environment for the growth of patterns and the observation of emergent complex behaviour over the time of evolution. For some rules the periodic generation of patterns creates an animated sequence of pattern formations. This opens up possibility of generating animations based on the development of pattern formation where both symmetries and the element of surprise coexist. This capability was observed in [27] where CA are described as "self-generating computer graphics movies". This is a new way of generating imagery which has no precedent in human culture [26]. The role of symmetry in art, architecture and its association with aesthetic preferences is a well known concept [21]. The iterative application of transition function

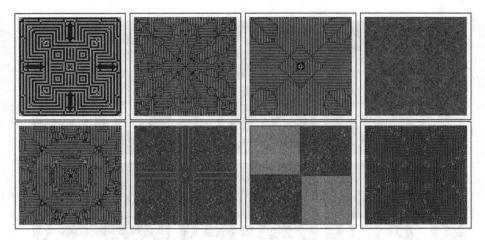

**Fig. 1.** Sample CA generated symmetrical patters

over initial configuration, especially in multi-state CA, can generate complex symmetrical patterns [12,22] which are extremely challenging to construct using conventional mathematical methods. Figs. 1 and 2 show experimental patterns generated by the authors to demonstrate the generative capabilities of CA in creating symmetrical patterns.

## 3   Symmetry and Aesthetic

Symmetry, having proportionality and balance is an important element of aesthetics. The association of aesthetics and symmetry has been investigated extensively in literature. A study to investigate the effect of symmetry on interface judgements, and relationship between a higher symmetry value and aesthetic appeal for the basic imagery, showed that subjects preferred symmetric over non-symmetric images [4]. Further studies found that if symmetry is present in the face or the body, an individual is judged as being relatively more attractive and if the body is asymmetric the face is rated unattractive, even if the person doing the rating never sees the body [25,10]. Symmetry plays a crucial role in theories of perception and is even considered a fundamental structuring principle of cognition [15]. In the Gestalt school of psychology things [objects] are affected by where they are and by what surrounds them... so that things [objects] are better described as more than the sum of their parts [5]. The Gestalt principles emphasise the holistic nature of perception where recognition is inferred, during visual perception, more by the properties of an image as a whole, rather than its individual parts [13]. Thus, during the recognition process elements in an image are grouped from parts to whole based on Gestalt principles of perception such as proximity, parallelism, closure, symmetry, and continuation [23]. In particular, symmetric objects are more readily perceived [8]. It is not surprising that we humans find sensory delight in symmetry, given the world in which

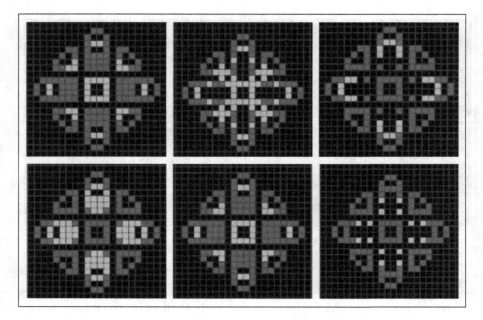

**Fig. 2.** Sample CA generated symmetrical patters

we evolved. In our world the animals that have interested us and our ancestors (as prey, menace, or mate) are overwhelming symmetric along at least one axis [24]. Evolutionary psychologists examine physical appearances like as symmetry, and perceived level of aesthetics as an indirect measure in mate selection [21,20]. In this view symmetrical faces are examined as more attractive faces. In other words symmetry is positively linked with both psychological and physiological health indicators [28]. In geometry symmetrical shapes are produced by applying four operations of translations, rotations, reflections, and glide reflections. However developing computational methods which generate symmetrical patterns is still a challenge since it has to connect abstract mathematics with the noisy, imperfect, real world; and few computational tools exist for dealing with real-world symmetries [16]. Applying evolutionary algorithms to produce symmetrical forms leaves the formulation of fitness functions, which generate and select symmetrical phenotypes, to be addressed . Lewis describes two strategies in evolutionary algorithms approach for generating and selecting symmetrical forms: " A common approach is to hope for properties like symmetry to gradually emerge by selecting for them. Another strategy is to build in symmetry functions which sometimes activate, appearing suddenly. However this leads to a lack of control, as offspring resulting from slight mutations (i.e., small steps in the solution space) bear little resemblance to their ancestors [14]".

The next section explains the swarm intelligence algorithm which will be used in detecting symmetrical patterns.

# 4    Swarm Intelligence Algorithm

The swarm intelligence algorithm used in this work is Stochastic Diffusion Search (SDS) [6,1] which is a probabilistic approach for solving best-fit pattern recognition and matching problems. SDS, as a multi-agent population-based global search and optimisation algorithm, is a distributed mode of computation utilising interaction between simple agents [19]. Its computational roots stem from Geoff Hinton's interest 3D object classification and mapping. See [11,17] for Hinton's work and [6,7] for the connection between Hinton mapping and SDS. SDS algorithm has been used in various fields including optimisation and generative arts (e.g. [2,3]).

In order to introduce SDS, a social metaphor, *the Mining Game*, is introduced.

## 4.1    The Mining Game

The mining game provides a simple metaphor outlining the high-level behaviour of agents in SDS:

A group of friends (miners) learn that there is gold to be found on the hills of a mountain range but have no information regarding its distribution. On their maps the mountain range is divided into a set of discrete hills and each hill contains a discrete set of seams to mine. Over time, on any day the probability of finding gold at a seam is proportional to its net wealth.

To maximise their collective wealth, the miners need to identify the hill with the richest seams of gold so that the maximum number of miners can dig there (this information is not available a-priori). In order to solve this problem, the miners decide to employ a simple Stochastic Diffusion Search.

- At the start of the mining process each miner is randomly allocated a hill to mine (his hill hypothesis, $h$).
- Every day each miner is allocated a randomly selected seam on his hill to mine.
- At the end of each day, the probability that a miner is happy is proportional to the amount of gold he has found.
- At the end of the day the miners congregate and over the evening each miner who is unhappy selects another miner at random to talk to. If the chosen miner is happy, he happily tells his colleague the identity of the hill he is mining (that is, he communicates his hill hypothesis, $h$, which thus both now maintain). Conversely, if the chosen miner is unhappy he says nothing and the original miner is once more reduced to selecting a new hypothesis - identifying the hill he is to mine the next day - at random.

In the context of SDS, agents take the role of miners; active agents being 'happy miners', inactive agents being 'unhappy miners and the agent's hypothesis being the miner's 'hill-hypothesis'. It can be shown that this process is

isomorphic to SDS, and thus that the miners will naturally self-organise and
rapidly congregate over hill(s) on the mountain range with a high concentration
of gold.

### 4.2  SDS Architecture

The SDS algorithm commences a search or optimisation by initialising its population (e.g. miners, in the mining game metaphor). In any SDS search, each
agent maintains a hypothesis, $h$, defining a possible problem solution. In the
mining game analogy, agent hypothesis identifies a hill. After initialisation two
phases are followed (for high-level SDS description see Algorithm 1):

- – Test Phase (e.g. testing gold availability)
- – Diffusion Phase (e.g. congregation and exchanging of information)

In the test phase, SDS checks whether the agent hypothesis is successful or not
by performing a partial hypothesis evaluation and returning a domain independent boolean value. Later in the iteration, contingent on the strategy employed,
successful hypotheses diffuse across the population and in this way information
on potentially good solutions spreads throughout the entire population of agents.

In the Test phase, each agent performs *partial function evaluation, pFE*,
which is some function of the agent's hypothesis; $pFE = f(h)$. In the mining
game the partial function evaluation entails mining a random selected region on
the hill, which is defined by the agent's hypothesis (instead of mining all regions
on that hill).

In the Diffusion phase, each agent recruits another agent for interaction and
potential communication of hypothesis. In the mining game metaphor, diffusion
is performed by communicating a hill hypothesis.

---

**Algorithm 1.** SDS Algorithm

---

```
01: Initialising agents()
02: While (stopping condition is not met)
03:     Testing hypotheses()
04:         Determining agents' activities (active/inactive)
05:     Diffusing hypotheses()
06:         Exchanging of information
07: End While
```

---

The next section details how SDS is instructed to detect symmetry in CA
generated patterns.

## 5  Experiments and Results

In this work Stochastic Diffusion Search is tasked to identify various types of
symmetry. The input to the system are some sample patterns to show the func-
tionality of the method and later some real world cellular automata generated
patterns are fed in the system to evaluate the overall performance of the algorithm in detecting symmetry.

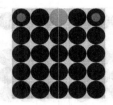

**Fig. 3.** Figure showing the search space (5 × 5); hypothesis in green; and the micro-features in blue

## 5.1 Applying SDS Algorithm

In order to adopt SDS to use for identifying symmetries, the following are considered:

- the search space comprises of the entire cells on the canvas (see Fig. 3 where the search space size is 5 × 5)
- SDS hypothesis is a cell index along one of the axes of a symmetry. See Fig. 3 where the hypothesis is highlighted in green (i.e. index = 0)
- the cells on either side of each axes of symmetry are considered micro-features[1] of the hypotheses (see Fig.3 where sample micro-features are highlighted in blue)

As shown in Fig. 4, there are four axes of symmetry in four-fold symmetrical patterns. Fig. 5 shows each of these axes separately.

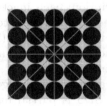

**Fig. 4.** Four axes of symmetry in a four-fold symmetrical pattern

The process through which the test and diffusion phases of SDS algorithm iterates is explained below:

**Initialisation Phase.** During the initialisation phase one of the symmetrical axes is chosen and is set as a model (to be used for comparing the cells on either sides). Then each agent is associated to a cell index which is between 0 and the length of the side of the screen (i.e. width or height). In other words each agent's hypothesis is set to one of the cells along the axis of symmetry.

---

[1] Micro-features are used in the test phase of SDS to determine the status of the agent (i.e. active or inactive).

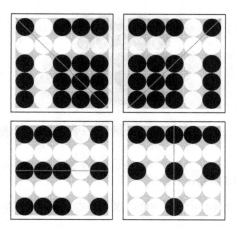

**Fig. 5.** Individual axes of symmetry

**Test Phase.** During the test phase, each agent, which is already allocated to an index on the axis of symmetry, picks a cell (micro-feature) from either side of the axis and checks if the mirror of the cell has the same value. If the difference between the two corresponding micro-features is zero, the agent becomes active, otherwise inactive.

**Diffusion Phase.** The process in the diffusion phase is the same as the one detailed in the algorithm description: each inactive agent picks an agent randomly from the population; if the randomly selected agent is active, the inactive agent adopts the hypothesis of the active agent (i.e. the cell index on the axis of symmetry), otherwise the inactive agent picks a random cell index between 0 and the length of the side of the canvas.

After $n$ number of iterations all agents converge on the points of symmetry.

One of the main features of SDS is partial function evaluation which here manifests itself in: each time checking one cell on one side of the symmetrical axis to its corresponding cell on the other side. Therefore even when an agent is active, in the next iteration it picks another micro-feature and checks the point from "a different perspective" to ensure that the symmetry holds.

Fig. 6 shows few iterations in which the cells are marked in blue (the current micro-features) are checked. This feature is also useful in dynamically changing environments where cells change their characteristics over time and as such might lose their symmetrical patterns.

The process can be repeated to test other axis of symmetry. Fig. 7 shows a pattern that is symmetrical on two points on one of the symmetrical axis. Therefore, the agents converge to the 'optimal' points. Fig. 7(1) shows that all agents except the one at the bottom are active (green); the micro-features selected for the inactive agents are clearly not identical (black on the left hand side and white on the right hand side). Therefore, now that the agent is inactive,

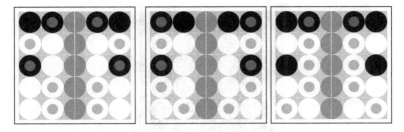

**Fig. 6.** Regular change in picking mico-features in the test phase

it selects another cell (during the diffusion phase) along the symmetrical line. It selects the one on top as shown on Fig. 7(2) where there are two micro-features on each side been tested by the algorithm (during the test phase). This process is repeated until all agents converge to the points where symmetry or partial symmetry is detected in the pattern (see Fig. 7(4)).

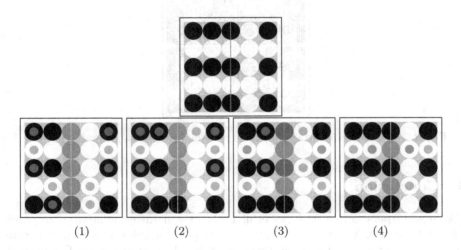

(1)            (2)            (3)            (4)

**Fig. 7.** Identifying partial symmetry

Using this approach, the algorithm allocate its resources "wisely" and repeatedly tests the already maintained points of interest against any asymmetrical discovery.

Fig. 8 shows a larger pattern which is fed into the system and the algorithm confirms its symmetrical nature against all four axes of symmetry.

**Fig. 8.** Detecting four-fold symmetry in a cellular automata generated pattern

# 6   Conclusion

CA provide perspective and powerful tools in generating computer graphics. The multi-state CA rule space is a vast set of possible rules which can generate interesting patterns with high aesthetic qualities. The interaction of CA rules at local level generates emergent global behaviour, that can sometimes demonstrate attractive complexity. Some characteristics of CA, such as the regularity and complexity of the rules that are employed locally, suggest that they could be well suited to generating computer graphics.

This paper demonstrates the capability of a swarm intelligence algorithm – Stochastic Diffusion Search – in detecting symmetrical patterns along various axes of symmetry. Evaluating the symmetry of cellular automata generated patterns is often a difficult task partly due the the large size of the search space or canvas, and partly due to the constantly changing, dynamic environment in which the cellular automata patterns are generated. These factors contribute to making the detection of symmetrical patterns computationally expensive. One of the main features of Stochastic Diffusion Search is partial function evaluation which is particularly useful when dealing with large problems with high dimensions. The performance of this algorithm is explained in the paper and the results are accordingly reported. In addition to identifying symmetry along one or all axes of symmetry (four-fold symmetry), the algorithm demonstrates its ability in identifying partial symmetry.

Following the introduction of this novel technique, among the future research topics are: conducting a comparison with other evolutionary and non-evolutionary techniques, computing the correlation between the size of search space and the computational complexity of the process, and applying this method on dynamically evolving cellular automata generated patterns.

# References

1. al-Rifaie, M.M., Bishop, M.: Stochastic diffusion search review. Paladyn, Journal of Behavioral Robotics 4(3), 155–173 (2013)
2. al-Rifaie, M.M., Bishop, M., Blackwell, T.: Information sharing impact of stochastic diffusion search on differential evolution algorithm. J. Memetic Computing 4(4), 327–338 (2012)
3. al-Rifaie, M.M., Bishop, M., Caines, S.: Creativity and autonomy in swarm intelligence systems. J. Cognitive Computation 4(3), 320–331 (2012)
4. Bauerly, M., Liu, Y.: Computational modeling and experimental investigation of effects of compositional elements on interface and design aesthetics. International Journal of Man-Machine Studies 64(8), 670–682 (2006)
5. Behrens, R.R.: Design in the visual arts. Prentice-Hall (1984)
6. Bishop, J.: Stochastic searching networks. In: Proc. 1st IEE Conf. on Artificial Neural Networks, pp. 329–331. IET, London (1989)
7. Bishop, J., Torr, P.: The stochastic search network. In: Neural Networks for Images, Speech and Natural Language, pp. 370–387. Chapman & Hall, New York (1992)
8. Carroll, M.J. (ed.): HCI Models, Theories, and Frameworks: Toward a multidisciplinary science. Morgan Kaufmann Publishers, San Francisco (2003)
9. Dawkins, R.: The blind watchmaker. New York: Norton & Company, Inc. (1986)
10. Gangestad, S.W., Thornhill, R., Yeo, R.A.: Facial attractiveness, developmental stability, and fluctuating asymmetry. Ethology and Sociobiology 15(2), 73–85 (1994)
11. Hinton, G.F.: A parallel computation that assigns canonical object-based frames of reference. In: Proceedings of the 7th International Joint Conference on Artificial Intelligence, vol. 2, pp. 683–685. Morgan Kaufmann Publishers Inc. (1981)
12. Javid, M.A.J., te Boekhorst, R.: Cell Dormancy in Cellular Automata. In: Alexandrov, V.N., van Albada, G.D., Sloot, P.M.A., Dongarra, J. (eds.) ICCS 2006. LNCS, vol. 3993, pp. 367–374. Springer, Heidelberg (2006)
13. Jiang, H., Ngo, C.W., Tan, H.K.: Gestalt-based feature similarity measure in trademark database. Pattern Recognition 39(5), 988–1001 (2006)
14. Lewis, M.: Evolutionary visual art and design. In: Romero, J., Machado, P. (eds.) The Art of Artificial Evolution. Natural Computing Series, pp. 3–37. Springer (2008)

15. Leyton, M.: Symmetry, causality, mind. Bradford Books, MIT Press (1992)
16. Liu, Y.: Computational symmetry. In: CMU Robotics Institute (2000)
17. McClelland, J.L., Rumelhart, D.E., Group, P.R., et al.: Parallel distributed processing. Explorations in the Microstructure of Cognition 2 (1986)
18. McCormack, J.: Interactive evolution of l-system grammars for computer graphics modelling. Complex Systems: from biology to computation, 118–130 (1993)
19. de-Meyer, K., Bishop, J.M., Nasuto, S.J.: Stochastic diffusion: Using recruitment for search. In: McOwan, P., Dautenhahn, K., Nehaniv, C.L. (eds.) Evolvability and interaction: evolutionary substrates of communication, signalling, and perception in the dynamics of social complexity, Technical Report 393, vol. 393, pp. 60–65 (2003)
20. Møller, A.P., Cuervo, J.J.: Asymmetry, size and sexual selection: meta-analysis, publication bias and factors affecting variation in relationships, p. 1. Oxford University Press (1999)
21. Møller, A.P., Thornhill, R.: Bilateral symmetry and sexual selection: a meta-analysis. Am. Nat. 151(2), 174–192 (1998)
22. Nowak, M.A.: Evolutionary dynamics: exploring the equations of life. Harvard University Press (2006)
23. Park, I.K., Lee, K.M., Lee, S.U.: Perceptual grouping of line features in 3-D space: A model-based framework. Pattern Recognition 37(1), 145–159 (2004)
24. Railton, P.: Aesthetic Value, Moral Value and the Ambitions of Naturalism. In: Aesthetics and Ethics, vol. 3, University of Maryland (2001)
25. Randy, T., Steven, G.: Human facial beauty. Human Nature 4, 237–269 (1993)
26. Roth, T.O., Deutsch, A.: Universal synthesizer and window: Cellular automata as a new kind of cybernetic image. In: Imagery in the 21st Century, pp. 269–288. The MIT Press (2011)
27. Rucker, R.: Seek!: Selected Nonfiction. Running Press Book Publishers (1999)
28. Shackelford, T.K., Larsen, R.J.: Facial symmetry as an indicator of psychological emotional and physiological distress. Journal of Personality and Social Psychology 72 (1997)
29. Sims, K.: Evolving virtual creatures. In: Proceedings of the 21st Annual Conference on Computer Graphics and Interactive Techniques, pp. 15–22. ACM (1994)
30. Todd, S., Latham, W., Hughes, P.: Computer sculpture design and animation. The Journal of Visualization and Computer Animation 2(3), 98–105 (1991)

# Vehicle Routing in a Forestry Commissioning Operation Using Ant Colony Optimisation

Edward Kent, Jason A.D. Atkin, and Rong Qu

Automated Scheduling Optimisation & Planning Group
The University of Nottingham, Nottingham NG8 1BB UK
{eqk,jaa,rxq}@cs.nott.ac.uk

**Abstract.** This paper formulates a vehicle routing problem where constraints have been produced from a real world forestry commissioning dataset. In the problem, vehicles are required to fully load wood from forests and then deliver the wood to sawmills. The constraints include time windows and loading bay constraints at forests and sawmills. The loading bay constraints are examples of inter-route constraints that have not been studied in the literature as much as intra-route constraints. Inter-route constraints are constraints that cause dependencies between vehicles such that more than one vehicle is required to perform a task. Some locations have a lot of consignments at similar times, causing vehicles to queue for loading bays. The aim is to produce an optimal routing of consignments for vehicles such that the total time is minimised and there is as little queuing at forests and sawmills as possible. In this paper, the problem has been formulated into a vehicle routing problem with time windows and extra inter-route constraints. An ant colony optimisation heuristic is applied to the datasets and yields feasible solutions that appropriately use the loading bays. A number of methods of handling the inter-route constraints are also tested. It is shown that incorporating the delay times at loading bays into the ant's visibility produces solutions with the best objective values.

**Keywords:** Ant Colony Optimisation, Forestry Commissioning, Inter-route Constraints.

## 1 Introduction

The problem discussed in this paper is a vehicle routing problem faced by a forestry commissioning operator in Dumfries, Scotland. The data has been provided by Optrak, a vehicle routing and consultancy company. This is a vehicle routing problem with time windows and loading bay capacity constraints.

Models of similar vehicle routing problems with time window constraints have been presented by Fisher et al [6] and by Solomon [11] and are used in this paper. The travel times in this problem are also non-euclidean, asymmetric and the triangle rule does not apply. Such conditions cause problems for many traditional heuristics such as those discussed by Solomon et al [10]. The loading bays capacity constraints are examples of inter-route constraints similar to the

A.-H. Dediu et al. (Eds.): TPNC 2014, LNCS 8890, pp. 95–106, 2014.
© Springer International Publishing Switzerland 2014

inter-tour resource constraints in Hempsch et al [7], which are much less studied in the literature than intra-route constraints [3]. This paper presents a number of methods to mitigate delays at the loading bays.

Smaller forestry commissioning operations have been solved using methods such as column generation (Epstein et al [4,5]) and mixed integer linear programming models. For larger optimisation problems it is common to turn to heuristics to produce good solutions.

An ant colony optimisation (ACO) heuristic, which is a population based search that is both "robust and versatile" [2], is used to find the routing of vehicles between consignments and minimise the inter-consignment duration and violations of constraints. The heuristic can be easily adapted to accommodate a variety of different constraints, specifically the loading bay constraints in this case. It was suggested by Epstein et al [4] that solutions with periodic vehicle arrivals at loading bays may be easier to use. A variety of methods have been developed in this research for handling the loading bay constraints during the construction of solutions, such as making consignments "invisible" if they cannot be fulfilled without causing waiting time. These methods are compared and analysed in this paper.

The rest of this paper is structured as follows: Section 2 describes the problem and the loading bay constraints faced by this problem. Section 3 describes the ant colony optimisation heuristic and a number of adaptations to handle the loading bay constraints. Section 4 shows the experimental results using various adaptations to the ant colony optimisation heuristic, and discusses the consequent loading bay usage. Section 5 concludes the findings in this paper.

## 2   Problem Description

### 2.1   Routing the Forestry Commissioning Operation

The problem presented in this paper is a vehicle routing problem with time windows and additional loading bay constraints. The objective is to minimise the total time to transport logs from a set of forests to a set of sawmills. Forests have been paired with sawmills a-priori into tuples called consignments. Each consignment describes a task that needs to be fulfilled by exactly one vehicle; wood must be picked up from the forest and then driven directly to the paired sawmill. Since the start and end locations of consignments differ from each other, the driving times are asymmetric, non-euclidean and the triangle inequality does not hold, making some heuristics that exploit these characteristics potentially unsuitable for this problem.

Multiple consignments may share the same forest or the same sawmill (or both). Also, some consignments may need to be fulfilled simultaneously by different vehicles, meaning that multiple vehicles can arrive simultaneously at a forest or sawmill with a limited number of loading bays. Inter-route constraints are used to model the usage of these loading bays, as described below.

## 2.2   Loading Bay Constraints

Let $\Pi_{ib}$ be a variable that is 1 if bay $b$ is used by order $i$ and 0 otherwise. Let $A_i$ be the pickup location of consignment $i$ and $l$ represent the loading duration, assumed to be a constant of one hour in this problem. Let $O$ represent the set of consignments and $B$ represent the set of loading bays.

$$(\Pi_{ib} + \Pi_{jb} \leq 1) \vee (A_i + l \leq A_j) \vee (A_j + l \leq A_i)$$
$$\forall b \in B, \forall i, j \in O, i \neq j, \text{(i and j share the same location)} \tag{2.1}$$

Constraints (2.1) state that if two different consignments $i$ and $j$ use the same loading bay at a forest/sawmill (pickup/delivery location), then either the finish time of the first consignment must be before the start time of the second consignment or vice versa. Figure 1 shows how the pickup loading bay constraint (2.1) is violated (the shaded area) if two consignment loading bay usage times overlap. A vehicle that arrives at a busy pickup/delivery location (with no free loading bays) is allowed to wait. However, it sometimes may be preferable for a vehicle to service a different consignment first and service this consignment later, when the location becomes free again.

## 3   Algorithm Description

This section describes the ACO heuristic and a number of adaptations and implementations that handle inter-route constraints.

### 3.1   Ant Colony Optimisation

Ant colony optimisation (ACO) is a population based adaptive constructive heuristic [2]. It was used in Mazzeo et al [8] to build routes for a capacitated vehicle routing problem (CVRP) (without inter-tour constraints) and obtained better results than Tabu Search in some cases. Riemann et al [9] also used an ACO heuristic in a similar way for vehicle routing problems.

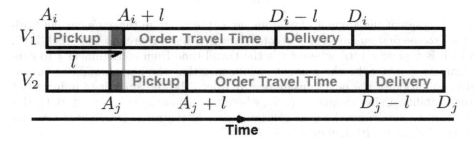

**Fig. 1.** The pickup constraint is violated when there is a loading bay usage overlap (e.g when $A_i + l > A_j \wedge A_i < A_j + l$. $A_i$: the arrival time of a vehicle at order $i$, $l$: the loading time.)

ACO uses a set of constructive agents called "ants" to create paths on a graph using knowledge ("pheromones") from previous iterations. After each iteration, for every solution, the pheromones on each arc of the graph are updated based on the fitness of the solutions that used that arc. Solutions that have a better fitness will add more pheromone to the arcs it uses than solutions that have a worse fitness.

Pheromones evaporate over time at a rate of $\rho$ to prevent the heuristic converging too early. Shorter arcs with strong pheromone will attract more ants per iteration than longer arcs with weak pheromone. When more ants traverse an arc throughout the iterations, the pheromone on the arc becomes stronger. Eventually the heuristic should identify a selection of arcs in good solutions.

In this paper, the ants in the ACO heuristic represent vehicles. Unlike the standard ACO heuristic for the travelling salesman problem (TSP) [2], more than one vehicle is needed to create a full solution for the VRP, so "ant groups" are formed that share a list of fulfilled consignments, preventing consignments from being scheduled more than once. A number of ant groups are performed in the same iteration and leave pheromones on arcs for use by later iterations of ant groups. The ACO algorithm can be found in Dorigo et al [2]. In this paper, the ACO heuristic has been further modified to handle time window constraints and loading bay constraints. Let $O$ denote the set of consignments. Each ant in an ant group starts at the depot and a probability of $p_j, \forall j \in O$ is determined for each unassigned consignment based on a number of things: the amount of pheromone on the arc that connects the ant's current position to the consignment, the length of this arc, whether waiting time is required for a vehicle to be serviced at the forest/sawmill for the consignment and, finally, whether the time windows can be met for both the pickup and delivery parts of the consignment. Consignments that cause constraint violations when added to the ant's route can be avoided by setting the probability $p_j$ to 0. Let $\Psi$ represent the set of consignments that are avoided by the ant. Given that the ant is at consignment $i$, $p_j$ can be calculated using function (3.1), for all $j \notin \Psi$.

$$p_j = \frac{\tau_{ij}^{\alpha} \eta_{ij}^{\beta}}{\sum_{k \in O \setminus \Psi} \tau_{ik}^{\alpha} \eta_{ik}^{\beta}} \tag{3.1}$$

Let $\tau$ represent the amount of pheromone on the arc from the ant's current position $i$ to the first customer in the consignment $j$. Let $\eta$ represent the "visibility", which is typically $1/t_{ij}$ where $t_{ij}$ is the travel time from consignment $i$ to consignment $j$. Let $\alpha$ be the amount of influence that the pheromone has on the determination of the next consignment and let $\beta$ be the amount of influence of the visibility. Using inequality (3.2), where r is a random number $r \in [0, 1)$, the decision to determine the next consignment $j$ in the route is weighted towards "better" choices with higher values of $p_j$.

$$\sum_{i=0}^{j-1} p_i \leq r \leq \sum_{i=0}^{j} p_i \quad j \in O \tag{3.2}$$

## 3.2   Constraint Handling

ACO heuristics can be implemented differently to fit particular constraints. For example, a "Heuristic function" is used in the place of the visibility in [1] to solve a vehicle routing problem with time windows and time dependent travel times (traffic conditions). This function includes the duration of the arc as well as the waiting time required to service the customers. A similar approach can be adopted to use loading bay waiting times to influence the ant's choice of consignment. During the construction of the route, an ant can check a loading bay to see if there is time available for both the sawmill and the forest visits for a consignment. The ant can also calculate the total duration of waiting time that will be required at the forest and the sawmill and use this in the decision making. The loading bay schedule is updated for that group each time an ant visits a particular place, to ensure that there are no loading bay conflicts and to calculate delays.

Three options for handling the loading bay constraints have been considered:

**Ignoring and Repairing.** In this method, the loading bay usage is ignored during the ACO heuristic so infeasible solutions can be created. A repairing procedure (such as a local search heuristic) is used to re-schedule the routes after each iteration to remove loading bay conflicts. This method does not require analysis of arrival times at customers until the repairing procedure, which may reduce the runtime. However, it may not be possible to re-arrange the consignments effectively in the repair procedure, or at least without a large increase in the solution's objective value.

**Avoiding Conflicts.** For any consignment $j$, let $\omega_j$ be the waiting time, which is the shortest time before the current ant can be serviced at consignment $j$. The simple avoidance method will set $p_j = 0$ for all consignments $j$ such that $\omega_j > 0$. Figure 2 shows how a loading bay usage window can be tested against a

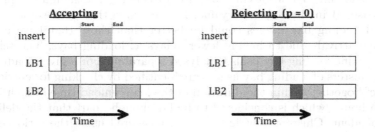

**Fig. 2.** A forest/sawmill $j$ with 2 loading bays, and an example of when a visit is accepted at the loading bay and and example of when a visit is rejected (when $p_j$ is set to 0)

customer's schedule. It shows an example of a customer with two loading bays. The first example (Accepting) shows that the loading bay usage (labelled insert) can be inserted into the second loading bay without any waiting time. The second example shows that the loading bay usage window cannot be directly inserted into the schedule without having to consider adding waiting time. This method avoids queuing entirely. However, for a hard dataset, queuing may be required to get to a feasible solution.

**Scheduling & Penalising Waiting Times with $W_1$ and $W_2$.** Let $\omega_j$ denote the waiting time for consignment $j$, as above. Rather than preventing the usage, an alternative approach is to penalise the delays. This can be achieved by using a weighted visibility $\eta_{ij}$ calculated by equation (3.3) where $W_1$ and $W_2$ are constants, rather than setting $\eta_{ij} = \frac{1}{t_{ij}}$ in equation (3.1).

$$\eta_{ij} = \frac{1}{W_1 t_{ij} + W_2 \omega_j} \tag{3.3}$$

For large values of $W_2$, waiting times can be avoided where possible since ants will be diverted, due to small values of visibility ($\eta_{ij}$). However, a strong penalty could impair the solution in a similar way to setting the probability ($p_j$) to 0. Consignments that cannot be scheduled without waiting times would be left until the end of the day because their corresponding probabilities have to compete with consignments that do not have waiting times. This can lead to infeasible solutions where these consignments miss their time windows.

### 3.3    Observing Loading Bay Usage

Although the main objective of the model is to reduce the total time (waiting and driving) the consecutive arrivals of the loading bays can be measured to give an insight into how well the loading bay capacity constraint handling techniques work. Solutions that have a large number of consecutive arrivals and no space between the loading operations may be harder to manage. Although this property is not measured in the objective value, it is possible that such solutions that have good loading bay usages could be better than those that have a lot of consecutive arrivals due to having fewer delays at loading bays. The schedule for each specific loading bay is also analysed separately. For a given loading bay schedule, clusters of loading bay usages are identified by checking for entries that are "close" together within the duration of the load/unload time (which in this case is an hour), which is considered to be far enough apart that the deliveries are independent. Clustered entries are then measured using the ratio between the loading time and the time between the entries. Figure 3 presents an example of clusters of loading bay schedule entries that are used in the calculation of the ratio. A solution that has a low average ratio means that there may be many consecutive entries in the loading bay schedules.

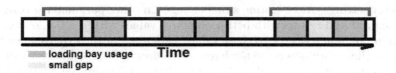

Fig. 3. A loading bay with a number of vehicle visits. The "close" visits have been clustered together, and the sum of the ratio of the time gap between the visits and the loading time is used in the calculation of the average ratio.

## 4    Computational Results

The six datasets which were used in this research were generated from real world data from south west Scotland. All datasets have a number of locations that are particularly busy (with many consignments in a short duration) with only one or two loading bays available. These datasets can be found at http://www.cs.nott.ac.uk/~rxq/benchmarks.htm. The purpose of these experiments is to analyse the different constraint handling techniques. A number of parameter settings for the penalty method are also tested, to analyse their effect on the objective values and the number of delays.

One experiment shows results without the loading bay constraints (for the purpose of comparing objective values). The other experiments use a waiting time penalty multiplier $W_2$ set to 0, 1 or 2. An experiment was also performed with $W_1 = 2$, to see whether better objective values can be achieved if the waiting time is not prioritised as much as the driving time.

### 4.1    Results

Results are given in tables 1-6 for different test datasets. Each row in each table gives the average results over ten runs of the ACO heuristic, with the same parameter settings. In each column, the parameter settings and the average values for the following properties are given: the average waiting time across all final ant groups in each run; the average objective function value for the best ant group in each run (in seconds); the average number of times there was a delay across all final ant groups; the average of the loading bay ratios across all final ant groups; the average (upper bound on the) optimality gap for the best ant group for each run. The lower bounds of each dataset were calculated in CPLEX, by assuming a single asymmetric TSP tour that goes through all consignments without time window constraints. Since CPLEX failed to find the optimal solution for any of the asymmetric TSP relaxations, the lower bound of the a-TSP was used to determine (the lower bound for) the optimality gap.

A variety of parameter settings were tried. Firstly, the number of ant groups was set to a low value (10) to view the effects of the parameter settings more quickly. $\rho$ was set to 0.99 with $\alpha = 0.5$ and $\beta = 5$ as suggested by Dorigo et al [2] for travelling salesman problems. However, these values failed to produce good results, which is unsurprising since it is well known that different problems often require different parameter settings. After testing small changes in other parameter settings, the heuristic produced results with better objective values with $\rho = 0.9$, $\alpha = 0.7$ and $\beta = 1.5$ in preliminary tests, so these values were used for the experiments. Small changes to these parameters did not have much effect upon the objective value, but changing $\alpha$ to values above 1.0 or $\beta$ to values below 1.0 produced worse solutions as the heuristic converged too quickly. $\rho$ is set to a lower value because only 1000 iterations were used in order to keep the runtime low.

**Table 1.** 300 Consignments, 40 Vehicles, 79 Points

| Expt. | $W_1$ | $W_2$ | Waiting Time | Objective | Delay | Ratios | Gap % |
|---|---|---|---|---|---|---|---|
| 1 | off | | N/A | 5.464E6 | N/A | N/A | 15.01 |
| 2 | avoid | | N/A | 5.512E6 | N/A | 0.46 | 15.74 |
| 3 | 1.0 | 0.0 | 5.463E5 | 5.493E6 | 9.51 | 0.4 | 15.45 |
| 4 | 1.0 | 1.0 | 5.412E5 | 5.48E6 | 9.49 | 0.4 | 15.26 |
| 5 | 1.0 | 2.0 | 5.451E5 | 5.485E6 | 9.5 | 0.4 | 15.33 |
| 6 | 2.0 | 1.0 | 5.38E5 | 5.485E6 | 9.59 | 0.4 | 15.32 |

**Table 2.** 350 Consignments, 40 Vehicles, 84 Points

| Expt. | $W_1$ | $W_2$ | Waiting Time | Objective | Delays | Ratio | Gap % |
|---|---|---|---|---|---|---|---|
| 1 | off | | N/A | 6.297E6 | N/A | N/A | 16.47 |
| 2 | avoid | | N/A | N/A | N/A | N/A | N/A |
| 3 | 1.0 | 0.0 | 6.656E5 | 6.431E6 | 26.6 | 0.36 | 18.2 |
| 4 | 1.0 | 1.0 | 6.697E5 | 6.43E6 | 26.74 | 0.36 | 18.19 |
| 5 | 1.0 | 2.0 | 6.691E5 | 6.431E6 | 26.66 | 0.36 | 18.21 |
| 6 | 2.0 | 1.0 | 6.649E5 | 6.435E6 | 26.72 | 0.36 | 18.25 |

**Table 3.** 400 Consignments, 40 Vehicles, 98 Points

| Expt. | $W_1$ | $W_2$ | Waiting Time | Objective | Delays | Ratio | Gap % |
|---|---|---|---|---|---|---|---|
| 1 | off | | N/A | 7.016E6 | N/A | N/A | 12.58 |
| 2 | avoid | | N/A | 7.09E6 | N/A | 0.46 | 13.49 |
| 3 | 1.0 | 0.0 | 5.752E5 | 7.072E6 | 19.6 | 0.38 | 13.27 |
| 4 | 1.0 | 1.0 | 5.8E5 | 7.079E6 | 19.8 | 0.38 | 13.36 |
| 5 | 1.0 | 2.0 | 5.717E5 | 7.082E6 | 19.7 | 0.38 | 13.39 |
| 6 | 2.0 | 1.0 | 5.771E5 | 7.076E6 | 19.72 | 0.38 | 13.32 |

**Table 4.** 420 Consignments, 40 Vehicles, 93 Points

| Expt. | $W_1$ | $W_2$ | Waiting Time | Objective | Delays | Ratio | Gap % |
|---|---|---|---|---|---|---|---|
| 1 | off | | N/A | 6.961E6 | N/A | N/A | 13.33 |
| 2 | avoid | | N/A | 7.036E6 | N/A | 0.45 | 14.25 |
| 3 | 1.0 | 0.0 | 4.305E5 | 7.026E6 | 24.56 | 0.38 | 14.13 |
| 4 | 1.0 | 1.0 | 4.271E5 | 7.033E6 | 24.66 | 0.38 | 14.21 |
| 5 | 1.0 | 2.0 | 4.367E5 | 7.031E6 | 24.74 | 0.38 | 14.19 |
| 6 | 2.0 | 1.0 | 4.308E5 | 7.036E6 | 24.75 | 0.38 | 14.24 |

**Table 5.** 420 Consignments, 40 Vehicles, 95 Points

| Expt. | $W_1$ | $W_2$ | Waiting Time | Objective | Delays | Ratio | Gap % |
|---|---|---|---|---|---|---|---|
| 1 | off | | N/A | 7.249E6 | N/A | N/A | 12.25 |
| 2 | avoid | | N/A | 7.371E6 | N/A | 0.45 | 13.69 |
| 3 | 1.0 | 0.0 | 4.395E5 | 7.343E6 | 29.7 | 0.37 | 13.37 |
| 4 | 1.0 | 1.0 | 4.36E5 | 7.332E6 | 29.59 | 0.37 | 13.24 |
| 5 | 1.0 | 2.0 | 4.458E5 | 7.328E6 | 29.72 | 0.37 | 13.2 |
| 6 | 2.0 | 1.0 | 4.405E5 | 7.345E6 | 29.8 | 0.37 | 13.4 |

**Table 6.** 420 Consignments, 40 Vehicles, 95 Points

| Expt. | $W_1$ | $W_2$ | Waiting Time | Objective | Delays | Ratio | Gap % |
|---|---|---|---|---|---|---|---|
| 1 | off | | N/A | 7.573E6 | N/A | N/A | 12.34 |
| 2 | avoid | | N/A | N/A | N/A | N/A | N/A |
| 3 | 1.0 | 0.0 | 5.262E5 | 7.692E6 | 33.8 | 0.38 | 13.7 |
| 4 | 1.0 | 1.0 | 5.165E5 | 7.699E6 | 33.91 | 0.37 | 13.78 |
| 5 | 1.0 | 2.0 | 5.209E5 | 7.685E6 | 33.85 | 0.38 | 13.62 |
| 6 | 2.0 | 1.0 | 5.249E5 | 7.692E6 | 33.91 | 0.37 | 13.7 |

## 4.2  Discussion

The "avoid queuing" method failed to produce any feasible solutions for datasets 2 and 6. The time windows could not be met for these datasets because ants avoid consignments that require queuing, so these consignments were assigned later in the route and the time windows were missed. There may exist solutions where vehicles travel times cause arrivals to be outside of each others loading bay usage times. However, the ant colony algorithm could not find any of these solutions for datasets 2 and 6.

For other datasets, this approach produced feasible solutions because the time windows were lenient enough, or the loading bays were more plentiful. However, the objective values were worse than the other loading bay constraint handling methods. There are no delays for these solutions that are caused by loading bays because vehicles do not drive to consignments that have no loading bays available at the time of the vehicle's arrival. This causes the vehicles to drive to consignments that are further away and thus, routes are longer in these solutions. However, the loading bay ratio was the best in these solutions, meaning that the loading bays are less busy. Figure 4 shows an example of two loading bay schedules; the first example shows vehicles that arrive at similar times, and so the ratio of time between the loading bay usage and the total loading time is small because the loading bay usage is consecutive. The second has vehicles that arrive outside of each other's loading bay usage times, thus there are gaps between the entries and so the ratio is larger. The "ignoring queuing" method

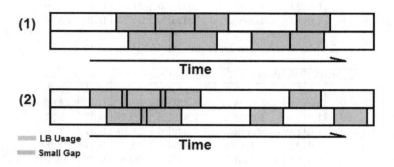

**Fig. 4.** Possible Effects of $W_2$ or of Avoiding Queuing. In (1), $W_2 = 0$ and thus the vehicles arrive in similar times and have to wait for the loading bay to be free. In (2), $W_2 = 2$ or the ants avoid queuing. The vehicles arrive slightly further apart, meaning there is no queuing.

produces better objective values because the loading bay constraints are relaxed, so the heuristic does not add waiting time to the entries at busy periods. The ratio of the loading time and gaps between the loading times is not measurable because entries are able to overlap. Of course, this makes the solutions infeasible in practice.

**Considering $W_1$ and $W_2$.** The objective values and loading bay ratios of the solutions obtained when different parameter settings of $W_1$ and $W_2$ are used are similar. For this reason, a number of Mann-Whitney U tests were performed on the results of the experiments on each dataset to test the difference in the results. Specifically, for two given sets of data, a percentage is given for the number of entries in the set that are larger than entries in the other. A percentage of $U = 100\%$ means that all entries in the first set are larger than those in the second set.

The objectives appear to vary with the different parameter settings. For example, comparing $W_2 = 0$ and $W_2 = 2$ gives $U = 30\%$ in dataset 3 and $U = 83\%$ in dataset 3. This means that objective values for $W_2 = 0$ were generally smaller than the objective values when $W_2 = 2$ for dataset 3, but for dataset 5 they were generally larger. However, over all tests over all datasets with settings $W_2 = 0$ and $W_2 = 2$, five of these datasets had larger objective values when $W_2 = 0$ because $U > 50\%$. Similarly, four out of six datasets had a result of $U > 50\%$ for tests between $W_2 = 0$ and $W_2 = 1$. This implies that penalising waiting times can potentially aid the heuristic to find good solutions more so than setting $W_2 = 0$. Ignoring waiting time by setting $W_2 = 0$ means that the heuristic is able to accept solutions that have large waiting times, worsening the objective values. For the comparisons between $W_1 = 1$ and $W_1 = 2$, four out of six datasets showed that the objective values were larger for $W_1 = 2$. These four datasets were also the same four datasets where the objective values were larger when $W_2 = 0$ for the tests between $W_2 = 1$ and $W_2 = 0$. Thus, the behaviour of the objective values is similar when setting $W_1 = 2$ or $W_2 = 0$.

A number of Mann-Whitney U tests showed that the loading bay ratios were better when $W_2 = 0$. This is because, when the waiting time at loading bays is penalised, consignments that have no loading bays available are avoided until the end of the day. Many vehicles then arrive at similar times at the end of the day causing queuing at the loading bays. The Mann-Whitney U test results for the loading bay ratios also coincided with the Mann-Whitney U tests for the waiting times; the waiting time is worse when the loading bay ratios are small.

## 5    Conclusion

In this paper, a forestry commissioning routing problem was presented based on real world problem datasets. The problem is a Vehicle Routing Problem with time windows and inter-route constraints. These inter-route constraints consist of loading bay capacity limitations at pickup and delivery points, meaning that only a limited number of vehicles are able to be serviced simultaneously. The forestry commissioning routing problem was explained and the loading bay constraints were shown. These constraints contained information to ensure that loading bays were used properly.

An Ant Colony Optimisation heuristic was used and a number of problem-specific modifications to the heuristic were tested. These modifications were created to handle the (inter-route) loading bay constraints to avoid loading bay queues, ignore the inter-route constraints, or penalise waiting times. Results showed that, for less constrained problems, queuing can be avoided, but only at the cost of increased objective function values. Penalising the waiting time by setting $W_2 = 1$ or $W_2 = 2$ in the visibility function was found to produce solutions with better objective values and having no cost for waiting time. Setting $W_2 = 0$ could result in solutions with long waiting times. Similarly, using a large penalty for travel times ($W_1 = 2$), was also found to decrease solution value, for the same datasets for which having no delay cost did so. The best objective values were attained for the parameter settings $W_1 = 1$ and $W_2 = 1$ or $W_2 = 2$.

The simple penalisation method for handling the loading bay constraints that are present in this model can also be adopted in other heuristics. The waiting times can be calculated and then included into the objective function of any heuristic with a penalty value. This method may also work well in other problems that have inter-route constraints and is worth further investigation.

# References

1. Donati, A.V., Montemanni, R., Casagrande, N., Rizzoli, A.E., Gambardella, L.M.: Time dependent vehicle routing problem with a multi ant colony system. European Journal of Operational Research 185(3), 1174–1191 (2008)
2. Dorigo, M., Maniezzo, V., Colorni, A.: Ant System: Optimization by a Colony of Cooperating Agents. IEEE Transactions on Systems, Management and Cybernetics. Part B, Cybernetics: A publication of the IEEE Systems, Management and Cybernetics Society 26(1), 29–41 (1996)
3. Drexl, M.: Synchronization in Vehicle Routing - A Survey of VRPs with Multiple Synchronization Constraints. Transportation Science 46(3), 1–58 (2011)
4. Epstein, R., Morales, R., Seron, J., Verso, P.T.R.A.: A Truck Scheduling System Improves Efficiency in the Forest Industries. Institute for Operations Research and the Management Sciences 1996(26), 1–12 (1996)
5. Epstein, R., Sero, J., Weintraub, A.: Use of OR Systems in the Chilean Forest Industries. Interfaces 29(1), 7–29 (1999)
6. Fisher, M.L., Jörnsten, K.O., Madsen, O.B.G.: Vehicle Routing with Time Windows: Two Optimization Algorithms. Operations Research 45(3), 488–492 (1997)
7. Hempsch, C., Irnich, S.: Vehicle routing problems with inter-tour resource constraints. In: The Vehicle Routing Problem: Latest Advances and New Challenges, pp. 421–444. Springer (2008)
8. Mazzeo, S., Loiseau, I.: An Ant Colony Algorithm for the Capacitated Vehicle Routing Problem. Electronic Notes in Discrete Mathematics 18, 181–186 (2004)
9. Reimann, M.: D-Ants: Savings Based Ants Divide and Conquer the Vehicle Routing Problem. Computers & Operations Research 31(4), 563–591 (2004)
10. Solomon, M.M.: Algorithms for the Vehicle Routing and Scheduling Problems with Time Window Constraints. Operations Research 35(2), 254–265 (1987)
11. Solomon, M.M., Desrosiers, J.: Time window constrained routing and scheduling problems. Transportation Science 22(1), 1–13 (1988)

# Extrapolated States, Void States, and a Huge Novel Class of Distillable Entangled States

Michel Boyer[1] and Tal Mor[2]

[1] DIRO, Université de Montréal, Canada
boyer@iro.umontreal.ca
[2] Technion, Israel
talmo@cs.technion.ac.il

**Abstract.** A nice and interesting property of any pure tensor-product state is that each such state has distillable entangled states at an arbitrarily small distance $\epsilon$ in its neighbourhood. We say that such nearby states are $\epsilon$-entangled, and we call the tensor product state in that case, a "boundary separable state", as there is entanglement at any distance from this "boundary". Here we find a huge class of separable states that also share that property mentioned above – they all have $\epsilon$-entangled states at any small distance in their neighbourhood. Furthermore, the entanglement they have is proven to be distillable.

**Keywords:** quantum computing and quantum information, entanglement, distillability.

## 1 Introduction

The search for interesting entangled states always fascinated researchers in quantum information processing. A few interesting examples are the Werner states [8], bound entangled states [6,1], and the W-states [2].

Obviously, any pure tensor product state has entangled states near it, at any distance. Also, a Werner-state $\lambda/3[\rho_{\psi_+} + \rho_{\varphi_+} + \rho_{\varphi_-}] + (1 - \lambda)[\rho_{\psi_-}]$ (built from the four Bell states) with $\lambda = 1/2$ has entangled states near it, at any distance.

Is the property of being separable yet having entangled states nearby at any distance common? Or is it rare? Furthermore, what can we learn about the type of entanglement that those nearby entangled states have? For two qubits, it is known [4] that the entanglement is always distillable. For qudits, cf proposition 6.

## 2 Notations and Terminology

### 2.1 Boundary Separable States and $\epsilon$-Entangled States

We call *boundary separable state* a separable density operator $\rho_b$ such that for *any* $\epsilon > 0$, there is an entangled state $\rho_e$ for which $\delta(\rho_b, \rho_e) \leq \epsilon$, where $\delta$ is the

A.-H. Dediu et al. (Eds.): TPNC 2014, LNCS 8890, pp. 107–118, 2014.

trace distance $(\delta(\rho_\epsilon, \rho_b) = \frac{1}{2}\mathrm{Tr}|\rho_\epsilon - \rho_b|)$, i.e. there are entangled states arbitrarily close to $\rho_b$. Notice that for any density operator $\rho_1$, and $0 \le \epsilon \le 1$, if

$$\rho_\epsilon = (1 - \epsilon)\rho_b + \epsilon\rho_1 \tag{1}$$

then $\delta(\rho_\epsilon, \rho_b) = \frac{\epsilon}{2}\mathrm{Tr}|\rho_1 - \rho_b| = \epsilon\delta(\rho_1, \rho_b)$ and thus

$$\delta(\rho_\epsilon, \rho_b) \le \epsilon .$$

The trace distance between $\rho_\epsilon$ given by (1) and the (boundary) separable state $\rho_b$ is at most $\epsilon$ but it may be much smaller than $\epsilon$; it is $\epsilon$ iff $\delta(\rho_1, \rho_b) = 1$ i.e. if $\rho_b$ and $\rho_1$ are orthogonal (have orthogonal support).

An entangled state $\rho_e$ such that there is a boundary separable state $\rho_b$ for which $\delta(\rho_e, \rho_b) \le \epsilon$ will be called $\epsilon$-*entangled*; it is at trace distance at most $\epsilon$ from a boundary separable state. As an example, the Werner state with $\lambda = 1/2$ is a boundary separable state and mixing it with $\rho_{\psi_-}$ gives epsilon-entangled states.

There are separable states $\rho_b$ for which there exists a state $\rho_1$ such that all the states $\rho_\epsilon$ given by (1) are entangled for $\epsilon$ small enough, $\epsilon \ne 0$: there is a continuous path starting from $\rho_b$ and going straight in the direction of $\rho_1$ whose initial section contains only $\epsilon$-entangled states. Note that for $\epsilon = 0$ the resulting state $\rho_0$ is the boundary separable-state $\rho_b$ itself; $\rho_0 = \rho_b$. As an example, again, the Werner state with $\lambda = 1/2$ is a boundary separable state, such that mixing it with $\rho_{\psi_-}$ as in (1) gives epsilon-entangled states, and there is continuous path from this Werner state and all the way to the fully entangled state $\rho_{\psi_-}$.

## 2.2   "Extrapolated States" and "Void States"

Given any two states $\rho_0$ and $\rho_1$, the operators $\rho_t = (1 - t)\rho_0 + t\rho_1$ are clearly always hermitian with trace 1; when $0 \le t \le 1$, they are (mixed) states, all on a straight line segment between $\rho_0$ and $\rho_1$; those mixed states are obtained by *interpolation* (convex combination) of two states. Let us now introduce three additional definitions:

a) When $t < 0$, $\rho_t$ is on the same straight line but is no longer between $\rho_0$ and $\rho_1$; in general, if $\rho_0 \ne \rho_1$ and all the eigenvalues of $\rho_0$ are strictly positive, then there are values of $t < 0$ such that $\rho_t$ is a state; we call such states *extrapolated states*.

Note that if $\rho_0 = |0\rangle\langle 0|$ and $\rho_1 = |1\rangle\langle 1|$, then $(1 - t)\rho_0 + t\rho_1 = (1 - t)|0\rangle\langle 0| + t|1\rangle\langle 1|$ is not a state (it is not positive semi definite) as soon as $t < 0$ (or $t > 1$).

There may be some value $m < 0$ such that $\rho_t$ is no longer positive semi-definite, thus no longer a state (hence it is not a physical entity), for $t < m$, while it is still semi-definite for $t = m$.

The condition that the eigenvalues of $\rho_0$ be all positive is sufficient for defining extrapolated states, but not necessary. One can extrapolate carefully-chosen states that have some 0 eigenvalues. Extrapolation somewhat behaves like subtraction: if $t < 0$, then $\rho_t = (1 + |t|)\rho_0 - |t|\rho_1$. We will be interested only with extrapolations with $t < 0$ though $t > 1$ could also provide extrapolations.

b) A *void state* is a quantum state that has exactly one zero eigenvalue. Namely, when diagonalized, it has exactly one zero on the diagonal.

c) A *k-void state* (of dimension $N > k$) is a quantum state that has exactly $k$ zero eigenvalues[1].

# 3  Two Qubits

Our first example of 2-party boundary separable-states (and the derived $\epsilon$-entangled states) is obtained by starting from a completely mixed state and "fully subtracting" one of the eigenstates, to obtain a separable void state. Our second example uses a different—yet very interesting state to start with—the thermal state. As in the first example, a void-state is generated from the thermal state (via extrapolation) by subtracting one of the eigenstates. Our third example uses a 2-void state instead of a simple (1-)void state (and we also discuss here the case of 3-void state which in this case is a tensor product state). Our last two 2-qubit examples provide generalizations to less trivial cases. Since two qubit states that are entangled are all distillable [4], the states obtained are thus also distillable.

## 3.1  Example 1 – The Extrapolated Pseudo-Pure State of Two Qubits

Mixing a completely mixed state $\rho_0$ with an arbitrary state $\rho_1$ to yield the pseudo pure state (PPS) $\rho = (1 - t)\rho_0 + t\rho_1$ is found to be extremely useful in quantum information processing (e.g. in NMR quantum computing). To the best of our knowledge, an extrapolated state of the form $\rho = (1 + |t|)\rho_0 - |t|\rho_1$ was never used. This "extrapolated pseudo pure state" (EPPS), whenever it is a legal quantum state, shares with the conventional PPS the fact that applying any unitary transformation acts only on $\rho_1$.

An interesting special case of this EPPS is when $|t|$ is exactly sufficiently large to make one eigenvalue disappear (become zero). If $\rho_1$ is a pure tensor product state, then the resulting $\rho$ is a void state. We assume here that the subtracted tensor product state is written in the computational basis, e.g., it is $|11\rangle\langle11|$ and $m = t = -1/3$.

**Proposition 1.** *If the standard basis is the eigenbasis of a state $\rho$ on $\mathcal{H}_2 \otimes \mathcal{H}_2$, and if the eigenvalue of $|11\rangle$ is 0, and the other three eigenvalues are $1/3$, then there are states arbitrarily close to $\rho$ that are entangled. [The same holds, with obvious adjustments, for any other tensor-product eigenstate that has a zero eigenvalue.]*

---

[1] Note that a separable $N - 1$-void state is a tensor product state.

We avoid proving this proposition as we later (in example 4) prove a more general result, containing the above (and also example 2) as special cases. The above mentioned (very basic) example is mainly given for historical reasons, as it was the first example we found.

For $j$ fixed, let

$$\rho = \frac{4}{3}\left[\frac{1}{4}\sum_{i=0}^{3}|i\rangle\langle i|\right] - \frac{1}{3}|j\rangle\langle j| = \frac{1}{3}\sum_{i=0;i\neq j}^{3}|i\rangle\langle i|$$

This is obtained by choosing $|j\rangle$ (viewed as a two bit integer from $0 = 00_2$ to $3 = 11_2$) to be any product state $j \equiv j_{AB} = j_A \otimes j_B$, where the two parties are $A$ for Alice's qubit and $B$ for Bob's. In fact, for all values of $t$ between 0 and $-1/3$, the hermitian operators

$$\rho_t = (1-t)\left[\frac{1}{4}\sum_{i=0}^{3}|i\rangle\langle i|\right] + t|j\rangle\langle j|$$

are separable states; for $t < -1/3$, $\rho_t$ is no longer a state since it is no longer positive semi definite, the eigenvalue of $|j\rangle$ becoming negative. Finally, if $|j\rangle = |11\rangle$, proposition 1 tells us that there are entangled states arbitrarily close to

$$\frac{1}{3}\sum_{i=0}^{2}|i\rangle\langle i|.$$

## 3.2    Example 2 – The Thermal State of Two Qubits

The thermal state on two qubits is the state

$$\rho_\Theta = \frac{(1+\eta)^2}{4}|00\rangle\langle 00| + \frac{1-\eta^2}{4}\left[|01\rangle\langle 01| + |10\rangle\langle 10|\right] + \frac{(1-\eta)^2}{4}|11\rangle\langle 11|$$

The state $|11\rangle$ is a 0-eigenstate of $\rho_p = (1+p)\rho_\Theta - p|1\rangle\langle 1|$ if $(1-\eta)^2(p+1) = 4p$ and a proposition similar to proposition 1 can be written for $\rho_p$. However, both cases of Sections 3.1 and 3.2 will be dealt with, by a generalization done in example 4.

The thermal state will get more attention later on, when we discuss $N$ qubits.

## 3.3    Example 3 — 2-Void State

Example 3, using a 2-void state, is as follows:

**Proposition 2.** *In $\mathscr{H}_2 \otimes \mathscr{H}_2$ there are entangled states arbitrarily close to the state $\rho = \frac{1}{2}\left[|01\rangle\langle 01| + |10\rangle\langle 10|\right]$.*

*Proof.* Here again, $|11\rangle$ is an eigenstate of $\rho$ of 0 eigenvalue. Let $\rho_1 = |\psi_+\rangle\langle\psi_+|$ with $|\psi_+\rangle = \frac{1}{\sqrt{2}}[|01\rangle + |10\rangle]$ and $\rho_\epsilon = (1-\epsilon)\rho + \epsilon\rho_1$. Then $(T \otimes I)(\rho_\epsilon)$, where T is the transpose operator, is

$$
(T \otimes I)
\begin{bmatrix}
0 & 0 & 0 & 0 \\
0 & 1/2 & \epsilon/2 & 0 \\
0 & \epsilon/2 & 1/2 & 0 \\
0 & 0 & 0 & 0
\end{bmatrix}
=
\begin{bmatrix}
0 & 0 & 0 & \epsilon/2 \\
0 & 1/2 & 0 & 0 \\
0 & 0 & 1/2 & 0 \\
\epsilon/2 & 0 & 0 & 0
\end{bmatrix}
$$

with characteristic equation $(\lambda - 1/2)^2(\lambda^2 - \epsilon^2/4) = 0$ and eigenvalues $1/2$, $\epsilon/2$ and $-\epsilon/2$; by the Peres criterion[2] [7], $\rho_\epsilon$ is thus entangled for all $1 > \epsilon > 0$ and, of course, $\delta(\rho, \rho_\epsilon) \leq \epsilon$.

In fact, there was no need to solve the characteristic equation to show that $(T \otimes I)(\rho_\epsilon)$ is not positive semi definite. That can be seen directly from the matrix of $(T \otimes I)(\rho_\epsilon)$ because there is a 0 on the main diagonal for which the corresponding row and column are not zero: This is a consequence of the following well known lemma with $|\varphi\rangle = |11\rangle$ and $|\psi\rangle = |00\rangle$; indeed $\langle 11| (T\otimes I)(\rho_\epsilon) |11\rangle = 0$ but $\langle 11| (T \otimes I)(\rho_\epsilon) |00\rangle \neq 0$.

**Lemma 3.** *Let $A$ be a hermitian operator on $\mathscr{H}$; if there are $|\varphi\rangle$ and $|\psi\rangle$ such that $\langle\varphi|A|\varphi\rangle = 0$ and $\langle\varphi|A|\psi\rangle \neq 0$ then $A$ is not positive semi definite.*

*Proof.* See appendix C.

### 3.4   Example 4 — A Generalization

Example 4 generalizes examples 1, 2 and 3:

**Proposition 4.** *If the standard basis is the eigenbasis of a state $\rho$ on $\mathscr{H}_2 \otimes \mathscr{H}_2$, and if the eigenvalue of $|11\rangle$ is 0, then there are states arbitrarily close to $\rho$ that are entangled. The same holds for any other eigenstate.*

*Proof.* Let indeed

$$
\rho = \lambda_{00} |00\rangle\langle00| + \lambda_{01} |01\rangle\langle01| + \lambda_{10} |10\rangle\langle10|
$$

i.e. $|11\rangle$ has eigenvalue $\lambda_{11} = 0$. Let

$$
\rho_1 = \rho_{\psi_+} = \frac{1}{2}\Big[|01\rangle\langle01| + |01\rangle\langle10| + |10\rangle\langle01| + |10\rangle\langle10|\Big]
$$

and $\rho_\epsilon = (1 - \epsilon)\rho + \epsilon\rho_1$. The matrix of $\rho$ being with real entries, its partial transpose with respect to the first system is $\rho$. The partial transpose of $\rho_1$ is

$$
(T \otimes I)(\rho_1) = \frac{1}{2}\big[|01\rangle\langle01| + |11\rangle\langle00| + |00\rangle\langle11| + |10\rangle\langle10|\big]. \tag{2}
$$

---

[2] Although Peres Criteria is well known, we provide it here, for completeness of the manuscript, in appendix A.

If follows that

$$\langle 11| (T \otimes I)(\rho_\epsilon) |11\rangle = 0, \qquad \langle 11| (T \otimes I)(\rho_\epsilon) |00\rangle = \frac{\epsilon}{2};$$

by lemma 3, $(T \otimes I)(\rho_\epsilon)$ is not positive semi definite if $\epsilon > 0$ and by the Peres criterion it follows that the state $\rho_\epsilon$ is then not separable; since $\delta(\rho, \rho_\epsilon) \leq \epsilon$, there are states arbitrarily close to $\rho$ that are not separable. $\qquad \square$

Notice that all that is needed is that $\lambda_{11} = 0$. Nothing prevents $\lambda_{10} = \lambda_{10} = 0$. That implies, after a suitable choice of basis for the two systems, that any product state has arbitrarily close entangled states; being two qubit states, they are also distillable [4], showing that there are arbitrarily close distillable states. By symmetry, the result clearly holds if any of the other eigenvalues is known to be 0 instead of $\lambda_{11}$.

## 3.5    A Generalization to Non-Trivial Bases

Example 5 generalizes the earlier examples to a non-trivial product basis, a basis that has no classical analog.

**Proposition 5.** *Let*

$$\rho = \lambda_{00} |00\rangle\langle 00| + \lambda_{01} |01\rangle\langle 01| + \lambda_{1+} |1+\rangle\langle 1+| + \lambda_{1-} |1-\rangle\langle 1-|$$

*If any of the eigenvalues is* 0, *then there are states arbitrarily close to $\rho$ that are entangled.*

*Proof.* This time we first prove if $\lambda_{00} = 0$ i.e. if

$$\rho = \lambda_{01} |01\rangle\langle 01| + \lambda_{1+} |1+\rangle\langle 1+| + \lambda_{1-} |1-\rangle\langle 1-|$$

Let again $\rho_1 = \frac{1}{2}\big[|01\rangle\langle 01| + |01\rangle\langle 10| + |10\rangle\langle 01| + |10\rangle\langle 10|\big]$ and $\rho_\epsilon = (1-\epsilon)\rho + \epsilon\rho_1$. Then $\langle 00|(T \otimes I)(\rho_\epsilon)|00\rangle = 0$ and $\langle 00|(T \otimes I)(\rho_\epsilon)|11\rangle = \epsilon/2$ so that $\rho_\epsilon$ is not positive semi-definite by Lemma 3 and $\rho_\epsilon$ is thus entangled by the Peres criterion. Had we written explicitly the matrix, we would have seen the following pattern

$$(T \otimes I)(\rho_\epsilon) \quad = \quad \begin{matrix} & \begin{matrix} 00 & \ 01 & \ 10 & \ 11 \end{matrix} \\ \begin{matrix} 00 \\ 01 \\ 10 \\ 11 \end{matrix} & \begin{pmatrix} 0 & & & \epsilon/2 \\ & & & \\ & & & \\ \epsilon/2 & & & \end{pmatrix} \end{matrix}$$

with a 0 entry on the main diagonal for which the line is not identically 0 and concluded that $(T \otimes I)(\rho_\epsilon)$ is not positive semi definite if $\epsilon \neq 0$.

In this proof, it was assumed that $\lambda_{00} = 0$ but the same result holds if the eigenvalue of any other basis element is 0; for instance, if the eigenvalue of $|1-\rangle$ is 0, then applying $X \otimes XH$ maps the basis onto itself and $|1-\rangle$ onto $|00\rangle$; for $|1+\rangle$ we need to apply $X \otimes H$, and for $|01\rangle$ we apply $I \otimes X$.

# 4   Two Qudits (Quantum Digits)

We now consider bipartite systems, with each part of dimension at least two. We shall restrict our attention to states with real matrices though a similar result holds without such a restriction. It still holds that separable void states with a separable 0 eigenvector are boundary separable states and have arbitrarily close distillable (entangled) states.

**Proposition 6.** *Let $\rho$ be a state of a bipartite system $\mathscr{H}_A \otimes \mathscr{H}_B$ that has a product state $|\varphi_1\psi_1\rangle$ as eigenstate with 0 eigenvalue; let us assume that $\rho$ is represented by a real matrix; let us also assume that the state $|\varphi_1\rangle$ has real coefficients. Then $\rho$ is a boundary separable state; moreover there are entangled states arbitrarily close to $\rho$ that are distillable.*

*Proof.* Let us simply denote $|1\rangle_A$ and $|1\rangle_B$ each of the state $|\varphi_1\rangle$ and $|\psi_1\rangle$ and even drop the indices $A$ and $B$ when there is no ambiguity. Each of the two Hilbert spaces $\mathscr{H}_A$ and $\mathscr{H}_B$ is assumed to be of dimension at least 2; there is thus in each space a state orthogonal to their respective state $|1\rangle$ that we may denote $|0\rangle$. In the general case, $T_A(|1\rangle\langle 0|) = |\bar{0}\rangle\langle\bar{1}|$ (the transpose in the $A$ system), where the bar means the complex conjugation (the transpose is the complex conjugate of the dagger). However, it was assumed that $|\bar{1}\rangle_A = |1\rangle_A$. Given a vector $|1\rangle_A$ with real coefficients we can always find $|0\rangle_A$ orthogonal to it with real coefficients, so that $T_A(|0\rangle\langle 1|) = |1\rangle\langle 0|$ and $T_A(|1\rangle\langle 0|) = |0\rangle\langle 1|$. We choose such a state $|0\rangle_A$ of $\mathscr{H}_A$. Let $|0\rangle_B$ be any state of $\mathscr{H}_B$ orthogonal to $|1\rangle_B$. Let now

$$\rho_1 = \frac{1}{2}\big[|01\rangle\langle 01| + |01\rangle\langle 10| + |10\rangle\langle 01| + |01\rangle\langle 01|\big].$$

and let $\rho_\epsilon = (1-\epsilon)\rho + \epsilon\rho_1$. Since the matrix of $\rho$ is assumed to be real, its partial transpose is $\rho$ itself: $(T_A \otimes I_B)(\rho) = \rho$. From the way $\rho_1$ was chosen, its partial transpose is the operator

$$(T_A \otimes I_B)(\rho_1) = \frac{1}{2}\big[|01\rangle\langle 01| + |00\rangle\langle 11| + |11\rangle\langle 00| + |10\rangle\langle 10|\big]$$

and it is again clear that in this more general case

$$\langle 11|\,(T_A \otimes I_B)(\rho_\epsilon)\,|11\rangle = 0, \qquad \langle 11|\,(T_A \otimes I_B)(\rho_\epsilon)\,|00\rangle = \frac{\epsilon}{2}$$

and thus $\rho_\epsilon$ is entangled because its partial transpose is not positive semi definite. We now prove that the entanglement of $\rho_\epsilon$ is distillable. For two qubits this is shown directly in [4], where it is proven that any two qubit entanglement is distillable. In the general case, then $P_A = |0\rangle\langle 0| + |1\rangle\langle 1|$ (with indices $A$ understood) be the projection $\mathscr{H}_A$ on $\mathrm{Span}(|0\rangle_A, |1\rangle_A)$, and $P_B = |0\rangle\langle 0| + |1\rangle\langle 1|$ (with indices $B$ understood) be the projection of $\mathscr{H}_B$ on $\mathrm{Span}(|0\rangle_B, |1\rangle_B)$. Then, with $n = 1$, the (non normalized) state $\rho'_\epsilon = (P_A \otimes P_B)\rho_\epsilon^{\otimes n}(P_A \otimes P_B)$ is clearly such that its partial transpose is not positive semi definite, giving an entangled normalized state $\hat{\rho}'_\epsilon$ of $\mathrm{Span}(|0\rangle_A, |1\rangle_A) \otimes \mathrm{Span}(|0\rangle_B, |1\rangle_B) \simeq \mathscr{H}_2 \otimes \mathscr{H}_2$. By a result of Horodecki [5] [cf appendix B], since $\hat{\rho}'_\epsilon$ is entangled, $\rho_\epsilon$ is distillable.  $\square$

The conditions that the states have real coefficients can in fact be removed and the conclusions of the proposition still hold. The proof is however more tricky since it is then no longer true that the state that $(T_A \otimes I_B)(\rho)$ is equal to $\rho$ and the construction of $\rho_1$ needs to take into account complex conjugations. In any case, all our examples are with real matrices and the more general result will not be needed.

# 5    States of Larger Dimensions

## 5.1    Extrapolated Pseudo-Pure States of $N$ Qubits

Let us consider again states of the form

$$\rho_t = (1 - t)\frac{I}{2^N} + t|11\ldots 1\rangle\langle 11\ldots 1|$$

where I is the identity matrix, but this time of size $2^N \times 2^N$, and $t < 0$. With $(1 - t_b) + 2^N t_b = 0$ i.e. $t_b = -\frac{1}{2^N - 1}$, $\rho_b = \rho_{t_b}$ becomes a 1-void state, with $|11\ldots 1\rangle$ as 0-eigenvector. The states $\rho_t$ for $t_b \leq t \leq 0$ are all clearly separable; their matrix is diagonal in the standard basis, with non negative eigenvalues. Only the eigenvalue of $|11\ldots 1\rangle$ decreases.

$\rho_b$ **Is a Boundary Separable State.** We choose arbitrarily the first bit and show that there are $\epsilon$ close entangled states for which the first qubit is entangled with the others. Let $|1\rangle = |1^{N-1}\rangle$, i.e. $N - 1$ bits equal to one. The eigenstate of $\rho_b$ with 0 eigenvalue is $|1^N\rangle = |1\rangle|1\rangle$. That state has real entries when expressed in the standard basis. So does the state $\rho$. Proposition 6 thus applies.

**Trace Distance Between $\epsilon$-Entangled States and the Completely Mixed State.** The trace distance between $\rho_b$ and $I/2^N$ is

$$\frac{1}{2}\,\mathrm{tr}\left|(1 - t_b)\frac{I}{2^N} + t_b|1^N\rangle\langle 1^N| - \frac{I}{2^N}\right| = \frac{|t_b|}{2}\,\mathrm{tr}\left|\frac{I}{2^N} - |1^N\rangle\langle 1^N|\right|$$

The trace of $\left|I/2^N - |1^N\rangle\langle 1^N|\right|$ is $(2^N - 1) \times 1/2^N + 1 - 1/2^N = 2 - 2/2^N$. The trace distance is thus

$$\delta(\frac{I}{2^N}, \rho_b) = \frac{1}{2^N - 1}\left(1 - \frac{1}{2^N}\right) = \frac{1}{2^N}$$

Conclusion: for any $\epsilon > 0$ there are entangled states at distance at most $2^{-N} + \epsilon$ of the completely mixed state. Indeed, by the triangle inequality,

$$\delta(\frac{I}{2^N}, \rho_\epsilon) \leq \delta(\frac{I}{2^N}, \rho_b) + \delta(\rho_b, \rho_\epsilon) \leq 2^{-N} + \epsilon$$

## 5.2  The $N$ Qubit Thermal State

The thermal state of one qubit is

$$\rho_\Theta = \begin{bmatrix} \frac{1+\eta}{2} & 0 \\ 0 & \frac{1-\eta}{2} \end{bmatrix} = \frac{1+\eta}{2} \, |0\rangle\langle 0| + \frac{1-\eta}{2} \, |1\rangle\langle 1|$$

The thermal state of $N$ independent qubits (with the same $\eta$) is

$$\rho_\Theta^N = \rho_\Theta^{\otimes N} = \sum_{i \in \{0,1\}^N} \left(\frac{1+\eta}{2}\right)^{N-|i|} \left(\frac{1-\eta}{2}\right)^{|i|} |i\rangle\langle i|. \tag{3}$$

where $|i|$ is the Hamming weight of the string $i$, i.e. the number of bits equal to 1 in $i$, each 1 giving a minus sign, and each 0 a plus sign. The thermal state is not only separable but it has an eigenbasis consisting of product states The smallest eigenvalue is given by the eigenvector $|i\rangle = |1^N\rangle$, i.e. all qubits are 1 and it is

$$\lambda_{|1^N\rangle} = \left(\frac{1-\eta}{2}\right)^N$$

which is exponentially small with $N$.

**Extrapolated States Close to the Thermal State.** Let us consider the extrapolated states

$$\varrho_t = (1-t)\rho_\Theta^N + t|1^N\rangle\langle 1^N|$$

for $t < 0$ ($t = -p$ for some positive real number $p$). They are all separable and when the eigenvalue of $|1^N\rangle\langle 1^N|$ becomes 0, $\varrho_t$ is a void state. That happens when $(1-t)\big[(1-\eta)/2\big]^N + t = 0$ i.e

$$t_b = -\frac{\lambda_{|1^N\rangle}}{1 - \lambda_{|1^N\rangle}} = -\lambda_{|1^N\rangle} - \lambda_{|1^N\rangle}^2 - \cdots$$

a very small value, equal to $-\lambda_{|1^N\rangle} = -((1-\eta)/2)^N$ if we neglect terms of higher order. The trace distance between $\varrho_b$ and $\rho_\Theta^N$ is

$$\delta(\varrho_b, \rho_\Theta^N) = \frac{1}{2} \operatorname{tr} \left| (1-t_b)\rho_\Theta^N + t_b|1^N\rangle\langle 1^N| - \rho_\Theta^N \right| = \frac{|t_b|}{2} \operatorname{tr} \left| \rho_\Theta^N - |1^N\rangle\langle 1^N| \right|$$

The eigenvectors of $\rho_\Theta^N - |1^N\rangle\langle 1^N|$ are those of $\rho_\Theta^N$ and the eigenvalues are left unchanged except for the eigenvector $|1^N\rangle$ whose eigenvalue of $\lambda_{|1^N\rangle}$ is decreased by 1 which implies that the sum of the absolute values of the eigenvalues is increased by $1 - \lambda_{|1^N\rangle}$ and

$$\delta(\rho_\Theta^N, \varrho_b) = \frac{|t_b|}{2} \left(2 - \lambda_{|1^N\rangle}\right) = \frac{1}{2} \frac{\lambda_{|1^N\rangle}}{1 - \lambda_{|1^N\rangle}} \left(2 - \lambda_{|1^N\rangle}\right) = \frac{1}{2}\left(\lambda_{|1^N\rangle} + \frac{\lambda_{|1^N\rangle}}{1 - \lambda_{|1^N\rangle}}\right)$$

$$= \lambda_{|1^N\rangle} + \frac{1}{2}\lambda_{|1^N\rangle}^2 + \frac{1}{2}\lambda_{|1^N\rangle}^3 \cdots$$

which is $\lambda_{|1^N\rangle}$ if we neglect terms of higher order. That distance is exponentially small with $N$.

$\varrho_b$ **Is a Boundary Separable State.** We now show that there are entangled states arbitrarily close to $\varrho_b$. We choose again arbitrarily the first bit and show that there are $\epsilon$ close entangled states for which the first qubit is entangled with the others. Let $|\mathbf{1}\rangle = |1^{N-1}\rangle$, i.e. $N-1$ bits equal to one, and let $|v\rangle$ be any $N-1$ bit string with at least one bit equal to zero. The eigenstate of $\varrho_b$ with 0 eigenvalue is $|1^N\rangle = |1\rangle|\mathbf{1}\rangle$. That state has real entries when expressed in the standard basis. So does the state $\varrho_b$. Proposition 6 thus applies again.

**Entangled States Close to the Thermal State.** We have just proven that or any $\epsilon > 0$, there are entangled states $\varrho_\epsilon$ such that $\delta(\varrho_b, \varrho_\epsilon) \leq \epsilon$. By the triangle inequality (since the trace distance is a distance in the sense of metric spaces), the distance between those states $\varrho_\epsilon$ and $\rho_\Theta^N$ is such that

$$\delta(\rho_\Theta^N, \varrho_\epsilon) \leq \delta(\rho_\Theta^N, \varrho_b) + \delta(\varrho_b, \varrho_\epsilon) \leq \delta(\rho_\Theta^N, \varrho_b) + \epsilon$$

which implies that for any $\epsilon > 0$ there are entangled states in a ball of trace-distance radius

$$\epsilon + \left(\frac{1-\eta}{2}\right)^N + \frac{1}{2}\left(\frac{1-\eta}{2}\right)^{2N} + \frac{1}{2}\left(\frac{1-\eta}{2}\right)^{3N} \cdots$$

around the thermal state $\rho_\Theta^N$ of $N$ qubits where $\left(\dfrac{1-\eta}{2}\right)^N = \lambda_{|1^N\rangle}$ is exponentially small in $N$.

# Appendix

## A    The Peres Separability Criterion

An $n$ partite state represented by a density operator on $\mathcal{H}_1 \otimes \cdots \otimes \mathcal{H}_n$ is said to be *separable* if it can be produced as follows: each party $i$ prepares locally $\rho_i^k$ with with probability $p_k$. More precisely a state $\rho$ of $\mathcal{H}_1 \otimes \cdots \otimes \mathcal{H}_n$ is separable if there exist states $\rho_i^k$ of $\mathcal{H}_i$ for $1 \leq i \leq n$ and probabilities $p_k$ ($p_k \geq 0$, $\sum_k p_k = 1$) such that

$$\rho = \sum_k p_k \, \rho_1^k \otimes \cdots \otimes \rho_n^k$$

For any state $\rho_1^k$, its transpose $\mathrm{T}(\rho_1^k)$, which is the complex conjugate of its dagger, is simply $\overline{\rho}_1^k$, its complex conjugate. If party 1 systematically sends $\overline{\rho}_1^k$ instead of $\rho_i^k$, the resulting state

$$\rho' = \sum_k p_k \, \overline{\rho}_1^k \otimes \cdots \otimes \rho_n^k$$

is also a (separable) state and is, in particular, positive semi-definite. Such a partial transposition can be applied to any number of subsystems. This leads to the Peres criterion [7] that states that a state is *entangled* i.e. is not separable if it admits a partial transpose that is not positive semi-definite.

Note that the opposite is not true: If a state admits a positive partial transpose it may be seperable, but it does not have to be entangled. Furthermore, if a state $\rho_{ppt-ent}$ is entangled and admits a positive partial transpose then it is not distillable (namely, one canot distill a singlet state out of many copies of $\rho_{ppt-ent}$ via local operations and classical communication). Such states are said to have "bound entanglement".

The partial transpose is easy to calculate when states are written in the braket notation. On a bipartite system, the density matrix can always be written as $\rho = \sum_{ij} |i\rangle\langle j| \otimes \rho_{ij}$ where $\rho_{ij}$ are non normalized and $|i\rangle$ is the standard basisr. The partial transpose $(T\otimes I)(\rho)$ of $\rho$ is $\sum_{ij} |j\rangle\langle i|\otimes\rho_{ij}$. If other states than the standard basis are used then if $\rho = \sum_{ij} |\varphi_i\rangle\langle\varphi_j| \otimes \rho_{ij}$, $(T \otimes I)(\rho) = \sum_{ij} |\overline{\varphi}_j\rangle\langle\overline{\varphi}_i| \otimes \rho_{ij}$: indeed $T(|\varphi_i\rangle\langle\varphi_j|)$, which is the complex conjugate of the dagger of $|\varphi_i\rangle\langle\varphi_j|$, is $|\overline{\varphi}_j\rangle\langle\overline{\varphi}_i|$ where $|\overline{\varphi}\rangle = \sum_i \overline{\alpha}_i|i\rangle$ if $|\varphi\rangle = \sum_i \alpha_i|i\rangle$.

To decide on the positivity of the partial transpose, we shall need the fact that the partial transpose of a hermitian operator is always hermitian. That follows from elementary calculation: if $A = \sum_{ij} |i\rangle\langle j|\otimes A_{ij}$, then $A^\dagger = \sum_{ij} |j\rangle\langle i|\otimes A_{ij}^\dagger = \sum_{ij} |i\rangle\langle j| \otimes A_{ji}^\dagger$ and $A$ is hermitian if and only if $A_{ij}^\dagger = A_{ji}$. It then follows that

$$(T \otimes I)(A)^\dagger = \left(\sum_{ij} |j\rangle\langle i| \otimes A_{ij}\right)^\dagger = \sum_{ij} |i\rangle\langle j| \otimes A_{ij}^\dagger = (T \otimes I)(A).$$

# B    Horodecki's Distillability Criterion

**Theorem 7.** *An arbitrary state $\rho$ of $\mathscr{H}_A \otimes \mathscr{H}_B$ is distillable if and only if there exists $n$ and projectors $P_A : \mathscr{H}_A^{\otimes n} \to \mathscr{H}_2$ and $P_B : \mathscr{H}_B^n \to \mathscr{H}_2$ (where $\mathscr{H}_2$ denotes a Hilbert space of dimension 2) such that if $\hat{\rho}'$ is the state obtained by normalizing the operator*

$$\rho' = (P_A \otimes P_B)\rho^{\otimes n}(P_A \otimes P_B)$$

*of the system $\mathscr{H}_2 \otimes \mathscr{H}_2$, then $\hat{\rho}'$ is entangled.*

Notice that it was proven in [3] that a state $\hat{\rho}'$ of $\mathscr{H}_2 \otimes \mathscr{H}_2$ is entangled if and only if it has a partial transpose that is not positive semi definite (the Peres criterion is then a characterization of entanglement as well as of distillability for bipartite states of two qubits).

# C    Proof of Lemma 3

*Proof.* Let us assume $A$ is positive semidefinite: $A = \sum_i \lambda_i|\varphi_i\rangle\langle\varphi_i|$ with $\lambda_i \geq 0$. If $\langle\varphi|A|\varphi\rangle = 0$, then $\sum_i \lambda_i|\langle\varphi|\varphi_i\rangle|^2 = 0$ and $\lambda_i\langle\varphi|\varphi_i\rangle = 0$ for all $i$ and thus $\langle\varphi|A|\psi\rangle = \sum_i \lambda_i\langle\varphi|\varphi_i\rangle\langle\varphi_i|\psi\rangle = 0$ for all $|\psi\rangle$.

# References

1. Bennett, C.H., DiVincenzo, D.P., Mor, T., Shor, P.W., Smolin, J.A., Terhal, B.M.: Unextendible Product Bases and Bound Entanglement. Phys. Rev. Lett. 82, 5385–5388 (1999), http://link.aps.org/doi/10.1103/PhysRevLett.82.5385
2. Dur, W., Vidal, G., Cirac, J.I.: Three Qubits Can Be Entangled in Two Inequivalent Ways. Phys. Rev. A 62, 062314 (2000), http://link.aps.org/doi/10.1103/PhysRevA.62.062314
3. Horodecki, M., Horodecki, P., Horodecki, R.: Separability of Mixed States: Necessary and Sucient Conditions. Physics Letters A 223(12), 1–8 (1996), http://www.sciencedirect.com/science/article/pii/S0375960196007062
4. Horodecki, M., Horodecki, P., Horodecki, R.: Inseparable Two Spin- 1 2 Density Matrices Can Be Distilled to a Singlet Form. Phys. Rev. Lett. 78, 574–577 (1997), http://link.aps.org/doi/10.1103/PhysRevLett.78.574
5. Horodecki, M., Horodecki, P., Horodecki, R.: Mixed-State Entanglement and Distillation: Is There a Entanglement in Nature? Phys. Rev. Lett. 80, 5239–5242 (1998), http://link.aps.org/doi/10.1103/PhysRevLett.80.5239
6. Horodecki, P.: Separability Criterion and Inseparable Mixed States with Positive Partial Transposition. Physics Letters A 232(5), 333–339 (1997), http://www.sciencedirect.com/science/article/pii/S0375960197004167
7. Peres, A.: Separability Criterion for Density Matrices. Phys. Rev. Lett. 77(8), 1413–1415 (1996), http://link.aps.org/doi/10.1103/PhysRevLett.77.1413
8. Werner, R.F.: Quantum States with Einstein-Podolsky-Rosen Correlations Admitting a Hidden-Variable Model. Phys. Rev. A 40, 4277–4281 (1989), http://link.aps.org/doi/10.1103/PhysRevA.40.4277

# Design of a Minimal System for Self-replication of Rectangular Patterns of DNA Tiles

Vinay K. Gautam[1], Eugen Czeizler[2], Pauline C. Haddow[1], and Martin Kuiper[3]

[1] CRAB lab, Department of Computer and Information Science
The Norwegian University of Science and Technology
Trondheim, Norway
[2] Department of Information and Computer Science
School of Science
Aalto University P.O. Box 15400, FI-00076 Aalto, Finland
[3] Department of Biology
The Norwegian University of Science and Technology
Trondheim, Norway
{vkgautam,pauline}@idi.ntnu.no
eugen.czeizler@aalto.fi, martin.kuiper@ntnu.no

**Abstract.** Complex nanostructures assembled from DNA tiles cannot be manufactured in large volumes without extensive wet-lab efforts. Self-replication of tile structures would offer a low-cost and efficient nanomanufacturing if it would be based on an automated dynamically controlled assembly and disassembly of tiles — an attribute that is lacking in existing tile self-assembly framework. Here we propose self-replication of rectangular two-dimensional patterns based on the abstract Tile Assembly Model, by designing a system of tiles which replicate a target pattern by replicating its "L"-shaped seed. Self-replication starts by the formation of a mold structure from a "L"-shaped seed of a target pattern. The mold consists of switch-enabled tiles that can be dynamically triggered to dissociate the seed and the mold templates. The dissociated mold and seed structures each further catalyse assembly of new templates of seed and mold structures, respectively, forming the basis of a cross-catalytic exponential replication cycle.

**Keywords:** Nature-inspired materials, Minimal self-replication, DNA tile, Self-assembly, Switch-enabled tiles.

## 1 Introduction and Motivation

DNA tile self-assembly [19] is an emerging paradigm for molecular computation and nanomanufacturing. DNA tiles [21], the building blocks of tile self-assembly, can be designed to interact with strength and specificity for the assembly of logically and/or algorithmically directed periodic and aperiodic two-dimensional (2-D) intricate patterns. Erik Winfree has introduced the abstract Tile Assembly Model (aTAM) [14] for theoretical assessment of the tile assembly process. In the aTAM framework, the assembly starts from a single seed tile and grows

A.-H. Dediu et al. (Eds.): TPNC 2014, LNCS 8890, pp. 119–133, 2014.

in 2-D as more tiles adjoin one-by-one to the growing structure. Given any desired rectangular tile pattern, where the tiles can be seen as coloured (or functionalised) over a finite set of colours (or secondary structures), one can always design a finite, though exhaustive, approximate-minimal set of tiles so as to reliably and uniquely assemble the target pattern [2].

A minimal self-replicating chemical system [8] includes two elements: a template molecule and a few substrate molecules capable of self-assembling an exact replica of the template molecule. The assembled replica must be able to dissociate from the template so as to result in two templates: the former template and the newly created template. These templates need to then be able to catalyse a reiteration of the process by self-assembly of two new replicates on the two templates. Such a process theoretically results in an exponential amplification of the number of templates, and could be adopted to design a minimal self-replication system of patterns in the tile self-assembly framework. However, tile assembly was proposed as a purely passive process where tiles are incapable of self-triggering any post-assembly rearrangements. This prohibits the dynamic assembly and disassembly of tile structures, which is essential for the self-replication in the tile assembly framework.

In previous work on self-replication, Schulman and Winfree [15,16] demonstrated the self-replication in the tile self-assembly framework. The underlying principle is that an externally forced random fragmentation of a self-assembling lattice of tiles would create two new nucleation sites for regrowth of lattices. Such a lattice growth followed by fragmentation would eventually result into an amplified number of copies of the sequences. One approach for a post-assembly dissociation of a tile is the use of an enzyme that can selectively break apart fragments from an assembled tile structure. The self-replication of 2-D shapes using such an enzyme- and staged self-assembly model was first demonstrated by Abel et al. [1]. Although this is a shape-independent replication mechanism applicable to both a precise and an infinite yield, usage of enzymes could pose practical limitations.

Another paradigm of active tile self-assembly, without the use of enzymes, is emerging by the joining of tile assembly methodology with associated control of dynamic strand displacement circuitry [13,22,4]. In this framework, tiles can not only assemble in complex patterns through cooperative binding, but tile substructures can also be triggered to disassemble and reassemble. Exponential self-replication of 2-D rectangular patterns of origami tiles [9] using such a framework, namely the Signal Tile Assembly Model (STAM) [13,12], was demonstrated by Keenan et al. [7]. The STAM is derived from the aTAM [14] where tiles are modified to enable signalling and glue activation. A signal propagates through the tile lattice by sending controlled signals to activate and deactivate binding between two connected or remotely placed tiles. A signal-controlled dissociation of tile assemblies provides the basis for separating template from the replicated molecule. Although the technique provides an innovative approach for enzyme-free self-replication of both 2-D and 3-D structures, design and implementation of such tiles and their self-assembly would pose significant practical challenges [9,13].

We have drawn motivation from these pattern self-replicators to propose a design of a minimal system of self-replication for 2-D rectangular patterns within the framework of the aTAM [14]. The design adheres to simplicity and implementation feasibility in four aspects: 1) double crossover (DX) tiles are used; 2) all glues are of strength 1; 3) tiles do not carry signals; 4) the replication process is enzyme free. Pattern replication starts with formation of a mold structure around the "L"-shaped seed with the help of a set of SWitch-Enabled Tiles (SWET) that can be activated to switch their binding state from bound (ON) to free (OFF). Further, the assembled mold gets dissociated from the seed structure by a toehold-mediated switching control, which is cyclically triggered at precise time intervals. The dissociated mold structure grows a new copy of the "L"-shaped seed while the dissociated seed structure reiterates the process. The remaining pattern is grown on these self-replicating seed structures by supplying the system with an appropriate set of pattern forming tiles. The terms seed ("L"-shaped seed) and pattern have been interchangeably used in the rest of the article.

## 2    A Model of Switch-Enabled Tile Assembly

The abstract Tile Assembly Model (*aTAM*) [14], introduced by Winfree, provides a framework where a 2-D target pattern can be self-assembled with the help of a finite set of tiles. In the aTAM, a tile is represented as a unit square with its four edges, North (N), East (E), South (S) and West (W), labelled from $\Sigma$, where $\Sigma$ is a finite set of 'glues', including the special empty glue "0". Therefore, a Tile $t$ can be represented by the quadruple $\{\sigma_N(t), \sigma_E(t), \sigma_S(t), \sigma_W(t)\}$. A zero value of the glue denotes the absence of a sticky-end i.e., zero binding strength. We assume that our tile system is deterministic, and works under the $temperature - 2$ assumption. Moreover, all the glues/sticky-ends used herein are assumed to be of *strength 1*.

**Physical Basis of Switch-Enabled Tile Assembly.** The concept of glue activation/deactivation has earlier been demonstrated by [10,4], by introducing innovative mechanisms of protection and deprotection of tile sticky-ends. Signal passing and glue activation/deactivation was explored in STAM [13]. In the STAM framework, control signals pass through the tiles in order to activate or deactivate the glues of remotely lying tiles. Such a signal traversal involves several concomitant strand displacement steps. Further, in the STAM framework, tiles carry the control signals, and the activation/deactivation of a remotely lying tile would therefore depend on the success of a set of consecutive activation/deactivation events between tiles lying in the signal propagation path.

In order to design a tile assembly system with attributes of active assembly where tiles can activate/deactivate their glues through a localised strand displacement reaction, we introduce the concept of SWitch-Enabled Tile(SWET) shown in Figure 1(a). A (DX-)tile can be converted to a SWET by extending its sticky-end (S) with a short length switching toehold (SW) that serves as a local switch between two tiles, where switching is controlled by a global signal cyclically generated by an especially designed chemical oscillator system described in Section 4. The switching toehold is used to mediate the binding-breaking (ON-OFF) process in-between a SWET and a DX-tile, see Figure 1(b). In the 'ON' state, a SWET is able to bind a tile using as sticky end the domain $(ij)$, where sections $i$, $j$, $t_s$ are arbitrarily chosen to be 3, 7 and 3 nucleotides long, respectively, and complementary sections are marked by (*). A periodically available DNA strand $(j^*, t_s^*, sgc_1)$ changes the binding state from 'ON' to 'OFF', where the two tiles would eventually break apart.

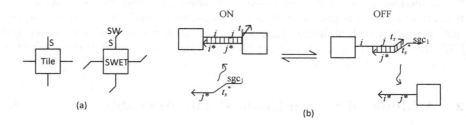

**Fig. 1.** (a) A normal tile and a SWET tile, (b) Toehold-mediated ON-OFF switching between a simple tile and a SWET tile

The toehold-mediated switching of the SWET, from ON to OFF and vice versa is essential for accomplishing dynamic assembly-disassembly of the tile structures. Such a control can be achieved by a cyclic and abrupt increase in the supply of the inhibitor signal i.e., the DNA strand $(j^*, t_s^*, sgc_1)$ in Figure 1(b). This dynamic process can be implemented using an Oregonator autocatalytic reaction-system [3], which in turn can be implemented using DNA molecules as reported in [18]. Moreover, the methodology from [18], based itself on the strand displacement technique, allows for various adjustments of the autocatalytic system parameters, including the length and the amplitude of the cyclic signal, as well as the steepness of its descent. In Section 4 we introduce an ODE-based numeric simulation for the dynamics of one such paired SWET and inhibitor signal showing that indeed the de-activation of the SWET is both cyclic and abrupt as shown in Figure 4.

## 3   Proposed Self-replication System

In this section we define a minimal self-replicating system for rectangular patterns of tiles as shown in Figure 2. Let $P$ be the pattern to be replicated, and structure $S$ as its "L"-shaped South-West border, named in the following as *seed*. Although the seed is usually assumed to be a single tile in various other tile assembly frameworks, herein we consider an "L"-shaped structure as seed. This is due to the fact that the glues placed on the interior border of such an "L"-shaped structure uniquely identify the entire rectangular tile-pattern within, assuming the system is deterministic.

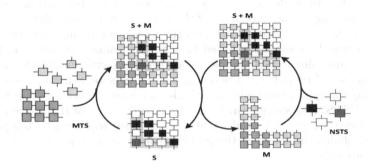

**Fig. 2.** Minimal self-replicating system of rectangular patterns

The replication process starts by supplying a pre-assembled rectangular pattern (P), which includes its seed structure (S), and a set of mold forming tiles (MTS). We require that the pattern contains a unique, red-coloured tile on its lower-left corner position, which is not used on any other position inside the pattern. Observe that the MTS consists of a pre-assembled corner supertile (CST) that is stable at temperature-2, and is designed to bind (using two strength-1 glues) on the special red-coloured tile. Thus, the CST initiates the mold formation, using as template the seed structure $S$. The mold assembly further proceeds as more tiles cooperatively join one by one until the entire South-West boundary of the seed structure is covered by a double layer of tiles, creating a seed-mold complex $(S+M)$. Tiles forming the inner layer of the mold are designed as SWET type with switch enabled glue on the side that binds with the seed (pattern). The assembled seed-mold complex undergoes a controlled dissociation, splitting into the seed $S$ and the mold $M$ structures. Observe that the dissociated mold structure have two layers of tiles ensuring its stability under temperature-2 assembly framework.

In the next replication cycle, the dissociated seed structure $(S)$ repeats the left hand side pathway, and thereby, creates two $(S+M)$ complexes, whereas the dissociated mold structure $(M)$ drives the right hand side pathway supplied by a pattern forming tile set (NSTS). Indeed, assuming we have at our disposal a tile set capable of assembling the pattern (we call this set the Nano-Structure Tile Set (NSTS)), we use the mold to first reassemble the seed S (using tiles from

NSTS) and then we reassemble the complete pattern P (using the same NSTS). Thus, by supplying the system with sufficient many copies of the tiles within the MTS and NSTS tile sets, and by continuing the process for $n$ complete cycles, the replicator could theoretically produce $2^{n-1}$ copies of both the mold and the pattern structures (which is first the seed structure and then the complete pattern). In a potential experimental implementation, one has to provide for an expected time for both the mold formation process (from a template pattern) and the seed formation process (using the mold as a seed). Then, one adjusts the signal inhibitor cycle, which triggers the seed-mold dissociation such as to be at least as long as the maximum of the two expected time values.

Although the above system deals with the replication of only one pattern (P), the method can be easily generalised to other rectangular patterns. Indeed, in Section 5 we are going to assume that we are provided with an arbitrary finite set of patterns, any of them being a potential template for replication. Then, we are going to design appropriate-minimal Mold- and Nano-Structure- Tile Sets, i.e., MTS and NSTS, respectively, such that by inserting any of the above patterns within the system, or even a subset of them, it/they will act as a template for replication. Thus, the result of the process will be an amplification of only the inserted pattern(s).

## 4   Cyclic ON-OFF Activation of SWET

The centrepiece of the self-replicator is an especially designed autonomous chemical oscillator that cyclically releases an inhibitor signal (DNA strand $(j^*, t_s^*, sgc_1)$ in Figure 1(b)) so as to switch a SWET from ON to OFF and back. Oscillator-controlled ON to OFF switching of the SWET(s) dissociates templates at the end of each cycle. However, as long as the mold remains bound to the pattern with only a few residual glues from SWETs that escape OFF switching it would reassemble instantly with the pattern upon subsequent ON switching. This would result in an overall lower efficient replication cycle, as it removes free templates from the replication process. It is therefore essential that the switching from ON to OFF occurs abruptly and completely, resulting in a comprehensive splitting of all mold-pattern complexes. Herein, an Oregonator autocatalytic reaction-system [3] is used to introduce the dynamics of a chemical oscillator.

Oregonator reactions, adopted from Soloveichik et al. [18], are shown by reactions (1-6) in Table 1. The mass-action based oscillatory dynamics can be implemented by a set of DNA-strand displacement reactions using the mapping proposed in Soloveichik et al. [18]. One of the key features of DNA-strand displacement reactions is their modularity i.e., by attaching multiple moieties to a single DNA strand, a hierarchical system of DNA strand-displacement reactions can be realised. In order to drive the ON-OFF switching of SWET(s), the inhibitor signal moiety ($j^*, t_s^*, sgc_1$, shown in Figure 1) would be attached with the DNA strand representing the $X2$ species in the Oregonator reaction system. The resulting reversible kinetics of the switching process is given by reaction (7) in Table 1. A bimolecular toehold exchange [23] and a unimolecular thermodynamic dissociation process represent the kinetics of the forward reaction ($k_{fw}$)

and the backward reaction ($k_{bw}$), respectively. We chose $k_{fw}$ to be $4000M^{-1}s^{-1}$ for a toehold exchange involving both the invader and the incumbent toeholds with lengths 3 nt, based on the toehold exchange model reported by Zhang and Winfree [23]. The value of $k_{bw} = 0.1s^{-1}$ for a 3 nt long duplex is derived by interpolating dsDNA dissociation kinetics data reported by Morrison and Stols [11].

**Table 1.** Reactions (1)-(6) form the Oregonator model; the reversible reaction (7) models the OFF/ON switching of the SWET(s)

| # | Reaction | Rate constant | Species | Initial Concentration |
|---|---|---|---|---|
| (1) | $X2 \rightarrow X1$ | $k_1 = 0.0871s^{-1}$ | $X1$ | $[X1]_0 = 8.8 \times 10^{-10}M$ |
| (2) | $X2 + X1 \rightarrow \phi$ | $k_2 = 1.6 \times 10^9 M^{-1}s^{-1}$ | $X2$ | $[X2]_0 = 3.4 \times 10^{-7}M$ |
| (3) | $X1 \rightarrow 2X1 + X3$ | $k_3 = 520s^{-1}$ | $X3$ | $[X3]_0 = 10^{-9}M$ |
| (4) | $2X1 \rightarrow \phi$ | $k_4 = 3000M^{-1}s^{-1}$ | | |
| (5) | $X3 \rightarrow X2$ | $k_5 = 443s^{-1}$ | | |
| (6) | $X3 \rightarrow \phi$ | $k_6 = 2.676s^{-1}$ | | |
| (7) | $X2 + SWoff \rightarrow SWoff$ | $k_{fw} = 4000M^{-1}s^{-1}$; $k_{bw} = 0.1s^{-1}$ | $SWon$ $SWoff$ | $[SWon]_0 = 9.8 \times 10^{-5}M$ $[SWoff]_0 = 1.8 \times 10^{-6}M$ |

A deterministic and ODE-based numerical simulation of the dynamics of the $X1$, $X2$, and $X3$ species, shown in Figure 3, has been performed with the CO-PASI software suite [6]. From the deterministic time course simulations performed by the COPASI simulator, as depicted by the oscillations of the molecule species shown in Figure 4, it is clear that the ON-state SWET and inhibitor transitions from low to high and vice versa, are abrupt. A more realistic simulation capturing the stochasticity of chemical kinetics would give even steeper transitions. The time span in which a spike of the inhibitor signal has significant levels should be larger than the time required to complete a strand displacement process (ON to OFF switching of a SWET). As the oscillator module drives the switching module of the SWET, and both modules are implemented by strand-displacement reactions, a rational design of these reactions must satisfy different timing constraints. In order to realise such a self-replicator system with maximum yield and reliability in a wet-lab implementation, two criteria must be met. First, the dynamics of SWET switching from ON to OFF should be faster than the inhibitor signal dynamics. Second, the SWET switching from ON to OFF should be driven strongly and efficiently in the presence of the inhibitor signal, ideally approaching completion.

In the simulation shown in Figure 4, ON to OFF switching is 95% complete with arbitrarily chosen parameters of reversible kinetics ($k_{fw} = 4000M^{-1}s^{-1}$ and $k_{bw} = 0.1s^{-1}$ for a three nucleotide long switching toehold) given by reaction(7) in Table 1. In this case, a mold with up to 20 SWET tiles would likely retain one tile that remains in the ON state (meaning a point of binding between mold and pattern) during the switching cycle, constituting a possible re-engagement point for mold and pattern. Although this would cause a reduction of the overall replication efficiency, the ON to OFF switching proportions

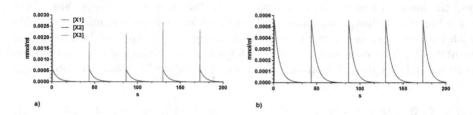

**Fig. 3.** The dynamics of the Oregonator model; the system parameters are those from Table 1 a) all three species X1, X2, and X3; the concentration of the $X1$ and $X3$ species is overlapping in most of the cases, though at different amplitudes; b) the oscillatory dynamics of the $X2$ species

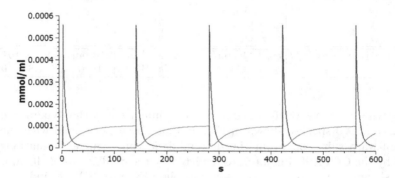

**Fig. 4.** Cyclic, abrupt, and virtually complete deactivation of a SWET tile using an inhibitor signal modulated by an Oregonator autocatalytic system. The blue line represents the dynamics of the inhibitor signal, while the purple one represents the concentration of the ON-state SWET. The total concentration (ON and OFF) of SWET is $10^{-4}M$.

can further be very significantly improved by increasing the switching toehold length [23] in the SWET. It therefore is reasonable to assume that a rationally designed DNA-strand displacement reaction network would be able to meet both the timing and efficiency demands of SWET-switching enabled template dissociation.

## 5    Tile Set Design and Implementation

In this section we present the design of tile sets and implementation details of the self-replication system for 2-D nanostructures. Let $\mathcal{P}$ be a finite set of rectangular patterns, each of them being a potential subject for replication. We can suppose without loss of generality that all the patterns have equal height, but variable lengths; otherwise we just complete the pattern using a special tile up to the desired height. We want to construct a finite collection of tiles, such that by inserting within this system one (or several) of the pattern-types in $\mathcal{P}$, these structures would act as a template and derive only the replication of the chosen pattern (or patterns).

In the following we suggest designs of two sets of tiles — the Nano-Structure Tile Set (*NSTS*) for the self-assembly of the pattern(s) to be replicated, see e.g. Figure 5, and the Mold Tile Set (*MTS*) consisting of SWET tiles for the template assembly of the mold along the boundary of the target nanostructure. All these tiles contain only temperature 1 glues, while the temperature of the entire system is 2. In other words, all tiles require a cooperative binding process from two input sides, in order to stably attach to an existing assembly (or seed/mold).

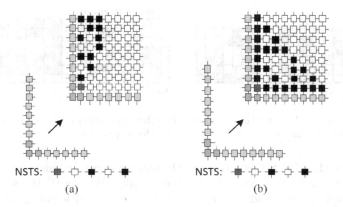

**Fig. 5.** Pattern assemblies starting from different "L"-shaped mold structures: (a) A three-bit binary counter pattern and a subset of the NSTS assembling it (b) the Sierpinski pattern, and a (possibly different) subset of NSTS assembling it. The two assemblies are initiated from (tile-content wise) different L-shaped mold structures.

## 5.1   Tile Set Design

**NSTS:** In order to derive an approximate-minimal tile set that can uniquely self-assemble the nanostructure pattern(s) to be replicated, we are going to employ known PATS search algorithms [5]. Recall that the Pattern self-Assembly Tile set Synthesis (PATS) problem asks to determine a set of coloured tiles such that starting from an "L"-shaped bordering seed structure, the tiles would self-assemble into a given rectangular coloured pattern. The task of finding such minimum-size tile sets is known to be NP-hard [2], even for the case when the coloured pattern is bounded to a predefined finite set of colours [17]. However, there exists an efficient search algorithm for finding approximate-minimal solutions for this problem [5].

Let $\mathcal{P} = \{P_1, P_2, ..., P_m\}$ be the finite set of patterns which might be subject to the replication process. We require (by possibly inserting a new line or column) that all of these patterns have on their lower left corner position a unique red-coloured tile which does not appear on any other positions inside the patterns. We now create a join pattern as shown in Figure 6, containing a bordered version of the above $m$ patterns. Namely, we introduce a new "grey" border-colour, and create lower- and left-bordered versions for each of the patterns, after which we horizontally concatenate all of them into a unique *Master Pattern, pattP*. By applying the PATS search algorithm on *pattP* and then removing all the "grey"-coloured tiles, we obtain the tiles of our NSTS tile set. Note that in the worst case scenario, this set of tiles consists at most as many elements as the disjoint union of all corresponding PATS solutions for each of the individual $P_i$ patterns.

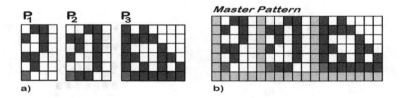

**Fig. 6.** (a) A set of three patterns subjected to the replication process; (b) The *master pattern* created by the concatenation of the bordered patterns

**MTS:** Once the NSTS tile set is established, we can construct the Mold Tile Set. This set can be split into the Bottom-Border (BottomB) tile set, forming the lower part of the mold, the Left-Border (LeftB) set, forming the left side, and the corner supertile (CST) serving as a seed for the mold assembly.

The CST seed can be seen as a merger of 8 tiles forming two layers of tiles around the corner — an inner layer of the mold seed (ILMS) having tiles that assemble with the seed of the pattern and an outer layer of the mold seed (OLMS) supporting the inner layer. The inner layer consists of ILMS-North (a SWET enabled with switching on its East glue), ILMS-middle, and ILMS-East (a SWET enabled with switching on its North glue), forming a corner-type structure; represented in green inside all of the above Figures. The outer layer consists of five tiles that are designed as to assemble with the tiles of the inner layer and form a stable structure at temperature-2. In both cases, we require that the East glue of the MS-North tile and the North glue of the MS-East tile agree with the corresponding West and South glues, respectively, of the special red-coloured tile from the NSTS tile set. Also, we define two new glues, $mb$ and $mt$, and require that the North glue of the ILMS-North tile is $mt$, while the East glue of the ILMS-East tile is $mb$.

Consider now the Bottom-NSTS (B-NSTS) and the Left-NSTS (L-NSTS) sets consisting of those tiles in NSTS that appear in the bottom line, respectively the left column, of any of the $P_i$ patterns; alternatively, we can choose these sets as the entire NSTS tile set. We define the Bottom-Glue (BG) and the Left-Glue (LG) sets as containing all South glues of tiles within B-NSTS, and all West glues of tiles within L-NSTS, respectively.

The BottomB tile set (within MTS) contains $|BG|$ tiles that form inner layer of the bottom border. For each glue $a \in BG$ we create a SWET with glue $a$ on the North side that is enabled with switching control, and glue $mbi$ on both its East and West sides. Similarly, the LeftB tile set (within MTS) contains $|LG|$ tiles that form the inner layer on the left border. For each glue $b \in LG$ we create a corresponding SWET with glue $b$ on the East side that is enabled with switching control, and glue $mti$ on its North and South sides. A fixed glue $mbf$ is designed for South sides of the tiles of the BottomB and LeftB tile sets, which provides a binding for the tiles forming outer layer of the mold.

## 5.2   Implementation of the Self-replication Process

We describe here the implementation of the self-replicator for an example case of a rectangular pattern of a 2-bit counter and its seed structure shown in Figure 7(a) and (b), respectively. It is assumed that a pre-assembled pattern or seed is available at the start of the self-replication process. Tile sets required for this replicator consist of NSTS and MTS as shown in Figure 7(c). The NSTS consists of pattern forming tiles (marked by a, b, c and d) and the MTS consists of MS seed, BottomB and LeftB tiles of type SWET. A cross-catalytic cycle of self-replication involving intermediate states *I to VII* is illustrated in Figure 7(d).

The self-replication process starts with mold formation where the CST (seed of mold structure) binds at the corner of the L-shaped seed of the pattern, as shown in state *I*. The mold structure grows further as more tiles from LebtB and BottomB tile sets join as shown in states *II*, such that in stage *III* the nanostructure-mold complex is completely assembled. Recall that the tiles within MTS are all equipped with switching toeholds on their North edges. At the end of stage *III*, these switches are turned off by sending the inhibitor signal $(j^*, t_s^*, sgc_1)$, as described in Figure 1. As a result the nanostructure-mold complex dissociates into the L-shaped seed and the mold, as shown in states *IV* and *V* respectively. The dissociated seed structure resumes the cycle involving the states $(I, II, III, IV)$, whereas the newly created mold serves as a seed for the assembly of a new copy of the L-shaped seed that could also grow the rest of the pattern in parallel, see states *V, VI, VII, III*. This process leads to the creation of a new copy of the seed-mold complex, and therefore another cycle starts. The above two parallel cycles, i.e., $(I, II, III, IV)$ and $(V, VI, VII, III)$, can produce a monotonically increasing number of copies of both the nanostructure and the mold (i.e., $2^{n-1}$ such copies after $n$ cycles), if supplied with an unlimited amount of tiles from the sets NSTS and MTS. The replication system can also be tweaked to attain a precise replication gain just by stopping the Oregonator oscillator activity. This would result into halting both of the replication cycles. Thus, by stopping the Oregonator cycle at an appropriate time-point, one could provide an exact replication gain (of the form $2^N$, for some integer value $N$).

Taking the assumption that the tile assembly is deterministic, it can be further assumed that both the mold (cycle involving states *I, II, III, IV*) and the seed (cycle *V, VI, VII, III*) assemble in some finite time, say $T_m$ and $T_s$ respectively. For a reliable self-replication, the ON-OFF cycles of the Oregonator oscillator

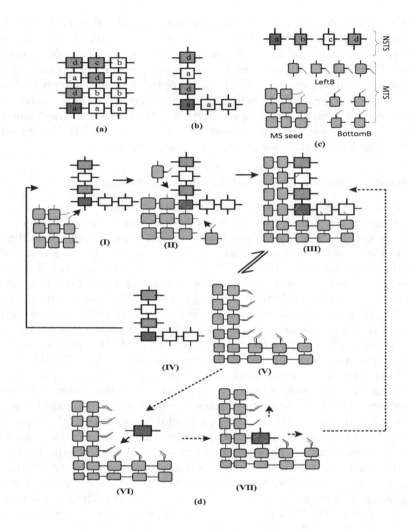

**Fig. 7.** Implementation of the replication process for a rectangular pattern of a 2-bit counter: (a) 2-bit binary counter pattern of tiles, (b) L-shaped seed structure of the pattern, (c) tile sets for replicator assembly and (d) cross-catalytic cycle of self-replication process

model described in Section 4 have to be synchronised with the times $T_m$ and $T_s$, for example, the ON period should be larger than the largest of the $T_m$, $T_s$. In order to test if the designed oscillator can be implemented for different time periods of oscillations so as to synchronise it with the above timing requirement, we performed a parameter scan only on the activation reaction, i.e., the backward rate constant $k_{bw}$ of reaction (7) in Table 1. We observed that the time of each

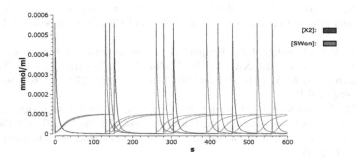

**Fig. 8.** A parameter scan for the rate constant $k_{bw}$ in Table 1 for the values $0.085, 0.1$, and $0.115s^{-1}$, respectively

cycle, in between two spikes of the inhibitor signal $X2$, becomes highly tunable, see e.g. Figure 8.

## 6 Conclusion and Future Work

To self-replicate 2-D rectangular patterns, we proposed a minimal self-replication system of DNA tiles under the aTAM framework. The replication mechanism is based on a cross-catalytic cycle, where an L-shaped seed of the desired pattern is replicated and the remaining pattern grows in parallel. The self-replicator is implemented with the help of DX-tiles and SWitching-enabled Tiles (SWET), which form the basis of an active tile assembly process where structures are dynamically assembled and disassembled with the help of an autonomous chemical oscillator that can be implemented using DNA strand displacement cascades. We also proposed a strategy for designing an approximate-minimal tile set in order to efficiently assemble a unique pattern (or a subset of patterns) out of a finite collection of possible patterns that might be subject to replication.

This work is a step forward in the direction of nanostructure self-replication, but assembly errors [20], which are common in the tile self-assembly process, pose an important potential problem that should be addressed in further work. A reliable self-replicator with error levels not exceeding a minimum threshold may further open up new directions for investigation of fundamental principles behind reproduction and selection-driven evolution.

## References

1. Abel, Z., Benbernou, N., Damian, M., Demaine, E.D., Demaine, M.L., Flatland, R.Y., Kominers, S.D., Schweller, R.T.: Shape replication through self-assembly and RNase enzymes. In: SODA, pp. 1045–1064. SIAM (2010)
2. Czeizler, E., Popa, A.: Synthesizing minimal tile sets for complex patterns in the framework of patterned DNA self-assembly. Theor. Comput. Sci. 499, 23–37 (2013)

3. Field, R.J., Niyes, R.M.: Oscillations in chemical systems iv. limit cycle behavior in a model of a real chemical reaction. Journal of Chemical Physics 60, 1877–1884 (1974)

4. Gautam, V.K., Haddow, P.C., Kuiper, M.: Reliable self-assembly by self-triggered activation of enveloped DNA tiles. In: Dediu, A.-H., Martín-Vide, C., Truthe, B., Vega-Rodríguez, M.A. (eds.) TPNC 2013. LNCS, vol. 8273, pp. 68–79. Springer, Heidelberg (2013)

5. Göös, M., Lempiäinen, T., Czeizler, E., Orponen, P.: Search methods for tile sets in patterned DNA self-assembly. J. Comput. Syst. Sci. 80(1), 297–319 (2014)

6. Hoops, S., et al.: COPASI - a complex pathway simulator. Bioinformatics 22(24), 3067–3074 (2006)

7. Keenan, A., Schweller, R., Zhong, X.: Exponential replication of patterns in the signal tile assembly model. In: Soloveichik, D., Yurke, B. (eds.) DNA 2013. LNCS, vol. 8141, pp. 118–132. Springer, Heidelberg (2013)

8. von Kiedrowski, G.: A self-replicating hexadeoxynucleotide. Angewandte Chemie International Edition in English 25(10), 932–935 (1986)

9. Liu, W., Zhong, H., Wang, R., Seeman, N.C.: Crystalline two-dimensional DNA-origami arrays. Angewandte Chemie International Edition 50(7082), 264–267 (2011)

10. Majumder, U., LaBean, T.H., Reif, J.H.: Activatable tiles: Compact, robust programmable assembly and other applications. In: Garzon, M.H., Yan, H. (eds.) DNA 2007. LNCS, vol. 4848, pp. 15–25. Springer, Heidelberg (2008)

11. Morrison, L.E., Stols, L.M.: Sensitive fluorescence-based thermodynamic and kinetic measurements of DNA hybridization in solution. Biochemistry 32(12), 3095–3104 (1993)

12. Padilla, J.E., Patitz, M.J., Pena, R., Schweller, R.T., Seeman, N.C., Sheline, R., Summers, S.M., Zhong, X.: Asynchronous signal passing for tile self-assembly: Fuel efficient computation and efficient assembly of shapes. In: UCNC, pp. 174–185 (2013)

13. Padilla, J., Liu, W., Seeman, N.C.: Hierarchical self assembly of patterns from the robinson tilings: DNA tile design in an enhanced tile assembly model. Natural Computing 11(2), 323–338 (2012)

14. Rothemund, P.W.K., Winfree, E.: The program-size complexity of self-assembled squares. In: Proceedings of the Thirty-second Annual ACM Symposium on Theory of Computing, STOC 2000, pp. 459–468. ACM (2000)

15. Schulman, R., Winfree, E.: Self-replication and evolution of DNA crystals. In: Capcarrère, M.S., Freitas, A.A., Bentley, P.J., Johnson, C.G., Timmis, J. (eds.) ECAL 2005. LNCS (LNAI), vol. 3630, pp. 734–743. Springer, Heidelberg (2005)

16. Schulman, R., Yurke, B., Winfree, E.: Robust self-replication of combinatorial information via crystal growth and scission. Proceedings of the National Academy of Sciences 109(17), 6405–6410 (2012)

17. Seki, S.: Combinatorial optimization in pattern assembly. In: Mauri, G., Dennunzio, A., Manzoni, L., Porreca, A.E. (eds.) UCNC 2013. LNCS, vol. 7956, pp. 220–231. Springer, Heidelberg (2013)

18. Soloveichik, D., Seelig, G., Winfree, E.: DNA as a universal substrate for chemical kinetics. Proceedings of the National Academy of Sciences 107(12), 5393–5398 (2010)

19. Winfree, E.: Algorithmic Self-Assembly of DNA. Ph.D. thesis, California Institute of Technology, Pasadena, USA (1998)

20. Winfree, E., Bekbolatov, R.: Proofreading tile sets: Error correction for algorithmic self-assembly. In: Chen, J., Reif, J.H. (eds.) DNA 2003. LNCS, vol. 2943, pp. 126–144. Springer, Heidelberg (2004)
21. Winfree, E., Liu, F., Wenzler, L., Seeman, N.C.: Design and self-assembly of two-dimensional DNA crystals. Nature 394(6693), 539–544 (1998)
22. Zhang, D.Y., Hariadi, R.F., Choi, H.M., Winfree, E.: Integrating DNA strand-displacement circuitry with DNA tile self-assembly. Nature Communications 4 (2013)
23. Zhang, D.Y., Winfree, E.: Control of DNA strand displacement kinetics using toehold exchange. Journal of the American Chemical Society (2009)

# Unconditionally Secure Quantum Bit Commitment Protocol Based on Incomplete Information

Naya Nagy[2] and Marius Nagy[1,2]

College of Computer Engineering and Science
Prince Mohammad Bin Fahd University
Al Azeziya, Eastern Province, KSA
mnagy@pmu.edu.sa
School of Computing, Queen's University
Kingston, Ontario, Canada
{nagy,marius}@cs.queensu.ca

**Abstract.** This paper is reversing the current belief on Quantum Bit Commitment. Several papers have claimed and given a formal proof that quantum bit commitment is impossible. Nevertheless, the hypotheses of the formal mathematical model are too restrictive and do not exhaustively reflect the original definition of the problem. They share the same unnecessary restriction that the responsibility of hiding information and committing to a bit value is attributed to the *same* communicating partner. The protocol described here fully abides to the original description of the bit commitment problem.The two communicating partners share responsibilities, one partner is mostly responsible for hiding information and the other one for committing to the bit value. The security of the protocol derives from quantum properties such as the unclonability of unknown states, the indistinguishability of non-orthogonal states and also from randomly discarding and permuting qubits. The protocol is safe from classical attacks and quantum attacks using entanglement. The level of security can be made arbitrarily large by using more qubits. This result opens the door for a whole set of cryptographic applications using bit commitment as a building block: remote coin tossing, zero-knowledge proofs and secure two-party computation.

**Keywords:** bit commitment, protocol, quantum, measurements, permutation, entanglement.

## 1 Introduction

The field of quantum cryptography is best known for its results in two major directions: *key distribution* and *bit commitment*. It is interesting to note that the foundations of both directions were laid in the same seminal paper by Bennett and Brassard in 1984 [1]. However, the destinies of the two results would prove to be far from similar. A variety of quantum key distribution protocols were

A.-H. Dediu et al. (Eds.): TPNC 2014, LNCS 8890, pp. 134–143, 2014.

proposed after the initial BB84, making key distribution the most successful practical application of quantum mechanics to information processing.

On the other hand, things were not so straightforward with quantum bit commitment. The classical problem of bit commitment can be described intuitively as follows. Alice places a bit of her choice into a "safe" or "box" that she locks up, before handing it over to Bob (the *commit* step). By guarding the "box", Bob makes sure that Alice cannot change the bit she committed to. At a later time, when Bob wants to find out the value Alice has locked in the box, he asks Alice for the key (the *decommit* step). From the very beginning (BB84) it was realized that entanglement would offer the ideal attack strategy on any quantum bit commitment protocol, allowing someone to actually avoid commitment right until the decommit step. Researchers in the field have tried ever since to some-how circumvent this difficulty by resorting to a wide range of ideas, from some clever use of measurements and classical communication to combining quantum mechanics with other physical theories in order to achieve their goal.

Perhaps the best known exponent of the early efforts to achieve an unconditionally secure protocol for quantum bit commitment was the BCJL protocol, developed in 1993 [4]. The future was looking bright for quantum cryptography following this result, since many important applications could be realized based on bit commitment (see [6] for example). The bad news came in 1996, when Mayers [10] and, independently, Lo and Chau [8] discovered a flaw in the BCJL protocol. Even worse, Mayers proved a more general result, stating that an unconditionally secure quantum bit commitment protocol is impossible [11].

It may have been the importance of bit commitment for the general field of cryptography or the intuition that the success of quantum key distribution could be replicated for quantum bit commitment that still pushed people to look for a solution. Several protocols were proposed that try to restrict the behavior of the cheater in some way so as to obtain a secure bit commitment scheme [3,5,7]. It turned out that all these protocols were falling under the scope of Mayers' impossibility result. This led to a general belief that the principles of quantum mechanics alone cannot be used to create an unconditionally secure bit commitment protocol. Therefore, recent advances on the topic either exploit realistic physical assumptions like the dishonest party being limited by "noisy storage" for quantum information [12] or combine the power of Einstein's relativity with quantum theory [9]. Secure bit commitment using quantum theory alone is still believed to be impossible.

The difficulty of the problem stems from the lack of trust between the parties. Alice may want to defer commitment until the decommit phase and Bob may want to find out Alice's commitment during the commit phase. First, Alice should be forced to commit during the commit phase, and Bob should be secure of the necessity of Alice's commitment. Bob should be able to test Alice's fairness. Secondly, Bob should not have enough information to allow him to find Alice's commitment during the commit phase. Alice should be able to ensure that she is not revealing too much information to Bob.

These two major properties of any correct quantum bit commitment solution, namely, binding Alice to her choice and hiding this choice from Bob, are considered mutually exclusive by Mayers. He states that in any protocol that is hiding, the quantum states of the safe containing either 0 or 1 must be very similar (if not identical) since otherwise Bob would be able to discern the difference and gain knowledge about the committed bit prematurely. But the very fact that the two states are virtually the same gives Alice the possibility to keep her options open and postpone her *commitment* for later on.

In this paper, we show that quantum bit commitment is indeed possible if Alice and Bob share the responsibilities of ensuring binding and concealing: Alice is responsible to hide her choice, while Bob must make sure that Alice cannot change her mind in the decommit step. Both properties can be achieved by resorting to incomplete information. Thus, the quantum state of the "safe" does not have to be identical (or close to identical) for the two possible values of the committed bit, but they have to *appear* as such to Bob, because he does not have complete information about it. Similarly, incomplete information about the "structure" of the "safe" prevents Alice from cheating in the decommit step. Thus, the key to achieving bit commitment through quantum means lies in a protocol in which none of the two parties has complete information on the "safe" throughout the entire commit phase.

The remainder of this paper is organized as follows. The next section describes in detail the steps Alice and Bob should go through when they want to honestly execute our quantum bit commitment protocol. Section 3 analyzes the security of the protocol, proving that it is both binding and concealing. In particular, we show how Bob can enforce the binding property without compromising the concealing property. A discussion on why this protocol falls outside the scope of Mayers impossibility result is offered in section 4. The main ideas that made this result possible and its significance for the field of quantum cryptography are summarized in the concluding section.

## 2   Protocol Description

We choose to describe our protocol in general terms, without restricting to a particular physical embodiment for a qubit (such as photon polarization or particle spin). Consequently, in what follows we will refer to $\{|0\rangle, |1\rangle\}$ as the normal computational basis and to $\{H|0\rangle = \frac{1}{\sqrt{2}}(|0\rangle + |1\rangle), H|1\rangle = \frac{1}{\sqrt{2}}(|0\rangle - |1\rangle)\}$ as the Hadamard basis.

### 2.1   Commit Phase

The Commit Phase, depicted in Fig. 1, is comprised of the following steps:

1. Bob generates a sequence of $N$ qubits in the state $|0\rangle \otimes |0\rangle \otimes \cdots \otimes |0\rangle \otimes H|0\rangle \otimes H|0\rangle \otimes \cdots \otimes H|0\rangle$, where $N$ is some positive even integer. The first $N/2$ qubits in the sequence are all in state $|0\rangle$, while the qubits in the second half are

ALICE                                              BOB

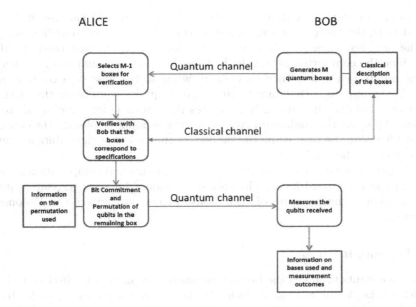

**Fig. 1.** Commit Phase of the protocol

all in state $H|0\rangle$. Bob sends a random permutation of this sequence to Alice. This step is repeated $M$ times (for some positive integer $M$), such that in the end Alice will have received from Bob $M$ sequences, each sequence consisting of $N/2$ qubits in state $|0\rangle$ and $N/2$ qubits in state $H|0\rangle$, in random order. In an intuitive description of this step, Bob hands out to Alice a number of $M$ "boxes", each different from the others (different permutation), yet all sharing the same characteristics (an equal number of qubits in each of the two possible states).

2. Alice verifies that the "boxes" she received correspond to the agreed specifications. In detail, one of the $M$ sequences ("boxes") received is saved for the actual commit step, while all remaining sequences are verified in order to determine if Bob executed the protocol honestly. For each of the $M - 1$ sequences selected for verification, Alice asks Bob to disclose, qubit by qubit, whether it was prepared in state $|0\rangle$ or in state $H|0\rangle$. Then, she can proceed to measure each qubit in the proper basis: the normal computational basis for a $|0\rangle$ qubit and the Hadamard basis for a $H|0\rangle$ qubit. In the first place, in each group (or sequence), $N/2$ qubits must have been prepared in state $|0\rangle$ and $N/2$ in state $H|0\rangle$. Secondly, all measurements must yield a value of 0, otherwise Bob has not been honest in telling the states in which the qubits were prepared. If both conditions are satisfied, Alice is confident that Bob has abided by the protocol rules and as such, she concludes that the last ($M$-th box) also contains $N/2$ qubits in state $|0\rangle$ and $N/2$ qubits in state $H|0\rangle$ in

a random order. Alice then proceeds to the next step. Otherwise, if Alice's test fails, the protocol is abandoned as Bob has been proven dishonest.

3. The only sequence left after the verification step is the box used by Alice to hide the committed bit inside. If Alice decides to commit to 0, she leaves the qubits in the sequence untouched, while in the case of a commitment to 1, she applies a Hadamard gate to all $N$ qubits composing that last sequence. Finally, she randomly permutes the qubits before sending them to Bob. Applying the Hadamard gate or not corresponds to placing the committed bit inside the box, while the random permutation of the qubits amounts to "locking the box".

4. Bob measures each received qubit either in the normal computational basis or in the Hadamard basis. The choice is random for each measured qubit. Bob records the outcome of each measurement and awaits the Decommit phase.

## 2.2  Decommit Phase

When Alice wants to unveil the bit she committed to, she has to disclose to Bob, for each of the $N$ qubits sent, its index in the original sequence. In order to be satisfied that Alice executed the protocol honestly, Bob proceeds to the following verification.

Based on the index information provided by Alice, Bob can determine for each qubit if it was measured in the "correct" basis or not: for a qubit that was originally in state $|0\rangle$ the correct basis is the normal computational basis, while for a qubit whose state was originally $H|0\rangle$ the correct basis is the Hadamard basis. Now, if Alice committed to 0, all the qubits measured in the "correct" basis must yield a value of 0. The other measurements will yield a 0 or a 1 with equal probability. On the other hand, if Alice committed to 1, then the qubits measured "incorrectly" must all yield a value of 0 and the others have an equal chance to be observed as 0 or as 1. Any other scenario for the measurement outcomes (in the ideal case of an error-free environment) points to a dishonest participant to the protocol.

# 3  Correctness

The protocol described above is both *binding* and *concealing*. Let us start by showing the concealing property first.

## 3.1  Concealing Property

Since Bob is the one initiating the protocol, it appears that he is in the position to set things to his advantage. In theory, he could distinguish between a commitment to 0 and a commitment to 1, if the sequence selected as "the box" is not balanced between $|0\rangle$ and $H|0\rangle$ states. The closer we are to a constant sequence (all qubits $|0\rangle$ or all qubits $H|0\rangle$), the higher the chances for Bob to guess the committed bit correctly. Consider, for example, a sequence (box) made up of $N$ qubits, all in state $|0\rangle$. If Alice commits to 0, this exact sequence is sent to Bob, otherwise a sequence made up of $N$ qubits in state $H|0\rangle$ will be sent. Bob, when receiving the $N$ qubits, measures all of them in the normal computational basis. If all measurements yield a 0, Bob is highly confident that the committed bit is 0 because, for a commitment to 1, he expects a $50 - 50$ probability distribution between 0 and 1 in the outcomes obtained.

In summary, Bob's chances to correctly guess the committed bit are directly proportional to how unbalanced the sequence selected to act as the box is. Thus, the probability of a correct guess varies between 0.5 (completely random guess) and a value which can be brought as close to 1 as desired by increasing the number of qubits in the sequence. This is also reflected in how close the density matrix corresponding to a commitment to 0 is to the density matrix for the case where Alice commits to 1. For a balanced sequence, the two density matrices are identical:

$$\rho_0 = \frac{1}{2}|0\rangle\langle 0| + \frac{1}{2}|1\rangle\langle 1| = \frac{1}{2}(\frac{|0\rangle + |1\rangle}{\sqrt{2}})(\frac{\langle 0| + \langle 1|}{\sqrt{2}}) + \frac{1}{2}(\frac{|0\rangle - |1\rangle}{\sqrt{2}})(\frac{\langle 0| - \langle 1|}{\sqrt{2}}) = \rho_1.$$
(1)

On the other hand, the density matrices are at a maximum distance from one another when the sequence is constant.

Now, Bob faces the following dilemma in his cheating strategy: the more counterfeited boxes he prepares (sequences that are not balanced between $|0\rangle$ and $H|0\rangle$), the more chances one of them will be used by Alice, but at the same time the more chances to be detected by Alice during the verification step. Formally, we can distinguish between the following two cases:

1. Bob chooses to play safely and from the $M$ sequences prepared, only a *constant* number, say $c$, do not correspond to the agreed specifications. Here, *constant* means that, always, only $c$ sequences are "counterfeited", regardless of what the value for $M$ is. In this situation, the probability $\varepsilon_1$ that Alice will choose one of the counterfeited boxes to place the committed bit inside can be made infinitesimally small by increasing $M$ (the number of boxes she chooses from):

$$\varepsilon_1 = \frac{c}{M}$$
(2)

Thus, for a maximum allowed probability of picking a counterfeited box $\varepsilon_1$, the total number of boxes must satisfy the inequality:

$$M \geq \left\lceil \frac{c}{\varepsilon_1} \right\rceil$$
(3)

For example, suppose that Bob always prepares $c = 10$ counterfeited boxes and we would like to limit the probability of picking a counterfeited box to $\varepsilon_1 = 0.01$. Then the total number of boxes to choose from should be at least 1000.

2. Bob plays aggressively and from the $M$ boxes prepared, a certain fraction $f$ are counterfeited. In this case, even if one of the counterfeited boxes is set aside by Alice for the commit step, the other $f \cdot M - 1$ will undergo the verification step. By definition, a counterfeited box is a sequence in which *at least* one qubit does not correspond to the agreed specifications. What is the actual state of such a qubit is irrelevant, as long as there is a certain non-zero probability $p$ that Alice will catch Bob when verifying that qubit. Again, by increasing the value of $M$, the probability of catching Bob can be brought as close to 1 as desired, or equivalently, the probability $\varepsilon_2$ of Bob escaping detection can be made arbitrarily small:

$$\varepsilon_2 = (1 - p)^{fM-1} \tag{4}$$

Therefore, if we want to keep the probability of Bob escaping detection to at most $\varepsilon_2$, then a lower bound on the total number of boxes used in the protocol is given by

$$M \geq \left\lceil \frac{1 + \log_{1-p} \varepsilon_2}{f} \right\rceil \tag{5}$$

Note that the above formula assumes that there is just one "incorrect" qubit in each counterfeited box. If there are more, like, for example, the whole sequence is constant, then the lower bound is obviously smaller. Also, the number of counterfeited boxes does not have to vary linearly with $M$, the analysis remains valid for any increasing function of $M$. Going through a concrete example again, let us assume that 10% of the boxes prepared by Bob are counterfeited and there is a 25% chance of detecting a "forged" qubit when verified. Under these circumstances, in order to catch Bob with a probability of 99%, the total number of boxes to choose from should be at least 171.

Consequently, there is no winning strategy for Bob: with an arbitrarily high probability (controlled by the value of parameter $M$), either he will be detected as dishonest or none of his counterfeited boxes will be selected by Alice. This result can be formally expressed as the following theorem:

**Theorem 1.** $\lim\limits_{M \to \infty} \varepsilon_1 \cdot \varepsilon_2 = 0$

*Proof.* The proof follows from the two cases discussed above. The more counterfeited boxes Bob prepares, the higher the chances he will be caught. In other words, in order to keep the probability of escaping detection above a certain threshold $\tau$

$$\lim\limits_{M \to \infty} \varepsilon_2 \geq \tau, \tag{6}$$

Bob cannot create more than a certain number $\eta$ of counterfeited boxes (where $\eta$ is a function of $\tau$). But in that case, the chance to select one of the counterfeited boxes to place the bit inside drops to zero as $M$ grows unbounded:

$$\lim_{M\to\infty} \varepsilon_1 = \lim_{M\to\infty} \frac{\eta}{M} = 0. \tag{7}$$

$\square$

Note that in the above analysis, Bob is free to use any states he wants, with no restrictions. Even entangled states will do him no good, since all measurements performed by Alice must consistently yield a 0, with no exception. There is no entangled state that will always be observed as 0, no matter how it is measured.

## 3.2 Binding Property

The only chance for Alice to postpone commitment until the decommit phase is to know the "structure" of the "box" she has used, that is, to know exactly what the quantum state of each qubit is in the sequence received from Bob. That way, when Bob asks for the index of each qubit received and measured, she can always pick a convenient index in the sequence, corresponding to a qubit that matches her late commitment. Unfortunately for Alice, there is no reliable way of distinguishing between $|0\rangle$ and $H|0\rangle$, as they are non-orthogonal quantum states. Without this knowledge, if she tries to be dishonest, there is always a probability of being revealed as a cheater for each qubit verified by Bob. Therefore, by increasing the value of $N$ (number of qubits composing each sequence), the probability of catching a dishonest Alice can be made arbitrarily high:

$$\lim_{N\to\infty} (1 - p^N) = 1, \tag{8}$$

where $p = 0.75$ is the probability per qubit that Alice passes Bob's verification.

Again, note that entanglement is of no use to Alice, since no entangled state will consistently collapse (when measured) to the outcome expected by Bob.

## 4 Discussion

Since we have just shown that bit commitment through quantum means alone is still possible, despite a contrary belief that has lasted for almost 20 years, the obvious question is : How can this result be reconciled with Mayers' impossibility result? The answer can be found in the framework in which that result was obtained, a framework that is not general enough to encompass all possible protocols. To be more explicit, Mayers shows that in any protocol that is concealing, Alice can cheat in a modified procedure *commit'* by keeping everything at the quantum level and "never sending a register away to the environment except when this register contains a classical bit that she must transmit to Bob via the environment, using the phone for instance" [11]. The same is assumed for Bob in a modified procedure *commit"*. Under these assumptions, the fact that the expected value of the fidelity between the reduced density matrices on Bob's side is arbitrarily close to 1 implies that Alice can apply a unitary transformation to steer the quantum state of her subsystem towards 0 or 1 in the decommit phase.

Our protocol does not fit this framework, because a key ingredient in it is the fact that both Alice and Bob have to keep classical information (in the commit phase) that is not to be sent to the other party. This classical information is the missing information that prevents the other party from cheating. At the end of the Commit Phase, all information in the system is actually classical, and Alice cannot transform the state of the system from 0 to 1 without the information in Bob's custody (that is, the original quantum states of the qubits composing the box chosen). Similarly, Bob cannot distinguish between a box containing a 0 and a box containing a 1 without knowing the permutation applied by Alice. Because no reduction exists that transforms our protocol into an equivalent one in which no classical information is required (except for what needs to be communicated classically), this protocol falls outside the scope of Mayers impossibility result.

## 5    Conclusion

We showed in this paper how a secure quantum bit commitment protocol can be realized. The key idea that made this result possible was that at any time during the protocol before the decommit phase, none of the two parties has complete information on the box used to hide the committed bit. Although the box is quantum in nature, the "description" of the box is distributed to both Alice and Bob, as classical information. Without knowledge of the information stored by the other party, none of them is capable of mounting an effective cheating strategy. The quantum nature of the box is essential because quantum mechanical properties, like unclonability and indistinguishability of non-orthogonal quantum states, are essential to ensuring the security of the protocol. Our scheme comes with two security parameters, each controlling one of the two critical properties of the protocol. The number $M$ of boxes (or sequences) created initially by Bob controls the concealing property: the higher the value of $M$, the lower the probability of Bob being able to cheat and identify the committed bit prematurely. The number of qubits in a sequence (or the size of the box), on the other hand, controls the binding property: the larger the value for $N$, the lower the probability that Alice will guess correctly the "structure" of the box and thus, be able to pick the value of the bit in the decommit phase. A secure bit commitment protocol realizable through quantum means alone has huge implications for the field of quantum cryptography. Remote coin tossing, which might be used for long-distance gambling, is immediately realizable based on bit commitment (see [2] for example). Quantum oblivious mutual identification [6], another important result built on secure quantum bit commitment can be exploited to avoid frauds from typing PIN codes to dishonest teller machines. Other applications may range from ensuring the security of remote voting to global financial trading. The future looks bright again for the field of quantum cryptography.

# References

1. Bennett, C.H., Brassard, G.: Quantum cryptography: Public key distribution and coin tossing. In: Proceedings of IEEE International Conference on Computers, Systems and Signal Processing, Bangalore, India, December, pp. 175–179. IEEE, New York (1984)
2. Brassard, G., Crépeau, C.: Quantum bit commitment and coin tossing protocols. In: Menezes, A., Vanstone, S.A. (eds.) CRYPTO 1990. LNCS, vol. 537, pp. 49–61. Springer, Heidelberg (1991)
3. Brassard, G., Crépeau, C.: 25 years of quantum cryptography. SIGACT News 27(3), 13–24 (1996)
4. Brassard, G., Crépeau, C., Jozsa, R., Langlois, D.: A quantum bit commitment scheme provably unbreakable by both parties. In: Proceedings of the 34th Annual IEEE Symposium on Foundations of Computer Science, pp. 362–371. IEEE Press (1993)
5. Crépeau, C.: What is going on with quantum bit commitment? In: Proceedings of Pragocrypt 1996: 1st International Conference on the Theory and Applications of Cryptology, Prague (October 1996)
6. Crépeau, C., Salvail, L.: Quantum oblivious mutual identification. In: Guillou, L.C., Quisquater, J.-J. (eds.) EUROCRYPT 1995. LNCS, vol. 921, pp. 133–146. Springer, Heidelberg (1995)
7. Kent, A.: Permanently secure quantum bit commitment protocol from a temporary computation bound (December 1997), los Alamos preprint archive, quant-ph/9712002
8. Lo, H.-K., Chau, H.F.: Is quantum bit commitment really possible? Physical Review Letters 78, 3410–3413 (1997)
9. Lunghi, T., Kaniewski, J., Bussières, F., Houlmann, R., Tomamichel, M., Kent, A., Gisin, N., Wehner, S., Zbinden, H.: Experimental bit commitment based on quantum communication and special relativity. Physical Review Letters 111, 180504 (2013)
10. Mayers, D.: Unconditionally secure quantum bit commitment is impossible. In: Fourth Workshop on Physics and Computation – PhysComp 1996, Boston (November 1996)
11. Mayers, D.: Unconditionally secure quantum bit commitment is impossible. Physical Review Letters 78, 3414–3417 (1997)
12. Ng, N.H.Y., Joshi, S.K., Ming, C.C., Kurtsiefer, C., Wehner, S.: Experimental implementation of bit commitment in the noisy-storage model. Nature Communications 3(1326) (December 27, 2012)

# Quantum and Reversible Verification of Proofs Using Constant Memory Space

Marcos Villagra[*] and Tomoyuki Yamakami

Department of Information Science, University of Fukui
3-9-1 Bunkyo, Fukui, 910-8507 Japan

**Abstract.** Non-interactive verification of proofs or certificates by deterministic verifiers in polynomial time with mighty provers is used to
characterize languages in NP. We initiate the study of the computational complexity of similar non-interactive proof-verification procedures
by quantum and reversible verifiers who are permitted to use only a
constant amount of memory storage. By modeling those weak verifiers
as quantum and reversible finite automata, we investigate fundamental
properties of such non-interactive proof systems and demonstrate that
languages admitting proof systems in which verifiers must scan the input
in real time are exactly regular languages. On the contrary, when we allow verifiers to move their tape heads in all directions, the corresponding
proof systems are empowered to recognize non-stochastic, non-context-
free, and NP-complete languages.

**Keywords:** quantum computing, Merlin-Arthur proof system, quantum
finite automaton, reversible finite automaton, NP, stochastic language.

## 1 Merlin-Arthur Proof Systems with Constant Space

Computational verification of a "proof" or "certificate" has been studied for five
decades using various models of two-party communication and computation,
where a *proof* refers to a piece of information that may contain sufficient data
to help a party verify the correctness of a target property (or a statement). Our
special interest lies on a communication game in which a party (called Merlin or
a prover) prepares such a proof, either correct or erroneous, and passes it on to
another party (called Arthur or a verifier), who operates a quantum computer
using only limited memory space for the purpose of verifying the correctness
of the proof. In particular, we are interested in the case where the space of
memory storage is upper-bounded by a certain absolute constant, independent
of inputs. Roughly speaking, a language $L$ is said to *admit* an *MA proof system*
if there exists a constant-space machine (Arthur) such that, for every input $x$ in
$L$, whenever a prover (Merlin) provides him a "correct" proof, Arthur verifies its
correctness and eventually accepts $x$; on the contrary, for every input $x$ outside

---

[*] This author is supported by a research fellowship of the Japan Society for the Promotion of Sciences (JSPS).

A.-H. Dediu et al. (Eds.): TPNC 2014, LNCS 8890, pp. 144–156, 2014.

of $L$, no matter what proof is passed on by Merlin, Arthur refutes the proof and eventually rejects $x$. Alternatively, we say that such an MA proof system *recognizes* $L$.

In the past literature, a more general model of *interactive proof (IP) systems* using memory-restricted verifiers has been studied extensively. Dwork and Stockmeyer [2] conducted an initial study on the strengths and weaknesses of IP systems whose verifiers are particularly limited to 2-way probabilistic finite automata (or 2pfa's, in short). Taking quantum finite automata as verifiers, Nishimura and Yamakami [7,8] investigated *quantum interactive proof (QIP) systems*. In those proof systems, the number of interactions between a prover and a verifier can be viewed as crucial computational resource that affects the power of language recognition. Recent literature (e.g., [8,10,14]) has been also focused on variants of QIP systems with weak verifiers.

Marriott and Watrous [5] studied *quantum Merlin-Arthur (QMA) proof systems*, which are a non-interactive model in which a quantum prover passes an "entire" quantum proof to a quantum verifier at the start of a verification procedure and the verifier checks the validity of the proof with no further communication with the prover. Nevertheless, little attention has been paid to non-interactive proof systems whose verifiers are "quantum finite automata."

Merlin is used to take various forms. In a model of *deterministic Merlin*,[1] he chooses a (possibly non-recursive) function assigning a proof to each input and sends such a proof to Arthur for its verification. When Arthur runs any 1-way[2] deterministic finite automaton (or 1dfa, in short) working on a pair of inputs and proofs, the associated MA proof system naturally induces nondeterministic computation and becomes equivalent in power to 1-way nondeterministic finite automata (or 1nfa's). When Arthur operates any *1-way reversible finite automaton* (or 1rfa), because of its similarity, we intend to refer to its associated MA proof system as a *1-way nondeterministic reversible automaton* (or 1nrfa).

Unlike 1dfa verifiers, 1rfa verifiers are quite sensitive to their *halting condition*. As in the case of 2-way finite automata, we can generally assume that our finite-automaton verifiers halt as soon as they enter halting states (i.e., either accepting or rejecting states). In comparison, when verifiers are forced to read off an entire input before checking a halting condition, the associated MA proof systems form a model known as *classical acceptance*. To emphasize the use of this classical-acceptance model, we append the special suffix "-cla", resulting in, e.g., 1nrfa-cla. It appears that the ability of 1nrfa-clas's is quite restrictive when recognizing languages.

This paper also studies a model of *quantum Merlin*, in which he is allowed to apply any quantum operation to prepare a proof in the form of a (possibly

---

[1] Here, the terminology "deterministic Merlin" is used purposely in comparison with "randomized Merlin" (who generates a probability distribution of proofs) and "quantum Merlin" (who generates a quantum state) discussed in the past literature.

[2] In this paper, the term "1-way" means that a tape head of a given machine moves from left to right without stopping at any computation step. This condition is sometimes called "real-time" in the literature.

reduced) quantum state, which he passes it on to Arthur. We consider only the case where Arthur is modeled as a *measure-once 1-way quantum finite automaton* (or mo-1qfa) [6], a *measure-many 1-way quantum finite automaton* (or 1qfa) [4], or a *2-way quantum finite automaton* (or 2qfa) [4]. The choice of those quantum automaton models is to make our later arguments simple and concise as well as to clarify the essential roles of quantum computation for proof verification.

For technicality, we can naturally differentiate two types of quantum Merlin. The first quantum Merlin generates a proof in the form of a *pure* quantum state, passes it on to Arthur, and does nothing afterwards. The second quantum Merlin prepares a proof, sends Arthur only a portion of the proof (in a form of *reduced* quantum state), and additionally applies any quantum operation to his privately-retaining quantum data at every step when Arthur makes a move. As quantum mechanics dictates, since the second quantum Merlin correlates his retaining data with Arthur's received data by way of *quantum entanglement*, Merlin may potentially interfere with Arthur's verification procedure simply by modifying his own data privately. To distinguish those two types, we call Merlin of the second type *active (quantum) Merlin* and the first type *non-active Merlin*.

## 2   A Short List of Major Contributions

A brief and informal list of the major contributions of this paper is given below.

**(i) MA Proof Systems with 1rfa Verifiers.** We show that the family 1NRFA of all languages recognized by 1nrfa's (namely, MA proof systems with 1rfa verifiers) coincides with the family REG of regular languages (Theorem 1). Moreover, we show two impossibility results: the existence of a regular language that admits no 1nrfa-cla (Theorem 4) and the non-closure property of 1NRFA-CLA under complementation (Proposition 6). Those results are, in fact, direct consequences of a variant of *pumping lemma*, targeting languages recognized by 1nrfa-cla's (Lemma 2). We prove this lemma by employing a semigroup-theoretical argument (outlined in Lemma 3).

**(ii) QMA Proof Systems with 1qfa Verifiers.** We show that the family QMA(1qfa) of all languages admitting 1qfa-verifier QMA proof systems coincides with REG (Theorem 7). In our QMA proof systems, active quantum Merlin is shown to be no more powerful than non-active quantum Merlin (Proposition 13). We also demonstrate an important property, in which a "long" quantum proof can be compressed into a much "shorter" proof without altering the behavior of the corresponding verifier (Lemma 11).

**(iii) QMA Proof Systems with 2qfa[3] Verifiers.** It is known that 2qfa's can recognize all regular languages and certain non-regular languages [4]. In 2qfa-verifier QMA proof systems, if a proof-tape head of a verifier is allowed to stay still, then we can show that the associated QMA proof systems recognize non-stochastic languages (Theorem 17) and non-context-free languages. Moreover, if

---

[3] A 2qfa has a read-only input-tape head that can move to the right, to the left, or stay still while scanning the tape.

the proof-tape head can further move in all directions, then the associated proof systems recognize even NP-complete languages (Lemma 19).

# 3   Quantum Merlin-Arthur Proof Systems

Due to page limit, we assume the reader's familiarity with basic concepts of quantum finite automata. Let $\Sigma$ refer to an *input alphabet* and let $\Gamma$ refer to another (possibly the same) *proof alphabet*. The notation $\lambda$ indicates both the *empty string* and the *blank symbol*. Furthermore, $\mathbb{N}$, $\mathbb{R}$, $\mathbb{C}$, and $\mathbb{A}$ respectively denote the sets of all nonnegative integers, of all real numbers, of all complex numbers, and of all algebraic complex numbers. In particular, $\tilde{\mathbb{C}}$ expresses the set of all *polynomial-time computable* complex numbers (i.e., both real and imaginary parts are approximable in time polynomial in a given precision parameter).

**Quantum Merlin and Quantum Finite Automata.** In our QMA proof system, Merlin (a prover) and Arthur (a verifier) access two tapes (i.e., an input tape and a proof tape) and Arthur operates two tape heads on those tapes. An *input tape* is a read-only infinite tape that holds an input string, surrounded by two designated end-markers ($\cent$ and $\$$). A *proof tape* is also a read-only infinite tape that holds a proof (or a certificate) given by Merlin before Arthur's verification procedure begins. For technical reasons, we assume that the input tape is *circular* and that the proof tape is infinite on both ends. Although the proof tape is infinite, the number of non-blank cells is always finite. As a basic computation model, we request Arthur to scan the proof tape from left to right (unless staying stationary). For convenience, we refer to this as the "no-move-back" requirement because, later in Section 6, we will lift this requirement to investigate the power of the verifiers.

Let $\mathcal{H}_{input} = span\{|\cent x\$\rangle : x \in \Sigma^*\}$ be a Hilbert space used to describe inputs. Let $\mathcal{H}_p = span\{|w\rangle : w \in \Gamma^*\}$ denote a Hilbert space composed of Merlin's (quantum) proofs. Quantum Merlin accesses an input in $\mathcal{H}_{input}$ and prepares in $\mathcal{H}_p$ a proof, which is simply a pure quantum state.

As noted in Section 1, we model Arthur as quantum finite automata, particularly, mo-1qfa's, 1qfa's, or 2qfa's. In a 2qfa model, Arthur owns his private Hilbert space $\mathcal{H}_A = span\{|q, h, \ell\rangle : (q, h, \ell) \in Q \times \mathbb{N} \times \mathbb{Z}\}$, where $Q$ is a finite set of internal states, $h$ is the position of an input-tape head, and $\ell$ is the position of a proof-tape head. Although $\mathcal{H}_p \otimes \mathcal{H}_{input} \otimes \mathcal{H}_A$ represents an entire QMA proof system, we often omit $\mathcal{H}_{input}$ when fixating an input string throughout an entire computation. Now, Arthur $\mathcal{A}$ is expressed as an 8-tuple $\mathcal{A} = (Q, \Sigma, \{\cent, \$\}, \delta, q_0, Q_{acc}, Q_{rej}, \Gamma)$, where $\delta$ maps $Q \times \check{\Sigma} \times \Gamma \times Q \times D_1 \times D_2$ to $\mathbb{C}$, where $\check{\Sigma} = \Sigma \cup \{\cent, \$\}$, $D_1 = \{-1, 0, 1\}$, and $D_2 = \{0, 1\}$. Meanwhile, we fix an input $x = x_1 x_2 \cdots x_n$ and set $x_0 = \cent$ and $x_{n+1} = \$$. The function $\delta$ naturally induces a *transition matrix* $U_\delta^{(x)}$ acting on $\mathcal{H}_p \otimes \mathcal{H}_A$ as follows. Given $s \in \Gamma^*$ and $(q, h, \ell) \in Q \times [0, n+1]_{\mathbb{Z}} \times \mathbb{N}$, this matrix $U_\delta^{(x)}$ transforms $|s\rangle|q, h, \ell\rangle$ to $\sum_{(p,d,d')} \delta(q, x_h, s, p, q', d, d')|s\rangle|p, h + d \pmod{n+2}, \ell + d'\rangle$, where the sum is taken over $Q \times D_1 \times D_2$ and $[0, n+1]_{\mathbb{Z}} = \{0, 1, 2, \ldots, n+1\}$.

When proof $|\phi\rangle$ is given, a *computation* of $\mathcal{A}$ proceeds as follows. The *initial state* of the entire system is $|\psi_0\rangle = |\phi\rangle|q_0,0,0\rangle \in \mathcal{H}_p \otimes \mathcal{H}_A$. Arthur keeps applying $U_\delta^{(x)}$ and a projective measurement $\Pi$ *in turn* until a certain halting state (i.e., either an accepting state or a rejecting state) is reached. The probability $p_{acc,t}(x,|\phi\rangle)$ of accepting $x$ with this proof $|\phi\rangle$ within $t$ steps is the sum of probabilities, over all $i \in [1,t]_\mathbb{Z}$, with which $\mathcal{A}$ accepts $x$ at step $i$. The *acceptance probability* $p_{acc}(x,|\phi\rangle)$ is further defined to be $\lim_{t\to\infty} p_{acc,t}(x,|\phi\rangle)$. Likewise, we define $p_{rej,t}(x,|\phi\rangle)$ and $p_{rej}(x,|\phi\rangle)$.

Generally, we say that a QMA system $(P,\mathcal{A})$ *recognizes* language $L$ (or alternatively, $L$ *admits* $(P,\mathcal{A})$) if there exist a constant $\varepsilon \in [0,1/2)$ such that

- [completeness] for all $x \in L$, there exists a proof $|\phi\rangle$ satisfying $p_{acc}(x,|\phi\rangle) \geq 1 - \varepsilon$; and
- [soundness] for all $x \notin L$ and any proof $|\phi\rangle$, $p_{rej}(x,|\phi\rangle) \geq 1 - \varepsilon$.

In accordance with the notation of QIP(2qfa) in [8], we write QMA(2qfa) to express the family of all languages recognized by 2qfa-verifier QMA systems and we define QMA(2qfa, poly-time) to be a subclass of QMA(2qfa) by demanding that the expected running time of Arthur's verification procedure should be at most $p(|x|)$ for a certain fixed polynomial $p$. Furthermore, when Arthur is forced to use amplitudes taken from set $K$, we write, e.g., $\text{QMA}_K(2\text{qfa})$.

In the case where Arthur operates any 1qfa, Arthur's private Hilbert space $\mathcal{H}_A$ becomes $span\{|q\rangle : q \in Q\}$. The *(global) time evolution* of a 1qfa-verifier QMA proof system is described formally as follows. Let $\mathcal{V} = (H_p \otimes H_A) \times \mathbb{R} \times \mathbb{R}$. A vector $\Psi = (|\psi\rangle, p_{acc}, p_{rej})^T$ in $\mathcal{V}$ means that the QMA proof system is currently in quantum state $|\psi\rangle$ with *cumulative* acceptance probability $p_{acc}$ and with *cumulative* rejection probability $p_{rej}$. A *norm* $\|\Psi\|$ of $\Psi$ is $(\||\psi\rangle\|^2 + p_{acc} + p_{rej})^{1/2}$ (see, e.g., [3,12]). At each step $i \in \{0,\ldots,n+1\}$, the time evolution operator $T_i^{(x_i)}$ modifies vector $(|\psi\rangle, p_{acc}, p_{rej})^T$ to another vector $(\Pi_{non}U_i^{(x_i)}|\psi\rangle, p_{acc} + \|\Pi_{acc}U_i^{(x_i)}|\psi\rangle\|^2, p_{rej} + \|\Pi_{rej}U_i^{(x_i)}|\psi\rangle\|^2)^T$, where $\Pi_{non}$ is a projector associated with non-halting states. Given any input $x$, the initial vector is $\Psi_0 = (|\psi_0\rangle,0,0)^T$ and the vector $\Psi_{i+1}$ after step $i$ becomes $T^{(x_0x_1\cdots x_i)}\Psi_0$, where $T^{(x_0x_1\cdots x_i)}$ denotes $T_i^{(x_i)}T_{i-1}^{(x_{i-1})} \cdots T_0^{(x_0)}$.

As a variant of QMA(2qfa), we define QMA(1qfa) by substituting 1qfa verifiers for 2qfa verifiers in the definition of QMA(2qfa). Likewise, when Arthur runs any mo-1qfa, we use the notation QMA(mo-qfa).

**Deterministic Merlin and Reversible Finite Automata.** In an MA proof system, when Merlin behaves deterministically and Arthur operates a deterministic verification procedure, we naturally obtain a crucial concept of "nondeterminism" as in the proof-verification characterization of NP problems. Similarly, using deterministic Merlin and 1rfa verifiers, we can obtain two "nondeterministic" language families, denoted by 1NRFA and 1NRFA-CLA, in the following fashion. Here, Arthur is modeled as a *1-way reversible finite automaton* (or 1rfa, in short) $\mathcal{A} = (Q, \Sigma, \{\mathcal{c}, \$\}, \delta, q_0, Q_{acc}, Q_{rej}, \Gamma)$ equipped with proof alphabet $\Gamma$ and two endmarkers $\mathcal{c}, \$ \notin \Sigma$. In what follows, we fix an input $x \in \Sigma^n$.

Since Arthur operates a 1rfa, we treat deterministic Merlin as a (not necessarily recursive) function $\eta : \Sigma^* \to \Gamma^*$ that, on each input $x$, produces a proof $\eta(x)$ of length exactly $|x|$. Notice that each proof is *uniquely determined* from the choice of the function $\eta$ and input $x$.

Since an input-tape head of a 1rfa verifier always moves rightward without stopping, we naturally require its proof-tape head to behave in the same manner. This requirement makes it possible to truncate two tapes (i.e., input tape and proof tape); as a result, we can take the following simple definition. Once proof $w$ is given to Arthur, the computation of the proof system proceeds as if $(x, w)$ is a single input. Let $x = x_1 x_2 \cdots x_n$ and $w = w_1 w_2 \cdots w_n$. Pictorially, $\mathcal{A}$ has one single tape consisting of two tracks (i.e., an input track and a proof track) holding a string $[\begin{smallmatrix} x \\ w \end{smallmatrix}]$ made up of $[\begin{smallmatrix} x_1 \\ w_1 \end{smallmatrix}][\begin{smallmatrix} x_2 \\ w_2 \end{smallmatrix}] \cdots [\begin{smallmatrix} x_n \\ w_n \end{smallmatrix}]$ and a single tape head scans symbol $[\begin{smallmatrix} x_i \\ w_i \end{smallmatrix}]$ at each step (as in the case of advice [12]). The transition function $\delta$ maps $Q \times \check{\Sigma}_\Gamma$ to $Q$, where $\check{\Sigma}_\Gamma = \{[\begin{smallmatrix} \sigma \\ \gamma \end{smallmatrix}] \mid \sigma \in \Sigma, \gamma \in \Gamma\} \cup \{\cent, \$\}$. For ease of later description, we define $[\begin{smallmatrix} x_0 \\ w_0 \end{smallmatrix}] = \cent$ and $[\begin{smallmatrix} x_{n+1} \\ w_{n+1} \end{smallmatrix}] = \$$. At the $i$th step with $0 \leq i \leq n+1$, if $\mathcal{A}$'s current internal state is $q$ and $\delta$ satisfies $\delta(q, [\begin{smallmatrix} x_i \\ w_i \end{smallmatrix}]) = q'$, then the next internal state of $\mathcal{A}$ becomes $q'$. Moreover, we demand that $\delta$ is *reversible*; namely, for every tuple $(q, q', [\begin{smallmatrix} \sigma \\ \gamma \end{smallmatrix}])$, $\delta(q, [\begin{smallmatrix} \sigma \\ \gamma \end{smallmatrix}]) = \delta(q', [\begin{smallmatrix} \sigma \\ \gamma \end{smallmatrix}])$ implies $q = q'$.

By obvious analogy with nondeterminism, unless there is any confusion, we also call a 1rfa-verifier MA proof system with deterministic Merlin a *1-way nondeterministic reversible automaton* (or 1nrfa, in short). The notation 1NRFA thus expresses the family of all languages admitting certain 1nrfa's. When we use a classical-acceptance model discussed in Section 1, the associated proof system is succinctly called a *1nrfa-cla*[4] and the notation 1NRFA-CLA is used for the family of all languages recognized by those 1nrfa-cla's.

# 4    Reversible Computation with Deterministic Merlin

In classical automata theory, it is known that nondeterminism does not improve the computational power of *1-way deterministic finite automata* (or 1dfa's). In terms of MA proof systems, this means that any proof given by deterministic Merlin does not help 1dfa verifiers recognize target languages. In contrast, deterministic Merlin still enhances the ability of both 1rfa verifiers and 1rfa-cla verifiers to recognize languages. More specifically, we prove:

**Theorem 1.** 1RFA $\subsetneq$ 1NRFA = REG.

To prove Theorem 1, first note that the separation 1RFA $\neq$ 1NRFA follows from the equality 1NRFA = REG. The containment 1NRFA $\subseteq$ REG can be shown by a straightforward simulation of every 1nrfa by an appropriate 1nfa. For the converse containment, we take any 1dfa and, for each of its transitions, we add a fresh proof symbol to guarantee the reversibility of a 1rfa verifier.

Let us turn our attention to 1NRFA-CLA. Since 1NRFA = REG by Theorem 1, a standard pumping lemma holds for any language in 1NRFA. However, languages in 1NRFA-CLA satisfy a much stronger pumping lemma stated below.

---

[4] Our 1rfa-cla's are also known as permutation automata or group automata [1].

**Lemma 2 (Pumping Lemma).** *Let $L \in$ 1NRFA-CLA. For any $u, v, w \in \Sigma^*$, there exists $k \in \mathbb{N}^+$ such that $uv \in L$ implies $uw^{ik}v \in L$ for all $i \in \mathbb{N}^+$.*

To prove the lemma, we will utilize a semigroup-theoretical property of 1nrfa-cla's. In what follows, we assume the reader's familiarity with basics of *semigroup theory* (see, e.g., [9]). Let $\mathcal{A}$ be a 1nrfa-cla and let $\mathcal{S}(Q)$ be a set of all bijections on a set $Q$ of internal states of $\mathcal{A}$. Since $\mathcal{A}$ is reversible, it is possible to define a mapping $\mu : \Sigma^* \times \Gamma^* \to \mathcal{S}(Q)$ so that, for every tuple $(p, q, x, w)$, $\mu(x, w)(p) = q$ holds if and only if there is a transition path between $p$ and $q$ on input $x$ and proof $w$. Let $\mathcal{M}$ be a set of all non-empty subsets of $\mathcal{S}(Q)$ and define a mapping $\varphi : \Sigma^* \to \mathcal{M}$ as $\varphi(x) = \{\mu(x, w) : w \in \Gamma^{|x|}\}$. Given two subsets $\mathcal{R}, \mathcal{T} \subseteq \mathcal{S}(Q)$, a product $\mathcal{R} \bullet \mathcal{T}$ is the set $\{r \circ t : r \in \mathcal{R}, t \in \mathcal{T}\}$, where $\circ$ denotes standard functional composition.

**Lemma 3.** *If $\mathcal{A}$ is a 1nrfa-cla that recognizes language $L$, then the above-defined $(\mathcal{M}, \bullet)$ is a finite monoid that recognizes $L$. Furthermore, for any state $q$ and any idempotent $e \in \mathcal{M}$, there exists a bijection $r \in e$ satisfying $r(q) = q$.*

Lemma 2 follows directly from Lemma 3. First, for any $m \in \mathcal{M}$, define a *right action* of $m$ on $Q$ as a binary operator $\cdot : Q \times \mathcal{M} \to \mathcal{P}(Q)$ satisfying that $q' \in q \cdot m$ exactly when there exists $r \in m$ such that $r(q) = q'$. This right action has the following distributivity property: for any $m, s \in \mathcal{M}$ and any $q \in Q$, $(q \cdot m) \cdot s = q \cdot (m \bullet s)$.

*Proof of Lemma 2.* We proceed by induction on $i$. Let us consider the base case of $i = 1$. Let $\mathcal{A}$ be a 1nrfa-cla for $L$ and take a finite monoid $(\mathcal{M}, \bullet)$ from Lemma 3. Assuming that $uv \in L$, it follows that $q_{acc} \in q_0 \cdot (\varphi(¢u) \bullet \varphi(v\$))$ for a certain accepting state $q_{acc}$. Assume that $q \in q_0 \cdot \varphi(¢u)$ for a certain internal state $q$. Since $\mathcal{M}$ is finite, for every string $w \in L$, there exists a positive integer $k$ such that the element $\varphi(w)^k$ is idempotent. Lemma 3 then implies that $q \in q_0 \cdot (\varphi(¢u) \bullet \varphi(w)^k)$ and $q_{acc} \in q \cdot \varphi(v\$)$. Thus, we obtain $uw^kv \in L$.

For the induction step, assume by the induction hypothesis that the lemma holds for $i \geq 1$ and that $q_{acc} \in q_0 \cdot (\varphi(¢u) \bullet \varphi(w^{ik}) \bullet \varphi(v\$))$. Take $q \in q_0 \cdot (\varphi(¢u) \bullet \varphi(w^{ik}))$. By Lemma 3, we obtain $q \in q_0 \cdot (\varphi(¢u) \bullet \varphi(w^{ik}) \bullet \varphi(w)^k)$ because $\varphi(w)^k$ is idempotent. Since $q_{acc} \in q \cdot \varphi(v\$)$ holds, $uw^{(i+1)k}v \in L$ follows. □

To demonstrate the usefulness of Lemma 2, we intend to exhibit two quick applications of the lemma. Firstly, we show the existence of regular languages that cannot be recognized by any 1nrfa-cla.

**Theorem 4.** 1NRFA-CLA $\subsetneq$ REG.

This theorem is obtained directly by studying the following three regular languages: $One = \{w1 : w \in \{0,1\}^*\}$ and $L_{01} = \{0\}^*\{1\}^*$ defined over a binary alphabet $\{0,1\}$, and $Two = \{w2 : w \in \{0,1\}^*\}$ over a ternary alphabet $\{0,1,2\}$.

**Lemma 5.** *$One, Two$, and $L_{01}$ are not in* 1NRFA-CLA.

*Proof.* We will prove only the case of $L_{01}$. Assume that $L_{01} \in$ 1NRFA-CLA. Choose $uv \in L_{01}$. Letting $u = 01$, $v = \lambda$ and $w = 0$, Lemma 2 implies that $010^k \in L_{01}$ for an appropriate number $k \in \mathbb{N}^+$. This contradicts the definition of $L_{01}$.    □

The second application concerns a non-closure property of 1NRFA-CLA.

**Proposition 6.** *The family* 1NRFA-CLA *is not closed under complementation.*

This proposition is proven by constructing a 1nrfa-cla for the language $\{0\}^+$ over a unary alphabet $\{0\}$. Obviously, its complement is finite. It is, however, possible to prove by Lemma 2 that no finite language exists in 1NRFA-CLA. Therefore, the complement of $\{0\}^+$ is not in 1NRFA-CLA; thus, Proposition 6 holds.

## 5    Power of Quantum Merlin

Unlike deterministic Merlin, quantum Merlin can prepare a *superposition* of classical proofs. The main result of this section is the following theorem.

**Theorem 7.**    *1.* 1NRFA-CLA $\subseteq$ QMA(mo-1qfa) $\subseteq$ 1NRFA.
*2.* 1NRFA = QMA(1qfa) = REG.

Theorem 7 follows from Lemmas 8, 9, and 10 given below. Hereafter, we will show those supporting lemmas. Firstly, since mo-1qfa's are 1qfa's, we obtain the following.

**Lemma 8.** QMA(mo-1qfa) $\subseteq$ QMA(1qfa).

It is also possible to directly simulate every 1nrfa (resp., 1nrfa-cla) by an appropriate pair of quantum Merlin and 1qfa (resp., mo-1qfa) verifier.

**Lemma 9.**    *1.* 1NRFA-CLA $\subseteq$ QMA(mo-1qfa).
*2.* 1NRFA $\subseteq$ QMA(1qfa), *or equivalently* REG $\subseteq$ QMA(1qfa).

The next goal is to show that a 1qfa verifier playing with quantum Merlin is no more powerful in language recognition than any 1dfa alone is. More precisely, we want to prove the following key containment.

**Lemma 10.** QMA(1qfa) $\subseteq$ REG.

Before proving Lemma 10, we will show two useful properties. Given any proof $|\phi\rangle$, let $\Psi_0^\phi$ denote $|\phi\rangle|q_0\rangle$ in $\mathcal{H}_p \otimes \mathcal{H}_A$. When Arthur halts, the entire system on input $x$ results in $T^{(\mathfrak{c}x\$)}\Psi_0^\phi$. Let $\mathcal{H}_{p,n} = span\{|w\rangle : w \in \Gamma^n\}$ for any nonnegative integer $n$. Clearly, for any $m \neq n$, $\mathcal{H}_{p,n}$ and $\mathcal{H}_{p,m}$ are orthogonal subspaces of $\mathcal{H}_p$.

**Lemma 11.** *Let $n$, $m$, and $t$ be nonnegative integers. For any triplet $(x, y, z) \in \Sigma^n \times \Sigma^m \times \Sigma^t$ and any quantum states $|\phi\rangle \in \mathcal{H}_{p,n+t}$ and $|\phi'\rangle \in \mathcal{H}_{p,m+t}$, there exist two quantum states $|\tilde{\phi}\rangle \in \mathcal{H}_{p,n}$ and $|\tilde{\phi}'\rangle \in \mathcal{H}_{p,m}$ satisfying $\|T^{(\text{¢}xz)}\Psi_0^\phi - T^{(\text{¢}yz)}\Psi_0^{\phi'}\| \leq \frac{1}{\sqrt{2}}\|T^{(\text{¢}x)}\Psi_0^{\tilde{\phi}} - T^{(\text{¢}y)}\Psi_0^{\tilde{\phi}'}\|$.*

**Lemma 12.** *[4] Let $D = \{v \in \mathcal{V} : \|v\| \leq 1\}$, where $\mathcal{V} = (\mathcal{H}_p \otimes \mathcal{H}_A) \times \mathbb{R} \times \mathbb{R}$ as defined in Section 3. Let $E \subseteq D$. If there exists a constant $\epsilon > 0$ satisfying $\|v - v'\| > \epsilon$ for all pairs $v, v' \in \mathcal{V}$, then $E$ is finite.*

In the following proof of Lemma 10, we intend to show that $\Sigma^*$ is partitioned into finitely many equivalence classes by a given language. This partition technique was previously used for 1qfa's in [4] and 1qfa's with advice in [12]. Here, our technical achievement relies on an application of Lemma 11.

*Proof of Lemma 10.* Let $L \in \text{QMA}(\text{1qfa})$ and, for each $\epsilon \in [0, 1/2)$, let $\mathcal{A}_\epsilon$ be a 1qfa verifier recognizing $L$ with error probability at most $\epsilon$. For any pair $(x, y) \in \Sigma^* \times \Sigma^*$, we define a closeness relation $x \cong_L y$ when $\|T^{(\text{¢}xz\$)}\Psi_0^\phi - T^{(\text{¢}yz\$)}\Psi_0^{\phi'}\| < \epsilon$ holds for any $z \in \Sigma^*$ and any two quantum states $|\phi\rangle \in \mathcal{H}_{|x|+|z|}$ and $|\phi'\rangle \in \mathcal{H}_{|y|+|z|}$. Moreover, we write $x \equiv_L y$ exactly when, for any $z \in \Sigma^*$, $xz \in L$ holds if and only if $yz \in L$ holds. Here, we want to claim that $x \cong_L y$ implies $x \equiv_L y$ for any pair $(x, y)$. This claim can be proven by contradiction using Lemma 11.

Let $S \subseteq \Sigma^*$ be any set and assume that, for each pair $(x, y) \in S^2$, $x \not\cong_L y$ holds. By Lemma 12, $S$ is finite. Let $d$ be the largest size of such $S$. Assume that $|\Sigma^*/\equiv_L| > d$. Let $x_1, \ldots, x_{d+1} \in \Sigma^*$ be strings such that $x_i \not\equiv_L x_j$ for every distinct pair $i, j \in [d+1]$ and let $S = \{x_1, \ldots, x_{d+1}\}$. The previous claim implies that $x_i \not\cong_L x_j$ for every distinct pair $(i, j)$. Hence, the set $S$ must have cardinality at most $d$, a contradiction. Therefore, the number of equivalence classes in $\equiv_L$ is finite. It is known that $L$ is regular if and only if the number of equivalence classes in $\equiv_L$ is finite. From this fact, we conclude that $L$ is regular. $\square$

As remarked in Section 1, we distinguish two types of quantum Merlin. For the time being, we call current quantum Merlin defined in Section 3 *non-active*. Active Merlin, by contrast, produces a pure quantum state, say, $|\phi\rangle$ in his own private workspace, sends only a "portion" of $|\phi\rangle$ to Arthur by retaining the rest, and modifies it at every step when Arthur moves. For clarity, we use the notation active-QMA(mo-1qfa) and active-QMA(1qfa) to emphasize the use of active quantum Merlin. Surprisingly, we can prove that active Merlin is equivalent in computational power to non-active Merlin.

**Proposition 13.** *1.* active-QMA(mo-1qfa) = QMA(mo-1qfa).
*2.* active-QMA(1qfa) = QMA(1qfa).

Proposition 13 relies on the following key lemma.

**Lemma 14.** *Let $\mathcal{A}$ be an mo-1qfa verifier in a QMA proof system with active quantum Merlin. The acceptance and rejection probabilities of $\mathcal{A}$ are independent* *of any change of private workspace data by Merlin during a computation. The same holds even if $\mathcal{A}$ is either a 1qfa verifier or a 2qfa verifier.*

The lemma follows from a fact that, since Merlin's local operators $\{P_i\}_{i \geq 0}$ acting on his own private workspace do not apply to $\mathcal{H}_p \otimes \mathcal{H}_A$, it is possible to swap the order of Merlin's operators $P_i$ and Arthur's operators.

# 6    Proof Verification by 2qfa's

We will study properties of QMA systems when verifiers are 2qfa's. We start with a closure property of QMA(2qfa). In comparison, it is not known whether the family 2QFA of languages recognized by 2qfa's alone is closed under union.

**Proposition 15.** *The family* QMA(2qfa) *is closed under union.*

**Lemma 16.** *Let $t$ be any function from $\mathbb{N}$ to $\mathbb{N}$.*

1. QMA(2qfa, $t$-time) $\subseteq$ QIP(2qfa, $t$-time).
2. *In particular,* QMA$_{\tilde{\mathbb{C}}}$(2qfa, poly-time) $\subseteq$ QIP$_{\tilde{\mathbb{C}}}$(2qfa, poly-time) $\subseteq$ NP.

Although intuitively clear, Lemma 16(1) still requires an argument that (i) no cheating-prover can fool a verifier even in the presence of *entanglement* and (ii) an honest-prover demands the information on the proof-tape head of the verifier to be dumped alongside the messages sent to the prover. Lemma 16(2) follows from [8, Theorem 5.3] and a $\tilde{\mathbb{C}}$-version of Lemma 16(1). Since QIP$_{\tilde{\mathbb{C}}}$(2qfa, poly-time) $\subseteq$ NP [8], it follows from Lemma 16(1) that QMA$_{\tilde{\mathbb{C}}}$(2qfa, poly-time) $\subseteq$ NP.

Let us quickly discuss the power of QMA(2qfa). Consider the following language $DUP = \{ww : w \in \{0,1\}^*\}$, which is known to be non context-free. Now, we claim that $DUP$ is in QMA$_{\mathbb{A}}$(2qfa). This claim obviously leads to a simple separation: QMA$_{\mathbb{A}}$(2qfa) $\not\subseteq$ CFL. To show this claim, it suffices to construct a unidirectional 2qfa verifier $M$ recognizing $DUP$ as follows. On input $w = xy$, $M$ checks by moving its head rightward whether the input is of even length. When reading $\phi$, it splits with equal amplitudes the computation into two paths. In those two paths, we check whether $x = y$ using the given proof that marks the boundary between $x$ and $y$. Moreover, consider the language $L_{YS} = \{a^{m-1}ba^{km} : m, k \in \mathbb{N}^+ \wedge m > 1\}$. This language was shown to be non-stochastic [11]. It is possible to show that $L_{YS}$ is recognized by a certain 2qfa-verifier $\mathbb{A}$-amplitude QMA system. This yields the following conclusion. Let SL$_{\mathbb{R}}$ denote the family of all *stochastic languages* (whose probabilities are all drawn from $\mathbb{R}$).

**Theorem 17.** QMA$_{\mathbb{A}}$(2qfa) $\not\subseteq$ SL$_{\mathbb{R}}$

Let us recall that an input-tape head of our 2qfa verifier moves in all directions but its proof-tape head is limited to moving in one direction. What happens if we further allow the proof-tape head to move *in all directions*? To answer this question, we first modify our original definition of 2qfa verifier by allowing its transition function $\delta$ to be a mapping from $Q \times \check{\Sigma} \times \Gamma \times Q \times D_1 \times \{-1, 0, 1\}$

to $\mathbb{C}$. Let QMA(2qfa, 2-way-proof) be the family of all languages recognized by 2qfa-verifier QMA systems using 2-way proof-tape heads. Clearly, QMA(2qfa) $\subseteq$ QMA(2qfa, 2-way-proof) holds; however, it is not clear that even QIP(2qfa) includes QMA(2qfa, 2-way-proof), because a cheating-prover may potentially fool a verifier when Arthur moves its proof-tape head in the left direction.

Here, we want to argue that QMA(2qfa, 2-way-proof) $\subseteq$ L is unlikely.

**Theorem 18.** *If* $\text{QMA}_\mathbb{A}(2qfa, 2\text{-way-proof}) \subseteq L$, *then* $L = NP$.

Let us prove this theorem. First, we introduce a special language, called *CNF-SAT*, which is a set of suitable encodings of CNF formulas. More precisely, let $\Sigma_4 = \{-, +, 0, \wedge\}$ be our alphabet and define the language *CNF-SAT* over $\Sigma_4$ as the set of all strings of the form $c_1 \wedge c_2 \wedge \cdots \wedge c_m$ with $c_i \in \{-, +, 0\}^k$ for certain indices $k, m \in \mathbb{N}^+$ that satisfy the following. We say that $c_i = c_{i,1}c_{i,2}\cdots c_{i,k} \in \{-, +, 0\}^k$ *represents* a disjunctive clause $C_i$ if $C_i$ has the form $(\bigvee_{j \in S_+(i)} x_j) \vee (\bigvee_{j \in S_-(i)} \overline{x_j})$, where $S_+(i) = \{j \in [1,k]_\mathbb{Z} : c_{i,j} = +\}$, $S_-(i) = \{j \in [1,k]_\mathbb{Z} : c_{i,j} = -\}$. We demand that the Boolean formula $C_1 \wedge C_2 \wedge \cdots \wedge C_m$ represented by $c_1 \wedge c_2 \wedge \cdots \wedge c_m$ is satisfiable. It is known from the arXiv version of [13] that *CNF-SAT* is NP-complete under L-reductions. Theorem 18 follows immediately from Lemma 19, which deals with *CNF-SAT*.

**Lemma 19.** *CNF-SAT* $\in \text{QMA}_\mathbb{A}(2qfa, 2\text{-way-proof})$.

*Proof Sketch.*    Given an input $x \in$ *CNF-SAT*, Merlin first provides Arthur with the information on an assignment to all variables in the CNF formula, say, $C_1 \wedge C_2 \wedge \cdots \wedge C_n$ associated with $x$. Arthur who runs a 2qfa $M = (Q, \Sigma, \{\rlap{\textcent}, \$\}, \delta, q_0, Q_{acc}, Q_{rej})$, where $\Gamma = \{0, 1, \rlap{\textcent}, \$\}$, checks that, for each clause $C_i$ in the given formula, $C_i$ is indeed satisfied with the help of the proof. Moreover, at each time when Arthur finishes checking one clause, he resets the proof-tape head position so that he can start checking the next clause. Since he uses the same assignment given as the proof to check each clause, the target formula must be satisfied. When $x \notin$ *CNF-SAT*, no matter what proof Merlin gives Arthur, Arthur correctly refutes any unsatisfied input.    $\square$

**Theorem 20.** $\text{QMA}_{\tilde{C}}(2qfa, \text{poly-time}, 2\text{-way-proof}) \subseteq \text{NEXP}$.

**Lemma 21.** *Let* $t : \mathbb{N} \to \mathbb{N}$ *be any time-constructible function.* $\text{QMA}_{\tilde{C}}(2qfa, t\text{-time}, 2\text{-way-proof}) \subseteq \text{NTIME}(2^{O(t(n))}t(n)\text{poly}(n, \log t(n)))$.

Theorem 20 follows by choosing any polynomial as $t$ in Lemma 21.

In what follows, we will prove Lemma 21. For any function $t : \mathbb{N} \to \mathbb{N}$, a *t-bounded 2qfa M* is obtained from a 2qfa by requiring the following two conditions: (1) we "cut" all computation paths of $M$ after exactly $t(n)$ steps and (2) we treat any computation path that does not halt within $t(n)$ steps as "non-halting." Let QMA(2qfa, $t$-bounded) be the family of all languages recognized by $t$-bounded 2qfa's.

**Proposition 22.** *Let* $t : \mathbb{N} \to \mathbb{N}$ *be any function.*
QMA(2qfa, 2-way-proof, $t$-time) $\subseteq$ QMA(2qfa, 2-way-proof, $O(t)$-bounded).

Note that, by setting $t$ to be any polynomial, Proposition 22 yields the containment $\text{QMA}_{\tilde{C}}$(2qfa, 2-way-proof, poly-time) $\subseteq$ QMA, where QMA was defined in [5]. Proposition 22 follows from Lemma 23.

**Lemma 23.** *Let* $(M, \mathcal{A})$ *be any 2qfa-verifier QMA system recognizing language* $L$ *in expected running time* $t(n)$ *with error probability at most* $\epsilon$. *For any* $x \in \Sigma^*$, *if we cut the running time of* $\mathcal{A}$ *by* $t(n)/\epsilon$, *then the same system* $(M, \mathcal{A})$ *recognizes* $L$ *with error probability at most* $\epsilon(2 - \epsilon)$.

*Proof Sketch.* By Markov's inequality follows $Pr[\text{number of steps} \geq t(n)/\epsilon] \leq \epsilon$. If we cut all computation paths exactly after $t(n)/\epsilon$ steps, then at least a $1 - \epsilon$ fraction of computation paths end in halting states. Hence, the probability of either accepting or rejecting any string is at least $(1 - \epsilon)^2 = 1 - \epsilon(2 - \epsilon)$. □

Return to the proof of Lemma 21. By [8, Proposition 5.5], Merlin needs a unitary operation whose dimension is at most $|Q||\Gamma|^{t(n)}n$ to generate a proof, where $Q$ is Arthur's set of internal states and $\Gamma$ is a proof alphabet. Similarly to [8, Proposition 5.7], Lemma 21 follows using Proposition 22.

# References

1. Brodsky, A., Pippenger, N.: Characterizations of 1-way quantum finite automata. SIAM J. Comput. 31(5), 1456–1478 (2002)
2. Dwork, C., Stockmeyer, L.: Finite state verifiers I: the power of interaction. J. ACM 39(4), 800–828 (1992)
3. Gruska, J.: Quantum Computing. McGraw-Hill (2000)
4. Kondacs, A., Watrous, J.: On the power of quantum finite state automata. In: Proc. of FOCS 1997, pp. 66–75 (1997)
5. Marriott, C., Watrous, J.: Quantum Arthur-Merlin games. Computational Complexity 14(2), 122–152 (2005)
6. Moore, C., Crutchfield, J.P.: Quantum automata and quantum grammars. Theor. Comput. Sci. 237(1–2), 275–306 (2000)
7. Nishimura, H., Yamakami, T.: An application of quantum finite automata to interactive proof systems (extended abstract). In: Domaratzki, M., Okhotin, A., Salomaa, K., Yu, S. (eds.) CIAA 2004. LNCS, vol. 3317, pp. 225–236. Springer, Heidelberg (2005)
8. Nishimura, H., Yamakami, T.: An application of quantum finite automata to interactive proof systems. J. Comput. System Sci. 75(4), 255–269 (2009)
9. Sakarovitch, J.: Elements of Automata Theory. Cambridge University Press (2000)
10. Yakaryilmaz, A.: Public-qubits versus private-qubits. Tech. Rep. TR12-130, Electronic Colloquium on Computational Complexity (2012)
11. Yakaryilmaz, A., Say, A.C.C.: Unbounded-error quantum computation with small space bounds. Inform. Comput. 279(6), 873–892 (2011)
12. Yamakami, T.: One-way reversible and quantum finite automata with advice. Inf. Comput. (in press, 2014), An extended abstract appeared in: Dediu, A.-H., Martín-Vide, C. (eds.) LATA 2012. LNCS, vol. 7183, pp. 526–537. Springer, Heidelberg (2012)

13. Yamakami, T.: Oracle pushdown automata, nondeterministic reducibilities, and the hierarchy over the family of context-free languages. In: Geffert, V., Preneel, B., Rovan, B., Štuller, J., Tjoa, A.M. (eds.) SOFSEM 2014. LNCS, vol. 8327, pp. 514–525. Springer, Heidelberg (2014), A complete version appeared at arXiv:1303.1717 (2013)
14. Zheng, S., Gruska, J., Qiu, D.: Power of the interactive proof systems with verifiers modeled by semi-quantum two-way finite automata, arXiv:1304.387 (2013)

# Solving 2D-Pattern Matching with Networks of Picture Processors

Henning Bordihn[1], Paolo Bottoni[2],
Anna Labella[2], and Victor Mitrana[3],[*]

[1] Department of Computer Science, University of Potsdam,
August-Bebel-Str. 89, 14482 Potsdam, Germany
henning@cs.uni-potsdam.de
[2] Department of Computer Science, "Sapienza" University of Rome
Via Salaria 113, 00198 Rome, Italy
{bottoni,labella}@di.uniroma1.it
[3] Faculty of Mathematics and Computer Science, University of Bucharest
Str. Academiei 14, 010014, Bucharest, Romania
mitrana@fmi.unibuc.ro

**Abstract.** We propose a solution based on networks of picture processors to the problem of picture pattern matching. The network solving the problem can be informally described as follows: it consists of two subnetworks, one of them extracts simultaneously all subpictures of the same size from the input picture and sends them to the second subnetwork. The second subnetwork checks whether any of the received pictures is identical to the pattern. We present an efficient solution based on networks with evolutionary processors only, for patterns with at most three rows or columns. Afterwards, we present a solution based on networks containing both evolutionary and hiding processors running in $\mathcal{O}(n + m + kl + k)$ computational (processing and communication) steps, where the input picture and the pattern are of size $(n, m)$ and $(k, l)$, respectively.

## 1 Introduction

Picture languages defined by different mechanisms have been studied extensively in the literature. Two-dimensional matrix and array models describing pictures have been proposed in [15,16,19,17]. On the other hand, models defining pictures that are connected arrays, but not necessarily rectangular, have been proposed as early as 70's [14] and a hierarchy of these grammars was considered in [18]. A new model of recognizable picture languages, extending to two dimensions the characterization of the one-dimensional recognizable languages in terms of alphabetic morphisms of local languages, has been introduced in [7]. Similarly to the string case, characterizations of recognizable picture series were proposed, see, e.g. [5,12]. An early survey on automata recognizing rectangular picture languages is [8], a bit more recent one considering different mechanisms defining

---

[*] Supported by the Visiting Professor Programme - "Sapienza" University of Rome and the Alexander von Humboldt Foundation.

A.-H. Dediu et al. (Eds.): TPNC 2014, LNCS 8890, pp. 157–168, 2014.

picture languages, not necessarily rectangular, is [14] and an even more recent and concise one is [6].

This work is a continuation of [4], where networks of evolutionary picture processors acting on rectangular pictures as *acceptors* are considered. The paper [4] is a first attempt to extend the investigation started in [10], where the data is organized in the form of linear strings, and continued in a series of papers (see [9] for a recent survey) to rectangular pictures. In [4], networks of evolutionary picture processors where each node is either a row/column substitution node or a row/column deletion node are considered. The action of each node on the data it contains is precisely defined. For instance, if a node is a row substitution node, then it can substitute a letter by another letter in either the top row only, the bottom row only, or an arbitrary row. Moreover, if there are more occurrences of the letter to be substituted in the row on which the substitution rule acts, then each such occurrence is substituted in different copies of that picture. An implicit assumption is that arbitrarily many copies of every picture are available. A similar informal explanation concerns the column substitution and deletion nodes. Local data is then transmitted over the network following a given protocol. Only data which can pass a filtering process can be communicated. This filtering process is regulated by input and output filters (defined by some very simple context conditions) associated with each node. All the nodes simultaneously send their data to, and receive data from, the nodes they are connected to. In [4] we showed that these networks can accept the complement of any local language, as well as languages that are not recognizable.

We consider here the pattern matching problem, which is largely motivated by different aspects in low-level image processing [13], and try to solve it in a parallel and distributed way with networks of picture processors. The network solving the problem can be informally described as follows: it consists of two subnetworks, one of them extracts simultaneously all subpictures of the same size from the input picture and sends them to the second subnetwork. In its turn, the second subnetwork consists of two subnetworks; one of them checks whether any of the received pictures is identical to the pattern, while the other one halts the computation if none of the received pictures is identical to the pattern. If the pattern is of size $(k, l)$, with $1 \leq k \leq 3$, and $l \geq 1$, we present an efficient solution running in $\mathcal{O}(n + m + l)$ computational (processing and communication) steps, provided that the input picture is of size $(n, m)$. Moreover, this solution can be extended at no further cost w.r.t. the number of computational steps to any finite set of patterns all of them of the same size.

We introduce a new operation and its inverse that can convert a visible row/column into an invisible one and vice versa. The two operations which seem to be relevant with respect to picture processing (see, e.g. "zoom-in", "zoom-out") are called *mask* and *unmask*, respectively. We show how this variant of networks of picture processors is able to solve efficiently (in $\mathcal{O}(n + m + kl + k)$ computational steps) the problem of pattern matching of an arbitrary pattern of size $(k, l)$ in a given rectangular picture of size $(n, m)$. Again, the solution can be extended at no further cost w.r.t. the number of computational steps to any finite set of patterns all of them of the same size.

## 2    Basic Definitions

The basic terminology and notations concerning two-dimensional languages are taken from [6]. The set of natural numbers from 1 to $n$ is denoted by $[n]$. The set of all finite subsets of a set $A$ is denoted by $2^A$. The cardinality of a finite set $A$ is denoted by $card(A)$. Let $V$ be an alphabet, $V^*$ the set of one-dimensional strings over $V$ and $\varepsilon$ the empty string. A *picture* (or a two-dimensional string) over the alphabet $V$ is a two-dimensional array of elements from $V$. We denote the set of all pictures over the alphabet $V$ by $V_*^*$, while the empty picture will be still denoted by $\varepsilon$. A two-dimensional language over $V$ is a subset of $V_*^*$.

Let $\pi$ be a picture in $V_*^*$; we denote the number of rows and the number of columns of $\pi$ by $\overline{\pi}$ and $|\pi|$, respectively. The pair $(\overline{\pi}, |\pi|)$ is called *the size* of the picture $\pi$. The size of the empty picture $\varepsilon$ is obviously $(n, m)$ with $nm = 0$. The set of all pictures of size $(m, n)$ over the alphabet $V$, where $m, n \geq 1$, is denoted by $V_m^n$. The symbol placed at the intersection of the $i$th row with the $j$th column of the picture $\pi$, is denoted by $\pi(i, j)$.

Let $\pi$ be a picture of size $(m, n)$ over $V$; for any $1 \leq i \leq k \leq m$ and $1 \leq j \leq l \leq n$ we denote by $^{[i,j]}\pi_{[k,l]}$ the *subpicture* of $\pi$ having its left-hand upper corner in $\pi(i, j)$ and right-hand lower corner in $\pi(k, l)$ (it starts and ends at $(i, j)$ and $(k, l)$ in $\pi$, respectively). For any values $i > k$ or $j > l$, we set $^{[i,j]}\pi_{[k,l]} = \varepsilon$. Furthermore, we simply write $\pi$ instead of $^{[1,1]}\pi_{[m,n]}$.

For any alphabet $V$ and a symbol $a \in V$, we denote by $\text{æ}$ the *invisible* copy of $a$; furthermore, we set $\text{¥} := \{\text{æ} \mid a \in V\}$. We say that a picture $\pi \in (V \cup \text{¥})_m^n$ is *well defined* if there exists $1 \leq i \leq k \leq m$ and $1 \leq j \leq l \leq n$ such that all elements of $^{[i,j]}\pi_{[k,l]}$ are from $V$ and all the other elements of $\pi$ are from $\text{¥}$. In this case, we say that $^{[i,j]}\pi_{[k,l]}$ is the *maximal visible subpicture* of $\pi$. A rather intuitive way to understand a well defined picture $\pi$ is to consider that some rows and/or columns of $\pi$ are hidden but not deleted. Note that any picture over $V$ is a well defined picture. For the rest of this paper, we deal with well defined pictures only. The minimal alphabet containing all visible symbols appearing in a picture $\pi$ is denoted by $alph(\pi)$.

Let $V$ be an alphabet; a rule of the form $a \to b$, with $a, b \in V \cup \{\varepsilon\}$ is called an *evolutionary rule*. We say that a rule $a \to b$ is: a) a *substitution rule* if both $a$ and $b$ are not $\varepsilon$; b) a *deletion rule* if $a \neq \varepsilon$, $b = \varepsilon$; c) an *insertion rule* if $a = \varepsilon$, $b \neq \varepsilon$. In this paper we shall ignore insertion rules because we want to process every given picture in a space bounded by the size of that picture. We denote the sets of substitutions and deletions by $Sub_V = \{a \to b \mid a, b \in V\}$ and $Del_V = \{a \to \varepsilon \mid a \in V\}$, respectively. Given a rule $\sigma$ as above and a picture $\pi \in (V \cup \text{¥})_m^n$, we define the following *actions* of $\sigma$ on $\pi$ following [4].

If $\sigma \equiv a \to b \in Sub_V$, then $\sigma^{\leftarrow}(\pi)$ is the set of all pictures $\pi'$ such that the following conditions are satisfied:

(1.) There exist $1 \leq u \leq v \leq m$ and $1 \leq s \leq t \leq n$ such that $^{[u,s]}\pi_{[v,t]}$ is the maximal visible subpicture of $\pi$,

(2.a.) There exists $u \leq i \leq v$ such that $\pi(i,s) = a$; then $\pi'(i,s) = b$, and $\pi'(j,l) = \pi(j,l)$ for all $(j,l) \in ([m] \times [n]) \setminus \{(i,s)\}$.

(2.b.) If the leftmostcolumn of $^{[u,s]}\pi_{[v,t]}$ does not contain any occurrence of $a$, then $\sigma^{\leftarrow}(\pi) = \{\pi\}$.

Informally, $\sigma^{\leftarrow}(\pi)$ is the set of all pictures that can be obtained from $\pi$ by replacing an occurrence of $a$ by $b$ in the leftmost column of the maximal visible subpicture of $\pi$. Note that $\sigma$ is applied to all occurrences of the letter $a$ in the leftmost column of the maximal visible subpicture of $\pi$ in different copies of the picture $\pi$. We say that the rule $\sigma$ is applied to the leftmost column of the maximal visible subpicture of $\pi$.

In an analogous way, we define $\sigma^{\rightarrow}(\pi)$, $\sigma^{\uparrow}(\pi)$, $\sigma^{\downarrow}(\pi)$, $\sigma^{+}(\pi)$, as the set of all pictures obtained by applying $\sigma$ to the rightmost column, to the first row, to the last row, and to any column/row of the maximal visible subpicture of $\pi$.

If $\sigma \equiv a \rightarrow \varepsilon \in Del_V$, then $\sigma^{\leftarrow}(\pi)$ is the picture obtained from $\pi$ by deleting the $i^{\text{th}}$ column of $\pi$ provided that the maximal visible subpicture of $\pi$ starts at the position $(i,j)$ in $\pi$, for some $j$, and the $i^{\text{th}}$ column of $\pi$ contains an occurrence of $a$. If the leftmost column of the maximal visible subpicture of $\pi$ does not contain any occurrence of $a$, then $\sigma^{\leftarrow}(\pi) = \pi$. We say that the deletion rule $\sigma$ is applied to the leftmost column of the maximal visible subpicture of $\pi$.

Analogously, $\sigma^{\rightarrow}(\pi)$, $\sigma^{\uparrow}(\pi)$, and $\sigma^{\downarrow}(\pi)$ is the picture obtained from $\pi$ by applying $\sigma$ to the rightmost column, to the first row, and to the last row of the maximal visible subpicture of $\pi$, respectively. Furthermore, $\sigma^{|}(\pi)$ ($\sigma^{-}(\pi)$) is the set of pictures obtained from $\pi$ by deleting an arbitrary column (row) containing an occurrence of $a$ from $\pi$. If more than one column (row) of $\pi$ contains $a$, then for each such column (row), there is a copy of $\pi$ in $\sigma^{|}(\pi)$ ($\sigma^{-}(\pi)$) having this column (row) deleted. If $\pi$ does not contain any occurrence of $a$, then $\sigma^{|}(\pi) = \{\pi\}$ ($\sigma^{-}(\pi) = \{\pi\}$).

For every rule $\sigma$, symbol $\alpha \in \{\leftarrow, \rightarrow, \uparrow, \downarrow, |, -, +\}$, and $L \subseteq (V \cup \not{V})^{*}_{*}$, we define the $\alpha$-action of $\sigma$ on $L$ by $\sigma^{\alpha}(L) = \bigcup_{\pi \in L} \sigma^{\alpha}(\pi)$. Given a finite set of rules $M$, we define the $\alpha$-action of $M$ on the picture $\pi$ and the language $L$ by:

$$M^{\alpha}(\pi) = \bigcup_{\sigma \in M} \sigma^{\alpha}(\pi) \quad \text{and} \quad M^{\alpha}(L) = \bigcup_{\pi \in L} M^{\alpha}(\pi),$$

respectively. In what follows, we shall refer to the rewriting operations defined above as *evolutionary picture operations* since they may be viewed as the 2-dimensional linguistic formulations of local gene mutations.

We now define a new operation on pictures and its inverse, namely *mask* and *unmask*. Let $\pi$ be a picture of size $(m,n)$ over $V \cup \not{V}$ and $a \in V$.

– $mask^{\leftarrow}(\pi)$ returns the picture obtained from $\pi$ by transforming all visible symbols from the leftmost column of the maximal visible subpicture of $\pi$ into their invisible copies. Analogously, one defines the mappings $mask^{\rightarrow}$, $mask^{\uparrow}$, and $mask^{\downarrow}$.

– $unmask^{\leftarrow}(\pi)$ returns the picture obtained from $\pi$ as follows. If $^{[i,j]}\pi_{[k,l]}$ is the maximal visible subpicture of $\pi$, then all invisible symbols $\pi(s, j - 1)$, $i \leq s \leq k$, become visible. If $j = 1$, then $unmask^{\leftarrow}(\pi) = \pi$. Analogously, one defines the mappings $unmask^{\rightarrow}$, $unmask^{\uparrow}$, and $unmask^{\downarrow}$.

For every $\alpha \in \{\leftarrow, \rightarrow, \uparrow, \downarrow\}$ and $L \subseteq (V \cup \yen)^*_*$, we define $mask^{\alpha}(L) = \{mask^{\alpha}(\pi) \mid \pi \in L\}$. Analogously, $unmask^{\alpha}(L) = \{unmask^{\alpha}(\pi) \mid \pi \in L\}$.

For two disjoint subsets $P$ and $F$ of an alphabet $V$ and a picture $\pi$ over $V$, we consider the following two predicates which we will later use to define two types of filters:
$$rc_s(\pi; P, F) \equiv P \subseteq alph(\pi) \wedge F \cap alph(\pi) = \emptyset$$
$$rc_w(\pi; P, F) \equiv alph(\pi) \cap P \neq \emptyset \wedge F \cap alph(\pi) = \emptyset.$$
The construction of these predicates is based on *context conditions* defined by the two sets $P$ (*permitting contexts/symbols*) and $F$ (*forbidding contexts/symbols*). Informally, both conditions require that no forbidding symbol is present in $\pi$; furthermore the first condition requires all permitting symbols to appear in $\pi$, while the second one requires that at least one permitting symbol appears in $\pi$.

For every picture language $L \subseteq V^*_*$ and $\beta \in \{s, w\}$, we define:
$$rc_{\beta}(L, P, F) = \{\pi \in L \mid rc_{\beta}(\pi; P, F) = \mathtt{true}\}.$$
An *evolutionary picture processor* over $V \cup \yen$ is a 5-tuple $(M, PI, FI, PO, FO)$, where:

– Either $M \subseteq Sub_V$ or $M \subseteq Del_V$. The set $M$ represents the set of evolutionary rules of the processor. As one can see, a processor is "specialized" into one type of evolutionary operation, only.

– $PI, FI \subseteq V$ are the *input* sets of permitting/forbidding symbols (contexts) of the processor, while $PO, FO \subseteq V$ are the *output* sets of permitting/forbidding symbols of the processor (with $PI \cap FI = \emptyset$ and $PO \cap FO = \emptyset$).

A *hiding picture processor* over $V \cup \yen$ is a 5-tuple $(M, PI, FI, PO, FO)$, where $M$ is either *mask* or *unmask*, while the other parameters are identical to those defined above for evolutionary processors.

An *accepting network of picture processors* (ANPP) is a 9-tuple
$$\Gamma = (V, U, G, N, \alpha, \beta, \underline{In}, \underline{Halt}, \underline{Accept}),$$
where:

– $V$ and $U$ are the input and network alphabet, respectively, $V \subseteq U$.
– $G = (X_G, E_G)$ is an undirected graph without loops with the set of vertices $X_G$ and the set of edges $E_G$. $G$ is called the *underlying graph* of the network. Although in network theory, several types of graphs are common like *complete, rings, stars, grids*, we focus here on complete underlying graphs (every two vertices are connected by an edge), so that we can replace the graph $G$ by the set of its nodes.
– $N$ is a mapping which associates with each node $x \in X_G$ the picture processor $N(x) = (M_x, PI_x, FI_x, PO_x, FO_x)$.
– $\alpha : X_G \longrightarrow \{\leftarrow, \rightarrow, \uparrow, \downarrow, |, -, +\}$; $\alpha(x)$ gives the action mode of the rules of node $x$ on the pictures existing in that node.
– $\beta : X_G \longrightarrow \{s, w\}$ defines the type of the *input/output filters* of a node. More precisely, for every node, $x \in X_G$, the following filters are defined:

– input filter: $\rho_x(\cdot) = rc_{\beta(x)}(\cdot; PI_x, FI_x)$,
– output filter: $\tau_x(\cdot) = rc_{\beta(x)}(\cdot; PO_x, FO_x)$.

That is, $\rho_x(\pi)$ (resp. $\tau_x(\pi)$) indicates whether or not the picture $\pi$ can pass the input (resp. output) filter of $x$. More generally, $\rho_x(L)$ (resp. $\tau_x(L)$) is the set of pictures of $L$ that can pass the input (resp. output) filter of $x$.

– $\underline{In}$, $\underline{Halt}$, $\underline{Accept} \in X_G$ are the *input* node, the *halting* node, and the *accepting* node of $\Gamma$, respectively. Note that it is not obligatory the three nodes be different from one another.

We say that $card(X_G)$ is the size of $\Gamma$. A *configuration* of an ANPP $\Gamma$ as above is a mapping $C : X_G \longrightarrow 2^{U_*^*}$ which associates a finite set of pictures with every node of the graph. A configuration may be understood as the sets of pictures which are present in any node at a given moment. Given a picture $\pi \in V_*^*$, the initial configuration of $\Gamma$ on $\pi$ is defined by $C_0^{(\pi)}(\underline{In}) = \{\pi\}$ and $C_0^{(\pi)}(x) = \emptyset$ for all $x \in X_G - \{\underline{In}\}$.

A configuration can change via either a *processing step* or a *communication step*. When changing via a processing step, each component $C(x)$ of the configuration $C$ is changed in accordance with the set of rules $M_x$ associated with the node $x$ and the way of applying these rules, namely $\alpha(x)$. Formally, we say that the configuration $C'$ is obtained in *one processing step* from the configuration $C$, written as $C \Longrightarrow C'$, iff $C'(x) = M_x^{\alpha(x)}(C(x))$ for all $x \in X_G$.

When changing via a communication step, each node processor $x \in X_G$ sends one copy of each picture it has, which is able to pass the output filter of $x$, to all the node processors connected to $x$ and receives all the pictures sent by any node processor connected with $x$ provided that they can pass its input filter. Formally, we say that the configuration $C'$ is obtained in *one communication step* from configuration $C$, written as $C \vdash C'$, iff

$$C'(x) = (C(x) \setminus \tau_x(C(x))) \cup \bigcup_{\{x,y\} \in E_G} (\tau_y(C(y)) \cap \rho_x(C(y))) \text{ for all } x \in X_G.$$

Note that pictures that cannot pass the output filter of a node remain in that node and can be further modified in the subsequent evolutionary steps, while pictures that can pass the output filter of a node are expelled. Further, all the expelled pictures that cannot pass the input filter of any node are lost.

Let $\Gamma$ be an ANPP, the computation of $\Gamma$ on an input picture $\pi \in V_*^*$ is a sequence of configurations $C_0^{(\pi)}, C_1^{(\pi)}, C_2^{(\pi)}, \ldots$, where $C_0^{(\pi)}$ is the initial configuration of $\Gamma$ on $\pi$, $C_{2i}^{(\pi)} \Longrightarrow C_{2i+1}^{(\pi)}$ and $C_{2i+1}^{(\pi)} \vdash C_{2i+2}^{(\pi)}$, for all $i \geq 0$. Note that configurations are changed by alternative steps. By the previous definitions, each configuration $C_i^{(\pi)}$ is uniquely determined by $C_{i-1}^{(\pi)}$. A computation as above *halts* if there exists a configuration such that the sets of pictures existing in the halting node is non-empty. As we consider here ANPPs as problem solvers, for the rest of this paper we only deal with ANPPs that halt on every input. The *picture language decided* by $\Gamma$ is

$L(\Gamma) = \{\pi \in V_*^* \mid$ the computation of $\Gamma$ on $\pi$ halts with a non-empty accepting node$\}$.

An ANPP without hiding picture processors is called accepting network of evolutionary picture processors (ANEPP) in [4]. The computational power of ANEPPs has been investigated in [4]; we recall the following results, where the class of recognizable and local languages, respectively, have been defined in [7].

**Theorem 1.**
1. *There exist non-recognizable languages which can be accepted by ANEPPs.*
2. *The complement of every local language can be accepted by an ANEPP.*

# 3 Solving Picture Matching With ANPPs

A natural problem is to find a pattern (a fixed picture) in a given picture. This problem is widely known as the two-dimensional pattern matching problem and is largely motivated by different aspects in low-level image processing [13]. The more general problem of picture matching (it is not obligatory for the picture to be a two-dimensional array) is widely known in Pattern Recognition field and is connected with Image Analysis and Artificial Vision [11,20].

We discuss a solution to the problem of picture pattern matching based on the networks defined in the previous section. For the sake of a better understanding, we discuss first a solution based on ANEPP. A key step in our solution is to construct a network able to decide the singleton language formed by a given picture. If the given picture $\pi$ is of size $(k, n)$ or $(n, k)$ for any $1 \leq k \leq 3$ and $n \geq 1$, then an ANEPP can decide the language $\{\pi\}$.

**Theorem 2.** *Let $\pi$ be a picture of size $(k, n)$ for some $1 \leq k \leq 3$ and $n \geq 1$. The language $\{\pi\}$ can be decided by an ANEPP.*

*Proof.* Actually, we only prove the most difficult case, namely $k = 3$, the proofs of the other cases that can be easily deduced from this one are left to the reader. We construct the ANEPP $\Gamma$ deciding $\{\pi\}$ as follows. Let $V$ be the alphabet of $\pi$; the working alphabet of $\Gamma$ is:
$$U = V \cup \{a^{(i)}, \overline{a(i)}, \overline{a_{(i)}} \mid a \in V, 1 \leq i \leq n\} \cup \{[a, i] \mid a \in V, 1 \leq i \leq 4n\} \cup V'$$
$$V' = \{a' \mid a \in V\}.$$
The nodes of $\Gamma$ are distributed in four groups for a better understanding of their role.

Group 1.

$$\underline{In} : \begin{cases} M = \{\pi(1,1) \rightarrow \overline{\pi(1,1)^{(1)}}\}, \\ PI = V, FI = U \setminus V, \\ PO = \{\overline{\pi(1,1)^{(1)}}\}, FO = \emptyset, \\ \alpha =\uparrow, \ \beta = w. \end{cases}$$

Group 2.

$$x_{(i)} : \begin{cases} M = \{\pi(3,i) \rightarrow \overline{\pi(3,i)_{(i)}}\}, \\ PI = \{\overline{\pi(1,i)^{(i)}}, \overline{\pi(1,i+1)^{(i+1)}}\}, \\ FI = U \setminus (V \cup \{\overline{\pi(1,i)^{(i)}}, \overline{\pi(1,i+1)^{(i+1)}}\}), \\ PO = \{\overline{\pi(3,i)_{(i)}}\}, FO = \emptyset, \\ \alpha =\downarrow, \ \beta = s, \\ 1 \leq i \leq n-1 \end{cases}$$

$$x^{(i)} : \begin{cases} M = \{\pi(1,i) \to \overline{\pi(1,i)^{(i)}}\}, \\ PI = \{\overline{\pi(1,i-1)^{(i-1)}}\}, \\ FI = U \setminus (V \cup \{\overline{\pi(1,i-1)^{(i-1)}}\}), \\ PO = \{\overline{\pi(1,i)^{(i)}}\}, FO = \emptyset, \\ \alpha = \uparrow, \ \beta = s, \\ 2 \le i \le n \end{cases}$$

$$x(i) : \begin{cases} M = \{\pi(2,i) \to \overline{\pi(2,i)(i)}\}, \\ PI = \{\overline{\pi(1,i)^{(i)}}, \overline{\pi(3,i)_{(i)}}\}, \\ FI = \emptyset, \\ PO = \{\overline{\pi(2,i)(i)}\}, \\ FO = \emptyset, \\ \alpha = \leftarrow, \ \beta = s, \\ 1 \le i \le n \end{cases}$$

$$x_{del}^{(i)} : \begin{cases} M = \{\overline{\pi(1,i)^{(i)}} \to \varepsilon\}, \\ PI = \{\overline{\pi(2,i)(i)}\}, \\ FI = \emptyset, \\ PO = \emptyset, \\ FO = \{\overline{a^{(i)}}, \overline{a_{(i)}}, \overline{a(i)} \mid a \in V\}, \\ \alpha = \leftarrow, \ \beta = s, \\ 1 \le i \le n-1 \end{cases}$$

$$x_{(n)} : \begin{cases} M = \{\pi(3,n) \to \overline{\pi(3,n)_{(n)}}\}, \\ PI = \{\overline{\pi(1,n)^{(n)}}\}, \\ FI = U \setminus (V \cup \{\overline{\pi(1,n)^{(n)}}\}), \\ PO = \{\overline{\pi(3,n)_{(n)}}\}, \\ FO = \emptyset, \\ \alpha = \downarrow, \ \beta = s. \end{cases}$$

Group 3.

| Node | $M$ | $PI$ | $FI$ | $PO$ | $FO$ | $\alpha$ | $\beta$ |
|------|-----|------|------|------|------|----------|---------|
| $x_{err1}$ | $\{[a,i] \to [a,i+1] \mid$ $a \in V, 1 \le i \le 4n-1\}$ | $\{[a,1] \mid$ $a \in V\}$ | $\emptyset$ | $\{[a,4n]$ $\mid a \in V\}$ | $\emptyset$ | $+$ | $w$ |
| $x_{err2}$ | $\{[a,4n] \to a' \mid a \in V\} \cup$ $\{a \to a' \mid a \in V\}$ | $\{[a,4n]$ $\mid a \in V\}$ | $V'$ | $U$ | $\{[a,4n] \mid$ $a \in V\}$ | $+$ | $w$ |
| $x_{err}^{del1}$ | $\{a \to \varepsilon \mid a \in V\}$ | $V$ | $\{[a,4n]$ $\mid a \in V\}$ | $U$ | $\emptyset$ | $\leftarrow$ | $w$ |
| $x_{err}^{del2}$ | $\{a \to \varepsilon \mid a \in V\}$ | $V$ | $\{[a,4n]$ $\mid a \in V\}$ | $U$ | $\emptyset$ | $\leftarrow$ | $w$ |

The halting and the accepting node, which are grouped together, are defined respectively by

Group 4.

$$\underline{Halt} : \begin{cases} M = \emptyset, \\ PI = U \setminus V, \\ FI = V, \\ PO = \emptyset, \\ FO = \emptyset, \\ \alpha = *, \ \beta = s, \end{cases}$$

$$\underline{Accept} : \begin{cases} M = \{\overline{\pi(1,n)^{(n)}} \to \overline{\pi(1,n)^{(n)}}\}, \\ PI = \{\overline{\pi(1,n)^{(n)}}, \overline{\pi(2,n)(n)}, \overline{\pi(3,n)_{(n)}}\}, \\ FI = V \setminus \{\overline{\pi(1,n)^{(n)}}, \overline{\pi(2,n)(n)}, \overline{\pi(3,n)_{(n)}}\}, \\ PO = \emptyset, \\ FO = \{\overline{\pi(1,n)^{(n)}}, \overline{\pi(2,n)(n)}, \overline{\pi(3,n)_{(n)}}\}, \\ \alpha = *, \ \beta = s, \end{cases}$$

It is easy to note that the nodes from Group 2 and those from Group 3 will never exchange pictures with each other. We analyze the computation of this network on an input picture $\mu$ of size $(k,m)$ for some $k, m \ge 1$. In the input node $\underline{In}$, the following pictures are simultaneously produced: some pictures with $\pi(1,1)^{(1)}$ on the first row, provided that $\pi(1,1)$ appears in the first row of $\mu$, and several other pictures (at least one) all of them having exactly one symbol $[a,1]$ for some $a \in V$. We first assume that at least one picture with $\overline{\pi(1,1)^{(1)}}$ on its first row has been produced in $\underline{In}$ and follow the rest of the computation on such a picture. For simplicity we consider the case $k = 3$ and $m = n$. All the pictures with $\overline{\pi(1,1)^{(1)}}$ on the first row which go out from $\underline{In}$ can be received only by either $x^{(2)}$, if $n \ge 2$, or $x_{(n)}$, if $n = 1$. We assume $n \ge 2$ and continue the computation in $x^{(2)}$. Here an occurrence of $\pi(1,2)$ on the first row of all pictures is replaced by $\overline{\pi(1,2)}^{(2)}$. All pictures where an occurrence of $\pi(1,2)$ has been replaced by $\overline{\pi(1,2)}^{(2)}$ can leave $x^{(2)}$ and enter $x_{(1)}$ where an occurrence of $\pi(3,1)$ on the last row is replaced by $\overline{\pi(3,1)}_{(1)}$. Now all pictures arrive in $x(1)$ where an occurrence of $\pi(2,1)$ on the leftmost column is replaced by $\overline{\pi(2,1)(1)}$. Note that if a picture does not have an occurrence of the symbol that is to be replaced in any of the nodes $x^{(2)}$, $x_{(1)}$, and $x(1)$, then it remains forever in that node.

Pictures going out from $x(1)$ can enter $x_{del}^{(1)}$ only, where the leftmost column is deleted provided that $\overline{\pi(1,1)}^{(1)}$ is situated on that column. The second condition to continue the computation is that $\overline{\pi(3,1)}_{(1)}$ is also situated on the column

$$\pi(1,1)$$
$$\ldots\ldots$$

which is to be deleted in $x_{del}^{(1)}$. Therefore, the first column of $\mu$ must be $\pi(2,1)$.

$$\ldots\ldots$$
$$\pi(3,1)$$

Now the process described above resumes for all pictures going out from $x_{del}^{(1)}$, as all these pictures contain $\overline{\pi(1,2)}^{(2)}$ on their first row. Inductively, for every $1 \leq i \leq n-2$ every picture that has just gone out from $x_{del}^{(i)}$ must contain $\overline{\pi(1,i+1)}^{(i+1)}$ on its first row. Further on, it must follow the following itinerary through the network: $x^{(i+2)}$, $x_{(i+1)}$, $x(i+1)$, $x_{del}^{(i+1)}$.

We now analyze the case when the symbol on the first row of a picture going out from $x_{del}^{(n-1)}$ is $\overline{\pi(1,n)}^{(n)}$. This picture enters $x_{(n)}$ only, where an occurrence of $\pi(3,n)$ in the last row is replaced by $\overline{\pi(3,n)}_{(n)}$ and then enters $x(n)$ where an occurrence of $\pi(2,n)$ in the first column is replaced by $\overline{\pi(2,n)(n)}$. Now, if the

$$\pi(1,n)^{(n)}$$
picture is $\pi(2,n)(n)$, then it enters simultaneously *Halt* and *Accept*, otherwise
$$\pi(3,n)_{(n)}$$

it is lost. By these explanations we infer the followings:

– If $\mu$ is of size $(3,n)$, then both nodes *Halt* and *Accept* become non-empty after $4n - 1$ processing steps if and only if $\mu = \pi$.
– If $m < n$, then the computation on $\mu$ will be eventually blocked after at most $m - 1$ column deletions.
– If $m > n$, then the computation on $\mu$ will be eventually blocked after at most $n - 1$ column deletions.
– If $k < 3$, then the computation on $\mu$ is blocked after the first column deletion.
– If $k > 3$, then the computation on $\mu$ will be eventually blocked after at most $n - 1$ column deletions.

We now analyze the computation on a picture containing a symbol $[a, 1]$ which goes out from *In*. Such a picture enters $x_{err1}$, where $[a, 1]$ is replaced successively by $[a, 2]$, $[a, 3]$, $\ldots$, $[a, 4n]$. Hence, after $4n - 1$ processing steps all pictures in $x_{err1}$ contain a symbol $[a, 4n]$, for some $a \in V$. They can leave now $x_{err1}$ and enter $x_{err2}$ only. A picture in $x_{err2}$ can be transformed in two ways: a symbol from $V$ is replaced by its primed copy or $[a, 4n]$ is replaced by $a'$. In the former case, the picture cannot leave $x_{err2}$, while in the later, the picture leaves $x_{err2}$ and one copy enters $x^{del1}$ and another enters $x^{del2}$. In each of these nodes, the leftmost column is deleted provided that it contains a symbol from $V$. Now a "ping-pong" process starts between the two nodes $x^{del1}$ and $x^{del2}$. This process continues until either the picture becomes empty or the leftmost column does not contain any symbol from $V$. If the current picture contains symbols from $V'$ only, it enters $\underline{Halt}$ and the computation halts. By these explanations, we infer that $\underline{Halt}$ will always receive a picture from the nodes in Group 3 but not earlier than $4n$ processing steps.

In conclusion, the computation on $\mu$ always halts. It halts after either $4n - 1$ processing steps, which means that $\mu = \pi$, or $4n - 1 + k' + n' - 1 > 4n - 1$ processing steps, provided that the input picture is of size $(k', n')$, hence $\mu \neq \pi$. □

We give now a solution to the picture matching based on ANEPP, provided that the pattern is of size $(k, n)$ or $(n, k)$ for any $1 \leq k \leq 3$ and $n \geq 1$.

**Theorem 3.** *Let $\pi$ be a picture of size $(k, l)$ for some $1 \leq k \leq 3$ and $l \geq 1$. The language $\{\theta \mid \pi$ is a subpicture of $\theta\}$ can be decided by an ANEPP.*

*Proof.* We give only an informal description of the construction which is based on a pretty simple idea. The network defined in the proof of Theorem 2 will be used as a subnetwork as follows. The node $\underline{In}$ of that network is renamed $x_I$ all the other nodes remaining unchanged. The network we intend to construct contains nine nodes more:
– $\underline{In}$, which is a substitution node where a symbol is replaced by itself everywhere in the picture.
– two identical nodes deleting the leftmost column.
– two identical nodes deleting the rightmost column.
– two identical nodes deleting the uppermost row.
– two identical nodes deleting the undermost row.
All these nodes can receive pictures containing original symbols only such that as soon as a picture entered one node from any of the Groups 1,2,3, it cannot further returns to these nodes. As one can see, these new 9 nodes cut from the input picture arbitrary subpictures. Clearly, all subpictures of the same size are produced simultaneously. All subpictures of the same size received by the subnetwork are matched against the pattern $\pi$ in parallel. A short discussion is in order here. Assume that an input picture is of size $(m, n)$; all pictures of the same size $(k', l')$ will be sent to the subnetwork after exactly $(m - k') + (n - l') + 1$ processing steps. If at least one of these subpictures is identical to $\pi$, both halting and accepting node will eventually be non-empty after $m - k + n - l + 4l$ processing steps. In this case, the input picture is accepted. If the halting node is empty after $m - k + n - l + 4l$, it will definitely become non-empty after $m + n + 4l - 1$ processing steps. As $m + n + 4l - 1 > m - k + n - l + 4l$, the input picture is rejected. □

Note that the network constructed in the previous proof (nodes, rules, filters, symbols) does not depend on the input picture but on the pattern only.

Various algorithms exist for the exact two-dimensional matching problem. The fastest algorithms for finding a rectangular picture pattern of size $(k, l)$ in a given picture of size $(n, m)$ run in $\mathcal{O}(n \times m + k \times l)$ time, see, e.g., [3,21]. It is rather easy to note that an ANEPP which decides whether a pattern of size $(k, l)$, $1 \leq k \leq 3, l \geq 1$, appears in a given picture of size $(n, m)$ does this in $\mathcal{O}(n+m+l)$ computational (processing and communication) steps. On the other hand, the space complexity of the algorithm proposed in [21] is $\mathcal{O}(n \times m + k \times l)$, while in our case the number of pictures moving through the network is exponential. We recall that some biological phenomena are sources of inspiration for our model. In this context, it is considered to be biologically feasible to have sufficiently many identical copies of a molecule. By techniques of genetic engineering, in a linear number of laboratory operations one can get an exponential number of identical 2-dimensional molecules [1,2].

It is worth mentioning that the construction described above can be easily extended to an ANEPP able to detect, in the same number of computational steps, any pattern from a finite sets of pictures of the same size. It suffices to construct an independent subnetwork for each pattern.

**Theorem 4.** *Given a finite set $F$ of patterns of size $(k, l)$ and $(l, k)$ for all $1 \leq k \leq 3$ and $l \geq 1$, the pattern matching problem with patterns from $F$ can be solved by ANEPPs in $\mathcal{O}(n+m+l)$ computational (processing and communication) steps.*

However, this approach is not suitable for detecting patterns of a different size that those considered above. In the sequel, we show how the picture pattern matching can be completely solved with ANPP, that is with networks having both types of nodes: evolutionary processors and hiding processors. As the idea is the same, it suffices to construct an ANPP able to decide the singleton language formed by a given picture.

**Theorem 5.** *Let $\pi$ be a picture of size $(k, l)$, for some $k, l \geq 1$ over an alphabet $V$. The language $\{\pi\}$ can be decided by an ANPP.*

The idea of the proof is the same as that from the proof of Theorem 2, namely it consists in two disjoint subnetworks, one of them checking whether the input picture is identical to $\pi$, and the other one making a sufficiently long computation which ends in the halting node but allows the first network to complete its computation. The complete proof is left to the reader.

We are now able to give the complete solution based on ANPPs to the problem of picture matching:

**Theorem 6.** *Given a finite set $F$ of patterns of size $(k, l)$ and $(l, k)$ for any $k, l \geq 1$, the pattern matching problem with patterns from $F$ can be solved by ANPPs in $\mathcal{O}(n + m + kl + k)$ computational (processing and communication) steps.*

Clearly, the networks including both evolutionary and hiding processors seem to be more powerful than ANEPPs considered in [4]. A natural further step is to investigate the computational power and other computational properties of ANPPs.

# References

1. Adleman, L.M., Cheng, Q., Goel, A., Huang, M.: Running time and program size for self-assembled squares. In: Proc. 33rd ACM STOC, pp. 740–748 (2001)
2. Aggarwal, G., et al.: Complexities for generalized models of self-assembly. SIAM Journal on Computing 34, 1493–1515 (2005)
3. Amir, A., Benson, G., Farach, M.: Alphabet independent two dimensional matching. In: Proc. 24th ACM STOC, pp. 59–68 (1992)
4. Bottoni, P., Labella, A., Mitrana, V.: Networks of evolutionary picture processors. Fundamenta Informaticae 131, 337–349 (2014)
5. Bozapalidis, S., Grammatikopoulou, A.: Recognizable picture series. J. of Automata, Languages and Combinatorics 10, 159–183 (2005)
6. Giammarresi, D., Restivo, A.: Two-dimensional languages. In: Handbook of Formal Languages, pp. 215–267. Springer (1997)
7. Giammarresi, D., Restivo, A.: Recognizable picture languages. Int. J. Pattern Recognition and Artificial Intelligence 6, 241–256 (1992)
8. Inoue, I., Takanami, I.: A survey of two-dimensional automata theory. In: Dassow, J., Kelemen, J. (eds.) IMYCS 1988. LNCS, vol. 381, pp. 72–91. Springer, Heidelberg (1989)
9. Manea, F., Martín-Vide, C., Mitrana, V.: Accepting networks of evolutionary word and picture processors: A survey. In: Scientific Applications of Language Methods. Mathematics, Computing, Language, and Life: Frontiers in Mathematical Linguistics and Language Theory, vol. 2, pp. 523–560. World Scientific (2010)
10. Margenstern, M., Mitrana, V., Jesús Pérez-Jímenez, M.: Accepting Hybrid Networks of Evolutionary Processors. In: Ferretti, C., Mauri, G., Zandron, C. (eds.) DNA 2004. LNCS, vol. 3384, pp. 235–246. Springer, Heidelberg (2005)
11. Marriott, K., Meyer, B.E.: Visual Language Theory. Springer (1998)
12. Maürer, I.: Characterizations of recognizable picture series. Theoretical Computer Science 374, 214–228 (2007)
13. Rosenfeld, A., Kak, A.C.: Digital Picture Processing. Academic Press, New York (1982)
14. Rosenfeld, A., Siromoney, R.: Picture languages – a survey. Languages of Design 1, 229–245 (1993)
15. Siromoney, G., Siromoney, R., Krithivasan, K.: Abstract families of matrices and picture languages. Computer Graphics and Image Processing 1, 284–307 (1972)
16. Siromoney, G., Siromoney, R., Krithivasan, K.: Picture languages with array rewriting rules. Information and Control 22, 447–470 (1973)
17. Subramanian, K.G., Siromoney, R.: On array grammars and languages. Cybernetics and Systems 18, 77–98 (1987)
18. Wang, P.S.: Hierarchical structure and complexities of parallel isometric patterns. IEEE Trans. PAM I 5, 92–99 (1983)
19. Wang, P.S.: Sequential/parallel matrix array languages. Journal of Cybernetics 5, 19–36 (1975)
20. Wang, P.S., Bunke, H. (eds.): Handbook on Optical Character Recognition and Document Image Analysis. World Scientific (1996)
21. Zhu, R.F., Takaoka, T.: A technique for two-dimensional pattern matching. Communications of the ACM 32, 1110–1120 (1989)

# Unavoidable Sets and Regularity of Languages Generated by (1,3)-Circular Splicing Systems*

Clelia De Felice, Rocco Zaccagnino, and Rosalba Zizza

Dipartimento di Informatica, University of Salerno, Italy
{defelice,zaccagnino,zizza}@dia.unisa.it

**Abstract.** *Circular splicing systems* are a formal model of a generative mechanism of circular words, inspired by a recombinant behaviour of circular DNA. They are defined by a finite alphabet $A$, an initial set $I$ of circular words and a set $R$ of rules. Berstel, Boasson and Fagnot (2012) showed that if $I$ is context-sensitive and $R$ is finite, then the generated language is context-sensitive. Moreover, when $I$ is context-free and the rules are of a simple type (*alphabetic* splicing systems) the generated language is context-free. In this paper, we focus on the still unknown relations between regular languages and circular splicing systems with a finite initial set and a finite set of rules represented by a pair of letters ((1,3)-CSSH systems). We prove necessary conditions for (1,3)-CSSH systems generating regular languages. We introduce a special class of (1,3)-CSSH systems, *hybrid systems*, and we prove that if a hybrid system generates a regular language, then the full linearization of its initial set is unavoidable, a notion introduced by Ehrenfeucht, Haussler and Rozenberg (1983). Hybrid systems include two previously considered classes of (1,3)-CSSH systems: complete systems and transitive marked systems. Unavoidability of the full linearization of the initial set has been previously proved to characterize complete systems generating regular languages whereas transitive marked systems generating regular languages are characterized by a property of the set of rules. We conjecture that this property of the set of rules, along with unavoidability of the full linearization of the initial set, still characterizes hybrid systems generating regular languages.

**Keywords:** Nature-inspired models of computation, splicing systems, regular languages.

## 1 Introduction

Circular splicing systems were introduced in [14] along with various open problems related to their computational power (see [16,22] and [2] for a recent survey

---

* Partially supported by the *FARB* Project *"Aspetti algebrici e computazionali nella teoria dei codici e dei linguaggi formali"* (University of Salerno, 2012), the *FARB* Project *"Aspetti algebrici e computazionali nella teoria dei codici, degli automi e dei linguaggi formali"* (University of Salerno, 2013) and the *MIUR PRIN* 2010-2011 grant *"Automata and Formal Languages: Mathematical and Applicative Aspects"*, code H41J12000190001.

A.-H. Dediu et al. (Eds.): TPNC 2014, LNCS 8890, pp. 169–180, 2014.

on this topic). In the circular context, the splicing operation acts on two circular DNA molecules by means of a pair of restriction enzymes as follows. Each of these two enzymes is able to recognize a pattern inside one of the given circular DNA molecules and to cut the molecule in the middle of such a pattern. Two linear molecules are produced and then they are pasted together by the action of ligase enzymes. Thus, a new circular DNA sequence is generated [13,16,22,27]. For instance, circular splicing models the integration of a plasmid into the DNA of a host bacterium [15]. Depending on whether or not these ligase enzymes substitute the recognized pattern (in nature, both situations can happen), we have the Pixton definition or the Head and Păun definition, which will be used in this paper. Obviously a string of circular DNA can be represented by a circular word, i.e., by an equivalence class with respect to the conjugacy relation $\sim$, defined by $xy \sim yx$, for $x, y \in A^*$ [19]. The set of all strings equivalent to a given word $w$ is the full linearization of the circular word $^\sim w$. A circular language is a set of circular words. It is regular (resp. context-free, context-sensitive) if so is its full linearization, i.e., the union of the full linearizations of its elements.

The circular splicing operation is applied to two circular words and a circular word may be generated. A Păun circular splicing system is a triple $S = (A, I, R)$ where $A$ is a finite alphabet, $I$ is the *initial* circular language and $R$ is the set of rules $r$, represented as quadruples of words $r = u_1 \# u_2 \$ u_3 \# u_4$ [16]. The *circular language* generated by a circular splicing system $S$ (splicing language) is the smallest language which contains $I$ and is invariant under iterated splicing by rules in $R$. In this paper by a splicing system we always mean a *finite* Păun system $S$, i.e., a Păun circular splicing system with $I$ and $R$ being finite sets and with no additional hypotheses. It is known that the corresponding class of generated circular languages is not comparable with the class of regular circular languages [4,21,26] and it is contained in the class of context-sensitive circular languages [1]. In [1], the authors also proved that the splicing language is context-free if it is generated by an *alphabetic splicing system* (i.e., a splicing system such that in any rule $u_1 \# u_2 \$ u_3 \# u_4$, the words $u_j$ are letters or the empty word). In this framework, the following still open questions may be asked.

*Problem 1 (P1).* Given a splicing system, can we decide whether the corresponding generated language is regular?

*Problem 2 (P2).* Given a regular circular language, can we decide whether it is a splicing language?

*Problem 3 (P3).* Can we characterize the structure of the regular circular languages which are splicing languages?

A question similar to Problem 2 has been solved in [1]. Moreover, the above problems have been solved for unary languages [4,5].

In this paper, we tackle Problem 1 for a special class of alphabetic splicing systems, namely $(1, 3)$-CSSH systems. *Păun circular semi-simple splicing systems* (or *CSSH systems*), previously considered in [7,8,26], are such that both $u_1 u_2$, $u_3 u_4$ have length one for any rule $u_1 \# u_2 \$ u_3 \# u_4$. A $(1, 3)$-CSSH system is a CSSH system such that $u_2 = u_4 = 1$. Therefore $R$ is a symmetric binary relation on $A$. We recall that Problems 1–3 have been already considered for some classes of splicing systems, namely alphabetic, marked and complete systems. A $(1,3)$-CSSH system $S = (A, I, R)$ is complete if $R = A \times A$ whereas $S$ is marked if $I = A$ (see Section 3 for further details). The known results are summarized in the following table. For each of the above Problems 1–3, the array below indicates whether the answer is positive for the corresponding class of splicing systems (see [4], [1], [10] and [6] for the results in the first, second, third and fourth column respectively).

|    | Card($A$) = 1 | alphabetic | marked | complete |
|----|---------------|------------|--------|----------|
| P1 | yes           | ?          | yes    | yes      |
| P2 | yes           | yes        | yes    | ?        |
| P3 | yes           | ?          | yes    | ?        |

In this paper, we prove necessary conditions for $(1,3)$-CSSH systems generating regular languages. Then, we introduce *hybrid systems*. Roughly, a hybrid system $S = (A, I, R)$ is a $(1,3)$-CSSH system such that the undirected graph $(A, R)$ is connected and all letters in the words of $I$ appear in a rule of $R$. We prove that if a hybrid system generates a regular circular language, then the full linearization of $I$ is unavoidable, a notion introduced in [11]. Hybrid systems include complete systems and (transitive) marked systems. Unavoidability of the full linearization of $I$ has been previously proved to characterize complete systems generating regular languages whereas (transitive) marked systems generating regular languages are characterized by a property of the set of rules. We conjecture that this property of the set of rules, along with unavoidability of the full linearization of $I$, still characterizes hybrid systems generating regular languages.

The paper is organized as follows. Basics on words and splicing are collected in Section 2. Known results on Problem 1 with an outline of the results proved in this paper are in Section 3. A necessary condition for the regularity of languages generated by $(1,3)$-CSSH systems is stated in Section 4. Hybrid systems are defined in Section 5 where we also prove one of the main results. Another necessary condition for the regularity of languages generated by $(1,3)$-CSSH systems is given in Section 6. Finally, in Section 7 we discuss future perspectives that follow on from the above results.

## 2    Basics on Words and Splicing

We suppose the reader familiar with classical notions in formal languages [12,17,19,24]. We denote by $A^*$ the free monoid over a finite alphabet $A$ and we set $A^+ = A^* \setminus 1$, where 1 is the empty word. For a word $w \in A^*$, $|w|$ is the length of $w$ and for every $a \in A$, $w \in A^*$, we denote by $|w|_a$ the number of occurrences of $a$ in $w$. We also set $alph(w) = \{a \in A \mid |w|_a > 0\}$. A word $x \in A^*$ is a *factor* of $w \in A^*$ if there are $u_1, u_2 \in A^*$ such that $w = u_1 x u_2$. If $u_1 = 1$ (resp. $u_2 = 1$) then $x$ is a *prefix* (resp. *suffix*) of $w$. We denote by $\text{Pref}(L)$ the set of all prefixes of the words in $L$. A language is *regular* if it is recognized by a finite automaton.

Given $w \in A^*$, a circular word $^\sim w$ is the equivalence class of $w$ with respect to the *conjugacy* relation $\sim$ defined by $xy \sim yx$, for $x, y \in A^*$ [19]. The notations $|^\sim w|$, $|^\sim w|_a$, $alph(^\sim w)$ will be defined as $|w|$, $|w|_a$, $alph(w)$, for any representative $w$ of $^\sim w$. When the context does not make it ambiguous, we will use the notation $w$ for a circular word $^\sim w$. Let $^\sim A^*$ denote the set of all circular words over $A$, i.e., the quotient of $A^*$ with respect to $\sim$. Given $L \subseteq A^*$, $^\sim L = \{^\sim w \mid w \in L\}$ is the *circularization* of $L$ whereas, given a *circular language* $C \subseteq {}^\sim A^*$, every $L \subseteq A^*$ such that $^\sim L = C$ is a *linearization* of $C$. In particular, a linearization of $^\sim w$ is a linearization of $\{^\sim w\}$, whereas the *full linearization* $\mathrm{Lin}(C)$ of $C$ is defined by $\mathrm{Lin}(C) = \{w \in A^* \mid {}^\sim w \in C\}$. Notice that we will often write $^\sim w$ instead of $\{^\sim w\}$. Given a family of languages $FA$ in the Chomsky hierarchy, $FA^\sim$ is the set of all those circular languages $C$ which have some linearization in $FA$. For instance, if $Reg$ is the family of regular languages, then $Reg^\sim$ is the class of circular languages $C$ such that $C = {}^\sim L$ for some regular language $L$. If $C \in Reg^\sim$ then $C$ is a *regular circular language*. Analogously, we can define *context-free* (resp. *context-sensitive*) circular languages. It is classically known that given a regular (resp. context-free, context-sensitive) language $L \subseteq A^*$, $\mathrm{Lin}(^\sim L)$ is regular (resp. context-free, context-sensitive) [17,18]. As a result, a circular language $C$ is regular (resp. context-free, context-sensitive) if and only if $\mathrm{Lin}(C)$ is a regular (resp. context-free, context-sensitive) language [16].

A *Păun circular splicing system* is a triple $S = (A, I, R)$, where $A$ is a finite alphabet, $I$ is the *initial* circular language, with $I \subseteq {}^\sim A^*$, $I \neq \emptyset$, and $R$ is the set of *rules*, with $R \subseteq A^* \# A^* \$ A^* \# A^*$ and $\#, \$ \notin A$. Given a rule, $r = u_1 \# u_2 \$ u_3 \# u_4$ and circular words $^\sim w'$, $^\sim w''$, if there are linearizations $w'$ of $^\sim w'$, $w''$ of $^\sim w''$ and words $h, k$, such that $w' = u_2 h u_1$, $w'' = u_4 k u_3$, then the result of the splicing operation applied to $^\sim w'$ and $^\sim w''$ by $r$ is the circular word $^\sim w$ such that $w = u_2 h u_1 u_4 k u_3$. Therefore, we set $(^\sim w', {}^\sim w'') \vdash_r {}^\sim w$ and we say that $^\sim w$ is generated (or spliced) starting with $^\sim w'$, $^\sim w''$ and by using a rule $r$. The splicing operation is extended to circular languages in order to obtain the definition of circular splicing languages. Given a Păun circular splicing system $S$ and a circular language $C \subseteq {}^\sim A^*$, we set $\sigma'(C) = \{w \in {}^\sim A^* \mid \exists w', w'' \in C, \exists r \in R : (w', w'') \vdash_r w\}$. We also define

$$\sigma^0(C) = C,$$
$$\sigma^{i+1}(C) = \sigma^i(C) \cup \sigma'(\sigma^i(C)), \ i \geq 0,$$
$$\sigma^*(C) = \bigcup_{i \geq 0} \sigma^i(C).$$

Then, $L(S) = \sigma^*(I)$ is the circular language *generated* by $S$. A circular language $C$ is *Păun generated* (or $C$ is a *circular splicing language*) if a Păun circular splicing system $S$ exists such that $C = L(S)$. We will only consider finite circular splicing systems, i.e. with a finite initial set and a finite set of rules. Moreover, as observed in [6], in order to find a characterization of the circular splicing languages, there is no loss of generality in assuming that the set $R$ of the rules is *symmetric* (i.e., for each $u_1\#u_2\$u_3\#u_4 \in R$, we have $u_3\#u_4\$u_1\#u_2 \in R$). Thus, in what follows, we assume that $R$ is symmetric. However, for simplicity, in the examples of Păun systems, only one of either $u_1\#u_2\$u_3\#u_4$ or $u_3\#u_4\$u_1\#u_2$ will be reported in the set of rules. A finite circular splicing system $S = (A, I, R)$ is a *Păun circular semi-simple splicing system* (or *CSSH system*) if both $u_1u_2$, $u_3u_4$ have length one for any rule $u_1\#u_2\$u_3\#u_4$ in $R$ [7,8,26]. A (1,3)-CSSH system is a CSSH system such that $u_2 = u_4 = 1$.

# 3   Outline of the Results

In this paper, we will focus on (1, 3)-CSSH systems $S = (A, I, R)$. Therefore $R$ is a symmetric binary relation on $A$ and $(a_i, a_j)$ will be an abridged notation for a rule $a_i\#1\$a_j\#1$ in $R$. We suppose that $I$ does not contain the empty word (adding the empty word to $I$ will only add the empty word to $L(S)$ [10]). Moreover, set $alph(I) = \cup_{w \in I} alph(w)$ and $alph(R) = \{a_i \mid (a_i, a_j) \in R\}$. We also suppose that $alph(R) \subseteq alph(I)$ (i.e., for any rule $(a_i, a_j)$ there are $x, y \in I$ such that $a_i \in alph(x), a_j \in alph(y)$) and $alph(w) \cap alph(R) \neq \emptyset$, for any $w \in I$ (i.e., for any $w \in I$ there is $(a_i, a_j)$ in $R$ such that $a_i$ or $a_j$ is in $alph(w)$). Indeed, omitting rules or circular words in $I$ which do not intervene in the application of the splicing operation, will not change the language generated by a CSSH system, beyond the finite set of words removed from $I$. This result was incorrectly stated for Păun circular splicing systems in [10] but it is not difficult to see that it holds for CSSH systems.

As said, a characterization of circular splicing systems generating regular circular languages is known for two classes of (1, 3)-CSSH systems. These results are recalled below and were the starting point of our investigation. The definition of unavoidable set is needed. This notion appeared in a paper by Schützenberger [25], then explicitly introduced in [11] and considered also by other authors [9,23]. Notice that there are algorithms to check that a given finite set $Y$ is unavoidable (see Chapter 1 in [20]).

**Definition 4.** *Let $A$ be an alphabet, let $X, Y$ be subsets of $A^*$. $Y$ is unavoidable in $X$ if there exists $k_0 \in N$ such that for any $x$ in $X$, with $|x| > k_0$, there exists $y \in Y$ which is a factor of $x$, i.e., $x = x_1yx_2$. The integer $k_0$ is called an avoidance bound for $Y$. $Y$ is unavoidable if $Y$ is unavoidable in $A^*$. If $Y$ is not unavoidable, then it is avoidable.*

A (1, 3)-CSSH system $S = (A, I, R)$ is *complete* if $A = alph(I) = alph(R)$ and $R = A \times A$. There is a close relation between complete systems and pure unitary grammars introduced in [11]. Thanks to this relation, in [6] it has been proved that a complete system $S = (A, I, R)$ generates a regular circular language if and only if $Lin(I)$ is unavoidable. More generally, this condition characterizes monotone complete systems generating regular circular languages (a monotone complete system is a CSSH system such that for two fixed integers $i, j$, with $1 \leq i < j \leq 4$, one has $u_i = u_j = 1$ in any rule $u_1\#u_2\$u_3\#u_4$) [6].

A $(1,3)$-CSSH system $S = (A, I, R)$ is a *transitive marked system* if the undirected graph $(A, R)$ is connected and $I = A$. Let $G$ be the simple graph induced by $(A, R)$, i.e., obtained by dropping the self-loops - edges from a vertex to itself - in $(A, R)$. In [3,10], it has been proved that $S$ generates a regular circular language if and only if every connected subgraph of $G$ induced by a set of 4 vertices is not $P_4 = (\{a_1, a_2, a_3, a_4\}, \{(a_1, a_2), (a_2, a_3), (a_3, a_4)\})$. As a matter of fact, in [10], a solution to Problem 1 has been given for the more general classes of marked and extended marked systems.

In Section 5, we introduce hybrid systems. Roughly they are $(1,3)$-CSSH systems $S = (A, I, R)$ such that the undirected graph $(A, R)$ is connected and $A = alph(I) = alph(R)$. Thus, transitive marked systems are hybrid and so are complete systems. We conjecture that a hybrid system $S = (A, I, R)$ generates a regular circular language if and only if $\text{Lin}(I)$ is unavoidable and every connected subgraph of $(A, R)$, with no self-loops, induced by a set of 4 vertices is not $P_4$ (see Section 7). As a first step towards a solution of the conjecture, we prove that unavoidability of $\text{Lin}(I)$ is a necessary condition for regularity of $L(S)$ (see Section 5). This is a consequence of a more general result, stating the unavoidability of $\text{Lin}(I)$ in $\text{Pref}(\text{Lin}(L(S)))$ as a necessary condition for the regularity of the language $L(S)$ generated by a $(1,3)$-CSSH system $S$ (see Section 4). Finally, we prove another necessary condition for the regularity of the language generated by a $(1,3)$-CSSH system (see Section 6). The former necessary condition seems to be unrelated to the latter.

## 4     Regular Languages and Unavoidable Sets

In this section we will prove that if a $(1,3)$-CSSH system $S$ generates a regular circular language, then the full linearization of its initial set is unavoidable in a special set related to $L(S)$. This statement, along with all intermediate results, is a generalization of statements and results in [11]. In particular, the following proposition is well known [11].

**Proposition 5.** *Let $L$ be a regular language. There exists an integer $N$ such that if $uv \in L$, then there is $v' \in A^*$ such that $|v'| \leq N$ and $uv' \in L$.*

**Lemma 6.** *Let $S = (A, I, R)$ be a $(1,3)$-CSSH system, let $Y = \text{Lin}(I)$. If $w \in \text{Lin}(L(S))$, then there is $y \in Y$ which is a factor of $w$.*

*Proof.* Let $w \in \text{Lin}(L(S))$. We prove the statement by induction on $|w|$. If $w \in Y$ we have nothing to prove. Otherwise, by the definition of $L(S)$, $w \sim x_1 x_2$ with $x_1, x_2$ words in $\text{Lin}(L(S))$, both shorter than $w$. Therefore, we may assume $w = z x_2 t$ with $tz = x_1$. By induction hypothesis, there is $y \in Y$ which is a factor of $x_2$ and so also of $w$.

$\square$

**Definition 7.** *For any finite, nonempty $Y \subseteq A^*$, we set $\ell_Y = \max\{|v| \mid v \in Y\}$.*

The following lemma is close to a result proved in [11].

**Lemma 8.** *Let $S = (A, I, R)$ be a $(1,3)$-CSSH system, let $Y = \mathrm{Lin}(I)$. If $uv \in \mathrm{Lin}(L(S))$ and $|u| > (\ell_Y - 1)|v|$, then there is $y \in Y$ which is a factor of $u$.*

*Proof.* Let $uv \in \mathrm{Lin}(L(S))$ with $|u| > (\ell_Y - 1)|v|$. We prove the statement by induction on $|v|$. If $|v| = 0$, then our claim holds by Lemma 6. Otherwise, $uv \notin Y$ since $|uv| > \ell_Y$ and, by the definition of $L(S)$, $uv \sim x_1 x_2$ with $x_1, x_2$ words in $\mathrm{Lin}(L(S))$, both shorter than $uv$. Therefore, we may assume $uv = z x_2 t$ with $tz = x_1$. Recall that $zt$ is also in $\mathrm{Lin}(L(S))$. If $x_2$ is a factor of $u$, then the statement holds for $x_2 = x_2 \cdot 1$ (induction hypothesis) and so also for $u$. If $x_2$ is a factor of $v$, then $zt = uz't$ with $z't$ shorter than $v$. By induction hypothesis, applied to $zt$ and to its prefix $u$, there is $y \in Y$ which is a factor of $u$. Otherwise, set $u = zu_1$ and $v = v_1 t$, with $u_1 v_1 = x_2$, $u_1 \neq 1$, $v_1 \neq 1$. If $t = 1$, then $u = zu_1 = x_1 u_1$, hence the statement holds for $x_1 = x_1 \cdot 1$ (induction hypothesis) and so also for $u$. Assume $t \neq 1$. Thus $v_1$ and $t$ are both shorter than $v$. Since $|u| > (\ell_Y - 1)|v|$, we have $|u_1| > (\ell_Y - 1)|v_1|$ or $|z| > (\ell_Y - 1)|t|$. By using induction hypothesis, applied to $x_2$ in the first case and to $zt$ in the second case, there is a word $y$ in $Y$ which is a factor of a factor of $u$ and so $y$ is a factor of $u$. $\square$

**Proposition 9.** *Let $S = (A, I, R)$ be a $(1,3)$-CSSH system, let $Y = \mathrm{Lin}(I)$. If $L(S)$ is a regular circular language, then $Y$ is unavoidable in $\mathrm{Pref}(\mathrm{Lin}(L(S)))$.*

*Proof.* Let $L(S)$ be a regular circular language, where $S = (A, I, R)$ is a $(1,3)$-CSSH system. Let $N$ be the integer defined by Proposition 5 for $\mathrm{Lin}(L(S))$. We prove that $Y$ is unavoidable in $\mathrm{Pref}(\mathrm{Lin}(L(S)))$, with an avoidance bound $k_0 = N(\ell_Y - 1)$.

Let $u \in \mathrm{Pref}(\mathrm{Lin}(L(S)))$ with $|u| > k_0$. Then there is a word $v$ such that $uv \in \mathrm{Lin}(L(S))$. Moreover, by Proposition 5, we may assume that $|v| \leq N$. Thus, $|u| > N(\ell_Y - 1) \geq |v|(\ell_Y - 1)$ and, by Lemma 8, there is $y \in Y$ which is a factor of $u$. $\square$

## 5  Hybrid Systems

In this section we investigate *hybrid* systems, defined below.

**Definition 10.** *A hybrid system is a $(1,3)$-CSSH system $S = (A, I, R)$ such that*

*(1)  $A = alph(R) = alph(I)$,*
*(2)  For any $a_i, a_j \in A$ there are $b_1, \ldots, b_k \in A$, with $k \geq 2$, such that:*
  $b_1 = a_i$, $b_k = a_j$,
  $\forall h \in \{1, \ldots, k-1\}$,  $(b_h, b_{h+1}) \in R$.

*Example 11.* The $(1,3)$-CSSH system $S = (A, I, R)$, defined by $A = \{a, b\}$, $I = {}^\sim\{ab, a, b\}$ and $R = \{(a, b)\}$, is hybrid. For any $a_i, a_j \in A$, condition (2) is satisfied with $k = 3$ for $a_i = a_j$, with $k = 2$ otherwise. The $(1,3)$-CSSH system $S' = (A, I', R')$, where $I' = {}^\sim\{ab, a\}$ and $R' = \{(a, a)\}$, is not a hybrid system since $b$ is in $alph(I')$ but $b$ is not in $alph(R')$.

Corollary 13 is a direct consequence of Proposition 9 and of the following result.

**Proposition 12.** *If $S = (A, I, R)$ is a hybrid system, then* $\mathrm{Pref}(\mathrm{Lin}(L(S))) = A^*$.

*Proof.* Let $S = (A, I, R)$ be a hybrid system and let $w \in A^*$. We may assume $w = a_1 \cdots a_n$, with $a_i \in A$, $1 \le i \le n$. We prove our claim by induction on $n$. Since $Y = \mathrm{Lin}(I)$ is closed under the conjugacy relation and $A = alph(Y)$, we know that for any $a \in A$, there are words $y', z'$ such that $az', y'a \in Y$. In particular, there is a word $z'$ such that $a_n z' \in \mathrm{Lin}(L(S))$. This proves our claim if $n = 1$. Otherwise, by induction hypothesis, there is a word $x$ such that $a_1 \cdots a_{n-1} x \in \mathrm{Lin}(L(S))$. Let $a_n z' = y_1' c$, with $c \in A$. Since $S$ is hybrid, there are $b_1, \ldots, b_k \in A$, with $k \ge 2$, $b_1 = c$, $b_k = a_{n-1}$ and $(b_h, b_{h+1}) \in R$, with $1 \le h \le k-1$. Hence, there are also $y_h = y_h' b_h \in Y$, $2 \le h \le k-1$ (there may be no such integers $h$ if $k = 2$). Set $y_1 = a_n z' = y_1' c$. One can prove by induction on $k$ that the word $w' = y_1 y_2 \cdots y_{k-1}$ is in $\mathrm{Lin}(L(S))$. Indeed, this holds for $k = 2$ by hypothesis. Moreover, if $y_1 y_2 \cdots y_{j-1} y_j = y_1 y_2 \cdots y_{j-1} y_j' b_j$ is in $\mathrm{Lin}(L(S))$ then, by $(b_j, b_{j+1}) \in R$, we also have $y_1 y_2 \cdots y_j y_{j+1} = y_1 y_2 \cdots y_j' b_j y_{j+1}' b_{j+1}$ in $\mathrm{Lin}(L(S))$. Let $v, v'$ be words such that $w' = y_1 y_2 \cdots y_{k-1} = a_n v = v' b_{k-1}$. Hence $x a_1 \cdots a_{n-1}$ and $w' = y_1 y_2 \cdots y_{k-1} = v' b_{k-1}$ are both in $\mathrm{Lin}(L(S))$ and $(a_{n-1}, b_{k-1}) = (b_k, b_{k-1}) \in R$. By the definition of the splicing operation, the word $x a_1 \cdots a_{n-1} w' = x a_1 \cdots a_{n-1} a_n v$ is in $\mathrm{Lin}(L(S))$, which yields $a_1 \cdots a_{n-1} a_n v x \in \mathrm{Lin}(L(S))$. Thus $w$ is in $\mathrm{Pref}(\mathrm{Lin}(L(S)))$. □

**Corollary 13.** *Let $S = (A, I, R)$ be a hybrid system, let $Y = \mathrm{Lin}(I)$. If $L(S)$ is a regular circular language, then $Y$ is unavoidable.*

*Proof.* Let $S = (A, I, R), Y$ be as in the statement. By Proposition 9, $Y$ is unavoidable in $\mathrm{Pref}(\mathrm{Lin}(L(S)))$ and, by Proposition 12, $\mathrm{Pref}(\mathrm{Lin}(L(S))) = A^*$. □

Thanks to the previous result, we can state that the initial set of each hybrid system generating a regular circular language must contain a power of each letter of the alphabet.

**Corollary 14.** *Let $S = (A, I, R)$ be a hybrid system. If $L(S)$ is a regular circular language, then for any $a \in A$ there exists $n \in \mathbb{N}$ such that $a^n \in I$.*

*Proof.* Let $S = (A, I, R)$ be a hybrid system such that $L(S)$ is a regular circular language. Let $Y = \mathrm{Lin}(I)$. If there existed $a \in A$ such that $Y \cap a^* = \emptyset$, $Y$ would be avoidable. Indeed, for any $n \in \mathbb{N}$, no word in $Y$ would be a factor of $a^n$. □

# 6   A Necessary Condition for Regularity of Languages Generated by $(1,3)$-CSSH Systems

We now provide another necessary condition for regularity of languages generated by $(1,3)$-CSSH systems, which seems to be unrelated to the one given in Proposition 9.

*Remark 15.* Let $w$ be a word over $A$ such that $\mathrm{Card}(alph(w)) \geq 2$ and let $a$ be a letter in $alph(w)$. Then either there exists an occurrence of $a$ in $w$ which is followed by a different letter or there is a nonempty word $x$ over $A \setminus \{a\}$ such that $w = xa^t$, $t > 0$. In both cases there exists $w'$, $w' \sim w$, ending with $a$ and starting with a different letter.

In the proof of the following proposition, we need the Myhill-Nerode characterization of the regular sets [12]. We recall that the *right congruence relation* $\equiv_L$ *induced* by a language $L \subseteq A^*$ is defined as follows. For a word $w$, let $F_L(w) = \{x \in A^* \mid wx \in L\}$. Then, $w \equiv_L w'$ if and only if $F_L(w) = F_L(w')$. A language $L$ is regular if and only if $\equiv_L$ is of finite index, that is, the number of equivalence classes induced by $\equiv_L$ is finite.

**Proposition 16.** *Let $S = (A, I, R)$ be a $(1,3)$-CSSH, let $a \in A$. If $(a,b) \in R$ for all $b$ in $A \setminus \{a\}$ and $\mathrm{Lin}(I) \cap a^* = \emptyset$, then $L(S)$ is not regular.*

*Proof.* If $\mathrm{Card}(A) = 1$ we have nothing to prove. Thus, assume $\mathrm{Card}(A) > 1$. Let $a$ be a letter as in the statement. For any word $w$, set $\tau_a(w) = \frac{|w|_a}{|w|}$. Moreover, let $M = \max\{\tau_a(w) \mid w \in \mathrm{Lin}(I)\}$. We may prove by induction that $\tau_a(w) \leq M$, for any word $w$ in $\mathrm{Lin}(L(S))$. This is clearly true if $w \in \mathrm{Lin}(I)$. Otherwise, there is $w' \sim w$ such that $w' = w_1 w_2$, with $w_1, w_2 \in \mathrm{Lin}(L(S))$. Of course $\tau_a(w) = \tau_a(w')$ and moreover, by induction hypothesis, we have $|w_1|_a \leq M|w_1|$ and $|w_2|_a \leq M|w_2|$. Thus,

$$\tau_a(w') = \frac{|w'|_a}{|w'|} = \frac{|w_1|_a + |w_2|_a}{|w'|} \leq \frac{M|w_1| + M|w_2|}{|w'|} = M.$$

Let $w \in \mathrm{Lin}(I)$ be such $\tau_a(w) = M$. Since $alph(R) \subseteq alph(I)$ we have $M \neq 0$. If $\mathrm{Lin}(I) \cap a^* = \emptyset$, then $\mathrm{Card}(alph(w)) \geq 2$. Thus, there is $w'$, with $w' \sim w$ and such that $w' = bz$, where $z$ ends with $a$ and $b$ is a letter different from $a$ (see Remark 15). Since $(a,b) \in R$, the word $b^n z^n$ is in $\mathrm{Lin}(L(S))$ for any positive integer $n$. On the other hand , for any integer $m$, with $m > n$, we have

$$\tau_a(b^n z^m) = \frac{|b^n z^m|_a}{|b^n z^m|} > \frac{|b^n z^m|_a}{|b^m z^m|} = \tau_a(b^m z^m) = \tau_a((bz)^m) = M.$$

Therefore, the word $b^n z^m$ is not in $\mathrm{Lin}(L(S))$. In conclusion, $b^n \not\equiv_L b^m$, for any $n, m$, with $L = \mathrm{Lin}(L(S))$ and $m > n$. Hence there are an infinite number of classes induced by $\equiv_L$ and consequently $\mathrm{Lin}(L(S))$ is not regular.

$\square$

# 7   Future Perspectives

In this paper we have presented necessary conditions for the regularity of languages generated by $(1,3)$-CSSH systems. In particular, we have proved that if a hybrid system generates a regular circular language, then the full linearization of its initial set is an unavoidable set. One can ask whether the converse of this statement is also true. The answer is negative, as Example 20 shows. Since hybrid systems include both transitive marked systems and complete systems, we propose the following conjecture.

*Conjecture 17.* Let $S = (A, I, R)$ be a hybrid system, let $Y = \mathrm{Lin}(I)$. Let $G$ be the simple graph induced by the undirected graph $(A, R)$. The circular language $L(S)$ is regular if and only if $Y$ is unavoidable and every connected subgraph of $G$, induced by a set of 4 vertices, is not $P_4$.

Notice that, if the conjecture were true, then given a hybrid system $S = (A, I, R)$, we could decide whether $L(S)$ is regular. Indeed it is decidable whether or not a finite set is unavoidable [11] and, of course, the above mentioned condition on $(A, R)$ is also decidable.

We have no counter-examples to the above conjecture. On the contrary, next examples confirm it. The following result is needed: if $S = (A_1, I_1, R_1)$, $S' = (A_2, I_2, R_2)$ are two circular splicing systems such that $A_1 \subseteq A_2$, $I_1 \subseteq I_2$ and $R_1 \subseteq R_2$, then $L(S) \subseteq L(S')$ [10].

*Example 18.* Let $S = (A, I, R)$ be the hybrid system defined by $A = \{a, b\}$, $I = {}^{\sim}\{ab, a, b\}$ and $R = \{(a, b)\}$. By the definitions, $S$ is neither a marked system nor a complete system. Observe that $\mathrm{Lin}(I)$ is unavoidable and $P_4$ is not a subgraph of $(A, R)$. Let $S' = (A, I', R)$ with $I' = {}^{\sim}\{a, b\}$. Then, $\{a, b\}^+ \backslash (a^+ a \cup b^+ b) = \mathrm{Lin}(L(S')) \subseteq \mathrm{Lin}(L(S))$ [10]. Clearly $\mathrm{Lin}(L(S)) \subseteq \{a, b\}^+ \backslash (a^+ a \cup b^+ b)$, thus $\mathrm{Lin}(L(S)) = \{a, b\}^+ \backslash (a^+ a \cup b^+ b)$. In conclusion, $L(S)$ is a regular circular language.

*Example 19.* Let $S = (A, I, R)$ be the hybrid system defined by $A = \{a, b\}$, $I = {}^{\sim}\{ab\}$ and $R = \{(a, b)\}$. By the definitions, $S$ is neither a marked system nor a complete system. Morever, $L(S)$ is not a regular circular language since $\mathrm{Lin}(L(S)) \cap a^* b^* = \{a^n b^n \mid n > 0\}$ [1,2]. Observe that $P_4$ is not a subgraph of $(A, R)$ but $\mathrm{Lin}(I)$ is avoidable.

*Example 20.* Let $S = (A, I, R)$ be the hybrid system defined by $A = \{a, b, c, d\}$, $I = {}^{\sim}\{a, b, c, d, bc\}$ and $R = \{(a, b), (b, c), (c, d)\}$. By the definitions, $S$ is neither a marked system nor a complete system. Observe that $\mathrm{Lin}(I)$ is unavoidable and $P_4$ is a subgraph of $(A, R)$. Let $S' = (A, I', R)$ with $I' = {}^{\sim}\{a, b, c, d\}$. Then, $L(S') = L(S)$. Indeed, we know that $L(S') \subseteq L(S)$. Moreover, we can easily prove that any word $w$ in $L(S)$ is also in $L(S')$. This is clear if $w \in I$, otherwise we prove it by using induction on the number of applications of the splicing operation that yield $w$. Since $L(S')$ is not regular, neither is $L(S)$.

We end this section by observing that we can transform any $(1, 3)$-CSSH system $S = (A, I, R)$ into an equivalent $(1, 3)$-CSSH system $S_f = (A, I_f, R_f)$, with $alph(I_f) \subseteq alph(R_f)$ (as for the initial language in a hybrid system) and such that $L(S)$ is regular if and only if $L(S_f)$ is regular. The objective is to transform a $(1, 3)$-CSSH system into a more special system where the investigation of the generating language is easier.

# References

1. Berstel, J., Boasson, L., Fagnot, I.: Splicing systems and the Chomsky hierarchy. Theoretical Computer Science 436, 2–22 (2012)
2. Boasson, L., Bonizzoni, P., De Felice, C., Fagnot, I., Fici, G., Zaccagnino, R., Zizza, R.: Splicing systems from past to future: Old and new challenges (2015)
3. Bonizzoni, P., De Felice, C., Fici, G., Zizza, R.: On the regularity of circular splicing languages: a survey and new developments. Natural Computing 9(2), 397–420 (2010)
4. Bonizzoni, P., De Felice, C., Mauri, G., Zizza, R.: Circular splicing and regularity. Theoretical Informatics and Applications 38(3), 189–228 (2004)
5. Bonizzoni, P., De Felice, C., Mauri, G., Zizza, R.: On the power of circular splicing. Discrete Applied Mathematics 150(1-3), 51–66 (2005)
6. Bonizzoni, P., De Felice, C., Zizza, R.: A characterization of (regular) circular languages generated by monotone complete splicing systems. Theoretical Computer Science 411(48), 4149–4161 (2010)
7. Ceterchi, R., Martín-Vide, C., Subramanian, K.G.: On some classes of splicing languages. In: Jonoska, N., Păun, G., Rozenberg, G. (eds.) Aspects of Molecular Computing. LNCS, vol. 2950, pp. 84–105. Springer, Heidelberg (2003)
8. Ceterchi, R., Subramanian, K.G.: Simple circular splicing systems. Romanian Journal of Information Science and Technology 6(1-2), 121–134 (2003)
9. Choffrut, C., Culik II, K.: On extendibility of unavoidable sets. Discrete Applied Mathematics 9, 125–137 (1984)
10. De Felice, C., Fici, G., Zizza, R.: A characterization of regular circular languages generated by marked splicing systems. Theoretical Computer Science 410(47-49), 4937–4960 (2009)
11. Ehrenfeucht, A., Haussler, D., Rozenberg, G.: On regularity of context-free languages. Theoretical Computer Science 27, 311–332 (1983)
12. Harrison, M.D.: Introduction to Formal Language Theory. Addison-Wesley Longman (1978)
13. Head, T.: Formal language theory and DNA: an analysis of the generative capacity of specific recombinant behaviours. Bulletin of Mathematical Biology 49, 737–759 (1987)
14. Head, T.: Splicing schemes and DNA. In: Rozenberg, G., Salomaa, A. (eds.) Lindenmayer systems: impacts on theoretical computer science, computer graphics, and developmental biology, pp. 371–383. Springer (1992)
15. Head, T.: Circular suggestions for DNA computing. In: Carbone, A., Prusinkiewicz, P., Gromov, M. (eds.) Pattern formation in biology, vision and dynamics. World Scientific (2000)
16. Head, T., Păun, G., Pixton, D.: Language theory and molecular genetics: generative mechanisms suggested by DNA recombination. In: Rozenberg, G., Salomaa, A. (eds.) Handbook of Formal Languages, pp. 295–360. Springer (1997)

17. Hopcroft, J.E., Motwani, R., Ullman, J.D.: Introduction to Automata Theory, Languages, and Computation. Addison-Wesley series in computer science, 2nd edn. Addison-Wesley-Longman (2001)
18. Kudlek, M.: On languages of cyclic words. In: Jonoska, N., Păun, G., Rozenberg, G. (eds.) Aspects of Molecular Computing. LNCS, vol. 2950, pp. 278–288. Springer, Heidelberg (2003)
19. Lothaire, M.: Combinatorics on Words, 2nd edn. Cambridge University Press (1997) (1st edn. 1983)
20. Lothaire, M.: Algebraic Combinatorics on Words. Cambridge University Press (2002)
21. Pixton, D.: Regularity of splicing languages. Discrete Applied Mathematics 69(1-2), 101–124 (1996)
22. Păun, G., Rozenberg, G., Salomaa, A.: DNA computing - new computing paradigms. Texts in Theoretical Computer Science. Springer (1998)
23. Rosaz, L.: Inventories of unavoidable languages and the word-extension conjecture. Theoretical Computer Science 201(1-2), 151–170 (1998)
24. Sakarovitch, J.: Elements of Automata Theory. Cambridge University Press (2009)
25. Schützenberger, M.P.: On the synchronizing properties of certain prefix codes. Information and Control 7(1), 23–36 (1964)
26. Siromoney, R., Subramanian, K.G., Dare, V.R.: Circular DNA and splicing systems. In: Nakamura, A., Saoudi, A., Inoue, K., Wang, P.S.P., Nivat, M. (eds.) ICPIA 1992. LNCS, vol. 654, pp. 260–273. Springer, Heidelberg (1992)
27. Zizza, R.: Splicing systems. Scholarpedia 5(7), 9397 (2010)

# A Two-Dimensional Extension
# of Insertion Systems

Kaoru Fujioka

International College of Arts and Sciences
Fukuoka Women's University
1-1-1 Kasumigaoka Higashi-ku, Fukuoka 813-8529, Japan
kaoru@fwu.ac.jp

**Abstract.** Insertion systems are extended to two-dimensional models that are used to generate picture languages. Insertion rules are defined in terms of rows and columns. Using picture-insertion rules, we herein introduce two types of derivations that depend on the position at which the rules are applied. We obtain the relationships between the classes of languages generated by picture-insertion systems for each type of derivation and a number of two-dimensional computing models, such as tiling systems. Furthermore, we introduce regular control for the derivations in picture-insertion systems. Finally, we compare the classes of languages generated by picture-insertion systems with and without regular control.

**Keywords:** picture languages, insertion systems, tiling systems.

## 1 Introduction

A number of approaches to represent and generate picture languages (two-dimensional languages), such as tiling systems, automata, regular expressions, and grammars [11], [5], [9], [1], have been reported. Some of the ideas behind these approaches are based on concepts related to string languages, and the corresponding results are proved which are extended from language properties into two-dimensional languages.

On the other hand, insertion and deletion systems are computing models that are based on the field of molecular biology and can characterize any recursively enumerable language that was originally defined for string languages.

Several methods for generating two-dimensional languages based on insertion and deletion operations have been proposed [8]. In [2], an array single-contextual insertion deletion system for two-dimensional pictures (ASInsDelP) was introduced based on DNA computation. With an insertion rule consisting of context-checking picture $u$ and inserting picture $x$, a picture $\alpha u x u \beta$ is obtained from a given picture $\alpha u \beta$ by replicative transposition operation, which implies that columns are inserted by the insertion rule.

Computing models based on DNA molecules have evolved and increasingly complex structures have been introduced. Winfree [13] introduced a tile assembly model with DNA tile over two-dimensional arrays. A specialized model for DNA

A.-H. Dediu et al. (Eds.): TPNC 2014, LNCS 8890, pp. 181–192, 2014.

pattern assembly was proposed in [6] and theory of DNA pattern assembly has been recently developed.

In this paper, we focus on insertion operations with double context-checking strings while extending insertion systems from one dimension to two dimensions and then introduce picture-insertion systems to generate picture languages. The picture-insertion operation introduced herein is related to the (one-dimensional) insertion operations of the form $(u, x, v)$ to produce a string $\alpha u x v \beta$ from a given string $\alpha u v \beta$ with context $uv$ by inserting a string $x$ between $u$ and $v$ [10].

A derivation proceeds using picture-insertion rules in order to generate arrays. In one step of the derivation, pictures of the same size are inserted in either every row or every column. We introduce two modes of applying picture-insertion rules: alongside mode and independent mode. In the alongside mode, pictures are inserted in the same column (resp. row) for any row (resp. column). In the independent mode, there is no restriction as to the position of insertion regarding rows or columns.

Furthermore, we introduce regular control for the derivations and demonstrated that the proposed control properly increases the generative powers of picture-insertion systems.

## 2    Preliminaries

In this section, we introduce the notation and basic definitions used in this paper. The basics of formal language theory are available in [11] and [10].

For an alphabet $\Sigma$, a *picture* $p$ is a two-dimensional rectangular array of elements of $\Sigma$. $\Sigma^{**}$ (resp. $\Sigma^*$) is the set of all pictures (resp. strings) over $\Sigma$, including the empty picture (resp. empty string) $\lambda$. A *picture language* (resp. language) over $\Sigma$ is a subset of $\Sigma^{**}$ (resp. $\Sigma^*$).

For a picture $p \in \Sigma^{**}$, let $\ell_1(p)$ (resp. $\ell_2(p)$) be the number of rows (resp. columns) of $p$. For a picture $p$ in $\Sigma^{**}$, $|p| = (m, n)$ denotes the *size* of the picture $p$ with $m = \ell_1(p)$ and $n = \ell_2(p)$. In particular, for a string $w$ in $\Sigma^*$, $|w|$ denotes the length of $w$. For a string $w = a_1 a_2 \cdots a_n$, $w^T$ is a vertical string, such as $a_1$
$\vdots$ . For a picture $p$ with $|p| = (m, n)$, the transposition of $p$ is a picture $q$ with
$a_n$
$|q| = (n, m)$ such that rows and columns of $p$ are interchanged.

For any $h \le m$ and $k \le n$, $B_{h,k}(p)$ is the set of all sub-pictures of $p$ of size $(h, k)$.

For pictures $p$ and $q$, the *row and column concatenations* are denoted by $p \ominus q$ and $p \oplus q$, respectively, which are defined if $\ell_2(p) = \ell_2(q)$ (resp. $\ell_1(p) = \ell_1(q)$) holds. For $k \ge 0$, $p^{k\ominus}$ (resp. $p^{k\oplus}$) is the vertical (horizontal) juxtaposition of $k$ $p$'s. For picture languages $L_1$ and $L_2$, $L_1 \ominus L_2$ (resp. $L_1 \oplus L_2$) consists of pictures $p$ such that $p = p_1 \ominus p_2$ (resp. $p = p_1 \oplus p_2$) with $p_1 \in L_1$ and $p_2 \in L_2$.

Next, we present a number of two-dimensional computing models. A *tile* is a square picture of size $(2, 2)$. For a finite set $\theta$ of tiles over alphabet $\Gamma \cup \{\#\}$, $LOC(\theta)$ denotes the set $\{p \in \Gamma^{**} \mid B_{2,2}(\hat{p}) \subseteq \theta\}$, where $\hat{p}$ is a picture obtained by surrounding $p$ with the symbol $\#$. A picture language $L$ over $\Gamma$ is *local* if $L = LOC(\theta)$ for some tile set $\theta$.

For alphabets $\Gamma$ and $\Sigma$, a coding $\varphi : \Gamma^* \to \Sigma^*$ is a morphism such that for any $a$ in $\Gamma$, $\varphi(a) \in \Sigma$ holds. A projection $\pi : \Gamma^* \to \Sigma^*$ with $\Gamma \supseteq \Sigma$ is a morphism such that if $a$ is in $\Sigma$ then $\pi(a) = a$, otherwise $\pi(a) = \lambda$.

A *tiling system* is a tuple $\mathcal{T} = (\Sigma, \Gamma, \theta, \pi)$, where $\Sigma$ and $\Gamma$ are alphabets, $\theta$ is a finite set of tiles over the alphabet $\Gamma \cup \{\#\}$, and $\pi : \Gamma \to \Sigma$ is a projection. A language $L(\mathcal{T})$ defined by a tiling system $\mathcal{T}$ is $L(\mathcal{T}) = \pi(LOC(\theta))$. Let $REC$ be the class of picture languages generated by tiling systems.

Based on a pure context-free rule of the form $a \to \alpha$ with $a \in \Sigma$ and $\alpha \in \Sigma^*$ in one dimension, a *pure 2D context-free grammar* $G = (\Sigma, P_c, P_r, A)$ is considered in [12] , where $\Sigma$ is an alphabet, $P_c = \{t_{c_i} \mid 1 \leq i \leq m\}$, $P_r = \{t_{r_j} \mid 1 \leq j \leq n\}$, and $A \subseteq \Sigma^{**} - \{\lambda\}$ is a finite set of pictures over $\Sigma$. A *column table* $t_{c_i}$ ($1 \leq i \leq m$) is a set of pure context-free rules such that for any two rules $a \to \alpha$, $b \to \beta$ in $t_{c_i}$, $|\alpha| = |\beta|$ holds. Similarly, a *row table* $t_{r_j}$ ($1 \leq j \leq n$) is a set of pure context-free rules of the form $a \to \alpha^T$, $a \in \Sigma$, $\alpha \in \Sigma^*$ such that for any two rules $a \to \alpha^T$, $b \to \beta^T$ in $t_{r_j}$, $|\alpha| = |\beta|$ holds.

Let $P2DCFL$ be the class of picture languages generated by pure 2D context-free grammars.

A *context-free matrix grammar* $(G_1, G_2)$ consists of two grammars $G_1$ and $G_2$, where

- $G_1 = (H_1, I_1, P_1, S)$ is a context-free grammar, $H_1$ is a finite set of horizontal nonterminals, $I_1 = \{S_1, \cdots, S_k\}$ is a finite set of intermediate symbols with $H_1 \cap I_1 = \emptyset$, $P_1$ is a finite set of context-free rules, $S$ is the start symbol in $H_1$,
- $G_2 = (G_{21}, \cdots, G_{2k})$, where $G_{2i} = (V_{2i}, \Sigma, P_{2i}, S_{2i})$ with $1 \leq i \leq k$ is a regular grammar, $V_{2i}$ is a finite set of nonterminals with $V_{2i} \cap V_{2j} = \emptyset$ for $i \neq j$, $\Sigma$ is an alphabet, $P_{2i}$ is a finite set of regular rules of the form $X \to aY$ or $X \to a$ with $X, Y \in V_{2i}$, $a \in \Sigma$, $S_{2i}$ in $V_{2i}$ is the start symbol.

A *regular matrix grammar* is a context-free matrix grammar $(G_1, G_2)$, where both $G_1$ and $G_2$ are regular grammars. Let $CFML$ (resp. $RML$) be the class of picture languages generated by context-free (resp. regular) matrix grammars.

Let us conclude this section by presenting an insertion system for string languages [10], based on which we introduce a picture-insertion system in the next section. An *insertion system* is a tuple $\gamma = (\Sigma, P, A)$, where $\Sigma$ is an alphabet, $P$ is a finite set of *insertion rules* of the form $(u, x, v)$ with $u, x, v \in \Sigma^*$, and $A$ is a finite set of strings over $\Sigma$ called axioms.

We write $\alpha \Longrightarrow \beta$ if $\alpha = \alpha_1 u v \alpha_2$ and $\beta = \alpha_1 u x v \alpha_2$ for some insertion rule $(u, x, v) \in P$ with $\alpha_1, \alpha_2 \in \Sigma^*$. The reflexive and transitive closure of $\Longrightarrow$ is defined as $\Longrightarrow^*$. A language generated by $\gamma$ is defined as $L(\gamma) = \{w \in \Sigma^* \mid s \Longrightarrow^* w, \text{ for some } s \in A\}$.

Let $INS$ be the class of string languages generated by insertion systems.

# 3    Picture-Insertion Systems

We introduce a *picture-insertion system* with two types of tables consisting of insertion rules for columns and rows, as follows:

**Definition 1.** *A picture-insertion system is a tuple* $\gamma = (\Sigma, I_c, I_r, A)$, *where* $\Sigma$ *is an alphabet,* $I_c = \{t_{c_i} \mid 1 \leq i \leq m\}$, *(resp.* $I_r = \{t_{r_j} \mid 1 \leq j \leq n\}$*) is a finite set of column (resp. row) tables, and* $A$ *is a finite set of pictures over* $\Sigma$.

Each $t_{c_i}$ $(1 \leq i \leq m)$ is a set of C-type picture-insertion rules of the form $(u, w, v)$ with $u, v \in \Sigma^*$ and $w \in \Sigma^+$ such that for any two rules $(u, w, v)$ and $(x, z, y)$ in $t_{c_i}$, we have $|u| = |x|$, $|w| = |z|$, and $|v| = |y|$.

Each $t_{r_j}$ $(1 \leq j \leq n)$ is a set of R-type picture-insertion rules of the form $\begin{pmatrix} u, \\ w, \\ v \end{pmatrix}$ with $u^T, v^T \in \Sigma^*$ and $w^T \in \Sigma^+$ such that for any two rules $\begin{pmatrix} u, \\ w, \\ v \end{pmatrix}$ and $\begin{pmatrix} x, \\ z, \\ y \end{pmatrix}$ in $t_{r_j}$, we have $|u| = |x|$, $|w| = |z|$, and $|v| = |y|$.

Intuitively, a C-type (resp. R-type) rule refers to an insertion rule for a row (resp. column), then widen the column (resp. row) of pictures.

Next, we define two methods for applying insertion rules for pictures in order to obtain arrays.

**Definition 2.** *For pictures* $p_1$ *and* $p_2$ *in* $\Sigma^{**}$, *we say that* $p_1$ *derives* $p_2$ *denoted by* $p_1 \Longrightarrow_a p_2$ *with alongside mode if* $p_2$ *is obtained from* $p_1$ *by inserting pictures with the same column (resp. row) for each row (resp. column) using C-type (resp. R-type) insertion rules of some* $t_{c_i}$ *(resp.* $t_{r_j}$*) in* $I_c$ *(resp.* $I_r$*).*

*In a graphical representation of C-type picture-insertion rules, we have*

| $\alpha_1$ | $u_1$ | $v_1$ | $\beta_1$ |
|---|---|---|---|
| $\cdots$ | $\cdots$ | $\cdots$ | $\cdots$ |
| $\alpha_{k'}$ | $u_{k'}$ | $v_{k'}$ | $\beta_{k'}$ |
| $\cdots$ | $\cdots$ | $\cdots$ | $\cdots$ |
| $\alpha_k$ | $u_k$ | $v_k$ | $\beta_k$ |

$\Longrightarrow_a$

| $\alpha_1$ | $u_1$ | $w_1$ | $v_1$ | $\beta_1$ |
|---|---|---|---|---|
| $\cdots$ | $\cdots$ | $\cdots$ | $\cdots$ | $\cdots$ |
| $\alpha_{k'}$ | $u_{k'}$ | $w_{k'}$ | $v_{k'}$ | $\beta_{k'}$ |
| $\cdots$ | $\cdots$ | $\cdots$ | $\cdots$ | $\cdots$ |
| $\alpha_k$ | $u_k$ | $w_k$ | $v_k$ | $\beta_k$ |

*We note that different C-type (resp. R-type) insertion rules might be applied for rows (resp. columns) in the process of* $p_1 \Longrightarrow_a p_2$.

**Definition 3.** *For pictures* $p_1$ *and* $p_2$ *in* $\Sigma^{**}$, *we say that* $p_1$ *derives* $p_2$ *denoted by* $p_1 \Longrightarrow_i p_2$ *with the independent mode if* $p_2$ *is obtained from* $p_1$ *by inserting pictures for each row (resp. column) using C-type (reps. R-type) insertion rules of some* $t_{c_i}$ *(resp.* $t_{r_j}$*) in* $I_c$ *(resp.* $I_r$*).*

*In a graphical representation of C-type picture-insertion rules, we have*

| $\alpha_1$ | $u_1$ | $v_1$ | $\beta_1$ |
|---|---|---|---|
| ... | ... | ... | ... |
| $\alpha_{k'}$ | | $u_{k'}$ | $v_{k'}$ | $\beta_{k'}$ |
| ... | ... | ... | ... |
| $\alpha_k$ | $u_k$ | $v_k$ | $\beta_k$ |

$\Longrightarrow_i$

| $\alpha_1$ | $u_1$ | $w_1$ | $v_1$ | $\beta_1$ |
|---|---|---|---|---|
| ... | ...... | ... | ... |
| $\alpha_{k'}$ | $u_{k'}$ | $w_{k'}$ | $v_{k'}$ | $\beta_{k'}$ |
| ... | ...... | ... | ... |
| $\alpha_k$ | $u_k$ | $w_k$ | $v_k$ | $\beta_k$ |

*Different C-type (resp. R-type) insertion rules might be applied to rows (resp. columns) in the process of $p_1 \Longrightarrow_i p_2$.*

*Unlike the alongside mode in Definition 2, there is no restriction regarding the position at which to apply picture-insertion rules in the process of $p_1 \Longrightarrow_i p_2$.*

The reflexive and transitive closure of $\Longrightarrow_a$ (resp. $\Longrightarrow_i$) is defined as $\Longrightarrow_a^*$ (resp. $\Longrightarrow_i^*$). A picture language generated by $\gamma = (\Sigma, I_c, I_r, A)$ using the alongside mode (resp. independent mode) is defined as $L_a(\gamma) = \{w \in \Sigma^{**} \mid s \Longrightarrow_a^* w,$ for some $s \in A\}$ (resp. $L_i(\gamma) = \{w \in \Sigma^{**} \mid s \Longrightarrow_i^* w,$ for some $s \in A\}$).

Let $INPA$ (resp. $INPI$) be the class of picture languages generated by picture-insertion systems using the alongside mode (resp. independent mode).

# 4   Examples

In the following, we present examples of picture-insertion systems.

*Example 4.* Consider a picture-insertion system $\gamma_1 = (\Sigma, I_c, I_r, A)$, where $\Sigma = \{a, b\}$, $I_c = \{t_{c1}\}$ with $t_{c1} = \{(\lambda, ab, \lambda)\}$, $I_r = \{t_{r1}\}$ with $t_{r1} = \{\begin{pmatrix} a, \\ a, \\ \lambda \end{pmatrix}, \begin{pmatrix} b, \\ b, \\ \lambda \end{pmatrix}\}$, $A = \{\lambda\}$.

The picture language $L_a(\gamma_1)$ generated by $\gamma_1$ using the alongside mode is $\{w^{k\ominus} \mid w$ is Dyck's string language over $\{a, b\}$, $k \geq 0\}$. For example, the following pictures are generated using the alongside mode:

$ab,\ \begin{matrix} ab \\ ab \end{matrix},\ \begin{matrix} ab \\ ab \\ ab \end{matrix},\ aabb,\ \begin{matrix} aabb \\ aabb \\ aabb \end{matrix},\ aabbab,\ \begin{matrix} aabbab \\ aabbab \\ aabbab \end{matrix},\ \begin{matrix} aabbabab \\ aabbabab \\ aabbabab \\ aabbabab \end{matrix}.$

From the R-type insertion rules in $t_{r1}$ and the definition of the alongside mode, all of the row strings are the same.

On the other hand, we consider the picture language $L_i(\gamma_1)$ generated by $\gamma_1$ using the independent mode. For example, the following pictures are generated using the independent mode:

$ab,\ \begin{matrix} ab \\ ab \end{matrix},\ \begin{matrix} ab \\ ab \\ ab \end{matrix},\ aabb,\ \begin{matrix} aabb \\ abab \\ abab \end{matrix},\ aaabbb,\ \begin{matrix} aaabbb \\ ababab \\ ababab \end{matrix},\ \begin{matrix} aaaabbbb \\ aaaabbbb \\ ababab ab \\ ababab ab \end{matrix}.$

Any picture generated by $\gamma_1$ using the independent mode satisfies the condition that any row must consist of a Dyck language over $\Sigma$. From the definition of the independent mode, $L_i(\gamma_1)$ includes a picture with different row strings. Furthermore, we have the inclusion $L_a(\gamma) \subset L_i(\gamma)$.

As shown in Example 4, picture-insertion systems are two-dimensional generalizations of insertion systems in linear cases. Actually, for the case with $P_r = \emptyset$, the picture-insertion system generates strings using both the alongside mode and the independent mode. Then, a Dyck language is generated, as noted in Lemma 7. Note that a Dyck language is not regular (in a one-dimensional sense), which implies that both $INPA$ and $INPI$ include a picture language which is not regular.

*Example 5.* Consider a picture-insertion system $\gamma_2 = (\Sigma, I_c, I_r, A)$, where

$\Sigma = \{a, b, d, e\}$,

$I_c = \{t_{c1}, t_{c2}\}$,

$I_r = \{t_{r1}, t_{r2}\}$,

$t_{c1} = \{(u, ab, \lambda) \mid u \in \{a, b\}\} \cup \{(u, de, \lambda) \mid u \in \{d, e\}\}$,

$t_{c2} = \{(\lambda, ab, v) \mid v \in \{a, b\}\} \cup \{(\lambda, de, v) \mid v \in \{d, e\}\}$,

$t_{r1} = \left\{ \begin{pmatrix} u, \\ w, \\ \lambda \end{pmatrix} \mid w = (ad)^T, \ u \in \{a, d\} \right\} \cup \left\{ \begin{pmatrix} u, \\ w, \\ \lambda \end{pmatrix} \mid w = (de)^T, \ u \in \{d, e\} \right\}$,

$t_{r2} = \left\{ \begin{pmatrix} \lambda, \\ w, \\ v \end{pmatrix} \mid w = (be)^T, \ u \in \{b, e\} \right\} \cup \left\{ \begin{pmatrix} \lambda, \\ w, \\ v \end{pmatrix} \mid w = (be)^T, \ v \in \{b, e\} \right\}$,

$A = \{ \begin{smallmatrix} ab \\ de \end{smallmatrix} \}$.

The following are examples of the pictures generated by $\gamma$ using the alongside mode:

$$\frac{aabb}{ddee}, \ \frac{aaabbb}{dddeee}, \ \frac{abab}{dede}, \ \frac{ababab}{dedede}, \ \frac{\begin{smallmatrix} aabb \\ aabb \end{smallmatrix}}{\begin{smallmatrix} ddee \\ ddee \end{smallmatrix}}, \ \frac{\begin{smallmatrix} abab \\ dede \end{smallmatrix}}{\begin{smallmatrix} abab \\ dede \end{smallmatrix}}.$$

Note that the pictures generated by $\gamma_2$ using the alongside mode are *Chinese boxes*, which are nested boxes with two-dimensional Dyck analogue structures. The symbol $a$ (resp. $b$, $d$, and $e$) implies the upper left (resp. upper right, lower left, and lower right) corner of the box.

## 5    Properties and Comparisons of Picture-Insertion Systems Using the Alongside Mode

We first consider picture-insertion systems using the alongside mode and obtain the following result.

**Lemma 6.** *The class of $INPA$ is not closed under the operations of union, column catenation, or row catenation. The class is closed under transposition.*

*Proof.* Consider the picture language $L_a(\gamma_1)$ in Example 4 and the picture language $L_1$, which is obtained by replacing $b$ with $d$ in $L_a(\gamma_1)$.

Suppose that there is a picture-insertion system $\gamma' = (\{a, b, d\}, P'_c, P'_r, A')$ such that $L_a(\gamma_1) \cup L_1 = L_a(\gamma')$. For infinite pictures over $\{a, b\}$ in $L_a(\gamma_1)$, there is a picture-insertion rule $(u, w, v)$ with $|w|_a = |w|_b$. Similarly, for $L_1$, we have a picture-insertion rule $(x, z, y)$ with $|z|_a = |z|_d$. In order to generate only pictures in $L_a(\gamma_1) \cup L_2$, any picture-insertion rule $(u, w, v)$ with $|w|_a = |w|_b$ satisfies $|uv|_b > 0$. Otherwise, $\gamma'$ generates a picture $p$ which satisfies $|p|_b > 0$ and $|p|_d > 0$.

Similarly, for infinite pictures over $\{a, d\}$ in $L_1$, a picture-insertion rule $(x, z, y)$ with $|z|_a = |z|_d$ satisfies $|xy|_d > 0$.

Let $n = max\{|u|, |v|, |w| \mid (u, w, v)\}$ be a picture-insertion rule for $\gamma'\}$, $\ell_a = max\{\ell_1(\alpha) \mid \alpha \in A'\}$, and $N > n + \ell_a$. Consider the string $a^N aba^N b^{2N}$ in $L_1 \subset L_a(\gamma')$. There is no way to generate the string by a picture-insertion rule $(u, w, v)$ with $|uv|_b > 0$ and $|w|_a = |w|_b$ due to the substring $ab$ between $a^N$ and $a^N$.

The non-closure property under column catenation and row catenation can be determined by considering $L_a(\gamma_1) \ominus L_2$ and $L_a(\gamma_1) \oplus L_2$, respectively.

The closure property under transposition can be determined if we substitute column (resp. row) tables with row (resp. column) tables by replacing the rule $(u, w, v)$ (resp. $\begin{pmatrix} u^T, \\ w^T, \\ v^T \end{pmatrix}$ ) with $\begin{pmatrix} u^T, \\ w^T, \\ v^T \end{pmatrix}$ (resp. $(u, w, v)$) and consider transposition axiom.     □

From the construction of tiling systems, defined by the projection of local languages, tiling systems are considered to be two-dimensional generalizations of one-dimensional regular languages. In one-dimensional cases, for the class of regular languages denoted by $REG$, the proper inclusion $REG \subset INS$ holds, where $INS$ is the class of languages generated by insertion systems in one dimension. In contrast to the one-dimensional cases, for the class of picture languages generated by tiling systems denoted by $REC$, we obtain the following result.

**Lemma 7.** *The class of INPA is incomparable with the class of REC.*

*Proof.* Consider a picture-insertion system $\gamma_2 = (\Sigma, I_c, I_r, A)$, where $\Sigma = \{a, b\}$, $I_c = \{t_{c1}\}$ with $t_{c1} = \{(\lambda, ab, \lambda)\}$, $I_r = \emptyset$, $A = \{\lambda\}$ derived from Example 4.

The class of $REC$ coincides with that of regular languages if restricted to one dimension. A language $L_a(\gamma_2)$ in a one-dimensional language is a Dyck language which is not regular. Therefore, there is a picture-insertion system $\gamma_2$ such that $L_a(\gamma_2)$ is not generated by a tiling system.

Consider a picture language $L_s$ over $\{a, b\}$, where $L_s$ consists of squares, the positions in the main diagonal of which are covered by $a$ and the remaining squares are covered by $b$. From [11], $L_s$ is in the class of $REC$.

Suppose that there is a picture-insertion system $\gamma$ such that $L_s = L_a(\gamma)$. For a picture $w$ in $\{a, b\}^{**}$, there is a derivation $w \Longrightarrow_a w'$ using the C-type insertion rule such that $|w| = (m, m)$ and $|w'| = (m, m')$ with $m' > m$. For the picture $w'$ in $L_s$, $|w'| = (m, m')$ with $m \neq m'$ holds. Thus, we have a contradiction.

Thus, the lemma is proved.     □

We compare the class of $INPA$ to the class of $P2DCFL$ as follows.

**Lemma 8.** *The class of INPA is incomparable with the class of P2DCFL.*

*Proof.* Consider a pure 2D context-free grammar $G = (\Sigma, P_c, P_r, \{ \begin{smallmatrix} aba \\ ded \end{smallmatrix} \})$, where $\Sigma = \{a, b, d, e\}$, $P_c = \{t_c\}$, $P_r = \{t_r\}$ with $t_c = \{b \to aba, e \to ded\}$ and $t_r = \{a \to \begin{smallmatrix} a \\ d \end{smallmatrix}, b \to \begin{smallmatrix} b \\ e \end{smallmatrix}\}$ [12].

Suppose that there is a picture-insertion system $\gamma = (\Sigma, I_c, I_r, A)$ such that $L(G) = L_a(\gamma)$. Any row in $L(G)$ consists of strings such that $a^n b a^n$ or $d^n e d^n$ with $n \geq 1$.

There is no picture-insertion rule that can generate these strings, which can be proved by contradiction. Briefly, a picture-insertion rule $(u, w, v)$ with $w \in \{a\}^*$ (resp. $w \in \{d\}^*$) needed for infinitely long $a^n b a^n$ (resp. $d^n e d^n$) generates a string $a^i b a^j$ (resp. $d^i e d^j$) with $i \neq j$.

On the other hand, consider a picture-insertion system $\gamma_3 = (\{a, b\}, I_{c3}, I_{r3}, A_3)$ such that $I_{c3} = \{t_{c3}\}$ with $t_{c3} = \{(ab, ab, \lambda)\}$, $I_{r3} = \{t_{r3}\}$ with $t_{r3} = \{\left(\begin{smallmatrix} a, \\ a, \\ \lambda \end{smallmatrix}\right), \left(\begin{smallmatrix} b, \\ b, \\ \lambda \end{smallmatrix}\right)\}$, $A_3 = \{a^3 b^3 ab, a^3 b^3\}$. A picture language $L_a(\gamma_3)$ consists of pictures such that $(a^3 b^3 (ab)^n)^{m\ominus}$ with $m \geq 1$, $n \geq 0$. From [7][12], there is no pure 2D context-free grammar which generates $L_a(\gamma_3)$.

Thus, the lemma is proved.                                                    □

In the following, we consider two types of matrix grammars. First, from the picture language $L_a(\gamma_2)$ in Lemma 7 and the fact that a Dyck language is not regular in a one-dimensional sense, we obtain the following result.

**Corollary 9.** *There is a picture language in the class of INPA which is not in the class of RML.*

**Lemma 10.** *Every picture language in the class of RML is a coding of a language in the class of INPA.*

*Proof.* (Outline)
The proof is based on the idea that in a one-dimensional sense, the class of regular languages $REG$ is included in the class of insertion systems $INS$ [10].

Consider a regular matrix grammar $(G_1, G_2)$, where $G_1 = (H_1, I_1, P_1, S)$ and $G_2 = (G_{21}, \cdots, G_{2k})$ with $G_{2i} = (V_{2i}, \Sigma, P_{2i}, S_{2i})$ $(1 \leq i \leq k)$ are regular.

For regular languages $L(G_1)$ and $L(G_{2i})$ $(1 \leq i \leq k)$, there are picture-insertion systems $\gamma_1' = (I_1, P_1, A_1)$, $\gamma_{2i}' = (\Sigma, P_{2i}, A_{2i})$ and integers $n_1, n_{2i}$ such that $L(G_1) = L(\gamma_1')$, $L(G_{2i}) = L(\gamma_{2i}')$, and the axiom in $\gamma_1'$ (resp. $\gamma_{2i}'$) is no more than $n_1 - 1$ (resp. $n_{2i} - 1$). (See [10] for more details about how to define the integers $n_1$ and $n_{2i}$.)

Let $N$ be the least common multiple of $n_{2i}$ $(1 \leq i \leq k)$.

We construct a picture-insertion system with the additional symbols $\gamma = (\Sigma \cup \{S_{2i} \mid 1 \leq i \leq k\} \cup \{\#\}, I_c, I_r, A)$ and a coding $\varphi : (\Sigma \cup \{S_{2i} \mid 1 \leq i \leq k\} \cup \{\#\})^* \to \Sigma^*$ with $\varphi(a) = a$ for $a \in \Sigma$ and $\varphi(a) = \lambda$ otherwise.

Roughly speaking, the regular language $L(G_1)$ is simulated by C-type picture-insertion rules in $\gamma$ and the regular language $L(G_{2i})$ is simulated by R-type picture-insertion rules in $\gamma$. Finally, the coding $\varphi$ deletes the redundant symbols $S_{2i}$ (resp. $\#$) required to simulate $G_{2i}$ (resp. $G_1$).

A finite set of pictures $A$ satisfies $A = \{\begin{smallmatrix} w \\ \#^n \end{smallmatrix} \mid w \in A_1, |w| = n\}$. We construct C-type picture-insertion rules $(u, w, \lambda)$ and $(\#^m, \#^n, \lambda)$, where $(u, w, \lambda)$ is in $P_1$ concerning $\gamma_1'$ and $|u| = m$, $|w| = n$. The symbol $\#$ lies in the bottommost of each picture.

We construct R-type picture-insertion rules

- R1-type: $\begin{pmatrix} S_{2i}, \\ z_{2i}, \\ \# \end{pmatrix}$, where $z_{2i} \in L(G_{2i})$, $\ell_1(z_{2i}) \leq N - 1$

- R2-type: $\begin{pmatrix} u_{2i}, \\ w_{2i}, \\ \lambda \end{pmatrix}$, $\ell_1(u_{2i}) \leq N - 1$, $1 \leq \ell_1(w_{2i}) \leq N$ derived from $P_{2i}$.

Let $I_c$ (resp. $I_r$) consists of column (resp. row) tables, where each table includes all the C-type (resp. R-type) picture-insertion rules with the same length of triplet.

By the context-checking of picture-insertion rules, concerning R-type picture-insertion rules, the R1-type rules are applied first and only once. Then, R2-type picture-insertion rules are used to simulate $L(G_{2i})$.

The topmost row generated by $G_1$ can be simulated by C-type picture-insertion rules, and each column can be simulated by R-type picture-insertion rules. Finally, we eliminate the symbols $S_{2i}$ and $\#$ using the coding $\varphi$.    □

**Corollary 11.** *The class of $INPA$ is incomparable with the class of $CFML$.*

*Proof.* In the one-dimensional case, the class of insertion systems is incomparable with that of context-free languages. Thus, the corollary holds for these one-dimensional language relationships.    □

# 6   Properties and Comparisons of Picture-Insertion Systems Using the Independent Mode

Next, we consider picture-insertion systems using the independent mode and obtain the following results.

**Lemma 12.** *The class of $INPI$ is not closed under the operations of union, column catenation, or row catenation. The class is closed under transposition.*

*Proof.* Consider the picture languages $L_i(\gamma_1)$ in Example 4 and the picture language $L_4$ which is obtained by placing $d$ in the place of $b$ as for $L_i(\gamma_1)$.

The proof is similar to the proof for Lemma 6 for picture-insertion systems using the alongside mode.    □

For the generative powers, in the following, we compare picture-insertion systems with tiling systems.

**Lemma 13.** *The class of $INPI$ is incomparable with the class of $REC$.*

*Proof.* The proof is similar to the proof for Lemma 7.    □

**Lemma 14.** *The class of $INPI$ is incomparable with the class of $P2DCFL$.*

*Proof.* The proof is almost the same as Lemma 8.

Consider a pure 2D context-free grammar $G = (\Sigma, P_c, P_r, \{\, \begin{smallmatrix} a b a \\ d e d \end{smallmatrix} \,\})$ in Lemma 8. As in Lemma 8, we can prove by contradiction that there is no picture-insertion system $\gamma$ such that $L(G) = L_i(\gamma)$.

Next, we consider a picture-insertion system $\gamma_3 = (\{a, b\}, I_c, I_r, A)$ in Lemma 8. A picture language $L_i(\gamma_3)$ consists of pictures such that $(a^3 b^3 (ab)^n)^{m\ominus}$ with $m \geq 1$ and $n \geq 0$.

From the above two results, we obtain the claim.    □

*Note 15.* Consider a picture-insertion system $\gamma = (\Sigma, I_c, I_r, A)$, the C-type rule of which is of the form $(a, w, \lambda)$ with $a \in \Sigma$, $w \in \Sigma^*$, and the R-type rule is of the form $\begin{pmatrix} a, \\ w^T, \\ \lambda \end{pmatrix}$ with $a \in \Sigma$, $w^T \in \Sigma^*$.

Then, there is a pure 2D context-free grammar $G$ such that $L_i(\gamma) = L(G)$. The proof is obvious from the definition. For example, a C-type picture-insertion rule $(a, w, \lambda)$ can be simulated by the rule $a \to aw$. Therefore, a restricted insertion system using the independent mode is simulated by a pure 2D context-free grammar.

**Lemma 16.** *Both, $INPA$ and $INPI$ are incomparable.*

*Proof.* Consider the picture-insertion system $\gamma_1$ over $\Sigma = \{a, b\}$ in Example 4. We show that the picture language $L_a(\gamma_1)$ in $INPA$ is not in $INPI$.

Suppose that there is a picture-insertion system $\gamma$ such that $L_a(\gamma_1) = L_i(\gamma)$. Each column table in $\gamma$ consists of one C-type picture-insertion rule. For any string $w$ in a Dyck language, and C-type picture-insertion rule, the derivation in $\gamma$ proceeds deterministically, i.e., there should be only one place where the picture-insertion rule can be applied. Otherwise, the picture-insertion rule can generate a picture with different row strings.

For a C-type picture-insertion rule $(u, w, v)$ which satisfies $\alpha u v \beta \Longrightarrow_a \alpha u w v \beta$ with $\alpha, u, w, v, \beta \in \Sigma^*$ and $\alpha u v \beta, \alpha u w v \beta \in L_a(\gamma_1)$. For the string $\alpha u v \beta \alpha u v \beta$ in $L_a(\gamma_1)$, there are two substrings $uv$ in $\alpha u v \beta \alpha u v \beta$ for which we can apply the picture-insertion rule $(u, w, v)$. Thus, we have a contradiction.

On the other hand, we show that the picture language $L_i(\gamma_1)$ in $INPI$ is not in $INPA$. Suppose that there is a picture-insertion system $\gamma' = (\Sigma, I_c, I_r, A)$ such that $L_i(\gamma_1) = L_a(\gamma')$. Let $n = max\{\ell_1(\alpha) \mid \alpha \in A\} + max\{|uwv| \mid (u, w, v)$ be a C-type picture-insertion rule in $I_c\}$.

Consider a picture $\begin{smallmatrix} a^{2n} b^{2n} a b \\ a b a^{2n} b^{2n} \end{smallmatrix}$. For the first row $a^{2n} b^{2n} ab$, a picture-insertion rule is applied to the nested structure of $a^{2n} b^{2n}$ at least twice. On the other hand, for the second row $aba^{2n} b^{2n}$, the substring $ab$ without a nested structure is followed by $a^{2n} b^{2n}$. Therefore, there is no way to generate the picture using the alongside mode.

From the above two results, we obtain the claim.    □

# 7   Picture-Insertion Systems with Regular Control

We introduce an additional function for picture-insertion systems to control the application of picture-insertion rules. As is noted in [12], controlling the application with a regular language remains the generative power in general. However, the control for pure 2D context-free grammars properly increases their generative power. We apply regular control to picture-insertion systems and present the results below.

**Definition 17.** *A picture-insertion system with regular control $\gamma(R)$ is a tuple $(\gamma, R)$, where $\gamma = (\Sigma, I_c, I_r, A)$ is a picture-insertion system and $R$ is a regular language over $\Gamma$ with a set of table labels of $I_c$ and $I_r$.*

For pictures $p_1$ and $p_2$ in $\Sigma^{**}$, we write $p_1 \overset{t}{\Longrightarrow}_a p_2$ (resp. $p_1 \overset{t}{\Longrightarrow}_i p_2$) if $p_1$ derives $p_2$ using the alongside mode (resp. independent mode) using C-type (resp. R-type) insertion rules in the column table $t$ in $I_c$ (resp. $I_r$).

For a picture-insertion system $\gamma = (\Sigma, I_c, I_r, A)$ and a regular language $R$ over $\Gamma$, a regular control picture-insertion language $L_a(\gamma(R))$ using the alongside mode is a set of pictures $w \in \Sigma^{**}$ such that $S \overset{\alpha}{\Longrightarrow}_a w$, $\alpha \in \Gamma^*$, $\alpha \in R$. Similarly, a regular control picture-insertion language $L_i(\gamma(R))$ using the independent mode is a set of pictures $w \in \Sigma^{**}$ such that $S \overset{\alpha}{\Longrightarrow}_i w$, $\alpha \in \Gamma^*$, $\alpha \in R$.

Let $INPAC$ (resp. $INPIC$) be a set of regular control picture-insertion languages using the alongside mode (resp. independent mode).

*Example 18.* Consider a picture-insertion system $\gamma_1 = (\Sigma, I_c, I_r, A)$ in Example 4 and a regular language $R = \{(t_{c1} t_{r1} t_{r1})^n \mid n \geq 1\}$ with $t_{c1} = \{(\lambda, ab, \lambda)\}$ and
$$t_{r1} = \{ \begin{pmatrix} a, \\ a, \\ \lambda \end{pmatrix}, \begin{pmatrix} b, \\ b, \\ \lambda \end{pmatrix} \}.$$
The C-type insertion rule in $t_{c1}$ inserts picture $ab$ and widens two columns. Each R-type rule in $t_{r2}$ inserts the picture $a$ or $b$ and widens one row. The regular control language $(t_{c1} t_{r1} t_{r1})^n$ with $n \geq 1$ enables the generated pictures to be proportionate to the lengths of rows and columns.

**Lemma 19.** $INPA \subset INPAC$. $INPI \subset INPIC$.

*Proof.* From the definition of $INPAC$ and $INPIC$, the inclusions $INPA \subseteq INPAC$ and $INPI \subseteq INPIC$ are obvious.

As noted in Lemma 7, there is no picture-insertion system $\gamma$ such that $L(\gamma)$ consists of squares.

From Example 18, there is a picture language which consists of infinitely many square pictures in $INPAC$ and $INPIC$. Then, the proper inclusion is proved. □

The lemmas imply that regular control properly increases generative power for picture-insertion systems.

# 8    Concluding Remarks

In this paper, we introduced picture-insertion systems which generate picture languages and for the language classes generated by picture-insertion systems, we considered comparisons with two-dimensional computing models. Furthermore, in order to perform the derivations, we defined regular control of the picture-insertion systems, which properly increases the generative powers.

In the future, as in the one-dimensional case, picture insertion-*deletion* systems can be defined in which we can use not only picture-insertion operations but also *deletion* operations.

Using insertion systems together with some morphisms, characterizing and representation theorems have been given for the one-dimensional case [3] [4]. We discuss whether similar representation theorems are possible in the two-dimensional case.

**Acknowledgments.** The present study was supported by JSPS KAKENHI Grant Number 23740081.

# References

1. Cherubini, A., Crespi-Reghizzi, S., Pradella, M., Pietro, P.S.: Picture languages: Tiling systems versus tile rewriting grammars. Theoretical Computer Science 356(1-2), 90–103 (2006)
2. Easwarakumar, K.S., Murugan, A.: Possibilities of constructing two dimensional pictures in DNA computing: Part I. Int. J. Comput. Math. 82(11), 1307–1321 (2005)
3. Fujioka, K.: Morphic characterizations of languages in Chomsky hierarchy with insertion and locality. Inf. Comput. 209(3), 397–408 (2011)
4. Fujioka, K.: Morphic characterizations with insertion systems controlled by a context of length one. Theoretical Computer Science 469, 69–76 (2013)
5. Inoue, K., Nakamura, A.: Some properties of two-dimensional on-line tessellation acceptors. Information Science 13(2), 95–121 (1977)
6. Ma, X., Lombardi, F.: Synthesis of tile sets for DNA self-assembly. IEEE Trans. on CAD of Integrated Circuits and Systems 27(5), 963–967 (2008)
7. Maurer, H.A., Salomaa, A., Wood, D.: Pure grammars. Information and Control 44(1), 47–72 (1980)
8. Murugan, A., Easwarakumar, K.S.: Possibilities of constructing two dimensional pictures in DNA computing: Part II. Int. J. Comput. Math. 83(1), 1–20 (2006)
9. Pradella, M., Cherubini, A., Reghizzi, S.C.: A unifying approach to picture grammars. Information and Computation 209(9), 1246–1267 (2011)
10. Păun, G., Rozenberg, G., Salomaa, A.: DNA Computing. New Computing Paradigms. Springer (1998)
11. Rozenberg, G., Salomaa, A. (eds.): Handbook of formal languages. Springer-Verlag New York, Inc., New York (1997)
12. Subramanian, K.G., Ali, R.M., Geethalakshmi, M., Nagar, A.K.: Pure 2D picture grammars and languages. Discrete Appl. Math. 157(16), 3401–3411 (2009)
13. Winfree, E., Liu, F., Wenzler, L., Seeman, N.: Design and Self-assembly of Two-dimensional DNA Crystals. Nature 394, 539–544 (1998)

# Differential Evolution-Based Weighted Combination of Distance Metrics for $k$-means Clustering

Muhammad Marwan Muhammad Fuad

Forskningsparken 3, Institutt for kjemi, NorStruct
The University of Tromsø - The Arctic University of Norway, NO-9037 Tromsø, Norway
marwan.fuad@uit.no

**Abstract.** Bio-inspired optimization algorithms have been successfully used to solve many problems in engineering, science, and economics. In computer science bio-inspired optimization has different applications in different domains such as software engineering, networks, data mining, and many others. One of the main tasks in data mining is clustering, namely $k$-means clustering. Distance metrics are at the heart of all data mining tasks. In this paper we present a new method which applies differential evolution, one of the main bio-inspired optimization algorithms, on a time series $k$-means clustering task to set the weights of the distance metrics used in a combination that is used to cluster the time series. The weights are obtained by applying an optimization process that gives optimal clustering quality. We show through extensive experiments how this optimized combination outperforms all the other stand-alone distance metrics, all by keeping the same low complexity of the distance metrics used in the combination.

**Keywords:** Evolutionary Computing, Differential Evolution, Distance Metrics, $k$-means Clustering, Time Series Data Mining.

## 1 Introduction

*Global optimization* is a ubiquitous problem that has a very broad range of applications in engineering, economics, and others. In computer science optimization has different applications in software engineering, networking, data mining and other domains. Optimization can be defined as the action of finding the best-suited solution of a problem within given constraints. These constraints can be in the boundaries of the parameters controlling the optimization problem, or in the function to be optimized. Optimization problems can be classified according to whether they are: discrete/continuous/hybrid,constrained/unconstrained, single objective/multi-objective, unimodal (one extreme point) / multimodal (several extreme points).

Formally, an optimization task can be defined as follows: Let $\overrightarrow{X} = \left[ x_1, x_2, ..., x_{nbp} \right]$ be the candidate solution to the problem for which we are searching an optimal solution. Given a function $f : U \subseteq \mathbf{R}^{nbp} \to \mathbf{R}$, find the solution $\overrightarrow{X^*} = \left[ x_1^*, x_2^*, ..., x_{nbp}^* \right]$

A.-H. Dediu et al. (Eds.): TPNC 2014, LNCS 8890, pp. 193–204, 2014.

(*nbp* is the number of parameters) which satisfies $f\left(\overrightarrow{X^*}\right) \leq f\left(\overrightarrow{X}\right), \forall \overrightarrow{X} \in U$. The function *f* is called the *fitness function*, the *objective function*, or the *cost function*. It is worth mentioning here that it is a convention for optimization problems to be expressed as minimization problems since any maximization optimization problem can be transformed into a minimization problem.

*Metaheuristics* are probabilistic optimization algorithms which are applicable to a large variety of optimization problems. Many of these metaheuristics are inspired by natural processes, natural phenomena, or by the collective intelligence of natural agents, hence the term *bio-inspired*, also called *nature-inspired*, optimization algorithms.

Bio-inspired optimization can be classified into two main families; the first is *Evolutionary Algorithms* (EA). This family is probably the largest family of bio-inspired algorithms. EA are population based algorithms that use the mechanisms of Darwinian evolution such as selection, crossover and mutation. Of this family we cite *Genetic Algorithms* (GA), *Genetic Programming* (GP), *Evolution Strategies* (ES), and *Differential Evolution* (DE). The other family is *Swarm Intelligence* (SI). This family uses algorithms which simulate the behavior of an intelligent biological system. Of this family we mention *Particle Swarm Intelligence* (PSO), *Ant Colony Optimization* (ACO), and *Artificial Bee Colony* (ABC). Fig. 1 shows the main bio-inspired metaheuristics.

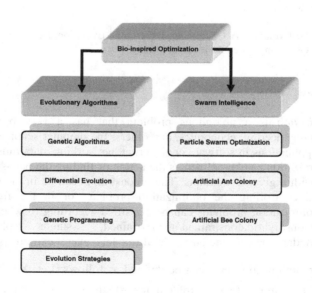

**Fig. 1.** Some of the main bio-inspired metaheuristics

Data mining is a field of computer science which handles several tasks such as classification, clustering, anomaly detection, and others. Processing these tasks usually requires extensive computing. As with other fields of computer science, different papers have proposed applying bio-inspired optimization to data mining tasks [11], [12], [13], [14], [15].

In this paper we apply one bio-inspired optimization technique on a particular task of time series data mining which is $k$-means clustering. This task includes using a distance metric or a similarity measure. In this work we use a weighted combination of distance metrics to cluster the time series. The novelty of our work is that the weights of the combination are obtained through an optimization process using differential evolution as an optimizer. The experiments we conducted clearly show how the proposed combination can enhance the quality of the $k$-means clustering of time series compared with the clustering quality obtained when using the distance metrics that constitute the combination as stand-alone distances.

The rest of the paper is organized as follows; the related work is presented in Section 2, in Section 3 we introduce the new algorithm, which we test in Section 4. We conclude this paper with Section 5.

## 2    Related Work

A *time series* is an ordered collection of observations at intervals of time points. These observations are real-valued measurements of a particular phenomenon.

Time series data mining handles several tasks such as classification, clustering, similarity search, motif discovery, anomaly detection, and others.

*Clustering*, also called *unsupervised learning*, is partitioning of the data objects into groups, or clusters, so that the objects within a cluster are similar to one another and dissimilar to objects in other clusters. [8]. There are several basic clustering methods such as *Partitioning Methods*, *Hierarchical Methods*, *Density-Based Methods*, and *Grid-Based Methods*. *k-means*, is a centroid-based partitioning technique which uses the *centroid* (also called *center*) of a cluster; $c_i$, to represent that cluster. Conceptually, the centroid of a cluster is its center point. The centroid can be defined in various ways such as by the mean of the objects assigned to the cluster. *k*-means is one of the most widely used and studied clustering formulations [9] . In *k*-means clustering we are given a set of $n$ data points in $d$-dimensional space $R^d$ and an integer $k$ and the problem is to determine a set of $k$ points in $R^d$, the centroids, so as to minimize the mean distance from each data point to its nearest center [9]. More formally, the $k$-means clustering error can be measured by:

$$E = \sum_{i=1}^{k} \sum_{j=1}^{n_j} d\left(u_{ij}, c_i\right)$$

(1)

Where $u_{ij}$ is the $i$th point in the $j$th cluster, and $n_j$ is the number of points in that cluster. The quality of the $k$-means clustering increases as the error given in relation (1) decrease. Fig. 2 shows the flow chart of the $k$-means algorithm.

The number of clusters is decided by the user, or application-dependent, or given by some cluster validity measure.

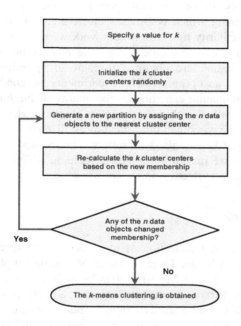

**Fig. 2.** Flow chart of the $k$-means clustering algorithm

The $k$-means starts by selecting the centroids $c_i$ , which are usually chosen randomly. In step two the membership of each of the $n$ data points is determined by assigning it to the nearest cluster centroid. In step three $c_i$ are re-calculated assuming the memberships obtained in step two are correct. If none of the $n$ data objects have changed its membership the algorithm stops otherwise it goes back to step tow. Fig. 3 shows an example of the different steps of the $k$-means clustering with $n=30$ and $k=3$.

The concept of similarity on which clustering, and other data mining tasks, is based is a fundamental one in data mining. In the similarity search problem a pattern or a query is given and the similarity search algorithm seeks to retrieve the data objects in the database that are "close" to that query according to some semantics that quantify this closeness. This closeness or similarity is quantified using a principal concept which is the *similarity measure* or its strongest form; the *distance metric*. Distance metrics satisfy the well-known metric axioms (non-negativity, symmetry, identity, triangle inequality). Metric spaces have many advantages, the most famous of which is that a single indexing structure can be applied to several kinds of queries and data types that are so different in nature. This is mainly important in establishing unifying models for the search problem that are independent of the data type. This makes metric spaces a solid structure that is able to deal with several data types [16]

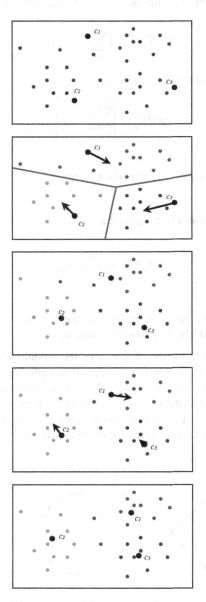

**Fig. 3.** The different steps of the $k$-means clustering algorithm

There are many similarity measures and distance metrics that are widely used in the field of time series data mining; the most-widely known is the *Minkowski distance*. This is actually a whole family of distances, the most famous of which are:

**i- Euclidean Distance ($L_2$)-** defined between time series $S$ and $T$ as:

$$L_2(S,T) = \sqrt{\sum_{i=1}^{n}(s_i - t_i)^2} \qquad (2)$$

**ii- Manhattan Distance ($L_1$)-** defined as:

$$L_1(S,T) = \left|\sum_{i=1}^{n}(s_i - t_i)\right| \qquad (3)$$

This distance is also called the *city block distance*.

**iii- Maximum Distance ($L_\infty$)-** defined as:

$$L_\infty(S,T) = \max_i\left(|s_i - t_i|\right) \qquad (4)$$

This distance is also called the *infinity distance* or the *chessboard distance*. Fig. 4 shows a few examples of the Minkowski distance.

It is important to mention here that one of the advantages of the members of the Minkowski distance is their low computational complexity which is $O(n)$. It is also important to emphasize, and this is related to the experimental section of our paper, that the aforementioned distances are all distance metrics. A last note about this, which is also related to the experimental section of this work, is that all these distances are applicable only to time series of the same length.

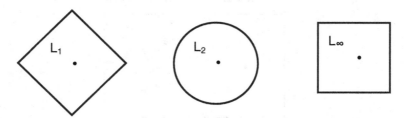

**Fig. 4.** From left to right; the Manhattan distance, the Euclidean distance, and the infinity distance

# 3    Using a Combination of Distance Metrics for $k$-Means Clustering

Instead of using one similarity measure or distance metric to handle data mining tasks, we can use a combination of several similarity measures or distance metrics to get better results. This idea has been proposed by several researchers before. In [2] the authors propose utilizing a similarity function defined as a weighted combination of several metrics to handle the similarity search problem. A similar idea was proposed in [3] where the authors present a retrieval method based on a weighted combination of feature vectors. However, these two works do not suggest using any optimization algorithm to determine the weights.

In this paper we propose utilizing a weighted combination of distance metrics to handle the $k$-means clustering task of time series data. The novelty of our method is: (i) the weights are determined as the outcome of an optimization process and (ii) it proposes a combination of distance metrics to handle a clustering task of time series data.

Formally, we perform a $k$-means clustering task of time using a combination $d$ which is defined as:

$$d(S,T) = \sum_{i=1}^{n} \omega_i d_i(S,T) \tag{5}$$

where $\omega_i \in [0,1]$.

Notice that we could also impose that $\sum_i \omega_i = 1$, but this would not make any difference as this latter condition is simply a normalized version of the one used in (5).

As mentioned earlier, we determine the weights $\omega_i$ through an optimization process, where the objective function to be maximized is the quality of the $k$-means clustering. The optimization algorithm we use is differential evolution.

## 3.1    Differential Evolution

Differential Evolution (DE) is an optimization method based on the principles of genetics and natural selection. DE is considered as one the most powerful stochastic optimization algorithms for continuous parameters [4]. DE has the same elements as a standard evolutionary algorithm; i.e. a population of individuals, selection according to fitness, crossover, and random mutation. DE creates an environment in which a population of individuals, representing solutions to a particular problem, is allowed to evolve under certain rules towards a state that minimizes the value of the fitness function.

As with other evolutionary algorithms, the first step of DE is defining the problem variables and the fitness function. The range of the variable values can be constrained or unconstrained. A particular configuration of variables produces a certain value of the fitness function and the objective of DE is to find the configuration that gives the optimal value of the fitness function.

DE has many variations, but in the following we present the classical DE. DE starts with a collection of randomly chosen individuals constituting a population, whose size is *popsize*. Each of these solutions is a vector of *nbp* dimensions and it represents a possible solution to the problem at hand. The fitness function of each individual is evaluated. The next step is optimization. In this step for each individual of the population, which we call the *target vector* $\vec{T_i}$ at this stage, three mutually distinct individuals $\vec{V_{r1}}, \vec{V_{r2}}, \vec{V_{r3}}$, and different from $\vec{T_i}$, are chosen at random from the population (hence the minimum value of *popsize* is 4). The *donor vector* $\vec{D}$ is formed as a weighted difference of two of $\vec{V_{r1}}, \vec{V_{r2}}, \vec{V_{r3}}$, added to the third; i.e. $\vec{D} = \vec{V_{r1}} + F(\vec{V_{r2}} - \vec{V_{r3}})$. $F$ is called the *mutation factor* or the *differentiation constant* and it is one of the *control parameters* of DE. $F$ is usually chosen from $[0,1[$.

The *trial vector* $\vec{R}$ is formed from elements of the target vector $\vec{T_i}$ and elements of the donor vector $\vec{D}$ according to different schemes such as the *exponential* and the *binomial* ones [1]. In the following we present the crossover scheme presented in [6] which we adopt in this paper; an integer *Rnd* is randomly chosen among the dimensions $[1, nbp]$. This guarantees that at least one of the dimensions will be changed. Then the trial vector $\vec{R}$ is formed as follows:

$$
t_i = \begin{cases} t_{i,r1} + F(t_{i,r2} - t_{i,r3}) & \text{if } (rand_{i,j}[0,1[ < C_r) \vee (Rnd = i) \\ t_{i,j} & \text{otherwise} \end{cases} \tag{6}
$$

where $i = 1,...,nbp$. $C_r$ is the *crossover constant*, which is another control parameter. The control parameters of DE are determined by the algorithm designer.

The next step of DE is selection. This step decides which of the trial vector and the target vector will survive in the next generation and which will die out. The selection is based on which of the two vectors; trial and target, yields a better value of the fitness function.

Crossover and selection repeat for a certain number of generations *NrGen*, which is the third control parameter of DE. Most algorithms add a *stopping criterion*, which terminates DE if met, even if *NrGen* has not been reached.

# 4    Experiments

We conducted extensive experiments using time series datasets of different sizes and dimensions available at UCR [10]. This archive makes up between 90% and 100% of all publicly available, labeled time series datasets in the world, and it represents the interest of the data mining/database community, and not just one group [5].

The distances we are using in the combination in relation (5) are the Euclidean distance, the Manhattan distance, and the maximum distance (relations (2), (3), and (4)).

In the time series data mining community *Dynamic Time Warping* (DTW) [7] is widely used, however we decided not to include it in the combination for several reasons; first, DTW is a similarity measure and not a distance metric, while $L_2$, $L_1$, $L_\infty$ are all distance metrics, so their combination will result in a distance metric, while combining a similarity measure (such as DTW) with distance metrics will result in a similarity measure (this can be easily proved mathematically). The second reason why we are not adding DTW to the combination is that DTW has a higher complexity, which is $O(mn)$ (or $O(n^2)$ if the two time series have the same length), whereas, the three other distances have a complexity, as mentioned in Section 2, of $O(n)$ . The third reason for not adding DTW is that it is applied to time series of different lengths, which is not the case with the other three distances. For all these reasons we decided to exclude DTW from the combination despite its widespread use in time series data mining, so our final combination is:

$$d(S,T) = \omega_1 L_1(S,T) + \omega_2 L_2(S,T) + \omega_3 L_\infty(S,T) \qquad (7)$$

We tested our method on a variety of datasets; the length of the time series varied between 60 (Synthetic_control) and 1639 (CinC_ECG_torso). The size of the training sets varied between 20 (SonyAIBORobot Surface) and 467 (ChlorineConcentration). The size of the testing sets varied between 30 (OliveOil) and 3840 (ChlorineConcentration), so as we can see, we tested our method on a wide range of datasets of different lengths and sizes to avoid getting biased results.

For each dataset the experiment consists of two phases; the training phase and the testing phase. In the training phase we perform an optimization process where the parameters of the optimization problem are the weights $\omega_i ; i \in [1,3]$. The objective function is the $k$-means clustering quality which we seek to maximize. The outcome of this optimization problem is the weights $\omega_i$ which give the optimal $k$-means clustering quality (c.f. Section 2).

In the testing phase, these optimal weights are used on the corresponding testing datasets to evaluate the quality of the $k$-means clustering.

As for the elements of the DE, we used the following : the population size *popsize* was 12, the number of generations *NrGen* was set to 100, the differentiation constant $F$ was set to 0.9, and the crossover constant $C_r$ was set to 0.5. The dimension of the problem *nbp*, as we mentioned earlier, is $\omega_i$. Table 1 summarizes the values of the control parameters of DE used in the experiments.

**Table 1.** The values of the control parameters of DE used in the experiments

| *popsize* | Population size | 12 |
|-----------|-----------------|-----|
| *NrGen* | Number of generations | 100 |
| *F* | Differentiation constant | 0.9 |
| *C$_r$* | Crossover constant | 0.5 |
| *nbp* | Number of parameters | 3 |

Table 2 shows the optimal weights for the three distances metric for the different training datasets after running the algorithm for 100 generations. As we can see the weights vary between 0 and 0.97, which proves that some distance metrics are more effective for clustering certain datasets than others.

In the next phase we use these weights shown in Table 2 on the corresponding testing datasets to get the *k*-means clustering quality. Table 3 shows the *k*-means clustering quality for the combination together with those for $L_2$, $L_1$, $L_\infty$ for comparison.

Table 3 shows that the clustering quality of the combination of the three distance metrics for all the datasets outperforms that of all the other three distance metrics for $L_2$, $L_1$, $L_\infty$ as stand-alone distance metrics, which proves the validity of our proposed algorithm.

**Table 2.** Weights assigned to each distance metric after 100 generations on the training datasets

| dataset | $\omega_1$ | $\omega_2$ | $\omega_3$ |
|---------|------|------|------|
| Synthetic_control | 0.34 | 0.39 | 0.76 |
| OSULeaf | 0.95 | 0.94 | 0.25 |
| Lighting2 | 0.57 | 0.09 | 0.97 |
| Lighting7 | 0.86 | 0.21 | 0.27 |
| SonyAIBORobotSurfac | 0.55 | 0.80 | 0.22 |
| FaceFour | 0.40 | 0.16 | 0.58 |
| ECG200 | 0.01 | 0.02 | 0.93 |
| Yoga | 0.34 | 0.88 | 0.11 |
| OliveOil | 0.72 | 0.83 | 0.87 |
| CinC_ECG_torso | 0.43 | 0.20 | 0.38 |
| ChlorineConcentration | 0.00 | 0.00 | 0.67 |
| Haptics | 0.63 | 0.51 | 0.26 |
| MedicalImages | 0.63 | 0.11 | 0.69 |
| Cricket_X | 0.02 | 0.01 | 0.88 |
| Cricket_Y | 0.36 | 0.12 | 0.76 |

**Table 3.** The $k$-means clustering quality of the combination and $L_2$, $L_1$, $L_\infty$ on the testing datasets

| dataset | k-means clustering quality | | | |
|---|---|---|---|---|
| | $L_1$ | $L_2$ | $L_\infty$ | combination |
| Synthetic_control | 0.57 | 0.71 | 0.64 | 0.73 |
| OSULeaf | 0.39 | 0.40 | 0.33 | 0.41 |
| Lighting2 | 0.56 | 0.63 | 0.63 | 0.65 |
| Lighting7 | 0.54 | 0.57 | 0.50 | 0.64 |
| SonyAIBORobotSurfac | 0.87 | 0.66 | 0.69 | 0.92 |
| FaceFour | 0.61 | 0.54 | 0.55 | 0.67 |
| ECG200 | 0.69 | 0.69 | 0.62 | 0.72 |
| Yoga | 0.50 | 0.48 | 0.48 | 0.51 |
| OliveOil | 0.57 | 0.57 | 0.57 | 0.58 |
| CinC_ECG_torso | 0.49 | 0.47 | 0.46 | 0.52 |
| ChlorineConcentration | 0.40 | 0.40 | 0.40 | 0.41 |
| Haptics | 0.33 | 0.32 | 0.32 | 0.34 |
| MedicalImages | 0.33 | 0.34 | 0.30 | 0.37 |
| Cricket_X | 0.30 | 0.27 | 0.30 | 0.31 |
| Cricket_Y | 0.31 | 0.32 | 0.36 | 0.38 |

## 5    Conclusion

In this paper, we presented a new algorithm for $k$-means clustering of time series data using a combination of weighted distance metrics. The weights of the combination are obtained through an optimization process where the optimizer is differential evolution; one of the most effective bio-inspired optimization algorithms for continuous optimization problems, all by keeping a low complexity of the combination. The extensive experiments we conducted show the superiority of our proposed combination over other, widely-used distance metrics, as stand-alone distance metrics.

As future work, we like to study how our proposed algorithm can be extended to cluster streaming data as an important application in time series data mining.

## References

1. Biswas, A., Dasgupta, S., Das, S., Abraham, A.: A Synergy of Differential Evolution And Bacterial Foraging Algorithm for Global Optimization. Neural Netw. World 17(6), 607–626 (2007)
2. Bustos, B., Skopal, T.: Dynamic Similarity Search in Multi-metric Spaces. In: Proceedings of the ACM Multimedia, MIR Workshop, pp. 137–146. ACM Press, New York (2006)
3. Bustos, B., Keim, D.A., Saupe, D., Schreck, T., Vranić, D.: Automatic Selection and Combination of Descriptors for Effective 3D Similarity Search. In: Proceedings of the IEEE International Workshop on Multimedia Content-based Analysis and Retrieval, pp. 514–521. IEEE Computer Society (2004)
4. Das, S., Suganthan, P.N.: Differential Evolution: A Survey of the State-of-the-Art. IEEE Trans. on Evolutionary Computation (February 2011)

5. Ding, H., Trajcevski, G., Scheuermann, P., Wang, X., Keogh, E.: Querying and Mining of Time Series Data: Experimental Comparison of Representations and Distance Measures. In: Proc of the 34th VLDB (2008)
6. Feoktistov, V.: Differential Evolution: in Search of Solutions (Springer Optimization and Its Applications). Springer- Verlag New York, Inc., Secaucus (2006)
7. Guo, A., Siegelmann, H.: Time-warped Longest Common Subsequence Algorithm for Music Retrieval. In: Proc. ISMIR (2004)
8. Han, J., Kamber, M., Pei, J.: Data Mining: Concepts and Techniques, 3rd edn. Morgan Kaufmann (2011)
9. Kanungo, T., Netanyahu, N.S., Wu, A.Y.: An Efficient K-means Clustering Algorithm: Analysis and Implementation. IEEE Transactions on Pattern Analysis and Machine Intelligence 24(7) (2002)
10. Keogh, E., Zhu, Q., Hu, B., Hao, Y., Xi, X., Wei, L., Ratanamahatana, C.A.: The UCR Time Series Classification/Clustering Homepage, http://www.cs.ucr.edu/~eamonn/time_series_data/
11. Muhammad Fuad, M.M.: ABC-SG: A New Artificial Bee Colony Algorithm-Based Distance of Sequential Data Using Sigma Grams. In: The Tenth Australasian Data Mining Conference - AusDM 2012, Sydney, Australia, December 5-7 (2012)
12. Muhammad Fuad, M.M.: Differential Evolution versus Genetic Algorithms: Towards Symbolic Aggregate Approximation of Non-normalized Time Series. In: Sixteenth International Database Engineering & Applications Symposium– IDEAS 2012, Prague, Czech Republic, August 8-10, pp. 8–10. BytePress/ACM (2012)
13. Muhammad Fuad, M.M.: Particle swarm optimization of information-content weighting of symbolic aggregate approximation. In: Zhou, S., Zhang, S., Karypis, G. (eds.) ADMA 2012. LNCS, vol. 7713, pp. 443–455. Springer, Heidelberg (2012)
14. Muhammad Fuad, M.M.: Towards Normalizing the Edit Distance Using a Genetic Algorithms–Based Scheme. In: Zhou, S., Zhang, S., Karypis, G. (eds.) ADMA 2012. LNCS, vol. 7713, pp. 477–487. Springer, Heidelberg (2012)
15. Muhammad Fuad, M.M.: Using Differential Evolution to Set Weights to Segments with Different Information Content in the Piecewise Aggregate Approximation. In: 16th International Conference on Knowledge-Based and Intelligent Information & Engineering Systems, KES 2012, San Sebastian, Spain, September 10-12. Frontiers of Artificial Intelligence and Applications (FAIA), IOS Press (2012)
16. Zezula et al.: Similarity Search - The Metric Space Approach, Springer (2005)

# Inferring Multiobjective Phylogenetic Hypotheses by Using a Parallel Indicator-Based Evolutionary Algorithm

Sergio Santander-Jiménez and Miguel A. Vega-Rodríguez

Department of Technologies of Computers and Communications,
University of Extremadura, Escuela Politécnica, Campus Universitario s/n,
10003 Cáceres, Spain
{sesaji,mavega}@unex.es

**Abstract.** The application of multiobjective optimization techniques to solve biological problems has significantly grown in the last years. In order to generate satisfying approximations to the Pareto-optimal set, two key problems must be addressed. Firstly, we must distinguish solution quality in accordance with the optimization goal, usually measured by means of multiobjective quality indicators. Secondly, we must undertake the development of parallel designs to carry out searches over exponentially growing solution spaces. This work tackles the reconstruction of phylogenetic relationships by applying an Indicator-Based Evolutionary Algorithm. For this purpose, we propose a parallel design based on OpenMP which considers the computation of hypervolume-based indicators in fitness assignment procedures. Experiments on four biological data sets show significant results in terms of parallel scalability and multiobjective performance with regard to other methods from the literature.

**Keywords:** Applications of Natural Computing, Parallel Computing, Indicator-Based Evolutionary Algorithm, Phylogenetic Inference.

## 1 Introduction

Current trends on bioinformatics must deal with optimization problems whose solution cannot be addressed in polynomial times. In this sense, the multiobjective nature of a wide range of biological processes requires the optimization of multiple criteria, which can support conflicting solutions for a same biological data. When dealing with multiobjective optimization problems (MOPs) [3], we seek to find those Pareto solutions $s$ in a decision space $X$ which optimize $n$ objective functions $f_1$, $f_2$ ... $f_n$ belonging to an objective space $Y$. A common way to compare solutions in a context where multiple objectives are involved is the application of the dominance relation. Given two solutions $s_1$ and $s_2$ to a MOP, $s_1$ dominates ($\succ$) $s_2$ iff $\forall\ i \in [1, 2...n]$, $f_i(s_1)$ is not worse than $f_i(s_2)$ and $\exists\ i \in [1, 2...n]$, $f_i(s_1)$ is better than $f_i(s_2)$. Those solutions which are non-dominated with regard to the overall decision space compose the Pareto-optimal set.

A.-H. Dediu et al. (Eds.): TPNC 2014, LNCS 8890, pp. 205–217, 2014.

Due to the large amount of possible solutions to be considered, most MOPs show NP-hard complexities which motivate the infeasibility of finding this set. Therefore, multiobjective approaches often rely on soft computing techniques to achieve good approximations to the Pareto-optimal set in reasonable times. However, when multiple time-demanding objective functions are taken into account, the development of parallel multiobjective metaheuristics is required [15].

This research focuses on the application of parallel multiobjective approaches to tackle one of the hardest biological problems: the reconstruction of phylogenetic hypotheses [9]. When inferring evolutionary relationships among species, phylogenetic methods have to deal with search spaces which grow exponentially with the number of species, along with computationally intensive evaluation procedures. Early bioinspired attempts to tackle these issues suggested the relevance of taking advantage of parallel architectures to reduce execution times [10]. As a result, multiple researches have proposed algorithmic designs for phylogenetics based on parallel [1] and natural computing [5]. In fact, current state-of-the-art proposals for single-criterion phylogenetic analysis focus heavily on these principles. We can highlight RAxML [14], a widely-used method for performing parallel phylogenetic analyses according to the maximum likelihood criterion.

One of the reasons which motivate the formulation of phylogenetic inference as a MOP is given by the need to solve those situations where different optimality criteria support conflicting evolutionary relationships [11]. Given the additional complexity of performing phylogenetic searches attending to multiple criteria simultaneously, the requirement of designing parallel bioinspired approaches becomes more remarkable. In [2], Cancino et al. addressed the problem of inferring phylogenetic hypotheses according to two principles: maximum parsimony and maximum likelihood. For this purpose, they applied a parallel multiobjective genetic algorithm known as PhyloMOEA, achieving significant performance when using master-worker designs under different parallel technologies.

Traditionally, runtime searches in dominance-based multiobjective methods like PhyloMOEA were governed by the classification of solutions based on Pareto rankings. The post-hoc assessment of the generated outcome can be carried out by using quality indicators which map a Pareto set to a real number for measuring its quality. In order to obtain improved solutions, modern multiobjective designs consider the idea of introducing quality indicators as fitness measurements to guide the search [16]. Taking into account this strategy, we address in this paper the inference of phylogenetic trees attending to parsimony and likelihood. For this purpose, we apply a parallel Indicator-Based Evolutionary Algorithm (IBEA) supported by the standard OpenMP to perform phylogenetic searches on multicore machines. The assessment of this approach will be carried out by experimentation on four real nucleotide data sets, making comparisons of parallel results, multiobjective performance, and biological quality with other parallel phylogenetic methods and dominance-based multiobjective proposals.

The remainder of this paper is organized as follows. The next section introduces the basis of phylogenetics, formulating the two optimality criteria to be considered. Section 3 discusses the concept of quality indicator and describes the parallel design of IBEA. Experimental results are presented and assessed in Section 4. Finally, conclusions and future work lines are provided in Section 5.

## 2  Inferring Phylogenetic Relationships

The current availability of sequence data from different species represents an opportunity for researchers to provide new hypotheses about the evolution of living organisms. Phylogenetic inference methods aim to describe evolutionary relationships by studying the molecular features observed in the species under review. Such features are characterized by data sets containing $N$ biological sequences of $L$ sites represented in accordance with a state alphabet $\alpha$, usually taken as $\alpha=\{A,C,G,T\}$ in the case of DNA-based inference. The results of the inference process are represented by using tree data structures known as phylogenetic trees. A phylogeny $T=(V,E)$ identifies evolutionary relationships between living and hypothetical organisms in the node set $V$ by means of branches in $E$.

Two main sources of complexity explain the NP-hard nature of this problem [9]. Firstly, the number of possible phylogenetic topologies is determined by the number of species $N$ in the input dataset. Data sets with more than ten species cannot be tackled by using exhaustive searches, as increasing values of $N$ lead to an exponential growth of the tree space. Secondly, the evaluation times required by the computation of objective functions grow linearly with the length $L$ of the input sequences. Due to the current need to analyze sequences involving hundreds and thousands of molecular sites, the assessment of solutions according to time-demanding criteria represents a noticeable source of complexity.

### 2.1  Optimality Criteria

The different principles supported by different phylogenetic methods often give as a result conflicting phylogenies for the same biological data [11]. A multiobjective approach must deal with the problem of inferring not a single solution according to a single objective function, but a set of multiple Pareto trees supported by multiple criteria simultaneously. As a result, bioinspired and parallel developments must be undertaken. In this research, we will consider two well-known principles to conduct multiobjective analyses: parsimony and likelihood.

The parsimony criterion seeks for the simplest explanation to the evolution of the input species. Such hypothesis is given by the phylogenetic tree which reduces the amount of state changes observed between related species. Given a biological dataset containing $N$ sequences of length $L$, this criterion aims to find the phylogeny $T=(V,E)$ which minimizes the parsimony length $P(T)$ [9]:

$$P(T) = \sum_{i=1}^{L} \sum_{(a,b)\in E} C(a_i, b_i), \tag{1}$$

where $(a, b) \in E$ refers to the evolutionary relationship between two nodes $a, b \in V$, $a_i$ and $b_i$ are the states at the $i$-th character of the sequences related to $a$ and $b$, and $C(a_i, b_i)$ quantifies the number of state changes between $a_i$ and $b_i$.

On the other hand, likelihood-based approaches are supported by the assumptions made by evolutionary models, which provide the probabilities of observing mutations at molecular level. Using this information in the inference process, likelihood procedures aim to find the phylogenetic tree which represents the most likely evolutionary history, the hypothesis which maximizes the likelihood statistical function. Given a dataset composed of $N$ sequences of $L$ characters whose states are defined according to an alphabet $\alpha$, and a phylogenetic topology $T=(V,E)$ rooted by $r \in V$ with descendant nodes $u, v \in V$, we define the likelihood of $T$ under the evolutionary model $\mu$ $L[T, \mu]$ in the following way [9]:

$$L[T,\mu] = \prod_{i=1}^{L} \sum_{x,y \in \alpha} \pi_x \left[ P_{xy}(t_{ru}) L_p \left( u_i = y \right) \right] \times \left[ P_{xy} \left( t_{rv} \right) L_p \left( v_i = y \right) \right], \quad (2)$$

where $\pi_x$ refers to the stationary probability of $x \in \alpha$, $P_{xy}(t)$ is the mutation probability from a state $x$ to $y$ within a time $t$, and $L_p(u_i = y)$, $L_p(v_i = y)$ the partial likelihoods of observing state $y$ at the $i$-th site in $u$ and $v$ sequences.

## 3    Parallel Indicator-Based Evolutionary Algorithm

In order to address phylogenetic inference as a MOP, we will apply an algorithmic approach based on the concept of quality indicator. This section introduces the algorithmic features of IBEA and proposes a parallel design for phylogenetics.

### 3.1    Quality Indicators

The performance of multiobjective algorithms is usually assessed by means of quality indicators. A quality indicator is defined as a function that maps the outcome of a multiobjective optimizer to a real number which can be used as a performance measure. Given an indicator $I$, the aim of the optimization process is to find the set of Pareto solutions $S$ which optimize the value $I(S)$. This concept can also be applied to distinguish the quality of different solutions by integrating the computation of quality indicators into fitness calculations. Under this assumption, Zitzler and Künzli proposed IBEA [16], a population-based metaheuristic which incorporates the information provided by quality indicators into the selection mechanism to improve multiobjective results.

A wide variety of quality indicators can be found in the literature [3]. One of the most widely-used and reliable multiobjective metrics is hypervolume. For a MOP involving two objectives, hypervolume gives the area of the objective space bounded by two reference points (ideal and nadir) which is dominated by the outcome of a multiobjective algorithm. Higher hypervolume values suggest better multiobjective quality. On the basis of this metrics, a hypervolume-based quality indicator named as $I_{HD}$ was proposed in [16]. Given two sets of Pareto solutions $R$ and $S$, we can compute $I_{HD}$ as follows:

$$I_{HD}(R, S) = \begin{cases} I_H(S) - I_H(R) & \text{if } \forall s \in S, \exists s' \in R : s' \succ s, \\ I_H(R + S) - I_H(R) & \text{otherwise.} \end{cases} \quad (3)$$

In this expression, $I_H(R)$ and $I_H(S)$ refer to the area of the objective space dominated by $R$ and $S$, respectively, with regard to a reference point $Z$, so $I_{HD}(R, S)$ represents the space dominated by $S$ but not by $R$. This definition can be applied to compare two solutions $s_i$ and $s_j$ directly, by considering $R = \{s_i\}$ as the set containing the solution $s_i$ and $S = \{s_j\}$ as the set composed of $s_j$.

## 3.2    Algorithmic Design

IBEA manages a population $P$ of individuals representing possible solutions to the problem, whose multiobjective quality is measured by means of quality indicators. Our proposal for phylogenetic inference will use the hypervolume-based indicator $I_{HD}$ for fitness measurement purposes. The input parameters for IBEA include the number of individuals in the population (*popSize*), the maximum number of evaluations considered as a stop criterion (*maxEvaluations*), crossover and mutation probabilities (*crossoverProb, mutationProb*), a scaling factor used in fitness computations ($\kappa$), and the $I_{HD}$ reference point ($Z$).

With the aim of adapting this algorithm to phylogenetic inference, individuals in $P$ are represented by using *NxN* symmetric floating-point matrices of genetic distances, where $N$ is the number of species under study. In a distance matrix $m$, each entry $m[i,j]$ represents the evolutionary distance of the path between the organisms $i$ and $j$. By processing such structures, we can perform searches over an auxiliary matrix space, mapping the obtained results into the tree topology space. For this reason, we apply BIONJ [9], a well-known tree-building method which takes as input the matrices processed by IBEA and generates the corresponding phylogenetic topologies. We have used the C++ bioinformatics library Bio++ [8] for implementation purposes.

The initialization of $P$ is performed by assigning initial matrices generated from randomly selected starter topologies contained in a repository of 1000 phylogenies. Afterwards, the main loop of IBEA operates over $P$ by applying indicator-based selection, generating new individuals by using distance-based crossover and mutation operators. Each generation involves the following tasks. Firstly, the current state of $P$ is examined by ranking each individual according to how useful it is attending to the considered quality indicator. The fitness assignment for an individual $P_i$ is carried out by normalizing its objective functions scores (parsimony and likelihood) to the interval $[0,1]$ and then summing up its $I_{HD}$ values with respect to each remaining individual $P_j$ [16] as follows:

$$P_i.Fitness = \sum_{P_j \in P \setminus \{P_i\}} -e^{-I_{HD}(\{P_j\},\{P_i\})/c \cdot \kappa}. \quad (4)$$

In this equation, $c$ refers to the maximum absolute indicator value, which is included to avoid widely spread indicator scores. By using these fitness values, an environmental selection is performed in a second step to keep the most promising *popSize* individuals. This mechanism is implemented by removing iteratively the individual $P_k$ with the smallest fitness value from $P$ until the size of the population fits the parameter *popSize*, updating the fitness values of the remaining individuals $P_i$ as: $P_i.Fitness = P_i.Fitness + e^{-I(\{P_k\},\{P_i\})/c \cdot \kappa}$.

From these *popSize* individuals, an offspring population $P'$ is generated by applying the following genetic operators. In the first place, parent selection is carried out by performing binary tournaments in accordance with the calculated fitness values. Offspring matrices are then generated by applying a uniform crossover operator which swaps randomly chosen rows from the parent matrices, along with a repair operator based on BLX-$\alpha$ [12] to preserve symmetry. Finally, the mutation operator applies the gamma distribution observed in genetic distances [10] to modify randomly chosen entries in the offspring matrices. After obtaining the resulting matrices $P_i'.m$, the corresponding phylogenetic trees $P_i'.T$ are inferred, optimized via topological rearrangements [6], and evaluated according to parsimony and likelihood. Both populations $P$ and $P'$ are combined and a new generation takes place. IBEA pseudocode is shown in Algorithm 1.

---

**Algorithm 1.** Parallel IBEA Pseudocode

---

```
 1. #pragma omp parallel (num_threads)
 2. P ← Initialize Population (popSize, dataset, num_threads), ParetoSet ← 0
 3. while ! stop criterion reached (maxEvaluations) do
 4.     #pragma omp single
 5.         P ← Scale Objective Values (bounds(P))
 6.     #pragma omp for schedule (schedulingType)
 7.         for i = 1 to |P| do
 8.             for j = 1 to |P| do
 9.                 indicatorValues[i][j] ← Compute I_HD Values (P_i, P_j, Z) /* i≠j */
10.             end for
11.         end for
12.     #pragma omp single
13.         P_i.Fitness ← Assign Fitness Values (indicatorValues) /* ∀i: i=1 to |P| */
14.         while |P| > popSize do
15.             k ← Remove the Individual with the Smallest Fitness Value (P)
16.             P_i.Fitness ← Update Fitness Values (indicatorValues, k) /* ∀i: i=1 to |P| */
17.         end while
18.     #pragma omp for schedule (schedulingType)
19.         for i = 1 to popSize do
20.             selectedParent_1, selectedParent_2 ← selectParents (P)
21.             P_i'.m ← Apply Crossover (selectedParent_1.m, selectedParent_2.m, crossoverProb)
22.             P_i'.m ← Apply Mutation (P_i'.m, mutationProb)
23.             P_i'.T ← Apply Tree-Building Method ("BIONJ", P_i'.m, dataset)
24.             P_i'.scores ← Evaluate Solution (P_i'.T, dataset)
25.         end for
26.     #pragma omp single
27.         P ← P ∪ P'
28.         ParetoSet ← updateParetoSet (P, ParetoSet)
29. end while
```

---

## 3.3  Parallel Approach

The pseudocode in Algorithm 1 describes an OpenMP-based parallel design for IBEA. The suitability of this algorithm to be parallelized is given by the fact that the loops for computing $I_{HD}$ values and generating offspring solutions show no dependencies between different iterations. By exploiting multicore architectures, we can reduce the times required by these loops, which contain the most computationally expensive steps of the algorithm. In this sense, the most time-demanding operations are given by the tree-building and optimization procedure and the parsimony and likelihood computations for evaluation purposes, which depend on the size of the matrix/topology and the length of the input sequences. Furthermore, the evaluation step often represents an interval of 60-80% over the overall execution time in most phylogenetic methods [1]. This is the reason which motivates the need to take advantage of parallelism in this context.

The parallel design of IBEA defines a pool of *num_threads* OpenMP threads which will be used in accordance with the needs of parallel processing. For this purpose, the directive *#pragma omp parallel* encloses the main loop of IBEA (line 1 in Algorithm 1). This idea aims to minimize those thread creation and destruction overheads which arise when *#pragma omp parallel for* directives are iteratively called inside a loop. While data-dependent functions and data structure management operations are carried out by using *#pragma omp single* directives, we apply *#pragma omp for* directives to distribute $I_{HD}$ computations (lines 6-11) and the generation of the offspring population $P'$ (lines 18-25) among OpenMP threads. Regarding this last step, load balance techniques are also introduced by defining a guided *scheduleType* in order to avoid idle threads when divergent times appear in the inference and evaluation of topologies.

## 4  Experimental Results

This section details the methodology we have used to evaluate IBEA, reporting the experimental results obtained by experimentation on four real biological data sets [2]: rbcL_55, 55 sequences (1314 nucleotides per sequence) of rbcL plastid gene; mtDNA_186, 186 sequences (16608 nucleotides per sequence) of human mitochondrial DNA; RDPII_218, 218 sequences (4182 nucleotides per sequence) of prokaryotic RNA; and ZILLA_500, 500 sequences (759 nucleotides per sequence) of rbcL plastid gene. Our analyses were carried out under the widely-used General Time Reversible (GTR+$\Gamma$) evolutionary model [9].

The hardware architecture considered in our experiments is composed of two 12-core AMD Opteron Magny-Cours 6174 processors at 2.2 GHz (a total of 24 processing cores) with 32GB DDR3 RAM, running Scientific Linux 6.1. We compiled our software by using GCC 4.4.5 with the GOMP_CPU_AFFINITY flag enabled to ensure CPU-thread affinity. The assessment of evolutionary algorithms needs to find, in a first step, the configuration of input parameters which allows the approach to maximize performance. For this purpose, we have studied by experimentation a range of different input values for each parameter, assessing the outcome of each configuration by using the hypervolume metrics.

In accordance with our experiments, the optimal settings found for IBEA are given by the following values: $maxEvaluations$=10000, $popSize$=96, $crossover$-$Prob$=70%, $mutationProb$=5%, $\kappa$=0.05, and $Z$=(2,2).

**Parallel Scalability.** Firstly, we will examine the scalability achieved by the OpenMP version of IBEA on system configurations involving 4, 8, 16, and 24 execution cores. For this purpose, 11 independent runs were carried out per dataset and system configuration, measuring parallel performance by applying two metrics: speedup and efficiency. Table 1 provides the observed median speedups (SU, columns 2, 4, 6, and 8) and efficiencies (Eff., columns 3, 5, 7, and 9), along with the serial times needed to complete a phylogenetic analysis on each dataset.

According to this table, IBEA is able to achieve meaningful scalabilities in all the analyzed data sets, obtaining efficiencies in the interval 70.14 - 86.36% for 24 cores. In order to show the relevance of the obtained results, Table 1 also reports a comparison with the POSIX-based multicore version of RAxML [14]. With the aim of making a fair comparison, experiments with RAxML were carried out under the same experimental conditions as IBEA, configuring RAxML in accordance with IBEA serial execution times. As can be observed, the parallel design of IBEA outperforms the speedup factors reported by RAxML when considering system sizes of 16 and 24 cores. A graphical representation of the scalabilities shown by IBEA and RAxML is given by Figure 1.

According to these results, our speedup factors show an improvement as we increase the number of species in the input dataset. This can be explained in accordance with the implications of the Amdahl's law for multicore machines. By considering growing number of species, the generation and evaluation of offspring solutions will involve more computations over growing matrix and tree data structures. As these operations take place inside parallel regions defined by *#pragma omp for* directives, an increase in the parallelizable fraction of this application is expected, leading the design to better parallel results.

**Table 1.** Speedup and efficiencies

| | 4 cores | | 8 cores | | 16 cores | | 24 cores | |
|---|---|---|---|---|---|---|---|---|
| | SU | Eff.(%) | SU | Eff.(%) | SU | Eff.(%) | SU | Eff.(%) |
| Algorithm | | | | | | | | |
| **rbcL_55 *(IBEA serial time = 5367.60 seconds)*** | | | | | | | | |
| IBEA | 3.66 | 91.56 | **6.95** | **86.87** | **12.32** | **77.01** | **16.83** | **70.14** |
| RAxML | **3.68** | **91.94** | 6.26 | 78.23 | 8.33 | 52.04 | 8.77 | 36.56 |
| **mtDNA_186 *(IBEA serial time = 47630.98 seconds)*** | | | | | | | | |
| IBEA | 3.83 | 95.83 | 7.21 | 90.12 | **12.90** | **80.60** | **17.56** | **73.17** |
| RAxML | **3.96** | **99.12** | **7.24** | **90.47** | 10.39 | 64.93 | 12.89 | 53.70 |
| **RDPII_218 *(IBEA serial time = 51657.38 seconds)*** | | | | | | | | |
| IBEA | **3.86** | **96.44** | **7.30** | **91.21** | **13.37** | **83.56** | **18.01** | **75.03** |
| RAxML | 3.52 | 88.06 | 6.54 | 81.72 | 9.31 | 58.19 | 11.35 | 47.27 |
| **ZILLA_500 *(IBEA serial time = 71754.79 seconds)*** | | | | | | | | |
| IBEA | **3.87** | **96.73** | **7.68** | **96.05** | **14.57** | **91.08** | **20.73** | **86.36** |
| RAxML | 3.73 | 93.33 | 5.99 | 74.89 | 7.41 | 46.33 | 7.72 | 32.17 |

**Table 2.** Speedup comparison with PhyloMOEA (16 cores)

| | PhyloMOEA | |
|---|---|---|
| Dataset | MPI | Hybrid |
| rbcL_55 | 7.30 | 8.30 |
| mtDNA_186 | 7.40 | 8.50 |
| RDPII_218 | 9.80 | 10.20 |
| ZILLA_500 | 6.70 | 6.30 |

| Dataset | IBEA |
|---|---|
| rbcL_55 | **12.32** |
| mtDNA_186 | **12.90** |
| RDPII_218 | **13.37** |
| ZILLA_500 | **14.57** |

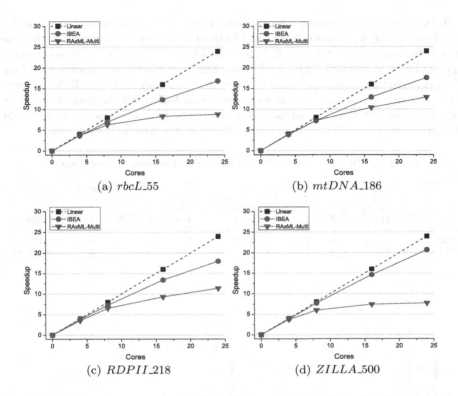

(a) $rbcL\_55$

(b) $mtDNA\_186$

(c) $RDPII\_218$

(d) $ZILLA\_500$

**Fig. 1.** Parallel performance - scalabilities with regard to the theoretical linear speedup

In order to make comparisons with other parallel multiobjective methods for phylogenetics, Table 2 introduces a comparison with the speedup factors reported by PhyloMOEA in [2] for 16 execution cores. Two parallel designs of PhyloMOEA were proposed in the literature: an MPI-based master-worker design and a hybrid OpenMP/MPI scheme. In accordance with Table 2, IBEA improves significantly the results published for both PhyloMOEA versions in all the considered data sets, showing the relevance of IBEA parallel implementation.

**Multiobjective Results.** The next step of this study is the multiobjective evaluation of the approach. For this purpose, we present a comparison with a well-known dominance-based multiobjective metaheuristic, NSGA-II [4]. We have implemented this algorithm by considering the same individual representation and crossover/mutation operators described for IBEA. This comparison has been conducted by performing 31 independent runs per dataset of each algorithm, evaluating their outcomes by using the hypervolume metrics. Due to the stochastic nature of these approaches, we will check for significant differences in hypervolume samples by applying a statistical methodology [13] based on Kolmogorov-Smirnov, Levene, Wilcoxon-Mann-Whitney, and ANOVA tests.

Table 3 shows the median hypervolume scores and interquartile ranges (IQR) obtained by IBEA (columns 2, 3) and NSGA-II (columns 4, 5), as well as the statistical testing results (columns 6, 7) and the ideal/nadir points used to compute hypervolume (columns 8-11). In addition, Figure 2 shows the hypervolume box plots reported by each algorithm. Our experiments suggest that IBEA achieves a statistically significant improvement over NSGA-II in all the considered data sets, pointing out that the introduction of quality indicators as a way to guide the inference process leads to considerable multiobjective performance.

**Table 3.** Multiobjective performance evaluation under hypervolume

| | Hypervolume metrics | | | | | | Hypervolume reference points | | | |
| | IBEA | | NSGA-II | | Statistical testing | | Ideal | | Nadir | |
| Dataset | Median Hyp. | IQR | Median Hyp. | IQR | P-value | Significant? | Pars. | Like. | Pars. | Like. |
|---|---|---|---|---|---|---|---|---|---|---|
| rbcL_55 | **71.31** | 0.07 | 71.01 | 0.22 | 1.64E-06 | Yes | 4774 | -21569.69 | 5279 | -23551.42 |
| mtDNA_186 | **69.81** | 0.11 | 69.69 | 0.09 | 1.40E-05 | Yes | 2376 | -39272.20 | 2656 | -43923.99 |
| RDPII_218 | **74.24** | 0.08 | 73.58 | 0.06 | 1.27E-11 | Yes | 40658 | -132739.90 | 45841 | -147224.59 |
| ZILLA_500 | **72.32** | 0.04 | 71.77 | 0.03 | 1.08E-11 | Yes | 15893 | -79798.03 | 17588 | -87876.39 |

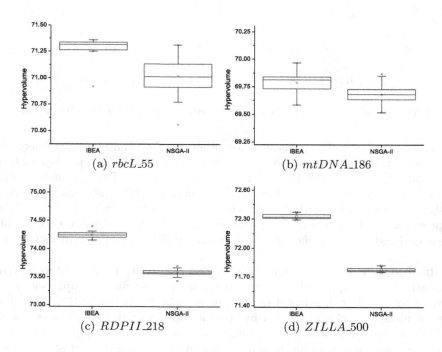

(a) $rbcL\_55$     (b) $mtDNA\_186$

(c) $RDPII\_218$     (d) $ZILLA\_500$

**Fig. 2.** Multiobjective performance - box plots for hypervolume

**Biological Comparisons.** Now we examine the biological quality of the phylogenetic topologies inferred by IBEA in the median hypervolume execution. To this end, we compare our maximum parsimony and likelihood trees with the ones generated by two single-criterion proposals from the literature: TNT [7] (for maximum parsimony) and RAxML (maximum likelihood). We will search for statistically significant differences in tree quality by applying a Kishino-Hasegawa-Templeton (KHT) test for parsimony and a Shimodaira-Hasegawa (SH) test for likelihood [9]. The results of applying these tests are given by Tables 4 and 5. From a biological perspective, the extreme Pareto trees inferred by IBEA are able to match the parsimony and likelihood quality found by the state-of-the-art tools TNT and RAxML, as no statistically significant differences are reported. Therefore, the indicator-based parallel approach allows an efficient exploitation of multicore resources, giving significant results not only from a multiobjective perspective, but also attending to biological criteria.

**Table 4.** KHT Comparison with TNT

| Dataset | Pars. Diff. | Std. Dev. | KHT output |
|---------|------|------|----------------------------|
| rbcL_55 | 0.00 | 8.95 | No stat. significant diff. |
| mtDNA_186 | 0.00 | 4.90 | No stat. significant diff. |
| RDPII_218 | 31.00 | 51.53 | No stat. significant diff. |
| ZILLA_500 | 0.00 | 12.81 | No stat. significant diff. |

**Table 5.** SH Comparison with RAxML

| Dataset | IBEA P-value | RAxML P-value | SH output |
|---------|---------|---------|----------------------------|
| rbcL_55 | 0.621 | 0.379 | No stat. significant diff. |
| mtDNA_186 | 0.380 | 0.620 | No stat. significant diff. |
| RDPII_218 | 0.592 | 0.408 | No stat. significant diff. |
| ZILLA_500 | 0.324 | 0.676 | No stat. significant diff. |

Finally, the study of biological results with regard to PhyloMOEA is given by Table 6. As PhyloMOEA only considers the Hasegawa-Kishino-Yano evolutionary model (HKY85+$\Gamma$), we have conducted new sets of 31 experiments per dataset with IBEA under this model. Our parsimony and likelihood trees outperform the ones generated by PhyloMOEA in all the considered data sets, showing the relevance of applying IBEA to address real phylogenetic analyses.

**Table 6.** Biological comparison with PhyloMOEA - HKY85+$\Gamma$ model

| Method | rbcL_55 Best pars. | Best like. | mtDNA_186 Best pars. | Best like. | RDPII_218 Best pars. | Best like. | ZILLA_500 Best pars. | Best like. |
|--------|----------|-----------|----------|-----------|----------|-------------|----------|-----------|
| IBEA | 4874 | -21821.11 | 2431 | -39888.07 | 41517 | -134260.26 | 16218 | -80974.93 |
| PhyloMOEA | 4874 | -21889.84 | 2437 | -39896.44 | 41534 | -134696.53 | 16219 | -81018.06 |

## 5 Conclusions

In this work, we have applied an indicator-based multiobjective metaheuristic to tackle the reconstruction of phylogenetic trees according to parsimony and likelihood. Due to the NP-hard nature of the problem, we have introduced a parallel design which aims to reduce the times required to perform real phylogenetic analyses on multicore machines. Experiments over four nucleotide data sets have pointed out a successful exploitation of a 24-core shared memory architecture, showing improved scalabilities with regard to other parallel phylogenetic methods of the literature. In addition, statistically reliable comparisons with NSGA-II and single-criterion biological approaches suggest that the introduction of quality indicators in multiobjective searches allows IBEA to infer high-quality Pareto trees attending to both multiobjective and biological perspectives.

As future research lines, we will focus on the design of new parallel and bioinspired developments for inferring phylogenetic histories. In this sense, the combination of swarm intelligence principles and quality indicators represents a promising line to maximize the multiobjective and biological quality of the inferred Pareto sets. Such designs will be implemented on the basis of parallel computing, introducing supercomputing and GPGPU/accelerator-based techniques to conduct multiobjective analyses over data sets with increasing complexity levels. Finally, we will undertake the comparison of the proposed approaches with other multiobjective metaheuristics available in the literature, along with other parallel biological methods.

**Acknowledgments.** This work was partially funded by the Spanish Ministry of Economy and Competitiveness and the ERDF (European Regional Development Fund), under the contract TIN2012-30685 (BIO project). Sergio Santander-Jiménez is supported by the grant FPU12/04101 from the Spanish Government.

# References

1. Bader, D.A., Stamatakis, A., Tseng, C.W.: Computational Grand Challenges in Assembling the Tree of Life: Problems and Solutions. In: Advances in Computers, vol. 68, pp. 127–176. Elsevier (2006)
2. Cancino, W., Jourdan, L., Talbi, E.-G., Delbem, A.C.B.: Parallel multi-objective approaches for inferring phylogenies. In: Pizzuti, C., Ritchie, M.D., Giacobini, M. (eds.) EvoBIO 2010. LNCS, vol. 6023, pp. 26–37. Springer, Heidelberg (2010)
3. Coello, C., Dhaenens, C., Jourdan, L.: Advances in Multi-Objective Nature Inspired Computing. Springer, Heidelberg (2010)
4. Deb, K., Pratap, A., Agarwal, S., Meyarivan, T.: A Fast and Elitist Multi–Objective Genetic Algorithm: NSGA-II. IEEE Trans. Evol. Comput. 6(2), 182–197 (2002)
5. Fogel, G.B.: Evolutionary Computation for the Inference of Natural Evolutionary Histories. IEEE Connections 3(1), 11–14 (2005)
6. Goëffon, A., Richer, J.M., Hao, J.K.: Progressive Tree Neighborhood Applied to the Maximum Parsimony Problem. IEEE/ACM Trans. Comput. Biol. Bioinform. 5(1), 136–145 (2008)
7. Goloboff, P.A., Farris, J.S., Nixon, K.C.: TNT, a free program for phylogenetic analysis. Cladistics 24(5), 774–786 (2008)
8. Guéquen, L., et al.: Bio++: efficient extensible libraries and tools for computational molecular evolution. Molecular Biology and Evolution 30(8), 1745–1750 (2013)
9. Lemey, P., Salemi, M., Vandamme, A.-M.: The Phylogenetic Handbook: a Practical Approach to Phylogenetic Analysis and Hypothesis Testing. Cambridge Univ. Press, Cambridge (2009)

10. Lewis, P.O.: A Genetic Algorithm for Maximum-Likelihood Phylogeny Inference Using Nucleotide Sequence Data. Mol. Biol. Evol. 15(3), 277–283 (1998)
11. Macey, J.R.: Plethodontid salamander mitochondrial genomics: A parsimony evaluation of character conflict and implications for historical biogeography. Cladistics 21(2), 194–202 (2005)
12. Poladian, L.: A GA for Maximum Likelihood Phylogenetic Inference using Neighbour-Joining as a Genotype to Phenotype Mapping. In: Genetic and Evolutionary Computation Conference, pp. 415–422 (2005)
13. Sheskin, D.J.: Handbook of Parametric and Nonparametric Statistical Procedures, 5th edn. Chapman & Hall/CRC Press, New York (2011)
14. Stamatakis, A.: RAxML Version 8: A Tool for Phylogenetic Analysis and Post-Analysis of Large Phylogenies. Bioinformatics 30(9), 1312–1313 (2014)
15. Talbi, E.-G., Mostaghim, S., Okabe, T., Ishibuchi, H., Rudolph, G., Coello Coello, C.A.: Parallel approaches for multiobjective optimization. In: Branke, J., Deb, K., Miettinen, K., Słowiński, R. (eds.) Multiobjective Optimization. LNCS, vol. 5252, pp. 349–372. Springer, Heidelberg (2008)
16. Zitzler, E., Künzli, S.: Indicator-Based Selection in Multiobjective Search. In: Yao, X., et al. (eds.) PPSN 2004. LNCS, vol. 3242, pp. 832–842. Springer, Heidelberg (2004)

# Combining Finite Element Method and L-Systems Using Natural Information Flow Propagation to Simulate Growing Dynamical Systems

Jean-Philippe Bernard[1], Benjamin Gilles[2], and Christophe Godin[1]

[1] Inria, Virtual Plants Project-Team, Université Montpellier 2, Bâtiment 5,
CC 06002, 860 rue de Saint Priest, 34095 Montpellier Cedex 5, France
[2] CNRS, Laboratoire d'Informatique, de Robotique et de Microélectronique de
Montpellier, Université Montpellier 2, Bâtiment 5, CC 06002, 860 rue de Saint Priest,
34095 Montpellier Cedex 5, France

**Abstract.** This paper shows how to solve a system of differential equations controlling the development of a dynamical system based on finite element method and L-Systems. Our methods leads to solve a linear system of equations by propagating the flow of information throughout the structure of the developing system in a natural way. The method is illustrated on the growth of a branching system whose axes bend under their own weight.

## 1 Introduction

Plants are complex branching organisms that undergo continuous development throughout their lifetime. To understand the key processes that control this development, a new type of modeling approach, called Functional-Structural Plant Models (FSPM) [8,19,17], has been developed in the last two decades. FSPMs combine a detailed description the plant architecture (in terms of axes or stem units) and physiological processes that participate to the branching system development (photosynthesis, water/sugar/mineral element transport, carbon allocation, bud growth, hormonal transport and regulation, interaction with gravity, etc.).

To build FSPMs, L-systems [16] have emerged as a dominant paradigm to describe both the development plant branching systems in time and to model the different bio-physical processes of interest [14,3]. L-systems make it possible to model the development of a plant by specifying rules of development for the different types of considered plant constituent in a declarative manner. At each time step, the language engine scans the constituents of the branching structure being computed and applies the developmental rule that corresponds to its type. Interestingly, at no moment the modeler needs to index the plant elements. As the rules are supposed to be local, it is sufficient in the rule specification to access the immediate neighbor components, for example referring in the rule to the predecessor and successor components of the current plant component.

A.-H. Dediu et al. (Eds.): TPNC 2014, LNCS 8890, pp. 218–230, 2014.

The propagation of a signal from the basis of the plant to the top provides a good example of such a principle of locality. Let a plant be represented a bracketed string I I [ I I ] I [ I ] I. This string represents a branching structure containing 7 components, all of type I (note that the structure contains no indexing of the components). Two consecutive I's represent two consecutive segments in the same axis of the plant, while a bracket indicates a branch inserted at the top of preceding left-hand component (Fig. 1). Then, let us imagine that the leftmost component in the string (at the plant basis) contains a signal $x = 1$, and that the signal $x$ is set to 0 in all the other components. To propagate the signal in time through the plant body, one needs to define a simple local rule such as (in pseudo-code form):

```
I   -->   { if predecessor().x == 1 then current().x = 1
          } produce I
```

meaning that a I symbol should be transformed over one time step in a I symbol (produce statement) after having set its internal signal value $x$ to 1 if the $x$ signal of the predecessor components in the plant was itself at set at 1. This local rule makes it possible to get completely rid of indexes when transferring information through the plant structure [13]. This specific feature of L-systems was used in the last decade to develop computational models for which the flow of information propagates in a natural way over the plant structure from component to component, e.g. [1] for the transport of carbon, [15] for the transport of water, and [10,5] for the reaction of plants to gravity. All these algorithms use finite difference methods (FDM) for which the plant is decomposed into a finite number of elements and quantities of interest (water content, sugar concentration, forces, displacements, etc.) correspond to discrete values attached to each component. Different FDM schemes have been developed for this based either on explicit or implicit methods [7,9].

FDM approaches use a local Taylor expansion to approximate differential equations and are easy to implement. However, the quality of the approximation between grid points is generally considered poor. The Finite Element Method is an alternative solution that uses an integral formulation. While more complex to implement, the quality of a FEM approximation is often higher than in the corresponding FDM approach [11]. In this paper, we intend to adapt the

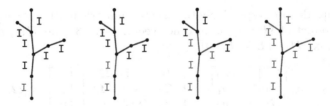

**Fig. 1.** Branch represented L-string I I [ I I ] I [ I ] I with information $x = 1$ (red segments) propagation to others segments (blue)

FEM approach to be used in the context of L-systems and natural computing, i.e. strictly respecting the paradigm of computational locality, and solving the differential equation by propagating information flows throughout the structure being computed. We illustrate and assess our generic approach on the problem of computing the effect of gravity on growing branching systems.

## 2  Natural Computing of Branch Bending Using Finite Difference Method (FDM) and L-Systems

### 2.1  Mechanical Model of Branch Bending

We model a branch as a set of inextensible elastic cantilever beams rigidly connected to each other and forming a branching network. Each beam represents a botanical axis and is conceptualized as a mean curve $\mathcal{C}$ of length $L$ with natural parameter $s \in [0, L]$ denoting the arc-length distance of a point $\boldsymbol{P}(s)$ from the base of the stem and a section $\mathcal{S}(s)$ (Fig. 2a).

Each point $\boldsymbol{P}(s)$ is associated with an orthonormal local frame $\mathcal{R}(s) = \{\boldsymbol{H}(s), \boldsymbol{L}(s), \boldsymbol{U}(s)\}$ (heading, left and up) similar to the Frenet's coordinate system [16]. We assume that vector $\boldsymbol{H}(s)$ is tangent to the rod axis and vectors $\boldsymbol{L}(s)$ and $\boldsymbol{U}(s)$ are $\mathcal{C}^0$-continuous with respect to $s$. Since all vectors $\boldsymbol{H}(s)$ have unit length the point $\boldsymbol{P}(s), s \in [0, L]$ is defined by:

$$\boldsymbol{P}(s) = \boldsymbol{P}(0) + \int_0^s \boldsymbol{H}(u)\, \mathrm{d}u. \tag{1}$$

Let $\boldsymbol{P}(s)$ and $\boldsymbol{P}(s + \mathrm{d}s)$ be two infinitesimally close points on the curve $\mathcal{C}$. Then the local frame $\mathcal{R}(s + \mathrm{d}s)$ can be obtained from $\mathcal{R}(s)$ by a rotation of axis $\Delta(s)$ and angle $\theta(s)$. It is convenient to represent this rotation by a vector $\boldsymbol{\Omega}(s)$, called the *generalized curvature*, whose direction is the rotation axis $\Delta(s)$ and whose norm is $\theta(s)$ (Fig. 2b) [10]. If the arc length $\mathrm{d}s$ is infinitesimal, this rotation can be factorized as a rotation around the tangent (twist) and a rotation around the normal (curvature) of the mean curve $\mathcal{C}$ at the point $\boldsymbol{P}(s)$. Starting from an initial frame $\mathcal{R}(0)$, the frames $\mathcal{R}(s)$ can be obtained thanks to the ordinary differential equation (2) [10]:

$$\mathrm{d}_s \mathcal{R}(s) = [\boldsymbol{\Omega}(s)]_\times \mathcal{R}(s), \tag{2}$$

where $[\boldsymbol{\Omega}(s)]_\times$ denote respectively the skew-symmetric matrix corresponding to the cross product of $\boldsymbol{\Omega}(s)$ with an other vector (Eq. (3))and $\mathcal{R}(s)$ denotes the column matrix $[\boldsymbol{H}(s), \boldsymbol{L}(s), \boldsymbol{U}(s)]$.

$$\boldsymbol{\Omega} \times \boldsymbol{v} = \begin{bmatrix} \Omega_0 \\ \Omega_1 \\ \Omega_2 \end{bmatrix} \times \begin{bmatrix} v_0 \\ v_1 \\ v_2 \end{bmatrix} = \begin{bmatrix} 0 & -\Omega_2 & \Omega_1 \\ \Omega_2 & 0 & -\Omega_0 \\ -\Omega_1 & \Omega_0 & 0 \end{bmatrix} \begin{bmatrix} v_0 \\ v_1 \\ v_2 \end{bmatrix} = [\boldsymbol{\Omega}]_\times \boldsymbol{v} \tag{3}$$

At rest, the branch geometry is characterized by its generalized curvature $\underline{\boldsymbol{\Omega}}$ and defines the reference configuration. At each point $\boldsymbol{P}(s)$, the elastic deformation of the material induces internal moments $\boldsymbol{M}^I(s)$ (departure from the rest

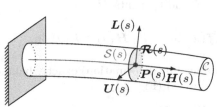
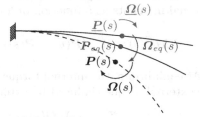

(a) Continuous representation of a beam: mean curve $\mathcal{C}$, section $\mathcal{S}(s)$ and frame $\mathcal{R}(s)$.

(b) Reference, calculated and equilibrium configurations.

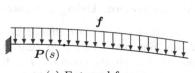
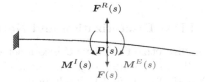

(c) External forces.

(d) Beam's reaction to the external stresses.

**Fig. 2.** Actors of the continuous model

configuration). We assume here for simplicity a linear constitutive law (Hooke's law). Classical beam theory [4] allows to compute those moments (Eq. (4)), as a function of the difference between the reference and actual generalized curvatures $\underline{\Omega}$ and $\Omega$:

$$M^I(s) = \mathcal{R}(s)\mathbb{C}(s)\mathcal{R}(s)^T\left(\underline{\Omega}(s) - \Omega(s)\right) = \mathbb{K}(s)\left(\underline{\Omega}(s) - \Omega(s)\right), \qquad (4)$$

where $\mathbb{K}(s)$ is the stiffness matrix. Note that the Hooke matrix $\mathbb{C}(s)$ expressed in the local frame $\mathcal{R}(s)$ is diagonal. Its coefficients are the twist rigidity $C_H(s)$ (in the plane $(L(s), U(s))$, as a function of section $\mathcal{S}(s)$ and shear modulus $G$) and the flexural rigidities $C_L(s)$ and $C_U(s)$ (respectively in the planes $(U(s), H(s))$ and $(H(s), L(s))$, as a function of section $\mathcal{S}(s)$ and young modulus $E$):

$$\mathbb{C}(s) = \begin{bmatrix} C_H(s) & \cdot & \cdot \\ \cdot & C_L(s) & \cdot \\ \cdot & \cdot & C_U(s) \end{bmatrix} \quad ; \quad \begin{cases} C_H(s) = G \int_{\mathcal{S}(s)} u^2 + v^2 \, dS \\ C_L(s) = E \int_{\mathcal{S}(s)} u^2 \, dS \\ C_U(s) = E \int_{\mathcal{S}(s)} v^2 \, dS \end{cases} , \qquad (5)$$

where $(u, v)$ are the coordinates in the plane $(L(s), U(s))$, with origin $P(s)$.

When external forces $f$ (such as the weight $f = \rho g$, Fig. 2c) are applied to the branch, external moments are induced. They result exclusively from the force densities $f([s, L])$ present downstream of $P(s)$. Denoting $F(s) = \int_s^L f(u) \, du$

the external force applied to segment $[s, L]$ due to gravity, we can express the external moments as a function of forces $\boldsymbol{F}$ and tangents $\boldsymbol{H}$:

$$\boldsymbol{M}^E(s) = \int_s^L \left(\boldsymbol{P}(u) - \boldsymbol{P}(s)\right) \times \boldsymbol{f}(u)\, \mathrm{d}u = \int_s^L \boldsymbol{H}(u) \times \boldsymbol{F}(u)\, \mathrm{d}u. \tag{6}$$

At equilibrium, the internal torque (induced by deformation) exactly balances the external torque (induced by external forces) (Fig. 2d):

$$\mathbb{K}(s)\left(\boldsymbol{\Omega}(s) - \boldsymbol{\Omega}_{eq}(s)\right) + \boldsymbol{M}^E(s) = \boldsymbol{0}, \tag{7}$$

where $\boldsymbol{\Omega}_{eq}$ denotes the generalized curvature at equilibrium:

$$\boldsymbol{\Omega}_{eq}(s) = \underline{\boldsymbol{\Omega}}(s) + \mathbb{K}(s)^{-1}\boldsymbol{M}^E(s). \tag{8}$$

## 2.2   FDM Discretization and Natural Integration Using L-Systems

Let us discretize the curve $\mathcal{C}$ into a set of $I + 1$ nodes $N_i$ of curvilinear abscissa $s_i, i = 0 \ldots I$ (usually regularly spaced though not necessarily) so that $N_0 = \boldsymbol{P}(0)$ and $N_I = \boldsymbol{P}(L)$. Each node is associated with its position $\boldsymbol{P}_i$, frame $\mathcal{R}_i$, external moments $\boldsymbol{M}_i^E$ or accumulated downstream forces $\boldsymbol{F}_i$. If distances $\mathrm{d}s_i = \|s_{i+1} - s_i\|$ are small enough, we can express (1), (2), and (6) thanks to Taylor's series at order 1 (Euler methods) [12].

Interestingly, point $\boldsymbol{P}_{i+1}$ and frame $\mathcal{R}_{i+1}$ can be recursively expressed in terms of the previous point $\boldsymbol{P}_i$ and frame $\mathcal{R}_i$, which allow us to compute these quantities in a single pass from the basis of the curve to its tip [18].

$$\boldsymbol{P}_{i+1} = \boldsymbol{P}_i + \mathrm{d}s_i\, \boldsymbol{H}_i, \tag{9}$$

$$\mathcal{R}_{i+1} = \mathcal{R}_i + \mathrm{d}s_i\, [\boldsymbol{\Omega}_i]_\times \mathcal{R}_i. \tag{10}$$

Likewise, external moments $\boldsymbol{M}_{i-1}^E$ and accumulated forces $\boldsymbol{F}_{i-1}$ can be recursively expressed in terms of $\boldsymbol{M}_i^E$ and $\boldsymbol{F}_i$ at the next node. Their computation can thus be carried out in a single pass from curve tip to basis.

$$\boldsymbol{M}_{i-1}^E = \boldsymbol{M}_i^E + \mathrm{d}s_{i-1}\, \boldsymbol{H}_i \times \boldsymbol{F}_i, \tag{11}$$

$$\boldsymbol{F}_{i-1} = \boldsymbol{F}_i + \int_{s_{i-1}}^{s_i} \boldsymbol{f}(u)\, \mathrm{d}u. \tag{12}$$

Due to large deformations, (7) is non-linear in terms of generalized curvature. To solve it, we use an explicit iterative method, and, specifically, a relaxation method [12] with a factor $r \in\, ]0, 1[$:

$$\boldsymbol{\Omega}^{t+1}(s) = (1 - r)\boldsymbol{\Omega}^t(s) + r(\underline{\boldsymbol{\Omega}}(s) + \mathbb{K}^t(s)^{-1}\boldsymbol{M}^{E^t}(s)), \tag{13}$$

with $\boldsymbol{\Omega}^0(s) = \underline{\boldsymbol{\Omega}}(s)$. The iterative process stops when the difference between two successive solutions is smaller than a tolerance $\|\boldsymbol{\Omega}^{t+1} - \boldsymbol{\Omega}^t\| < \varepsilon$.

The above recursive formulation makes it possible to define local L-system rules that will propagate in two pass across the branch structure, from node to node. The flow of computation goes as follows between two time steps:

```
Input: branch at time t
Output: branch at time t+1
do:
  L-system pass from tip to basis
    # computation of (11), (12), (13)
  L-system pass from basis to tip
    # computation of (9), (10)
until convergence condition of (13) reached
```

Sketch of a L-system rule used for the tip-to-basis pass

```
N --> { ds = abs( successor().s - current().s )
         current().F = successor().F  + ds * successor().f
            # ... computation of (11) and (13)
       } produce N
```

Sketch of a L-system rule used for the basis-to-tip pass

```
N --> { ds = abs( predecessor().s - current().s )
         current().P = predecessor().P + ds * predecessor.H
            # ... computation of (9), (10)
       } produce N
```

## 3 Natural Computing of Branch Bending Using Finite Element Method (FEM) and L-Systems

### 3.1 Computing Axis Bending by Axial Information Propagation with FEM

In FDM and FEM, continuous model domains are approximated using information at a finite number of discrete locations called nodes $N_i, i = 0, \ldots, I$. Whereas in FDM, solutions are only evaluated at nodes (and not elsewhere within the domain), in FEM the set of nodes correspond to the vertices of polygonal elements that tile the domain of interest. The solution is evaluated at each node using an integral formulation and interpolated over the whole domain using a basis of *shape functions* $\varphi_i$ associated with each node $N_i$) [2]. Here, our aim is to compute the generalized curvature $\Omega$ that characterizes the axis shape on the whole domain (i.e. on the curve $\mathcal{C}$). For this we decompose $\Omega$ on the set of shape functions:

$$\Omega(s) = \sum_{i=0}^{I} \Omega_i \varphi_i(s), \tag{14}$$

where $\Omega_i$ is a vector. Shape functions $\varphi_i$ are usually low order polynomials that are null on all node $N_j \neq N_i$ and have value 1 at node $N_i$. They are interpolating and form a partition of unity [2]. Their support is compact and their values at one node influences those of neighboring elements.

To compute values $\boldsymbol{\Omega}_i$ on nodes $N_i$, we have to solve the linear system $\mathbb{M}\boldsymbol{X} = \boldsymbol{B}$ defined by 15, [2]:

$$\sum_{i=0}^{I} \underbrace{\boldsymbol{\Omega}_i}_{=\boldsymbol{X}_i^T} \underbrace{\int_{\mathcal{C}} \varphi_i(s)\varphi_j(s)\,\mathrm{d}s}_{=\mathbb{M}_{ji}} = \underbrace{\int_{\mathcal{C}} \boldsymbol{\Omega}(s)\varphi_j(s)\,\mathrm{d}s + \int_{\mathcal{C}} \mathbb{K}(s)^{-1}\boldsymbol{M}^E(s)\varphi_j(s)\,\mathrm{d}s}_{=\boldsymbol{B}_j^T}, \quad (15)$$

where $\mathbb{M}_{ij}$ correspond to the energy of the cross influence of nodes $N_j$ and $N_i$ on the axis, $\boldsymbol{X}_i = \boldsymbol{\Omega}_i^T$ and $\boldsymbol{B}_i$ to the energy of forces along the axis which influence the generalized curvature $\boldsymbol{\Omega}_i$ of the node $N_i$. If the mass-matrix coefficient $\mathbb{M}_{ji}$ can be analytically computed (shape function are known) and expressed as a sum of integrals on each element, we have to compute numerically the right hand-side $\boldsymbol{B}_j$. Because this term is not linear, we split up each element in several integration areas and use midpoint method [12] to numericaly approach the integrals (note that one may also use the Gauss points method [12]).

Properties of mass-matrix (symmetric and positive definite) allow us to use a Cholesky decomposition [12] (product of a low triangular matrix with its transpose) to solve in two data propagation through the structure thanks to forward substitution (17) and backward substitution (18) algorithms [12].

$$\mathbb{M} = \mathbb{L}\mathbb{L}^T \quad , \quad \begin{cases} \mathbb{L}_{ij} = \dfrac{\mathbb{M}_{ij} - \sum_{k=0}^{j-1} \mathbb{L}_{ik}\mathbb{L}_{jk}}{\mathbb{L}_{jj}}, \forall 0 \leqslant j < i \leqslant I \\[3mm] \mathbb{L}_{ii} = \sqrt{\mathbb{M}_{ii} - \sum_{k=0}^{i-1} \mathbb{L}_{ik}^2}, \quad \forall 0 \leqslant i \leqslant I \end{cases} \quad (16)$$

$$\mathbb{L}\boldsymbol{Y} = \boldsymbol{B} \quad , \quad \boldsymbol{Y}_i = \dfrac{\boldsymbol{B}_i - \sum_{k=0}^{i-1} \mathbb{L}_{ik}\boldsymbol{Y}_k}{\mathbb{L}_{ii}}, \forall 0 \leqslant i \leqslant I \quad (17)$$

$$\mathbb{L}^T\boldsymbol{X} = \boldsymbol{Y} \quad , \quad \boldsymbol{X}_i = \dfrac{\boldsymbol{Y}_i - \sum_{k=i+1}^{I} \mathbb{L}_{ki}\boldsymbol{Y}_k}{\mathbb{L}_{ii}}, \forall I \geqslant i \geqslant 0 \quad (18)$$

Cholesky decomposition (16) and forward substitution (17) algorithms can be computed together with one pass, e.g. from basis-to-tip (resp. from tip to basis) and the backward substitution (18) algorithm can be computed with an a pass in the reverse direction, e.g. from tip to basis (resp. from basis to tip).

## 3.2   Extension to Branching Systems

We now need to extend the previous algorithm so that it can cope with branching organizations of beams that would represent plant structures. As in a branching structure, each element has only one parent, ramifications do not influence forward propagations (update of frames $\mathcal{R}(s)$ and points $\boldsymbol{P}(s)$).

Solving the linear system $\mathbb{M}\boldsymbol{X} = \boldsymbol{B}$ is more difficult in case of ramification than in the case of a single axis. Non-null elements $\mathbb{M}_{ij}$ in the matrix $\mathbb{M}$ correspond to branch segments between nodes $N_i$ and $N_j$ such that the product of the shape functions $\varphi_i$ and $\varphi_j$ along these segments is non-null. Therefore, the position of non-null elements in $\mathbb{M}$ depends on the indexing of the tree nodes. We consider two indexing strategies: a forward and a backward strategies indexing respectively the elements from basis to tip (matrix $M^f$) and from tip to basis (matrix $M^b$). Using either of indexing strategies, matrices have a block structure according to the set of nodes between two branching points (Fig. 3).

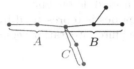

**Fig. 3.** Sets of nodes corresponding to each block of matrices $M^f$ and $M^b$

$$M^f = \begin{bmatrix} M^f_{AA} & & sym \\ M^f_{AB} & M^f_{BB} & \\ M^f_{AC} & \cdot & M^f_{CC} \end{bmatrix} \quad ; \quad M^b = \begin{bmatrix} M^b_{BB} & & sym \\ \cdot & M^b_{CC} & \\ M^b_{AB} & M^b_{AC} & M^b_{AA} \end{bmatrix}. \tag{19}$$

With the same notations, we can compute $L^f$ and $L^b$ the Cholesky decomposition matrices of $M^f = L^f L^{f^T}$ and $M^b = L^b L^{b^T}$ respectively. Then, building the direted acyclic graphs that correspond to data propagation in Cholesky decomposition algorithm. It is possible to show that only the Cholesky decomposition $L^b$ keeps non-null coefficients at exactly the same places as those of the original matrix $M^b$ (Fig. 4) [6].

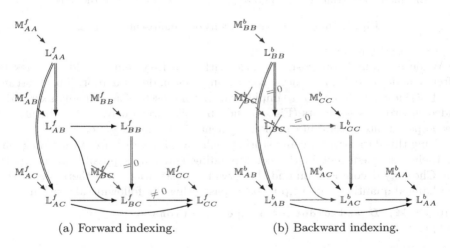

(a) Forward indexing.     (b) Backward indexing.

**Fig. 4.** Direted acyclic graphs that correspond to data propagation in Cholesky decomposition algorithm. With a forward indexing, $L^f_{BC} \neq 0$ whereas $M^f_{BC} = 0$ contrary to a backward indexing where $L^b_{BC} = 0 = M^b_{BC}$.

## 3.3   Natural Computing Using L-System

On an axis, elements and integration domains are segments. Since a node has influence only on its neighboring elements (possibly at order greater than 1), we can express our model in L-systems:

— a node is represented by a module of type N,
— an element between two nodes is represented by a module of type E,
— elements E are decomposed into integration segments represented by modules of type I.

Because two elements can be decomposed into two different number of integration segments, and a node influences always the same number of neighboring elements, we chose to use a multiscale L-string representation [3] to carry out the integral calculus. Thus the axis is represented at two scales: the scale of nodes and elements and the scale of integration points. The first scale is used to assemble the mass-matrix $\mathbb{M}^b$ and solve the linear system $\mathbb{M}^b X = B$ whereas the second scale is used to compute $B$.

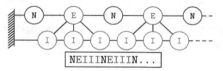

(a) Axis seen as multiscale L-string for FEM model (L-string and tree graph).

(b) Each L-string module corresponds to a part of the axis.

**Fig. 5.** Different representations of a multiscale L-string

stored in the node $N_i$.

When a ramification exists, we deal with it in L-system by adding brackets after a node N to begin a new axis having this node as a root. The L-string NEN[EN]EN corresponds to a simple branch composed of a segment axis E divided in two axis segments (Fig. 6a and 6b). Like previously, each element E is decomposed into several integration segments I at a lower scale.

Using this data structure and storing each row of matrices from their diagonal to their last coefficient in the corresponding node, it is possible to compute the Cholesky decomposition and the forward substitution (and therefore all the mechanical quantities) in a tip-to-basis pass using the following algorithm:

```
Input: M, B and order of shape functions n
Output: L and Y

init:
  N --> { current().L^{tmp} = current().M
          current().Y^{tmp} = current().B
        } produce N
```

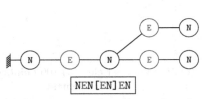

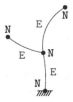

(a) L-string at elements and nodes scale for FEM model in case of ramification (L-string and tree graph).

(b) Each L-string module is equivalent to a part of the tree at elements and nodes scale.

**Fig. 6.** Different representations of a ramification L-string at nodes and elements scale

```
# Cholesky decomposition:
```

$$N \; \text{-->} \; \{ \; \texttt{current()}.\mathbb{L}_0 \; = \; \sqrt{\texttt{current()}.\mathbb{L}_0^{tmp}}$$

```
        for i = 1...n:
```

$$\texttt{current()}.\mathbb{L}_i \; = \; \frac{\texttt{current()}.\mathbb{L}_i^{tmp}}{\texttt{current()}.\mathbb{L}_0}$$

```
            forall k, p in { predecessors() of order k ≤ i }:
```

$$\texttt{p}.\mathbb{L}_i^{tmp} \; = \; \texttt{p}.\mathbb{L}_i^{tmp} \; - \; \texttt{current()}.\mathbb{L}_k \; * \; \texttt{current()}.\mathbb{L}_i$$

```
    } produce N


# Forward substitution:
```

$$N \; \text{-->} \; \{ \; \texttt{current()}.\mathbf{Y} \; = \; \frac{\texttt{current()}.\mathbf{Y}^{tmp}}{\texttt{current()}.\mathbb{L}_0}$$

```
            forall i, p in { predecessors() of order i ≤ n }:
```

$$\texttt{p}.\mathbf{Y}^{tmp} \; = \; \texttt{p}.\mathbf{Y}^{tmp} \; - \; \texttt{current()}.\mathbb{L}_i \; * \; \texttt{current()}.\mathbf{Y}$$

```
    } produce N
```

## 4   Results

We first tested our algorithm on a simple branching system composed of a rigid trunk, a horizontal branch and a secondary branch borne by the former one. The method is able to account for bending and twist, Fig. 7. Only few nodes were needed (here, only at each end of the branch and at each of its ramification nodes) to obtain curvature along the axis (Fig. 7d). Note that if we do not have enough integration points (Fig. 7b), the number of nodes and integration points are not enough to converge correctly.

To analyze this resolution issue, we compared our result to the model presented in the section 2 (green curves in Fig. 8). We present two simulations:

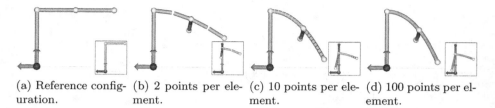

(a) Reference config- (b) 2 points per ele- (c) 10 points per ele- (d) 100 points per el-
uration.                ment.                   ment.                   ement.

**Fig. 7.** Branch bending with one ramification. 1 node (red spheres) at each end and ramification. Integration points are located on the midpoint of each brown segment (integration areas).

– one with only two nodes (at the beginning and at the end of the axis): we are only varying the number of integration points (blue curves in Fig. 8),
– another one where we are varying the number of nodes and where the number of integration points per element is fixed to 10 (red curves in Fig. 8).

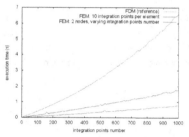

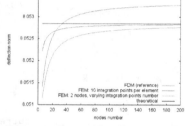

(a) Execution time (in seconds) as function of integration points number (in FDM, integration points and nodes numbers are the same).

(b) Convergence (norm of the deflection) as function of nodes number except for blue curve: as function of integration points number.

**Fig. 8.** Performances of our method on a single axis bending compared to FDM (reference mode, green curves). Two approaches are studied: nodes number fixed and increase the points integration numbers (2 nodes, blue curves); increase nodes number with fixed integration points number per element (red curves).

Fig. 8a shows us that our method is faster than a finite difference method. In general, the execution time increases roughly linearly with the number of integration points. Furthermore, for a given number of integration points, the less nodes we use the faster is our method. On Fig. 8b, we observe that our method converges more rapidly than a FDM method for a similar number of nodes. The error (distance between the simulated and the theoretical values) is a decreasing function of number of nodes. However, decreasing the number of integration points does not change the convergence speed but may affect the convergence itself (blue curve). A minimal density of integration points must therefore be used to obtain correct physical results.

Our method allows to compute branch bending with different kinds of growth rules (Fig. 9): we can play with reference curvature, material properties (density, Young and shear modulii, ... ), order of ramifications, children number at each ramification, sections, segment's length...

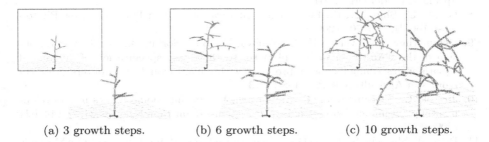

| (a) 3 growth steps. | (b) 6 growth steps. | (c) 10 growth steps. |

**Fig. 9.** Branch bending on growing tree with 2 perspectives

## 5  Conclusion

In this paper, we extended FDM to FEM integration in L-systems. For this we had to use a multiscale approach where the plant is represented at two scales to model both the nodes and the integration points of a FEM approach. We showed that we could solve symmetric and definite positive linear systems thanks to a Cholesky decomposition in L-systems, that made it possible to use the branching structure itself to propagate the numerical integration as a flow of information from the basis of the plant to the tip and reciprocally.

Our comparative analysis showed that our L-system FEM converges more rapidly for our application than L-system FDM (with same model). This approach, illustrated on a mechanical problem of branch bending, can be readily extended to the resolution of other systems involving differential equations on branching systems.

## References

1. Allen, M., Prusinkiewicz, P., DeJong, T.M.: Using L-systems for modeling source-sink interactions, architecture and physiology of growing trees: the L-PEACH Model. New Phyotologist 166, 869–880 (2005)
2. Bathe, K.: Finite Element Procedures. Prentice Hall (1996)
3. Boudon, F., Pradal, C., Cokelaer, T., Prusinkiewicz, P., Godin, C.: L-Py: an L-system simulation framework for modeling plant architecture development base on a dynamic language. Frontiers in Plant Science 3(76) (2012)
4. Chou, P.C., Pagano, N.J.: Elasticity: tensor, dyadic, and engineering approaches. Courier Dover Publications (1992)
5. Costes, E., Smith, C., Renton, M., Guédon, Y., Prusinkiewicz, P., Godin, C.: MAppleT: simulation of apple tree development using mixed stochastic and biomechanical models. Functional Plant Biology 35(10) (2008)

6. Featherstone, R.: Efficient Factorization of the Joint-Space Inertia Matrix for Branched Kinematic Trees. The International Journal of Robotics Research 24(6), 487–500 (2005)
7. Federl, P., Prusinkiewicz, P.: Solving differential equations in developmental models of multicellular structures expressed using L-systems. In: Bubak, M., van Albada, G.D., Sloot, P.M.A., Dongarra, J. (eds.) ICCS 2004. LNCS, vol. 3037, pp. 65–72. Springer, Heidelberg (2004)
8. Godin, C., Sinoquet, H.: Functional-structural plant modelling. The New Phytologist 166(3), 705–708 (2005)
9. Hemmerling, R., Evers, J.B., Smoleňova, K., Buck-Sorlin, G., Kurth, W.: Extension of the GroIMP modelling platform to allow easy specification of differential equations describing biological processes within plant models. Computers and Electronics in Agriculture 92(C), 1–8 (2013)    .
10. Jirasek, C., Prusinkiewicz, P., Moulia, B.: Integrating biomechanics into developmental plant models expressed using L-systems. Plant Biomechanics 24(9), 614–624 (2000)
11. Peiró, J., Sherwin, S.: Finite Difference, Finite Element and Finite Volume Methods for Partial Differential Equations. In: Springer Netherlands Handbook of Materials Modeling, Dordrecht, pp. 2415–2446 (2005)
12. Press, W.H., Teukolsky, S.A., Vettering, W.T., Flannery, B.P.: Numerical Recipes: The art of scientific computing. Cambridge University Press (1987)
13. Prusinkiewicz, P.: Geometric modeling without coordinates and indices. In: IEEE Computer Society Proceedings of the IEEE Shape Modeling International, pp. 3–4 (2002)
14. Prusinkiewicz, P.: Modeling plant growth and development. Modeling plant growth and development 7(1), 79–83 (2004)
15. Prusinkiewicz, P., Allen, M., Escobar-Gutierrez, A., DeJong, T.M.: Numerical methods for transport-resistance sink-source allocation models. Frontis 22, 123–137 (2007)
16. Prusinkiewicz, P. and Lindenmayer, A.: The algorithmic beauty of plants. Springer (1990)
17. Prusinkiewicz, P., Runions, A.: Computational models of plant development and form. The New Phytologist 193(3), 549–569 (2012)
18. Taylor-Hell, J.: Incorporating biomechanics into architectural tree models. In: 18th Brazilian Symposium on Computer Graphics and Image Processing, SIBGRAPI 2005. IEEE (2005)
19. Vos, J., Evers, J.B., Buck-Sorlin, G.H., Andrieu, B., Chelle, M., de Visser, P.H.B.: Functional-structural plant modelling: a new versatile tool in crop science. Journal of Experimental Botany 61(8), 2101–2115 (2010)

# Morphogenesis Model for Systematic Simulation of Forms' Co-evolution with Constraints: Application to Mitosis

Abdoulaye Sarr, Alexandra Fronville, and Vincent Rodin

UMR CNRS 6285, Lab-STICC, CID, IHSEV
Computer Science Department
Université de Brest
20 Avenue Le Gorgeu, Brest, France
{abdoulaye.sarr,alexandra.fronville,vincent.rodin}@univ-brest.fr

**Abstract.** We present a new approach to understand forms' emergence in a cellular system. We set the hypothesis that beyond the influence of mechanical forces and gene expression, constraints applied to the cells over time play a key role in the acquisition of specific shape. We consider that these constraints are the fundamental principles and basic cause of morphogenesis. In our model, it's due to these constraints that cells choose a particular direction while dividing, migrate or die. Our approach of morphogenesis based on constraints has been used to get effectively for a given form all possible evolutions by growth at latter times. Such work ensures to do some pattern prediction.

**Keywords:** Developmental systems, Virtual biology, Morphogenesis, Mathematical morphology, Viability theory.

## 1 Introduction

Facing the experimental complexity, understanding of the living is more and more focused on *in silico* models. The convenience of implementation of a *virtual lab* has made possible the formulation and testing of many hypotheses in *Biology*, particularly in *Morphogenesis*. This gave birth to a multitude of models in this area. But we note that they mostly aim to make an integration of the dynamic interactions between different spatial and/or temporal scales. This approach introduces some complexity in models that limits their understanding and effectiveness with respect to their purpose. Thus, we consider that the cell must be the focus, which determines both causalities and downgrades. In other words, as a first step of a better understanding, observations must be restricted to a single spatial and temporal scale of the biological organization.

Thanks to advances in microscopy and imaging, very detailed data on components and structures of living organisms are now available. Melani and al. achieved a tracking of cell nuclei and the identification of cell divisions in live zebra fish embryos using 3D+time images acquired by confocal laser scanning

A.-H. Dediu et al. (Eds.): TPNC 2014, LNCS 8890, pp. 231–242, 2014.

microscopy [5]. While the zebrafish embryo contains a few pairs of cells, we noticed:

1. a geometrical segmentation during cellular proliferation
2. a specific arrangement of cells at each stage

Theses observations allow us to formulate a set of principles so as to propose a model. First, the noticed geometrical segmentation allow us to adopt a 2D model, discrete in time and space to study the forms appearing in the early stages of morphogenesis. Besides, we make the hypothesis that we can define a morphological dynamic based only on spatial constraints of the cells. Furthermore, we assume that this dynamic is the fundamental principle of morphogenesis and is therefore able to describe all evolutions of a form, both those that modify it and those that maintain it.

The main contribution of this paper is to present the formalization and implementation of such a model. It's organized as follows, section 2 provides a quick overview of some existing models and finishes by our positioning with respect to these models. Section 3 presents the mathematical morphological dynamic relying on the viability theory [1]. Then we present in section 4 a system based on that model which allow to construct and reach over time all possible evolutions of a given form. Section 5 studies the coupling between constraints and organisms (*co-evolution*) with various types of constraints considered by epigenetics as very important to understand the development of living. Finally section 6 concludes this paper by giving some applications of this work and then highlighting the perspectives we should address in coming work.

## 2    Related Works

*Morphogenesis* is an important research field within *Developmental Biology*. It can be defined as the set of processes that generates shapes in the embryo. There exists many models in the area depending on the main factors considered in biological form creation and also the studied organisms (prokaryotes, animals, plant etc.).

*Tensegrity model* is for example interested in cells' shape changing. This model considers biomechanical forces between cells and the extracellular matrix. The stretching of cells adhering to the extracellular matrix may result from local reshuffle in this latter. According to this model, growth-generated strains and pressures in developing tissues regulate morphogenesis throughout development [3]. It is therefore the biomechanical forces which play the key role. For example by modulating cell differentiation, influencing the direction of division or deforming tissues. However, the question of cell diversity even arises before the acquisition of shape [7]. Indeed, when the embryo has only a few pairs of cells, we can see already a diversification of biochemical content or a diversification of embryonic cells morphology. That may be the result of genetic and molecular interactions. Indeed, the emergence of forms also stems from the acquisition of differential properties, of cell mobility and gene expression throughout cell development.

Among the mechanisms of cell morphogenesis, we have also *artificial Regulatory Networks*. They define a series of regulatory genes and structural genes. The firsts consists of a network of rules determining the evolution of the system and the latter are intended to each generate a simple specific pattern. They can be seen as a dynamic system following different trajectories in a state space [4]. However, even if the detailed knowledge of genomic sequences allow to determine where and when different genes are expressed in the embryo, it is insufficient to understand how the organism emerge [6].

So, focusing only on the cellular constraints, we tried to define a mechanism of morphogenesis including the cellular dynamics and allowing to describe and get all possible evolutions of a form over time.

# 3   Mathematical Morphological Dynamic

In *Mathematics*, the *viability theory* offers concepts and methods to control a dynamical system in a given fixed environment, in order to maintain it in a set of constraints of viability. Applied to *Morphogenesis*, this means that we should have at least one co-viable evolution of the cells' state and their environment based on each state-environment pair. This formalization allows us to establish rules in terms of `cell plus action`. The application of such rules by a cell, on the one hand is subject to the observance of an array of constraints and, on the other hand causes some biological effects both on the cell and the overall form.

$\mathcal{K} \subset \mathcal{P}(X)$[1] denotes the *morphological environment*[2] ($X = \mathbb{R}^2$ denotes the set of containment cells, contained in the complement of *vitellus* [3]).

Cells $x \in X \cup \emptyset$ are either characterized by their position (living cells) or by their death made of tissues $L$ which are subsets of cells ($L \in \mathcal{P}(X)$).

The subset of eight `genetic actions` $d$ of cells is:

$$\mathcal{A} := \{(1,0,0),(-1,0,0),(0,1,0),(0,-1,0),(0,0,1),(0,0,-1),(0,0,0),\emptyset\}$$

$\mathcal{A}$ is made of the six geometric directions, the origin and the empty set. Here, we restrict morphogenesis in the plan:

$$\mathcal{A} := \{(0,1),(0,-1),(1,0),(-1,0),(0,0),\emptyset\}$$

For convenience, we replace $(0,1)$, $(0,-1)$, $(1,0)$, $(-1,0)$, $(0,0)$ *and* $\emptyset$ respectively by 1, 2, 3, 4, 5 *and* 6.

$$\mathcal{A} := \{1,2,3,4,5,6\}$$

These `genetic actions` allow to describe cells' behaviour:

---

[1] Supplied with the structure of max-plus algebra for the operation $\cup$ and $+$ (where $K + \emptyset := \emptyset$ with $K$ a cell tissue).

[2] For instance, $\mathcal{K} := \{K \subset M\}$ is the family of subsets contained in a given subset $M$.

[3] In biology, the vitellus is the energy reserves used by the embryos during its development.

1. *Transitions* $x \mapsto x + d$, where $d \in \{1, 2, 3, 4\}$ (action)
2. *Quiescence* $x \mapsto x + 5 = x$ (no action)
3. *Apoptosis* $x \mapsto x + 6 = 6$ (programmed cell death)

This injunction $(d^{\curlyvee}, d^{\curlywedge})$ is described by the genetic inclusion

$$x \rightsquigarrow \{x + d^{\curlyvee}, x + d^{\curlywedge}\}$$

where the *mother* cell $x$

- first migrates from $x$ to $x + d^{\curlyvee}$ using the migration action $d^{\curlyvee} \in \mathcal{A}$ at a new position (including $x$ and $\{6\}$),
- then divides, giving birth to a cell at position $x + d^{\curlywedge}$ using the division action $d^{\curlywedge} \in \mathcal{A} \setminus \{5\}$ .

The composition of these actions produce a *mother-daughter* cell pair

$\{x + d^{\curlyvee}, x + d^{\curlywedge}\}$.

Hence the basic behaviours of the *mother* cell are described by:

1. *sterile migration* by taking $d^{\curlyvee} \in \mathcal{A}$ and $d^{\curlywedge} = 6$
2. *stationary division* by taking $d^{\curlyvee} = 5$ and $d^{\curlywedge} \in \mathcal{A}$
3. *migrating division* by taking $d^{\curlyvee} \in \mathcal{A} \setminus \{5\}$ and $d^{\curlywedge} \in \mathcal{A} \setminus \{5\}$

### 3.1   Gene and Status Expression

To define the **genetic actions** that cells must take in each time, we introduce **genetic processes**. They indicate the behaviours of cells over time while taking into account constraints they must face. The chosen actions in **genetic processes** is the basis of the morphological dynamic and lead to state changes for the cells. The possible states we define here are: proliferating, divided and quiescent cells. At the beginning of cycles (duration time for all cells to do an action), all cells are marked *"proliferating"*. When a mitosis occurs, the *mother* cell is marked *"divided"* while the *daughter* cell is marked *"quiescent"*. And only *proliferating cells* are enabled to make *mitosis*. Since we have associated a color to each **genetic process**, cells are coloured with respect to their current applied **genetic process** (*gene expression*) and in a color level according to their state (*status expression*). The color level codes are:

- light for the *"divided"*
- intermediate for the *"proliferating"*
- dark form the *"quiescent"*

Lifts from a **genetic process** to another make *differentiation* occurs for both *mother* and new created *daughter* cell. They adopt the associated color of the new **genetic process**. This mechanism ensures *gene expression* in forms.

In order to define the **genetic process**, we introduce the set of permutations $\sigma$ of the set $\mathcal{A}$ of **genetic actions**. A **genetic process** is the ordered sequence of actions $d_\sigma := \{d_{\sigma(1)}, ..., d_{\sigma(8)}\} \in \mathcal{A}$. We denote by $\mathcal{G}$ the subset of **genetic**

**processes** of the actions in $\mathcal{A}$ (subset of permutation of six elements). Operating a **genetic process** under a given criterion, either for migration or for division, means that the process scans successively $x + d_{\sigma(1)}, ..., x + d_{\sigma(8)}$ until the fist time when the criterion is satisfied. Since the empty set $\emptyset$ (action 6) belongs to any **genetic process**, any sequence of operations stops before the six **genetic actions** of the **genetic process**.

Before establishing the morphological evolutionary mechanism, we distinguish:

- the calendar (or algorithmic) time $n \geq 0$ that identifies the cycles
- and at each time $n$, a process time $j = 1, ..., j_m$ are the time process for each cell. That's why a cycle lasts as long as there are cells. This is mostly due to the requirement that at each process time, a cell pair cannot occupy the same position.

We can now define the **genetic regulon**. It's a map[4] associating with each triple $(n, L, x)$ the pair $(G^{\curvearrowright}(n, L, x), G^{\curvearrowleft}(n, L, x)) \in \mathcal{G} \times \mathcal{G}$ of **genetic processes** satisfying the non-overlapping property.

$$\begin{cases} \forall x \in L, \\ i \text{ is the time process when we first have } x + G^{\curvearrowright}(n, L, x)(i) \in x \cup \complement L, \\ j_i \text{ is the time process when we first have } x + G^{\curvearrowleft}(n, L, x)(j_i) \in \\ \{x \setminus x + G^{\curvearrowright}(n, L, x)(i)\} \cup \complement L, \end{cases}$$

The first property describes the migration of the *mother* cell, it can stay at the same position or move to an unoccupied position in the *morphological environment*. The second property describes the division and the birth of the *daughter* cell (it cannot take the position of any existing cell).

In what follows, we will describe the morphological evolutionary mechanism. We first define the local morphological dynamics and then the global morphological dynamics.

## 3.2 Local Morphological Dynamics

The **genetic regulons** $(G^{\curvearrowright}, G^{\curvearrowleft})$ are assumed either to be given or constructed to respectively regulate or describe viable evolutions. They are the input of the controlled morphological inclusion we are about to define. First, the map $H$ defined by:

$$H(G^{\curvearrowright}, G^{\curvearrowleft})(n, L, x) := (x + G^{\curvearrowright}(n, L, x)(i), x + G^{\curvearrowleft}(n, L, x)(j_i))$$

associates with any pair $(G^{\curvearrowright}, G^{\curvearrowleft})$ of **genetic processes** the *mother-daughter* cell pair and the transitions transform $\varphi(n, L, x; G^{\curvearrowright}, G^{\curvearrowleft})$ of the subset $L$ (representing the cell tissue at time $n$).

$$\varphi(n, L, x; G^{\curvearrowright}, G^{\curvearrowleft}) := L \cup H(G^{\curvearrowright}, G^{\curvearrowleft})(n, L, x)$$

It transforms $L$ at time $n$ after transitions of the cell $x \in L$.

---

[4] A single-valued map for the time, since no other parameters, biological ones, are involved at the stage of this study.

### 3.3    Global Morphological Dynamics

Let $K_n \in \mathcal{P}(x)$ be a subset constructed, described and coded by an ordered list $(x_1, \ldots, x_{p_{K_n}})$. Hence, we construct $\phi$ in the following way:

$K_n$ being given, we define the sequence $K_n(x_1) := \varphi(n, K_n, x1; G^{\curlywedge}, G^{\curlyvee})$.

$\forall p = 2, \ldots, p_{K_n},\ K_n(x_1, \ldots, x_p) := \varphi(n, K_n(x_1, \ldots, x_{p-1}), x_p; G^{\curlywedge}, G^{\curlyvee})$.

Thus we can set $\phi(n, K_n) := \varphi(K_n(x_1, \ldots, x_{p_{K_n}}); G^{\curlywedge}, G^{\curlyvee})$.

## 4    Sets of Evolutions

Giving a mathematical formalization of cells' actions and behaviours, defining the gene and status expressions and describing the morphological dynamics, we aim now to use this mathematical foundation to describe the possible evolutions of a form by growth. Indeed, we don't take into account *migration* and *death*. Hence, given an initial form, we construct and generate exhaustively its all evolutions at later times. It's also possible to keep only evolutions passing through specific paths while generating sets(see figure 1). To do so, a *filter catalogue* is set to be applied to some given sets of evolutions.

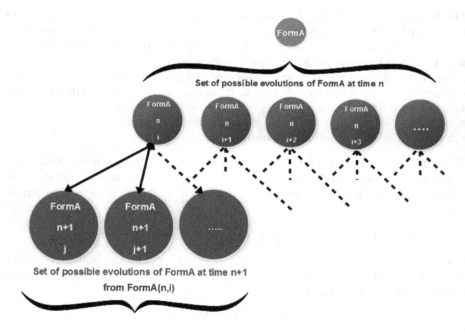

**Fig. 1.** Construction of the sets of evolutions over time

## 4.1   Implementation

The program is developed in C++, sets are represented with the library Boost Graph and the algorithm operates a redundancy control in sets to ensure that either a form or its different geometrical transformations (symmetries, rotations and translations) are stored only once (**reduced a set by 87%**). Since the sets' size increase asymptomatically, we have also developed a parallel implementation with Boost Thread, that allowed us a significant gain in execution time (**more that 30x faster**). The program offers a view on all details of each evolution:

- at each time which cell were created,
- which one created it
- and by which genetic action

Besides, while constructing evolutions, genetic processes are also constructed and thus allow to describe each evolution. Therefore, in the output results viewed with Scilab, we display the genetic process of each evolution. Furthermore, gene and status expressions can be observed in the evolutions by their colors and color levels. In the following figures for example, are represented the evolutions of a single cell when it becomes 2, 4, 8 and 16 cells.

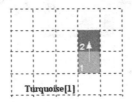

**Fig. 2.** Set of evolutions at 2 cells (size 1)

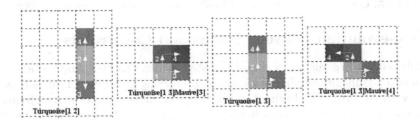

**Fig. 3.** Set of evolutions at 4 cells (size 4)

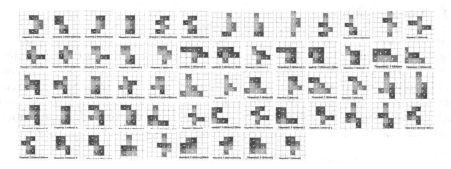

**Fig. 4.** Set of evolutions at 8 cells (size 61)

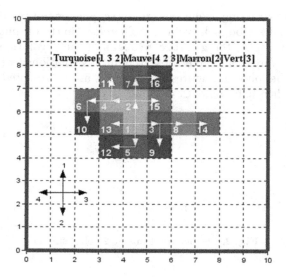

**Fig. 5.** One of the evolutions at 16 cells. The size of the entire set is 1029

## 5    Co-evolution between Forms and Constraints

A Multicellular organism is a complex system which can be defined as a composition of a significant number of elements interacting locally to produce a global behaviour. According to Doursat [2], whether inanimate structures or living organisms, all processes of form emergence are instances of decentralized morphological self-organization. When cells evolve, they modify their organism which in its turn impacts their behaviour. This is what biologists mean by *co-evolution* with constraints. Epigenetics considers that this coupling between organism and constraints can not be ignored in understanding the development of living organisms [8]. These constraints may arise from the environment, the dynamics or the form itself. To highlight the importance of this interaction between forms and constraints, we'll study two cases:

1. a co-evolution of commuting parts of a same form;
2. and form's evolutions in a very restrictive *morphological environment*

## 5.1  A Commutative Growth

We introduce an `evolution lock factor` (ELF) that handles the commutating process. We begin by defining a starting form where some cells are being allowed to divide (ELF is set to off) whereas the others are forbidden to divide (ELF is set to on): see figure 6.

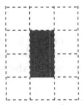

**Fig. 6.** The initial form with two cells: the dark coloured with an ELF set to on and the light coloured with an ELF set to off

Then, the possible evolutions of this form until the end of the cycle are obtained only by the possible transitions of the first ones with regard to the constraints making by the second ones (see figure 7). The proliferating cells give birth to proliferating cells too. At the end of the current cycle, here meaning that the **number of cells** $= 2^n$, we invert the ELF for each form of the current set. The proliferating part of the form becomes locked and the former locked part can now proliferate (see figure 8). Here, we lift the restrictions on the *mother* and *daughter* cells, they can divide as far as possible during the cycle. We thus have implemented an original co-evolution system ensured by commuting parts of the form through phases marked by the end of cycles. The gene expression method doesn't change for the commutative evolution but since we have only two possible cell state (`locked` and `free`), we thus have two color levels. For the cells whose the ELF is set to on, they are *dark coloured* and those for which the ELF is set to off are *light coloured*.

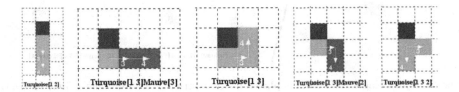

**Fig. 7.** The five possible evolutions at 4 cells of the initial form

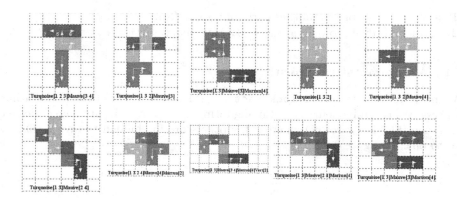

**Fig. 8.** Here are some possible evolutions at **8 cells** of the initial form. They are the result of the first **ELF's** inversion (done in the 4 cells forms). To seek the next evolutions, the **ELF** will be inverted in each of the total of **232 forms**.

The co-evolution with a constraint of commutative growth has a significant impact on forms' development. Indeed, without this constraint, from that initial form, it would be possible to get **369 forms of 8 cells**. Therefore, the commutative evolution reduces by **37%** the possibilities.

## 5.2    Growth in a Restrictive Morphological Environment

The more relevant and more natural way to highlight the influence of constraints on forms' development is to consider those arising from their *morphological environment*. Commonly, we make forms grow in a very basic environment that is a **2D Grid**. Here, we propose to change the environment a little quirky. Then we place a single cell in this restrictive environment to see how many possibles forms of 8 cells can we get from it (see figure 9).

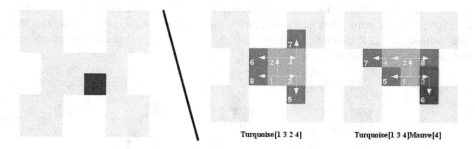

**Fig. 9.** *Left*: a single cell (blue) is placed in the restrictive environment (pink) to grow. *Right*: Growth of the single cell at 8 cells achieves only **2 forms**.

Considering the morphological dynamic defined in section 4, from a single cell, we had **61 forms of 8 cells**. So, the choice of a *quirky morphological environment* has drastically reduced (by **97%**) the potential of forms' development. Besides, in this *morphological environment* the biggest forms that we can reach are made by **12 cells** and are **only 5** (see figure 10), we can't go beyond.

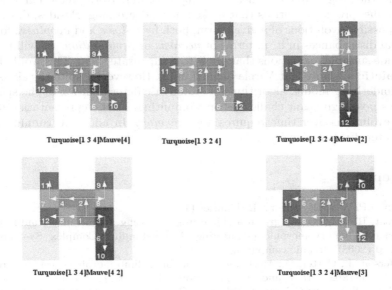

Turquoise[1 3 4]Mauve[4]      Turquoise[1 3 2 4]      Turquoise[1 3 2 4]Mauve[2]

Turquoise[1 3 4]Mauve[4 2]                    Turquoise[1 3 2 4]Mauve[3]

**Fig. 10.** Growth of the single cell stops at 12 cells. It achieves 5 forms. We can notice that within these forms, the proliferating cells (with a intermediate color level) can't no longer divide due to constraints imposed by the environment. Thus growth stops.

## 6   Discussion

To study and understand the developmental process at the early stage of the embryo when it contains just a few pairs of cells, constraints play a key role. In support of this hypothesis, we have presented a mathematical model based on the *viability theory* where the morphological dynamics depend on constraints. All cells' behaviours are able to be described in the model and according to the constraints, cells can apply one or another action. Due to constraints and applied actions, cells have respectively *status expression* and *gene expression* leading to a *differentiation* in colors and color levels. With this model, we developed a program to identify sets of forms that could be obtained from the growth of an initial form over the time. This is a systematic simulation where we use the existing computing powers, particularly with a parallel implementation on **multicores processor**, to explore the entire space of possibles. We have also highlighted the importance of constraints in cell development. Indeed, by restricting the *morphological environment* or by imposing a *commutative evolution* to forms, the possibilities of growth have been significantly reduced.

The interest is to have a view of all possible growth cases of any form. Having a starting form and a final form, the implementation of a method determining the **genetic processes** that allow to reach the latter from the first can be used either for *pattern prediction* or for *forms' growth controlling*.

We aim now to describe the possible evolutions of a form with another cellular dynamic: the programmed cell death or *apoptosis*. In pattern prediction, this will, for example, provides controls that make a form decreasing. Besides, describing sets of possible evolutions of a given form, both by *mitosis* and *apoptosis*, for any potential disturbances in it, in terms of *necrosis* or *proliferation*, we will be able to provide suitable regulations that allow to compensate them. This would be an **autopoietic system** that Varela defined in [9]. However, despite the simplicity of the underlying model, algorithms of systematic determination of the space of possibles pose significant challenges on Computing. First, representation of the sets of evolutions over time requires *huge memory*. In addition, running these sets is often *time consuming*.

# References

1. Aubin, J.P.: Viability theory. Birkhauser (1991)
2. Doursat, R.: Organically grown architectures: Creating decentralized, autonomous systems by embryomorphic engineering. Understanding Complex Systems, pp. 167–200 (2008), organic computing
3. Henderson, J., Carter, D.: Mechanical induction in limb morphogenesis: the role of growth-generated strains and pressures. Bone 31(6) (2002)
4. Kauffman, S.A.: The Origins of Order: self-Organization and Selection in Evolution. Oxford University Press, USA (1993)
5. Melani, C., Peyriéras, N., Mikula, K., Zanella, C., Campana, M., Rizzi, B., Veronesi, F., Sarti, A., Lombardot, B., Bourgine, P.: Cells tracking in the live zebrafish embryo. In: Conf. Proc. IEEE Eng. Med. Biol. Soc., vol. 1, pp. 1631–1634 (2007)
6. Müller, G., Newman, S.: Origination of organismal form: beyond the gene in developmental and evolutionary biology. MIT Press (2003)
7. Peyriéras, N.: Morphogenèse animale. Morphogénèse: L'origine des formes, pp. 179–201 (2006)
8. Varela, F.J.: Principles of Biological Autonomy. Developments in Marine Biology. North-Holland (1979)
9. Varela, F.J.: Autonomie et connaissance: essai sur le vivant. Seuil (1989)

# The Power of Extra Analog Neuron

Jiří Šíma*

Institute of Computer Science, Academy of Sciences of the Czech Republic
P.O. Box 5, 18207 Prague 8, Czech Republic
sima@cs.cas.cz

**Abstract.** In the effort to refine the analysis of computational power
of neural nets between integer and rational weights we study a hybrid
binary-state network with an extra analog unit. We introduce a finite
automaton with a register which is shown to be computationally equivalent to such a network. The main result is a sufficient condition for a
language accepted by this automaton to be regular which is based on the
new concept of a quasi-periodic power series. These preliminary results
suggest an interesting connection with the active research field on the
expansions of numbers in non-integer bases which seems to be a fruitful
area for further research including many important open problems.

**Keywords:** Neural computing, analog state, beta-expansion.

## 1 Introduction

The computational power of neural networks with the saturated-linear activation
function[1] depends on the descriptive complexity of their weight parameters [25,
30]. Neural nets with *integer* weights corresponding to binary-state networks
coincide with finite automata [3, 9, 11, 16, 29, 31]. *Rational* weights make the
analog-state networks computationally equivalent to Turing machines [11, 27],
and thus (by a real-time simulation [27]) polynomial-time computations of such
networks are characterized by the complexity class P. Moreover, neural nets
with arbitrary *real* weights can even derive "super-Turing" computational capabilities [25, 26]. For example, their polynomial-time computations correspond
to the nonuniform complexity class P/poly while any I/O mapping (including
undecidable problems) can be computed within exponential time. In addition, a
proper hierarchy of nonuniform complexity classes between P and P/poly has
been established for polynomial-time computations of neural nets with increasing
Kolmogorov complexity of real weights [4].

It follows that our understanding of the computational power of neural networks is satisfactorily fine-grained when changing from rational to arbitrary real
weights. In contrast, there is still a gap between integer and rational weights

---

* Research was supported by the projects GA ČR P202/10/1333 and RVO: 67985807.
[1] The results are valid for more general classes of activation functions [14, 24, 28, 32]
including the logistic function [13].

A.-H. Dediu et al. (Eds.): TPNC 2014, LNCS 8890, pp. 243–254, 2014.

which results in a jump from regular to recursive languages in the Chomsky hierarchy. It appears that Turing machines can be simulated by the neural networks that, apart from binary-state neurons interconnected via integer weights, include only *two* analog-state units with rational weights implementing two stacks of pushdown automata, a model equivalent to Turing machines [27]. A natural question arises: what is the computational power of hybrid binary-state networks with one extra analog unit having rational weights? Our investigation which was originally motivated by the quest of refining the analysis along this direction, has revealed interesting connections with other active research fields such as representations of numbers in non-integer bases [1, 2, 5, 7, 8, 15, 19, 20, 22, 23] and automata with multiplication [6, 10, 12, 17, 21]. In addition, our analysis leads to interesting open problems and even to new concepts which are worth investigating on their own.

The present paper which initiates our preliminary study, is organized as follows. In Section 2, we give a brief review of basic definitions concerning the language acceptors based on a hybrid model of binary-state neural networks with an extra analog unit. In Section 3, we introduce a new notion of a finite automaton with a register whose domain is partitioned into a finite number of intervals, each associated with a local state-transition function. This automaton is shown to be computationally equivalent by mutual simulations to a neural network with an analog unit. Our main technical result in Section 4 provides a sufficient condition when a finite automaton with a register accepts a regular language, which is based on the new concept of a quasi-periodic power series. In section 5, related results on so-called $\beta$-expansions of numbers in non-integer bases are surveyed and emerging directions for ongoing research are discussed.

## 2    Neural Language Acceptors with Extra Analog Unit

We will specify a hybrid model of a *binary-state neural network with an analog unit (NN1A)* $N$ which will be used as a formal language acceptor. The network consists of $s$ *units (neurons)*, indexed as $V = \{1, \ldots, s\}$, where $s$ is called the network *size*. All the units in $N$ are assumed to be binary-state *perceptrons (i.e. threshold gates)* except for the last $s$th neuron which is an *analog unit*. The neurons are connected into a directed graph representing the *architecture* of $N$, in which each edge $(i, j)$ leading from unit $i$ to $j$ is labeled with a rational *weight* $w(i, j) = w_{ji} \in \mathbb{Q}$. The absence of a connection within the architecture corresponds to a zero weight between the respective neurons, and vice versa.

The *computational dynamics* of $N$ determines for each unit $j \in V$ its *state (output)* $y_j^{(t)}$ at discrete time instants $t = 0, 1, 2, \ldots$. The states $y_j^{(t)}$ of the first $s - 1$ perceptrons $j \in V \setminus \{s\}$ are binary values from $\{0, 1\}$, whereas $y_s^{(t)}$ of analog unit $s \in V$ is a rational number from the unit interval $\mathbb{I} = [0, 1] \cap \mathbb{Q}$. This establishes the *network state* $\mathbf{y}^{(t)} = (y_1^{(t)}, \ldots, y_s^{(t)}) \in \{0, 1\}^{s-1} \times \mathbb{I}$ at each discrete time instant $t \geq 0$. At the beginning of a computation, the neural network $N$ is placed in an *initial state* $\mathbf{y}^{(0)}$ which may also include an external input. At discrete time instant $t \geq 0$, an *excitation* of any neuron $j \in V$ is defined as $\xi_j^{(t)} = \sum_{i=0}^{s} w_{ji} y_i^{(t)}$, including a rational *bias* value $w_{j0} \in \mathbb{Q}$ which can be viewed as the weight $w(0,j)$ from a formal constant unit input $y_0^{(t)} \equiv 1$. At the next instant $t+1$, the neurons $j \in \alpha_{t+1}$ from a selected subset $\alpha_{t+1} \subseteq V$ compute their new outputs $y_j^{(t+1)} = \sigma_j(\xi_j^{(t)})$ in parallel by applying an *activation function* $\sigma_j : \mathbb{R} \longrightarrow \mathbb{R}$ to $\xi_j^{(t)}$, whereas $y_j^{(t+1)} = y_j^{(t)}$ for the remaining units $j \in V \setminus \alpha_{t+1}$. For perceptrons $j \in V \setminus \{s\}$ with binary states $y_j \in \{0,1\}$ the *Heaviside* activation function $\sigma_j(\xi) = \sigma_H(\xi)$ is used where $\sigma_H(\xi) = 1$ for $\xi \geq 0$ and $\sigma_H(\xi) = 0$ for $\xi < 0$, while the analog-state unit $s \in V$ employs the *saturated-linear* function $\sigma_s(\xi) = \sigma_L(\xi)$ where

$$\sigma_L(\xi) = \begin{cases} 1 & \text{for } \xi \geq 1 \\ \xi & \text{for } 0 < \xi < 1 \\ 0 & \text{for } \xi \leq 0 \,. \end{cases} \tag{1}$$

In this way, the new network state $\mathbf{y}^{(t+1)}$ at time $t+1$ is determined.

Without loss of efficiency [18] we assume synchronous computations for which the sets $\alpha_t$, defining the computational dynamics of $N$, are predestined deterministically. Usually, sets $\alpha_t$ correspond to layers in the architecture of $N$ which are updated one by one (e.g., a feedforward subnetwork). In particular, we use a systematic periodic choice of $\alpha_t$ so that $\alpha_{t+d} = \alpha_t$ for any $t \geq 0$ where an integer parameter $d \geq 1$ represents the number of updates within one *macroscopic time step* (e.g., $d$ is the number of layers). We assume that the analog unit $s \in V$ is updated exactly once in every macroscopic time step, say $s \in \alpha_{d\tau}$ for every $\tau \geq 1$.

The computational power of neural networks has been studied analogously to the traditional models of computations so that the networks are exploited as acceptors of formal languages $L \subseteq \{0,1\}^*$ over the binary alphabet. For the finite networks the following I/O protocol has been used [3, 4, 9, 11, 24–27, 30, 31]. A binary input word (string) $\mathbf{x} = x_1 \ldots x_n \in \{0,1\}^n$ of arbitrary length $n \geq 0$ is sequentially presented to the network bit by bit via the first, so-called *input neuron* $1 \in V$. The state of this unit is externally set (and clamped) to the respective input bits at microscopic time instants, regardless of any influence from the remaining neurons in the network, that is, $y_1^{(d(\tau-1)+k)} = x_\tau$ for $\tau = 1, \ldots, n$ and every $k = 0 \ldots, d-1$ where an integer $d \geq 1$ is the *time overhead* for processing a single input bit which coincides with the microscopic time step. Then, the second, so-called *output neuron* $2 \in V$ signals at microscopic time instant $n$ whether the input word belongs to underlying language $L$, that is, $y_2^{(dn)} = 1$ for $\mathbf{x} \in L$ whereas $y_2^{(dn)} = 0$ for $\mathbf{x} \notin L$. Thus, a language $L \subseteq \{0,1\}^*$ is *accepted by NN1A* $N$, which is denoted by $L = L(N)$, if for any input word $\mathbf{x} \in \{0,1\}^*$, $\mathbf{x}$ is accepted by $N$ iff $\mathbf{x} \in L$.

## 3 Finite Automata with a Register

We introduce a (deterministic) *finite automaton with a register (FAR)* which is formally a nine-tuple $A = (Q, \Sigma, \{I_1, \ldots, I_p\}, a, (\Delta_1, \ldots, \Delta_p), \delta, q_0, z_0, F)$ where, as usual, $Q$ is a finite set of automaton *states* including a *start (initial) state*

$q_0 \in Q$ and a subset $F \subseteq Q$ of *accept (final) states*. We assume $\Sigma = \{0,1\}$ to be a binary *input alphabet*. In addition, the automaton is augmented with a register which stores a rational number $z \in \mathbb{I} = [0,1] \cap \mathbb{Q}$. Domain $\mathbb{I}$ is partitioned into a finite number of intervals $I_1, \ldots, I_p$, possibly of different types: open, closed, half-closed, or degenerate (containing a single point) bounded intervals with rational endpoints. Each such an interval $I_r$ is associated with a usual local state-transition function $\delta_r : Q \times \Sigma \longrightarrow Q$ which is employed if the current register value $z$ falls into this interval $I_r$.

Moreover, we have a rational *shift* function $\Delta_r : Q \times \Sigma \longrightarrow \mathbb{Q}$ for each interval $I_r$, $r = 1, \ldots, p$. The register is initialized to a *start (initial)* value $z_0 \in \mathbb{I}$, and during each state transition, its value $z \in \mathbb{I}$ is updated to $\sigma_L(az + \Delta_r(q,x)) \in \mathbb{I}$ by applying a linear mapping with saturation (1) having a fixed slope $a \in \mathbb{Q}$ called *multiplier* and an y-intercept $\Delta_r(q,x) \in \mathbb{Q}$ given by the shift function $\Delta_r$ for $z \in I_r$ which depends on current state $q \in Q$ and input bit $x \in \Sigma$. In summary, for current state $q \in Q$, register value $z \in \mathbb{I}$, and input bit $x \in \Sigma$, the global *state-transition function* $\delta : Q \times \mathbb{I} \times \Sigma \longrightarrow Q \times \mathbb{I}$ produces the new state and the new register value of automaton $A$ as follows:

$$\delta(q,z,x) = (\delta_r(q,x), \sigma_L(az + \Delta_r(q,x))) \quad \text{if } z \in I_r. \tag{2}$$

A binary input word $\mathbf{x} \in \Sigma^*$ is accepted by $A$ if automaton $A$, starting at initial state $q_0$ with start register value $z_0$, reaches a final state $q \in F$ by a sequence of state transitions according to (2) while reading the input $\mathbf{x}$ from left to right. A language $L \subseteq \{0,1\}^*$ is *accepted by FAR $A$*, which is denoted by $L = L(A)$, if for any input word $\mathbf{x} \in \Sigma^*$, $\mathbf{x}$ is accepted by $A$ iff $\mathbf{x} \in L$. The concept of FAR is reminiscent of today's already classical definition of finite automaton with multiplication [10]. In the following theorems, we will show by mutual simulations that the binary-state neural networks with analog unit introduced in Section 2 are computationally equivalent to the finite automata with register.

**Theorem 1.** *For any binary-state neural network with an analog unit, there is a finite automaton with a register such that both accept the same language.*

*Proof.* Let $L \subseteq \{0,1\}^*$ be a language accepted by NN1A $N$, that is, $L = L(N)$. We will construct a FAR $A$ such that $L(A) = L$. Let $Q = \{0,1\}^{s-2}$ be a finite set of automaton states corresponding to all possible binary states $(y_2^{(d\tau)}, \ldots, y_{s-1}^{(d\tau)})$ of neurons in $V \setminus \{1, s\}$ at macroscopic time $\tau \geq 0$, excluding the input and analog unit. The start state $q_0 = (y_2^{(0)}, \ldots, y_{s-1}^{(0)}) \in Q$ of $A$ is defined using the initial state of $N$ and $F = \{1\} \times \{0,1\}^{s-3}$ represents the set of accept states.

At any time instant $t \geq 0$, the computational dynamics of $N$ ensures $y_j^{(t+1)} = 1$ iff $\sum_{i=0}^{s-1} w_{ji} y_i^{(t)} + w_{js} y_s^{(t)} \geq 0$ for a non-input binary-state neuron $j \in \{2 \ldots, s-1\} \cap \alpha_{t+1}$. For $w_{js} \neq 0$, this condition can be rewritten as

$$y_j^{(t+1)} = 1 \text{ iff } \left(w_{js} > 0 \,\&\, y_s^{(t)} \geq c_j\left(\tilde{\mathbf{y}}^{(t)}\right)\right) \vee \left(w_{js} < 0 \,\&\, y_s^{(t)} \leq c_j\left(\tilde{\mathbf{y}}^{(t)}\right)\right) \tag{3}$$

where $\tilde{\mathbf{y}}^{(t)} = (y_1^{(t)}, \ldots, y_{s-1}^{(t)})$ and $c_j(\mathbf{y}) = (-\sum_{i=0}^{s-1} w_{ji} y_i)/w_{js} \in \mathbb{Q}$ for $\mathbf{y} \in \{0,1\}^{s-1}$. Let $C = \{(c_j(\mathbf{y}), 1 - \sigma_H(w_{js})) \in \mathbb{I} \times \{0,1\} \mid 1 < j < s \text{ such that } w_{js} \neq 0,$

$\mathbf{y} \in \{0,1\}^{s-1}\} \cup \{(0,0),(1,1)\}$ be a finite set of all possible values $c_j(\mathbf{y}) \in \mathbb{I}$ associated with the opposite signs of corresponding weights $w_{js}$, which is extended with the endpoints $0,1$ of $\mathbb{I}$. We sort the elements of $C$ lexicographically as $(0,0) = (c_1, s_1) < (c_2, s_2) < \ldots < (c_{p+1}, s_{p+1}) = (1,1)$, which defines the partition of $\mathbb{I}$ to rational intervals $I_1, \ldots, I_p$ as $I_r = [c_r, c_{r+1})$ if $s_r = 0 \,\& \, s_{r+1} = 0$, $I_r = [c_r, c_{r+1}]$ if $s_r = 0 \,\& \, s_{r+1} = 1$, $I_r = (c_r, c_{r+1})$ if $s_r = 1 \,\& \, s_{r+1} = 0$, and $I_r = (c_r, c_{r+1}]$ if $s_r = 1 \,\& \, s_{r+1} = 1$, for $r = 1, \ldots, p$. It follows from (3) that for any interval $I_r$ ($1 \leq r \leq p$) of this partition, for every neuron $j = 2, \ldots, s-1$ and for any $\tilde{\mathbf{y}}^{(t)} \in \{0,1\}^{s-1}$, the inequality $\sum_{i=0}^{s-1} w_{ji} y_i^{(t)} + w_{js} y_s^{(t)} \geq 0$ either holds for all $y_s^{(t)} \in I_r$ or it is not satisfied for all $y_s^{(t)} \in I_r$. This means that $y_s^{(t)} \in \mathbb{I}$ influences the state $y_j^{(t+1)}$ only by its membership to particular interval $I_r$ and not by its exact analog value.

We can define local state-transition functions $\delta_r : Q \times \Sigma \longrightarrow Q$ of $A$ for each interval $I_r$, $r = 1, \ldots, p$. Given an automaton state $q = (y_2^{(d(\tau-1))}, \ldots, y_{s-1}^{(d(\tau-1))}) \in Q$ corresponding to the network state $\mathbf{y}^{(d(\tau-1))}$ at microscopic time $\tau - 1$ when a current input bit $y_1^{(d(\tau-1))} = x_\tau \in \Sigma$ is read, and let $y_s^{(d(\tau-1))} \in I_r$, we know that $y_1^{(d(\tau-1)+k)} = y_1^{(d(\tau-1))}$ and $y_s^{(d(\tau-1)+k)} = y_s^{(d(\tau-1))}$ for every $k = 1, \ldots, d-1$, as the input and analog units are updated only at microscopic time instants. Hence, for this interval $I_r$, the neuron states $(y_2^{(d\tau)}, \ldots, y_{s-1}^{(d\tau)}) = q' \in Q$ depend only on state $q \in Q$ and input bit $x_\tau \in \Sigma$ using the computational dynamics of $N$, which define $\delta_r(q, x_\tau) = q'$.

Finally, the register of $A$ is initialized as $z_0 = y_s^{(0)} \in \mathbb{I}$. We define the multiplier $a = w_{ss} \in \mathbb{Q}$ and the shift functions $\Delta_r : Q \times \Sigma \longrightarrow \mathbb{Q}$ for $r = 1, \ldots, p$ as $\Delta_r(q, x) = \sum_{i=0}^{s-1} w_{si} y_i^{(d\tau-1)} \in \mathbb{Q}$ for $q = (y_2^{(d(\tau-1))}, \ldots, y_{s-1}^{(d(\tau-1))}) \in Q$ and $x = y_1^{(d(\tau-1))} = y_1^{(d\tau-1)} \in \Sigma$, and $y_s^{(d(\tau-1))} = y_s^{(d\tau-1)} \in I_r$, which is a correct definition since the network state $\mathbf{y}^{(d\tau-1)}$ is uniquely determined by the state $\mathbf{y}^{(d(\tau-1))}$ at the last microscopic time instant $\tau - 1$ using the computational dynamics of $N$. By induction on microscopic time $\tau$, the register of $A$ stores the current state $y_s^{(d\tau)}$ of analog unit $s \in V$, as its value $z = y_s^{(d(\tau-1))} = y_s^{(d\tau-1)} \in I_r$ is updated to $\sigma_L(az + \Delta_r(q, x)) = \sigma_s\left(w_{ss} y_s^{(d\tau-1)} + \sum_{i=0}^{s-1} w_{si} y_i^{(d\tau-1)}\right) = y_s^{(d\tau)}$ according to (2) and (1). This completes the definition of global state-transition function $\delta$ which ensures that $A$ simulates $N$. $\qquad \square$

**Theorem 2.** *For any finite automaton with a register, there is a binary-state neural network with an analog unit accepting the same language.*

*Proof.* Let $L \subseteq \{0,1\}^*$ be a language accepted by FAR $A = (Q, \Sigma, \{I_1, \ldots, I_p\}, a, (\Delta_1, \ldots, \Delta_p), \delta, q_0, z_0, F)$, that is, $L = L(A)$. We will construct a NN1A $N$ such that $L(N) = L$. Apart from the input, output, and analog neurons $\{1, 2, s\}$, the set of neurons $V$ contains four types of units corresponding to the automaton states from $Q$, to the given partition $I_1, \ldots, I_p$ of domain $\mathbb{I}$, to all triples from $Q \times \Sigma \times \{I_1, \ldots, I_p\}$, and to the endpoints $0 \leq c_2 \leq \cdots \leq c_p \leq 1$ of rational intervals from the partition (excluding the left endpoint $c_1 = 0$ of $I_1$ and the right endpoint $c_{p+1} = 1$ of $I_p$), respectively. For simplicity, we will identify the names of neurons with these objects, e.g. $c_r$ has two different meanings, once denoting neuron $c_r \in V$ and other times standing for rational number $c_r \in \mathbb{I}$. The initial network state $\mathbf{y}^{(0)} \in \{0,1\}^{s-1} \times \mathbb{I}$ is defined as an almost null vector except for the input unit receiving the first input bit $y_1^{(0)} = x_1 \in \Sigma = \{0,1\}$, the output neuron whose state $y_2^{(0)} = 1$ iff $q_0 \in F$, the neuron corresponding to the initial automaton state $q_0 \in Q$ with output $y_{q_0}^{(0)} = 1$, and the analog unit implementing the register initialized with its start value $y_s^{(0)} = z_0$.

Each microscopic time step of $N$ is composed of $d = 4$ updates. At the first time instant $4(\tau - 1) + 1$ within the microscopic step $\tau \geq 1$, each neuron $c_r$ $(1 < r \leq p)$ corresponding to the left endpoit of $I_r$ fires, i.e. $y_{c_r}^{(4(\tau-1)+1)} = 1$ iff either $y_s^{(4(\tau-1))} \geq c_r$ for left-closed interval $I_r$ or $y_s^{(4(\tau-1))} \leq c_r$ for left-open interval $I_r$, which is implemented by weights $w(s, c_r) = 1$ and biases $w(0, c_r) = -c_r$ for left-closed $I_r$, and $w(s, c_r) = -1$ and $w(0, c_r) = c_r$ for right-closed $I_r$, for every $r = 2, \ldots, p$. Thus, $\alpha_{4(\tau-1)+1} = \{c_2, \ldots, c_r\} \subseteq V$. At the second time instant $4(\tau - 1) + 2$, neuron $I_r$ $(1 \leq r \leq p)$ representing the interval $I_r$ from the partition of $\mathbb{I}$ fires, i.e. $y_{I_r}^{(4(\tau-1)+2)} = 1$ iff the current register value falls in $I_r$, that is, iff $y_s^{(4(\tau-1))} = y_s^{(4(\tau-1)+1)} \in I_r$. This is implemented by the following weights: $w(c_r, I_r) = 1$ if $I_r$ is left-closed whereas $w(c_r, I_r) = -1$ if $I_r$ is left-open, for $r = 2, \ldots, p$; $w(c_{r+1}, I_r) = 1$ if $I_r$ is right-closed whereas $w(c_{r+1}, I_r) = -1$ if $I_r$ is right-open, for $r = 1, \ldots, p-1$; $w(0, I_r) = -2$ if $I_r$ is closed, $w(0, I_r) = 0$ if $I_r$ is open, and $w(0, I_r) = -1$ otherwise, for $r = 2, \ldots, p-1$, while the biases of units $I_1$ and $I_p$ having only one incoming edge are by 1 greater than those defined for $I_2, \ldots, I_{p-1}$. Thus, $\alpha_{4(\tau-1)+2} = \{I_1, \ldots, I_r\} \subseteq V$.

At the third time instant $4(\tau - 1) + 3$, units in $\alpha_{4(\tau-1)+3} = Q \times \Sigma \times \{I_1, \ldots, I_p\} \subseteq V$ are updated so that the only firing neuron $(q, x, I_r) \in V$ among $\alpha_{4(\tau-1)+3}$ indicates the current triple of state $q \in V$, input bit $x \in \Sigma = \{0,1\}$, and the interval $I_r$ such that $y_s^{(4(\tau-1))} \in I_r$. For any $q \in Q$ and every $r = 1, \ldots, p$, this is simply implemented by weights $w(q, (q, x, I_r)) = w(I_r, (q, x, I_r)) = 1$ for any $x \in \Sigma$, $w(1, (q, 1, I_r)) = 1$, $w(1, (q, 0, I_r)) = -1$, and biases $w(0, (q, 1, I_r)) = -3$, $w(0, (q, 0, I_r)) = -2$. At the next time instant $4\tau$ when $\alpha_{4\tau} = Q \cup \{2, s\} \subseteq V$, the new automaton state is computed while the output neuron signals whether this state is accepting. For any $q, q' \in Q$, $x \in \Sigma$, and $r = 1, \ldots, p$, we define the weight $w((q, x, I_r), q') = 1$ iff $\delta_r(q, x) = q'$, and the bias $w(0, q') = -1$, while $w((q, x, I_r), 2) = 1$ iff $q \in F$, and $w(0, 2) = -1$. Finally, the register value is properly updated according to (2) using the weights $w_{ss} = a$ and $w((q, x, I_r), s) = \Delta_r(q, x)$ for any $q \in Q$, $x \in \Sigma$, and every $r = 1, \ldots, p$. This completes the construction of network $N$ simulating FAR $A$.    □

## 4    A Sufficient Condition for Accepting Regular Languages

In this section, we prove a sufficient condition when a finite automaton with a register accepts a regular language. For this purpose, we introduce a new concept of a quasi-periodic power series. We say that a power series $\sum_{k=0}^{\infty} b_k a^k$ is eventually *quasi-periodic* with *maximum period* $M \geq 1$ and *period sum* $P$

if there is an increasing infinite sequence of its term indices $0 \leq k_1 < k_2 < k_3 < \cdots$ such that $0 < m_i = k_{i+1} - k_i \leq M$ and for every $i \geq 1$, $P_i = (\sum_{k=0}^{m_i-1} b_{k_i+k} a^k)/(1 - a^{m_i}) = P$ where $k_1$ is the length of preperiodic part, that is, for any $0 \leq k_0 < k_1$, $P_0 \neq P$. For example, $\sum_{k=1}^{\infty} b_k a^k$ is eventually quasi-periodic with maximum period $m \geq 1$ if associated sequence $(b_k)_{k=1}^{\infty}$ is eventually periodic, that is, there exists $k_1 \geq 0$ such that $b_k = b_{k+m}$ for every $k \geq k_1$. For $|a| < 1$, one can calculate the sum of any eventually quasi-periodic power series as $\sum_{k=1}^{\infty} b_k a^k = \sum_{k=0}^{k_1-1} b_k a^k + \sum_{k=k_1}^{\infty} b_k a^k$ where $\sum_{k=k_1}^{\infty} b_k a^k = \sum_{i=1}^{\infty} a^{k_i} \sum_{k=0}^{m_i-1} b_{k_i+k} a^k = P \cdot \sum_{i=1}^{\infty} a^{k_i} (1 - a^{m_i})$, which gives

$$\sum_{k=1}^{\infty} b_k a^k = \sum_{k=0}^{k_1-1} b_k a^k + a^{k_1} P \tag{4}$$

since the absolutely convergent series $\sum_{i=1}^{\infty} a^{k_i}(1 - a^{m_i}) = \sum_{i=1}^{\infty}(a^{k_i} - a^{k_{i+1}})$ sums up to $a^{k_1}$. It follows that the sum (4) of eventually quasi-periodic power series does not change if any quasi-repeating block $b_{k_i}, b_{k_i+1}, \ldots, b_{k_{i+1}-1}$ satisfying $P_i = P$ is removed from associated sequence $(b_k)_{k=1}^{\infty}$ or if it is inserted in between two other quasi-repeating blocks, which means that these quasi-repeating blocks can also be permuted arbitrarily.

**Theorem 3.** *Let $A = (Q, \Sigma, \{I_1, \ldots, I_p\}, a, (\Delta_1, \ldots, \Delta_p), \delta, q_0, z_0, F)$ be a finite automaton with a register satisfying $|a| \leq 1$. Denote by $C \subseteq \mathbb{I}$ the finite set of all endpoints of rational intervals $I_1, \ldots, I_p$ and let $B = \bigcup_{r=1}^{p} \Delta_r(Q \times \Sigma) \cup \{0, 1, z_0\} \subseteq \mathbb{Q}$ be the finite set of all possible shifts including $0, 1$, and the initial register value. If every series $\sum_{k=0}^{\infty} b_k a^k \in C$ with all $b_k \in B$ is eventually quasi-periodic, then $L = L(A)$ is a regular language.*

*Proof.* We will construct a conventional finite automaton $A' = (Q', \Sigma, \delta', q_0', F')$ with binary input alphabet $\Sigma = \{0, 1\}$ simulating FAR $A$ so that $L(A') = L$, which shows that $L$ is regular. According to (2) and (1), a current register value

$$z = \sum_{k=0}^{h} b_k a^k \in \mathbb{I} \tag{5}$$

is uniquely determined by the complete history of shifts $b_0, b_1, \ldots, b_h \in B$ since the last time instant when either the register was initialized with start value $b_h = z_0$ or its value saturated at $b_h = 0$ or $b_h = 1$. For $a = 0$ or $|a| = 1$, the set of all possible register values proves to be finite, and henceforth assume $0 < |a| < 1$.

Let $C' = C \cap \{\sum_{k=0}^{\infty} b_k a^k \mid \text{all } b_k \in B\} = \{c_1, \ldots, c_\gamma\}$ be a subset of the interval endpoints from $C$ that are reached by eventually quasi-periodic series according to the assumption of the theorem, where $\gamma = |C'|$. We choose an integer $\kappa' \geq 0$ so that each such series $\sum_{k=0}^{\infty} b_k a^k \in C'$ meets $k_1 + 2M \leq \kappa' + 1$ where $k_1$ is the length of its preperiodic part and $M$ is its maximum period, while we set $\kappa' = 0$ if $\gamma = 0$. It follows that one can decide whether $\sum_{k=0}^{\infty} b_k a^k \notin C$ with all $b_k \in B$, based only on the first $\kappa' + 1$ terms $b_0, b_1, \ldots, b_{\kappa'}$. We observe that there exists an integer $\kappa \geq \kappa'$ such that for every series $\sum_{k=0}^{\infty} b_k a^k \notin C$

with all $b_k \in B$, the interval $I(b_0, b_1, \ldots, b_\kappa) = [z_\kappa + \sum_{k=\kappa+1}^{\infty} \min_{b \in B} (ba^k), z_\kappa + \sum_{k=\kappa+1}^{\infty} \max_{b \in B} (ba^k)]$ where $z_\kappa = \sum_{k=0}^{\kappa} b_k a^k$, does not contain any $c \in C$, since the opposite would force $c = \sum_{k=0}^{\infty} b_k a^k$ by Cantor's intersection theorem.

A finite set $Q' = Q \times B^\kappa \times \{<, =, >\}^\gamma$ is now composed of the states of $A$ which are extended with a *limited* history of register shifts $b_0, b_1, \ldots, b_\kappa \in B$ up to the last $\kappa$ state transitions. If $h < \kappa$, then $b_k = 0$ for every $k = h+1, \ldots, \kappa$. Moreover, a critical information $\varrho_j \in \{<, =, >\}$ is recorded from the "prehistory" when $h > \kappa$, which is specific to each $c_j \in C'$ for $j = 1, \ldots, \gamma$. In addition, let $q_0' = (q_0, z_0, 0, \ldots, 0, =, \ldots, =) \in Q'$ be an initial state of $A'$, while $F' = F \times B^\kappa \times \{<, =, >\}^\gamma \subseteq Q'$ represents the set of final states.

We define the transition function $\delta' : Q' \times \Sigma \longrightarrow Q'$ of $A'$ by using the local state transition and shift functions of $A$ as follows:

$$\delta'((q, b_0, \ldots, b_\kappa, \varrho_1, \ldots, \varrho_\gamma), x)$$
$$= \begin{cases} (\delta_r(q, x), \Delta_r(q, x), b_0, \ldots, b_{\kappa-1}, \varrho_1', \ldots, \varrho_\gamma') & \text{if } 0 < z_\kappa < 1 \\ (\delta_r(q, x), \sigma_L(z_\kappa), 0, \ldots, 0, =, \ldots, =) & \text{otherwise,} \end{cases} \tag{6}$$

for $q \in Q$, $b_0, \ldots, b_\kappa \in B$, $\varrho_1, \ldots, \varrho_\gamma \in \{<, =, >\}$, and $x \in \Sigma$. In the following we will describe two cases of choosing the parameter $r$ in definition (6) which depend on whether or not the arguments $b_0, \ldots, b_\kappa$ coincide with the first $\kappa + 1$ coefficients of a series from $C'$. We first consider the case when for any series $\sum_{k=0}^{\infty} b_k' a^k \in C'$ with all $b_k' \in B$,

$$b_k \neq b_k' \quad \text{for some } 0 \le k \le \kappa. \tag{7}$$

In this case, parameter $r$ is chosen so that $z_\kappa \in I_r$. Obviously, the actual register value (5) is approximated with $z_\kappa$ in (6), which gives a correct simulation of $A$ by $A'$ according to (2), as long as $h \le \kappa$ implying $z = z_\kappa$. Note that the register saturates properly at value $\sigma_L(z_\kappa) \in \{0, 1\}$ if $z_\kappa \le 0$ or $z_\kappa \ge 1$. Nevertheless, the correctness of the simulation must still be proven for $h > \kappa$, and henceforth assume $h > \kappa$. Condition (7) implies $\{z_\kappa, z\} \cap C = \emptyset$, and $\{z_\kappa, z\} \subseteq I(b_0, \ldots, b_\kappa)$. It follows from the definition of $\kappa$ that there is only one $r \in \{1, \ldots, p\}$ such that $I(b_0, \ldots, b_\kappa) \subset I_r$ while $I(b_0, \ldots, b_\kappa) \cap I_{r'} = \emptyset$ for the remaining $r' \neq r$, which gives $z_\kappa \in I_r$ iff $z \in I_r$ in this case.

Now consider the case when the arguments $b_0, \ldots, b_\kappa \in B$ do not satisfy condition (7), which means there exists a quasi-periodic series $\sum_{k=0}^{\infty} b_k' a^k = c_j \in C'$ with all $b_k' \in B$, maximum period $M \ge 1$, and period sum $P$ such that

$$b_k = b_k' \quad \text{for every } k = 0, \ldots, \kappa. \tag{8}$$

Let $0 \le k_1 < k_2 < k_3 < \cdots$ be the increasing infinite sequence of its term indices, which delimit the quasi-periods $m_i = k_{i+1} - k_i \le M$ with $P_i = P$ for $i \ge 1$, so that the shifts $b_0, \ldots, b_h \in B$ defining the register value (5) coincide with the coefficients of the series $\sum_{k=0}^{\infty} b_k' a^k = c_j \in C'$ up to the first $d$ quasi-repeating blocks for the maximum possible $d \ge 1$ over the permutations of these blocks, that is,

$$b_k = b_k' \quad \text{for every } k = 0, \ldots, k_{d+1} - 1, \tag{9}$$

where $\kappa \leq k_{d+1} - 1 \leq h$ according to (8). Recall that $c_j \in C'$ may serve as an endpoint of possibly three neighbor intervals $I_r$ including a degenerate one. According to (2), parameter $r$ in (6) can thus be chosen uniquely based on whether $z \varrho c_j$ for $\varrho \in \{<,=,>\}$. In particular, $z \varrho c_j$ rewrites to $z = (\sum_{k=0}^{k_1-1} b_k a^k + \sum_{i=1}^{d-1} a^{k_i} \sum_{k=0}^{m_i-1} b_{k_i+k} a^k + a^{k_d} \sum_{k=k_d}^{h} b_k a^{k-k_d}) \varrho c_j$ which reduces to $(a^{k_d} \sum_{k=k_d}^{h} b_k a^{k-k_d}) \varrho (a^{k_d} P)$ according to (9) and (4). Furthermore, we divide this inequality by $a^{k_d-k_1} \neq 0$ and add $\sum_{k=0}^{k_1-1} b_k a^k$ to both its sides, which yields

$$z' = \left( \sum_{k=0}^{k_1-1} b_k a^k + a^{k_1} \sum_{k=k_d}^{h} b_k a^{k-k_d} \right) \varrho' c_j \qquad (10)$$

where $\varrho' \in \{<,=,>\}$ differs from $\varrho \in \{<,>\}$ iff

$$a < 0 \quad \& \quad k_d - k_1 = \sum_{i=1}^{d-1} m_i \text{ is odd.} \qquad (11)$$

It follows that $z \varrho c_j$ can be replaced by $z' \varrho' c_j$ where $z'$ is determined by the history of shifts $b_0, \ldots, b_{k_1-1}, b_{k_d}, \ldots, b_{k_{d+1}}, \ldots, b_h$ according to (5) in which the terms $b_{k_1}, \ldots, b_{k_d-1}$ corresponding to the first $d-1$ quasi-repeating blocks of $\sum_{k=0}^{\infty} b'_k a^k = c_j$, are excluded.

By the definition of $\kappa'$, we know that $\kappa \geq \kappa' \geq k_1 + 2M - 1 \geq k_1 + m_d + m_{d+1} - 1 \geq k_1 + k_{d+2} - k_d - 1$ which gives $k_{d+2} - 1 \leq k_d + \kappa - k_1$. In addition, suppose that the history for $z'$ in (10) exceeds $\kappa + 1$ shifts (c.f. assumption $h > \kappa$ for $z$), that is, $k_1 + h - k_d > \kappa$ implying $h > k_d + \kappa - k_1$. This yields $z \neq c_j$ since otherwise $c_j$ could be expressed as a finite sum (5) with $h = k_{d+1} - 1$ producing a contradiction $\kappa' + 1 \leq \kappa + 1 < k_1 + k_{d+1} - k_d = k_1 + m_d \leq k_1 + M$. Hence, there is an index $k_{d+1} \leq k \leq k_{d+2} - 1$ such that $b_k \neq b'_k$ due to the maximality of $d$. By the definition of $\kappa$, condition $z \varrho c_j$ can further be reduced to

$$z'_\kappa = \left( \sum_{k=0}^{k_1-1} b_k a^k + a^{k_1} \sum_{k=k_d}^{k_d+\kappa-k_1} b_k a^{k-k_d} \right) \varrho' c_j \qquad (12)$$

which only includes the history of $\kappa + 1$ shifts from (10).

Based on the preceding analysis, we can now specify $\varrho'_1, \ldots, \varrho'_\gamma \in \{<,=,>\}$ in definition (6) of $\delta'$ which make the correct choice of parameter $r$ possible in the case of (8). According to (6), $\varrho_1, \ldots, \varrho_\gamma$ are set to default $=$ whenever the register value $z$ saturates at 0 or 1, including the initial state $q'_0$. The value of $\varrho_j$ for $1 \leq j \leq \gamma$ is then updated only if the arguments $b_0, \ldots, b_k \in B$ of $\delta'$ start with any quasi-repeating block $b'_{k_i}, \ldots, b'_{k_{i+1}-1}$ of a quasi-periodic series $\sum_{k=0}^{\infty} b'_k a^k = c_j \in C'$, which means $b_k = b'_{k_i+k}$ for every $k = 0, \ldots, m_i-1$ where $m_i = k_{i+1} - k_i$. Otherwise set $\varrho'_j = \varrho_j$. Moreover, the update of $\varrho_j$ depends on whether or not the block is followed by another quasi-repeating block of the series. If it is not the case, the value of $\varrho'_j$ is chosen to satisfy the inequality $(\sum_{k=0}^{k_1-1} b'_k a^k + a^{k_1} \sum_{k=0}^{\kappa} b_k a^k) \varrho'_j c_j$ anticipating (12) with $k_d = k_i$. If, on the other hand,

$b_0, \ldots, b_\kappa$ start with at least two quasi-repeating blocks of the series (i.e. $i < d$), then $\varrho'_j$ differs from $\varrho_j \in \{<, >\}$ iff $a > 0$ and $m_i$ is odd, complying with (11). It follows from (12) and (11) that inequality $z \, \varrho'_j \, c_j$ holds when the arguments $b_0, \ldots, b_\kappa$ meet (8), which automaton $A'$ exploits for deciding whether $z \in I_r$, particularly at the endpoint $c_j \in C'$ of interval $I_r$. This determines parameter $r$ in definition (6) for the case of (8) and completes the proof of the theorem.    □

## 5    Directions for Ongoing Research

In the effort to fill the gap in the analysis of computational power of neural nets between integer a rational weights we have investigated a hybrid model of a binary-state network with an extra analog unit. We have shown this model to be computationally equivalent to a finite automaton with a register. Our main result in Theorem 3 formulates a sufficient condition for a language accepted by this automaton to be regular. Our preliminary study leads to natural open problems for further research such as completing the statement in Theorem 3 for $|a| > 1$, finding a corresponding necessary condition for accepting regular languages, analyzing the algebraic properties of quasi-periodic power series, characterizing the full power of finite automata with register, e.g. by comparing them to finite automata with multiplication [10, 12] etc.

Even more important, our analysis of computational power of neural nets has revealed interesting connections with an active research on representations of numbers in non-integer bases (see [1, 2, 5, 7, 8, 15, 19, 20, 22, 23] including references there). In particular, a power series $\sum_{k=0}^{\infty} b_k a^k$ can be interpreted as a representation of a number from $[0, 1]$ in base $\beta = 1/a$ using the digits from a finite set $B$, which is called a $\beta$-*expansion* when $\beta > 1$ and $B = \{0, 1, \ldots, \lceil \beta \rceil - 1\}$ (usually starting from $k = 1$). Any number from $\left[0, \frac{\lceil \beta \rceil - 1}{\beta - 1}\right]$ has a $\beta$-expansion which need not be unique. Obviously, for any integer bases $\beta \geq 2$ when multiplier $a$ has the from $1/\beta$, the $\beta$-expansion of $c \in [0, 1]$ is eventually periodic iff $c$ is a rational number, which satisfies the assumption of Theorem 3. For simplicity, we further assume a binary set of digits $B = \{0, 1\}$ corresponding to $1 < \beta < 2$, that is, $\frac{1}{2} < a < 1$, although the analysis has partially been extended to sets of integer digits that can even be greater than $\lceil \beta \rceil - 1$ [15].

It has been shown [23] that for $\beta \in (1, \varphi)$ where $\varphi = (1 + \sqrt{5})/2$ is the golden ratio, which means for $0.618033 \ldots \leq a < 1$, any number from $[0, 1]$ has a continuum of distinct $\beta$-expansions including those not quasi-periodic, which breaks the assumption of Theorem 3. For $\beta \in (\varphi, q_c)$ where $q_c$ is the (transcendental) *Komornik-Loreti constant* (i.e. the unique solution of equation $\sum_{k=1}^{\infty} t_k q_c^{-k} = 1$ where $(t_k)_{k=1}^{\infty}$ is the *Thue-Morse sequence* in which $t_k \in \{0, 1\}$ is the parity of the number of 1's in the binary representation of $k$), that is, for $0.559524 \ldots < a < 0.618033 \ldots$, there are countably many numbers in $[0, 1]$ having eventually periodic unique $\beta$-expansions, which are candidate elements to $C$ in Theorem 3, while for $\beta \in (q_c, 2)$ corresponding to $\frac{1}{2} < a \leq 0.559524 \ldots$, the set of numbers from $[0, 1]$ having unique $\beta$-expansions has the cardinality of continuum and a positive Hausdorff dimension (although its Lebesgue measure remains zero) [7]. In addition, for $0 < a < \frac{1}{2}$ (i.e. $\beta > 2$ whereas $B = \{0, 1\}$), not every number from $[0, 1]$ has a $\beta$-expansion (in fact, the $\beta$-expansions create a Cantor-like set in this case), which can fulfill the assumption of Theorem 3 if the elements of $C$ do not have $\beta$-expansions.

Furthermore, for every $m \geq 2$, there exists $\beta_m \in [\varphi, 2)$ corresponding to $\frac{1}{2} < a_m < 0.618033\ldots$ such that there exists a number from $[0, 1]$ that has a periodic unique $\beta$-expansion of period $m$ if $a < a_m$, while there is no such a number for $a \geq a_m$ [2]. In addition, a so-called $greedy$ (resp. $lazy$) $\beta$-expansion has been considered which is lexicographically maximal (resp. minimal) for a given number. Denote by $\mathrm{Per}(\beta)$ a set of numbers having a quasi-periodic greedy $\beta$-expansions. If $\mathbb{I} \subseteq \mathrm{Per}(\beta)$, then $\beta$ is either a Pisot or a Salem number [22] where a $Pisot$ (resp. $Salem$) number is a real algebraic integer (a root of some monic polynomial with integer coefficients) greater than 1 such that all its Galois conjugates (other roots of such a unique monic polynomial with minimal degree) are in absolute value less than 1 (resp. less or equal to 1 and at least one equals 1). For any Pisot number $\beta$, it holds $\mathbb{I} \subseteq \mathrm{Per}(\beta)$, while for Salem numbers this implication is still open [8, 22]. It follows that for any non-integer rational $\beta$ (which is not a Pisot nor Salem number by the integral root theorem) corresponding to irreducible fraction $a = a_1/a_2$ where $a_1 \geq 2$ and $a_2$ are integers, there always exists a number from $\mathbb{I}$ whose (greedy) $\beta$-expansion is not quasi-periodic.

It appears that the computational power of neural nets with extra analog unit is strongly related to the results on $\beta$-expansions which still need to be elaborated and generalized, e.g. to arbitrary sets of digits $B$. This opens a wide field of interesting research problems which undoubtedly deserves a deeper study.

# References

1. Adamczewski, B., Frougny, C., Siegel, A., Steiner, W.: Rational numbers with purely periodic $\beta$-expansion. Bulletin of The London Mathematical Society 42(3), 538–552 (2010)
2. Allouche, J.P., Clarke, M., Sidorov, N.: Periodic unique beta-expansions: The Sharkovskiǐ ordering. Ergodic Theory and Dynamical Systems 29(4), 1055–1074 (2009)
3. Alon, N., Dewdney, A.K., Ott, T.J.: Efficient simulation of finite automata by neural nets. Journal of the ACM 38(2), 495–514 (1991)
4. Balcázar, J.L., Gavaldà, R., Siegelmann, H.T.: Computational power of neural networks: A characterization in terms of Kolmogorov complexity. IEEE Transactions on Information Theory 43(4), 1175–1183 (1997)
5. Chunarom, D., Laohakosol, V.: Expansions of real numbers in non-integer bases. Journal of the Korean Mathematical Society 47(4), 861–877 (2010)
6. Dassow, J., Mitrana, V.: Finite automata over free groups. International Journal of Algebra and Computation 10(6), 725–738 (2000)
7. Glendinning, P., Sidorov, N.: Unique representations of real numbers in non-integer bases. Mathematical Research Letters 8(4), 535–543 (2001)
8. Hare, K.G.: Beta-expansions of Pisot and Salem numbers. In: Proceedings of the Waterloo Workshop in Computer Algebra 2006: Latest Advances in Symbolic Algorithms, pp. 67–84. World Scientific (2007)

9. Horne, B.G., Hush, D.R.: Bounds on the complexity of recurrent neural network implementations of finite state machines. Neural Networks 9(2), 243–252 (1996)
10. Ibarra, O.H., Sahni, S., Kim, C.E.: Finite automata with multiplication. Theoretical Computer Science 2(3), 271–294 (1976)
11. Indyk, P.: Optimal simulation of automata by neural nets. In: Mayr, E.W., Puech, C. (eds.) STACS 1995. LNCS, vol. 900, pp. 337–348. Springer, Heidelberg (1995)
12. Kambites, M.E.: Formal languages and groups as memory. Communications in Algebra 37(1), 193–208 (2009)
13. Kilian, J., Siegelmann, H.T.: The dynamic universality of sigmoidal neural networks. Information and Computation 128(1), 48–56 (1996)
14. Koiran, P.: A family of universal recurrent networks. Theoretical Computer Science 168(2), 473–480 (1996)
15. Komornik, V., Loreti, P.: Subexpansions, superexpansions and uniqueness properties in non-integer bases. Periodica Mathematica Hungarica 44(2), 197–218 (2002)
16. Minsky, M.: Computations: Finite and Infinite Machines. Prentice-Hall, Englewood Cliffs (1967)
17. Mitrana, V., Stiebe, R.: Extended finite automata over groups. Discrete Applied Mathematics 108(3), 287–300 (2001)
18. Orponen, P.: Computing with truly asynchronous threshold logic networks. Theoretical Computer Science 174(1-2), 123–136 (1997)
19. Parry, W.: On the $\beta$-expansions of real numbers. Acta Mathematica Hungarica 11(3), 401–416 (1960)
20. Rényi, A.: Representations for real numbers and their ergodic properties. Acta Mathematica Academiae Scientiarum Hungaricae 8(3-4), 477–493 (1957)
21. Salehi, Ö., Yakaryılmaz, A., Say, A.C.C.: Real-time vector automata. In: Gąsieniec, L., Wolter, F. (eds.) FCT 2013. LNCS, vol. 8070, pp. 293–304. Springer, Heidelberg (2013)
22. Schmidt, K.: On periodic expansions of Pisot numbers and Salem numbers. Bulletin of the London Mathematical Society 12(4), 269–278 (1980)
23. Sidorov, N.: Expansions in non-integer bases: Lower, middle and top orders. Journal of Number Theory 129(4), 741–754 (2009)
24. Siegelmann, H.T.: Recurrent neural networks and finite automata. Journal of Computational Intelligence 12(4), 567–574 (1996)
25. Siegelmann, H.T.: Neural Networks and Analog Computation: Beyond the Turing Limit. Birkhäuser, Boston (1999)
26. Siegelmann, H.T., Sontag, E.D.: Analog computation via neural networks. Theoretical Computer Science 131(2), 331–360 (1994)
27. Siegelmann, H.T., Sontag, E.D.: On the computational power of neural nets. Journal of Computer System Science 50(1), 132–150 (1995)
28. Šíma, J.: Analog stable simulation of discrete neural networks. Neural Network World 7(6), 679–686 (1997)
29. Šíma, J.: Energy complexity of recurrent neural networks. Neural Computation 26(5), 953–973 (2014)
30. Šíma, J., Orponen, P.: General-purpose computation with neural networks: A survey of complexity theoretic results. Neural Computation 15(12), 2727–2778 (2003)
31. Šíma, J., Wiedermann, J.: Theory of neuromata. Journal of the ACM 45(1), 155–178 (1998)
32. Šorel, M., Šíma, J.: Robust RBF finite automata. Neurocomputing 62, 93–110 (2004)

# Model Predictive Control of Linear Parameter Varying Systems Based on a Recurrent Neural Network

Zheng Yan[1], Xinyi Le[2], and Jun Wang[2]

[1] Huawei Shannon Lab, Shenzhen, China
yanzheng@huawei.com
[2] Department of Mechanical and Automation Engineering,
The Chinese University of Hong Kong
Shatin, New Territories, Hong Kong
{xyle,jwang}@mae.cuhk.edu.hk

**Abstract.** This paper presents a model predictive control approach to discrete-time linear parameter varying systems based on a recurrent neural network. The model predictive control problem is formulated as a sequential convex optimization, and it is solved by using a recurrent neural network in real time. The essence of the proposed approach lies in its real-time computational capability with extended applicability. Simulation results are provided to substantiate the effectiveness of the proposed model predictive control approach.

**Keywords:** Recurrent neural network, model predictive control, linear parameter varying system.

## 1 Introduction

Linear parameter varying (LPV) systems constitute an important class of dynamical systems whose state space representations depend on time-varying, and often state-dependent, parameters [23]. LPV systems have attracted a lot of attention as they can capture the dynamic behaviors of many engineering problems in aeronautics, aerospace and mechanics [2, 16]. The LPV framework offers a middle ground between linear and nonlinear systems. Many nonlinear control systems can be synthesized in framework of LPV systems using linear control approaches with minor changes, such as the gain scheduling technique [22]. Due to the time-varying nature, it is desired to develop real time control methods for LPV systems to improve performances.

Model predictive control (MPC) is a popular model-based optimal control strategy that has achieved great successes in both academia and industries [17]. Unlike most control methods that compute off-line feedback laws, MPC iteratively predicts and optimizes system performances over a moving time window in real time. As such, optimal control signals are generated by solving a online sequential optimization problem. MPC has several attractive features for LPV

A.-H. Dediu et al. (Eds.): TPNC 2014, LNCS 8890, pp. 255–266, 2014.

systems such as its ability to deal with time-varying multivariable control problems, as well as its capability to take account of input and output constraints.

There are many results on MPC of LPV systems in the literature. For example, an MPC approach based on a convex optimization involving linear matrix inequalities was proposed where the LPV systems are treated as uncertain linear systems [10]. The MPC problem was formulated as a minimization of the upper bound of a finite horizon cost function based on relaxation matrices [11]. Bounds on the rate of variation of the time-varying parameters were taken into account in the MPC design and implementation [9]. An off-line MPC strategy was developed to reduce the online computational burden [3]. A parameter-dependent MPC approach was proposed by exploiting the time-varying parameters for feedback [28]. An MPC approach was developed based on nonlinearly parameterized Lyapunov functions [5]. However, these results share a common limitation: it was assumed that the time varying parameters varied inside a convex polytope with a finite number of vertices. This assumption can not be satisfied in many real-world applications such as flight control [16]. It is necessary and rewarding to further study MPC of LPV systems to extend the applicability.

Real-time optimization is a significant issue for MPC design and synthesis. Due to the large dimensions and stringent time requirement, numerical optimization methods may not be sufficiently efficient for solving MPC problems in real time. Neurodynamic optimization using recurrent neural networks (RNNs) emerged as a promising computational approach to real time optimization since middle 1980s. Neural networks are designed as goal-seeking computational models for optimization problems. The essence of neural optimization lies in its inherent nature of parallel and distributed information processing and the availability of hardware implementation. Various RNN models have been developed for constrained optimization, such as a one-layer neural network with a hard-limiting activation function [14], a neural network for nonlinear convex optimization with inequality constraints [24], an improved dual network [7], a finite-time convergent neural network [15], and neural networks for generalized convex optimization [6, 13, 12]. These RNNs have shown superior performance with guaranteed global convergence properties and low model complexity.

Some research on neural networks based MPC were carried out. The use of neural networks in MPC framework generally fall into three categories: (1) using neural networks for system identification [21, 8, 19], (2) using neural networks for real time optimization [4, 25–27], (3) using neural networks for off-line control law approximation [20, 1]. In these works, neural networks showed distinct advantages for MPC design.

In this paper, a recurrent neural network based MPC approach was proposed for LPV systems. The time varying parameters are explicitly taken into account for model prediction. The MPC problem is formulated as a convex optimization problem. A one-layer recurrent neural network model is applied for computing the optimal control input in real time. One major contribution of the proposed approach is that the conventional assumption on the topology of LPV systems is relaxed. Simulation results are included to demonstrate the characteristics of the proposed approach.

The rest of this paper is organized as follows: Section 2 discusses the problem formulation. Section 3 presents a neural network based MPC approach. Section 4 reports simulation results. Finally, Section 5 concludes this paper.

## 2   Problem Formulation

Consider a discrete LPV model as follows

$$x(k + 1) = A(\theta(k))x(k) + B(\theta(k))u(k), \tag{1}$$

where $x(k) \in \Re^n$ is the state vector, $u(k) \in \Re^m$ is the input vector, $\theta \in \Re^q$ is a vector of time-varying parameter, and $A(\theta(k))$ and $B(\theta(k))$ are matrices with compatible dimensions. The following assumptions hold throughout the discussion in this paper.

**Assumption 1.** $\theta(k)$ *is available at any time instant $k$.*

**Assumption 2.** $\theta(k + j)$ *can be determined by $x(k + i)$ and $u(k + i)$ for all $i \in \{0, 1, \ldots j\}$.*

It is worth pointing out that $\theta$ in (1) does not necessarily lie in a convex polytope. There may also be infinite many realizations of $\theta$ during the evolution of the system. There are many LPV systems fall into this category, such as LPV models obtained by state transformation where state coordinates are changed to remove nonlinearity in the dynamics.

MPC is an iterative optimization technique: at each sampling time $k$, the optimal control signals are obtained by solving a finite-horizon constrained optimization problem, using the current state as the initial state. The MPC problem for (1) is commonly formulated as:

$$\min_{u} \quad J(x, u) = \sum_{j=k}^{k+N-1} \ell(x(j) - r(j), u(j)) + F(x(N))$$

$$\text{s.t.} \quad x(j) \in \mathbb{X}, \ u(j) \in \mathbb{U}, \ j = k, \cdots, N - 1,$$

$$x(N) \in \mathbb{X}_f, \tag{2}$$

where $r(j)$ is a reference vector, $\ell(x, u)$ is a stage cost satisfying $\ell(0, 0) = 0$ and $\ell(x, u) > 0$ for all $(x, u) \neq 0$, $F(x(N))$ is a cost on the terminal state within the prediction horizon $N$, $\mathbb{X}$ and $\mathbb{U}$ are respectively state and input constraints, and $\mathbb{X}_f$ is a terminal constraint. The purpose for introducing $F$ and $\mathbb{X}_f$ is to ensure the closed-loop stability. The state and input constraints are commonly expressed as $\mathbb{X} = \{x | x_{\min} \leq x \leq x_{\max}\}$ and $\mathbb{U} = \{u | u_{\min} \leq u \leq u_{\max}\}$.

Denote $J(x, k, N)$ as the optimal value of the cost function in (2) at the time instant $k$, then using the optimal finite horizon cost as a Lyapunov function, a sufficient closed-loop stability condition can be obtained as following:

$$J(x, k, N) - J(x, k + 1, N) > 0, \forall x \neq 0. \tag{3}$$

The inequality (3) can be further rewritten as

$$J(x, k, N) - J(x, k+1, N) = \ell(x(k), u(k))$$
$$+ (J(x, k+1, N-1) - J(x, k+1, N)). \tag{4}$$

Define $\ell(x(k), u(k)) = x^T(k)Qx(k) + u^T(k)Ru(k)$ where $Q$ and $R$ are strict positive definite matrices, then the first term in (4) is positive. If $J(x, k+1, N-1) - J(x, k+1, N)$ is nonnegative, then the closed-loop system is asymptotically stable. Define the terminal cost in form of $F(x) = x^T Px$, a sufficient condition of ensuring the nonnegativity of $J(x, k+1, N-1) - J(x, k+1, N)$ can be obtained using the similar procedures in [29]:

$$Q + K^T RK + (A(\theta(k+N)) + B(\theta(k+N))K)^T P$$
$$\times (A(\theta(k+N)) + B(\theta(k+N))K) - P \le 0, \tag{5}$$

where $P$ is positive definite, $K$ is a feedback gain matrix such that the eigenvalues of $A(\theta(k+N)) + B(\theta(k+N))K$ lie within the unit ball. Note that the exact values of $A(\theta(k+N)) + B(\theta(k+N))$ cannot be precisely known at the current time instant $k$ as they are dependent on the value of $\theta(k+N)$ which is only measurable at the time instant $k+N$. A approximation strategy is proposed herein to remedy this problem. Under the MPC framework, a sequence of optimal control input $\bar{u}^*(k-1) = (u^*(k-1), u^*(k), \ldots, u^*(k+N-1))$ was obtained at the previous time instant $k-1$, but only $u^*(k-1)$ was applied as the actual control input. In addition, future states $x(k+j|k-1, j=1, \ldots, N$ can be predicted by by applying $\bar{u}^*(k-1)$. In view of the Assumption 2, the value of $\theta(k+j)$ can be numerically estimated based on $x(k+i|k-1)$ and $u^*(k+i)$ for all $i \in \{0, 1, \ldots j\}$. Denote $\theta(k+j|k)$ as the estimated value of $\theta$ at the future time instant $k+j$. The future states of the system (1) can be predicted as

$$x(k+1|k) = A(\theta(k))x(k) + B(\theta(k))u(k),$$
$$\vdots$$
$$x(k+j|k) = A(\theta(k+j-1|k))x(k+j-1|k)$$
$$+ B(\theta(k+j-1|k))u(k+j-1|k),$$
$$\vdots$$
$$x(k+N|k) = A(\theta(k+N-1|k))x(k+N-1|k)$$
$$+ B(\theta(k+N-1|k))u(k+N-1|k).$$

Therefore, the MPC problem (2) can be written as

$$\min_{u(k)} J(x(k), u(k)) = \sum_{j=1}^{N} \|r(k+j) - x(k+j|k)\|_Q^2$$

$$+ \sum_{j=0}^{N_u-1} \|\Delta u(k+j|k)\|_R^2 + x^T(k+N|k)Px(k+N|k)$$

$$\text{s.t. } \Delta u_{\min} \leq \Delta u(k+j|k) \leq \Delta u_{\max}, j = 0, 1, \ldots, N_u - 1,$$

$$u_{\min} \leq u(k+j|k) \leq u_{\max}, j = 0, 1, \ldots, N_u - 1,$$

$$x_{\min} \leq x(k+j|k) \leq x_{\max}, j = 1, 2, \ldots, N, \qquad (6)$$

where $\|\cdot\|$ denotes the Euclidean norm, Q and R are weight matrices with compatible dimensions, $\Delta u(k|) = u(k|k) - u(k-1|k)$, $N_u \leq N$ is a control horizon and it is assumed that $u(i|k) = u(N_u|k), \forall i = N_u + 1, \ldots, N - 1$.

Define the following vectors

$$\bar{x}(k) = [x(k+1|k) \ldots x(k+N|k)]^T \in \Re^{Nn},$$

$$\Delta \bar{u}(k) = [\Delta u(k|k) \ldots \Delta u(k+N_u-1|k)]^T \in \Re^{N_u m},$$

$$\bar{u}(k) = [u(k|k) \ldots u(k+N_u-1|k)]^T \in \Re^{N_u m},$$

$$\bar{r}(k) = [r(k+1|k) \ldots r(k+N|k)]^T \in \Re^{Np},$$

where $\bar{r}(k)$ is known in advance. For the sake of brevity, denote $\mathcal{A}_j = A(\theta(k+j|k))$, $\mathcal{B}_j = B(\theta(k+j|k))$ $j = 1, \cdots, N$. The predicted state vector $\bar{x}(k)$ can be expressed as follows

$$\bar{x}(k) = Sx(k) + Vu(k-1) + M\Delta\bar{u}(k), \qquad (7)$$

where

$$S = \begin{bmatrix} \mathcal{A}_1 \\ \mathcal{A}_2\mathcal{A}_1 \\ \vdots \\ \mathcal{A}_N \cdots \mathcal{A}_1 \end{bmatrix} \in \Re^{Np \times n},$$

$$V = \begin{bmatrix} \mathcal{B}_1 \\ \mathcal{B}_2 + \mathcal{A}_2\mathcal{B}_1 \\ \vdots \\ \mathcal{B}_N + \mathcal{A}_N\mathcal{B}_{N-1} + \ldots + \Pi_{i=2}^{N}\mathcal{A}_i\mathcal{B}_1 \end{bmatrix} \in \Re^{Np \times m},$$

$$M = \begin{bmatrix} \mathcal{B}_1 & \cdots & 0 \\ \mathcal{B}_2 + \mathcal{A}_2\mathcal{B}_1 & \cdots & 0 \\ \vdots & \ddots & \vdots \\ \mathcal{B}_N + \ldots + \Pi_{i=2}^{N}\mathcal{A}_i\mathcal{B}_1 & \ldots & \mathcal{B}_N + \ldots + \Pi_{i=N_u+1}^{N}\mathcal{A}_i\mathcal{B}_{N_u} \end{bmatrix} \in \Re^{Np \times N_u m}.$$

The terminal state within the prediction horizon $N$ can be expressed as

$$x(k+N|k) = \tilde{S}x(k) + \tilde{V}u(k-1) + \tilde{M}\Delta\bar{u}(k), \qquad (8)$$

where $\tilde{S}$, $\tilde{V}$, and $\tilde{M}$ are the last rows of $S$, $V$, and $M$, respectively. Therefore, the MPC of the LPV system (1) can be obtained by solving the following constrained optimization problem:

$$\min_{\Delta\bar{u}(k)} \ \|Sx(k) + Vs(k-1) + M\Delta\bar{x}(k)\|_Q^2 + \|\Delta\bar{u}(k)\|_R^2$$

$$+ \left\|\tilde{S}x(k) + \tilde{V}u(k-1) + \tilde{M}\Delta\bar{u}(k)\right\|_P^2,$$

$$\text{s.t.} \ \Delta\bar{u}_{\min} \leq \Delta\bar{u}(k) \leq \Delta\bar{u}_{\max},$$

$$\bar{u}_{\min} \leq \bar{u}(k-1) + \tilde{I}\Delta\bar{u}(k) \leq \Delta\bar{u}_{\max}$$

$$\bar{x}_{\min} \leq Sx(k) + Vu(k-1) + M\Delta\bar{u}(k)\bar{x}_{\max}, \tag{9}$$

where

$$\tilde{I} = \begin{bmatrix} I & 0 & \dots & 0 \\ I & I & \dots & 0 \\ \vdots & \vdots & \ddots & \vdots \\ I & I & \dots & I \end{bmatrix} \in \Re^{N_u m \times N_u m},$$

and $P$ can be obtained by solving the inequality

$$Q + K^T R K + (\mathcal{A}_N) + \mathcal{B}_N K)^T P(\mathcal{A}_N + \mathcal{B}_N K) - P \leq 0, \tag{10}$$

Up to this point, letting $\Delta\bar{u} = \Delta\bar{u}(k) \in \Re^{N_u m}$ for brevity, problem (9) can be put in a compact form as follows

$$\min \ \frac{1}{2}\Delta\bar{u}^T W \Delta\bar{u} + p^T \Delta\bar{u},$$

$$\text{s.t.} \ \Delta\bar{u}_{\min} \leq \Delta\bar{u} \leq \Delta\bar{u}_{\max},$$

$$E\Delta\bar{u} \leq b, \tag{11}$$

where

$$W = 2(M^T Q M + \tilde{M}^T P \tilde{M} + R) \in \Re^{N_u m \times N_u m},$$

$$p = 2M^T Q(Sx(k) + Vu(k-1))$$

$$+ 2\tilde{M}^T P(\tilde{S}x(k) + \tilde{V}u(k-1) \in \Re^{N_u m},$$

$$E = \begin{bmatrix} -\tilde{I} & \tilde{I} & -M & M \end{bmatrix}^T \in \Re^{(2N_u m + 2Nn) \times N_u m},$$

$$b = \begin{bmatrix} -\bar{u}_{\min} + \bar{u}(k-1) \\ \bar{u}_{\max} - \bar{u}(k-1) \\ -\bar{x}_{\min} + Sx(k) + Vu(k-1) \\ \bar{x}_{\max} - Sx(k) - Vu(k-1) \end{bmatrix} \in \Re^{2N_u m + 2Nn}.$$

As $Q$ and $R$ are chosen to be positive definite, $W$ is also positive definite. So the objective function in (11) is strictly convex. As $P$ is positive semi-definite, the feasible region defined by the constraints is convex. The problem (11) is shown to be a convex optimization problem, and the solution to (11) is unique and satisfies the Karush-Kauhn-Tucker (KKT) optimality conditions. The solution to (11) gives optimal control increment vector $\Delta\bar{u}$ which can be used to compute the optimal control vector $u^*(k)$.

## 3     A One-Layer Recurrent Neural Network

A one-layer recurrent neural network was developed based on the penalty function method in [12]. It is proved that the neural network can converge to the feasible region in finite time and can be globally convergent to the unique optimal solution of the problem (11). The neural network is applied for solving (11) to generate the optimal control incremental vector in real time.

Rewrite (11) in a general form:

$$\min \quad J(\Delta\bar{u}) = \frac{1}{2}\Delta\bar{u}^T W \Delta\bar{u} + p^T \Delta\bar{u},$$
$$\text{s.t.} \quad g(\Delta\bar{u}) \leq 0, \tag{12}$$

where

$$g(\Delta\bar{u}) = [g_1(\Delta\bar{u}), \ g_2(\Delta\bar{u}), \ g_3(\Delta\bar{u})]^T$$
$$= \begin{bmatrix} \Delta\bar{u} - \bar{u}_{\max} \\ -\Delta\bar{u} + \bar{u}_{\min} \\ E\Delta\bar{u} - b \end{bmatrix}$$

The dynamical equation of the neural network for solving (12) is described as follows

$$\frac{d}{dt}\Delta\bar{u} \in -\nabla J(\Delta\bar{u}) - \lambda\partial g^+(\Delta\bar{u}) \tag{13}$$

where $\nabla J = W\Delta\bar{u} + p$, which denotes the gradient of $J$, $\partial g^+$ denotes the generalized gradient of $g^+$, $g^+ = \sum_{i=1}^{3} \max(g_i(\Delta\bar{u}), 0)$, and $\lambda$ is a positive penalty parameter.

As shown in [12], the neural network (13) with any initial condition is guaranteed to be be convergent to the feasible region defined by $g(\Delta\bar{u}) \leq 0$ in finite time and stays there thereafter if $\lambda$ is sufficiently large. Moreover, the state of (13) converges to the unique optimal solution of (11) with initial condition. The estimation method for the lower bound of $\lambda$ is presented in [12].

The MPC approach to discrete-time LPV systems based on the one-layer neural network is summarized as follows:

1. Let $k = 1$. Set control time terminal $T$, prediction horizon $N$, control horizon $N_u$, and weighting matices $Q$ and $R$.
2. Compute the prediction model (7) based on the prediction of $\theta$.
3. Compute $P$ in view of (10).
4. Compute neural network matrices $\nabla J(\bar{u})$, $g(\bar{u})$, and $\partial g^+(\bar{u})$.
5. Solve the convex optimization problem (11) by using neural network (13) to obtain the optimal control input $u^*(k)$.
6. If $k < T$, set $k = k + 1$, go to Step 2; otherwise end.

## 4  Simulation Results

In this section, simulation results on two LPV systems are provided to substantiate the effectiveness of the proposed neural network based MPC approach.

*Example 1:* Consider a discrete-time two-mass-spring system which has many industrial applications such as flexible robot arms [30]:

$$
\begin{aligned}
x_1(k+1) =& x_1(k) + 0.1x_3(k), \\
x_2(k+1) =& x_2(k) + 0.1x_4(k), \\
x_3(k+1) =& -(0.05 + 5(x_2(k) - x_1(k))^2)x_1(k) \\
& + (0.05 + 5(x_2(k) - x_1(k))^2)x_2(k) + 0.1u(k), \\
x_4(k+1) =& (0.05 + 5(x_2(k) - x_1(k))^2)x_1(k) \\
& - (0.05 + 5(x_2(k) - x_1(k))^2)x_2(k),
\end{aligned}
\tag{14}
$$

where $x_1$ and $x_2$ are the positions of the two masses, $x_3$ and $x_4$ are the velocities, and $u$ is the control input. The system is subject to input constraint $|u| \leq 1$. The control objective is to steer all states to the origin from an initial state. Let $\theta(k) = 0.5 + 50(x_2(k) - x_1(k))^2$, an LPV model can be obtained for the nonlinear model (8).

$$
x(k+1) = A(\theta(k))x(k) + Bu(k),
\tag{15}
$$

where

$$
A(\theta(k)) =
\begin{bmatrix}
1 & 0 & 0.1 & 0 \\
0 & 1 & 0 & 0.1 \\
-0.1\theta(k) & 0.1\theta(k) & 1 & 0 \\
0.1\theta(k) & -0.1\theta(k) & 0 & 1
\end{bmatrix}, B = [0\ 0\ 0.1\ 0]^T.
\tag{16}
$$

The MPC of (15) is formulated in the form of (11) where $N = 25$, $N_u = 20$, $Q = I$, and $R = I$. $P$ is calculated as

$$
P =
\begin{bmatrix}
0.33 & * & * & * \\
0.09 & 0.70 & * & * \\
-0.06 & 0.20 & 0.25 & * \\
-0.19 & -0.06 & -0.11 & 0.31
\end{bmatrix}.
$$

Due to the parametric uncertainty, the nominal value of $\theta$ is assumed to be $\tilde{\theta}(k) = 0.45 + 55(x_2(k) - x_1(k))^2$. The initial state is $x(0) = [1\ 1\ 0\ 0]^T$ and the initial input is $u(0) = 0$. The optimization problem is repeatedly solved by using the neural network (13). To show the computational efficiency, the convergence of the neural network within the first sampling interval depicted in Fig. 1. The controlled state trajectories are depicted in Figs. 2-3, the control inputs are shown in Fig. 4. To compare the effectiveness of the proposed RNN based MPC approach, the LQR method is also applied for stabilizing (14). The input constraint is not always satisfied by using the LQR method (see Fig. 4). The proposed approach results in much better control performance.

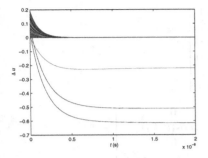

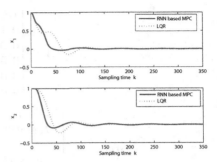

**Fig. 1.** RNN convergence during the first sampling interval in Example 1

**Fig. 2.** Positions in Example 1

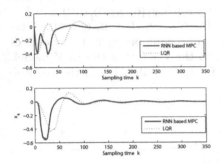

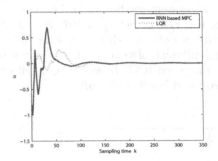

**Fig. 3.** Velocities in Example 1

**Fig. 4.** Control inputs in Example 1

*Example 2:* Consider a discrete-time model of a vertical takeoff and landing aircraft [18]:

$$x_1(k+1) = x_1(k) + t_s x_2(k)$$
$$x_2(k+1) = x_2(k) + t_s(-\sin(\alpha(k))u_1(k) + \cos(\alpha(k)u_2(k))$$
$$y_1(k+1) = y_1(k) + t_s y_2(k)$$
$$y_2(k+1) = y_2(k) + t_s(\cos(\alpha(k))u_1(k) + \sin(\alpha(k)u_2(k)) - g$$
$$\alpha(k+1) = \alpha(k) + t_s \omega(k)$$
$$\omega(k+1) = \omega(k) + t_s u_2(k)$$

where $x_1$ and $y_1$ are positions, $x_2$ and $y_2$ are velocities, $\alpha$ is the angle, $\omega$ is the the angular velocity, and $t_s$ the sampling period. This model can be equivalent put into an LPV form with

$$A = \begin{bmatrix} 1 & t_s & 0 & 0 & 0 & 0 \\ 0 & 1 & 0 & 0 & 0 & 0 \\ 0 & 0 & 1 & t_s & 0 & 0 \\ 0 & 0 & 0 & 1 & 0 & 0 \\ 0 & 0 & 0 & 0 & 1 & t_s \\ 0 & 0 & 0 & 0 & 0 & 1 \end{bmatrix}$$

$$B(\theta(k)) = \begin{bmatrix} 0 & 0 \\ -t_s \sin(\theta(k)) & t_s \cos(\theta(k)) \\ 0 & 0 \\ t_s \cos(\theta(k)) & t_s \sin(\theta(k)) - g/u_2 \\ 0 & 0 \\ 0 & t_s \end{bmatrix}$$

where $\theta(k) = \alpha(k)$. The constraint is $u_2 \geq 1$. The control objective is to stabilize the system to the origin. Let $x(0) = [x_1(0), x_2(0), y_1(0), y_2(0), \alpha(0), \omega(0)] = [2, 3, 4, 1, \pi/3, 1]$. Set $Q = 10I$, $R = I$, $N = 15$, $N_u = 5$, $P = 0$, $t_s = 0.1$. The control results are shown in Figs. 5-6. The constraint on $u_2$ is not violated. The fulfilment of this constraint is essential to the validity of the LPV model. The proposed RNN based MPC is effective for the stabilization of the vertical takeoff and landing aircraft.

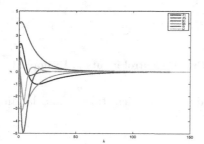

**Fig. 5.** State variables in Example 2

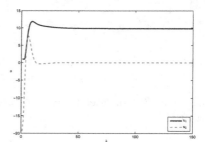

**Fig. 6.** Control inputs in Example 2

## 5 Conclusions

In this paper, a model predictive control approach is presented for a class of linear parameter varying systems based on a one-layer recurrent neural network. The time-varying parameter is estimated online and is explicitly exploited for system prediction. The model predictive control problem is formulated as a sequential convex optimization. A globally convergent neural network designed using the penalty function method is applied for solving the optimization problem in real-time. The effectiveness of the proposed approach is demonstrated by simulation results on linear parameter varying models.

**Acknowledgments.** The work described in the paper was supported by the Research Grants Council of the Hong Kong Special Administrative Region, China under Grants CUHK416812E.

# References

1. Akesson, B., Toivonen, H.: A neural network predictive controller. J. Process Contr. 16, 937–946 (2006)
2. Bamieh, B., Giarre, L.: Identification of linear parameter varying models. Int. J. Robust Nonlinear Control 12, 841–853 (2002)
3. Bumroongsri, P., Kheawhom, S.: An ellipsoidal off-line model predictive control strategy for linear parameter varying systems with applications in chemical processes. Systems & Control Letters 61, 435–442 (2012)
4. Cheng, L., Hou, Z., Tan, M.: Constrained multi-variable generalized predictive control using a dual neural network. Neural Comput. Appl. 16, 505–512 (2007)
5. Garone, E., Casavola, A.: Receding horizon control strategies for constrained lPV systems based on a class of nonlinearly parameterized Lyapunov functions. IEEE Trans. on Automatic Control 57, 2354–2360 (2012)
6. Guo, Z., Liu, Q., Wang, J.: A one-layer recurrent neural network for pseudoconvex optimization subject to linear equality constraints. IEEE Tran. Neural Networks 22, 1892–1900 (2011)
7. Hu, X., Wang, J.: An improved dual neural network for solving a class of quadratic programming problems and its k-winners-take-all application. IEEE Tran. Neural Networks 19, 2022–2031 (2008)
8. Huang, J., Lewis, F.: Neural network predictive control for nonlinear dynamic systems with time-delay. IEEE Tran. Neural Netw. 14, 377–389 (2003)
9. Jungers, M., Oliveira, R.C., Peres, P.L.: MPC for LPV systems with bounded parameter variations. International Journal of Control 84, 24–36 (2011)
10. Kothare, M.V., Balakrishnan, V., Morari, M.: Robust constrained model predictive control using linear matrix inequalities. Automatica 32, 1361–1379 (1996)
11. Lee, S.M., Park, J.H., Ji, D.H., Won, S.C.: Robust model predictive control for LPV systems using relaxation matrices. IET Control Theory & Applications 1, 1567–1573 (2007)
12. Li, G., Yan, Z., Wang, J.: A one-layer recurrent neural network for constrained nonsmooth invex optimization. Neural Networks 50, 79–89 (2014)
13. Liu, Q., Guo, Z., Wang, J.: A one-layer recurrent neural network for constrained pseudoconvex optimization and its application for dynamic portfolio optimization. Neural Networks 26, 99–109 (2012)
14. Liu, Q., Wang, J.: A one-layer recurrent neural network with a discontinuous hard-limiting activation function for quadratic programming. IEEE Tran. Neural Networks 19, 558–570 (2008)
15. Liu, Q., Wang, J.: Finite-time convergent current neural network with hard-limiting activation function for constrained optimization with piecewise-linear objective functions. IEEE Tran. Neural Networks 22, 601–613 (2011)
16. Marcos, A., Balas, G.J.: Development of linear-parameter-varying models for aircraf. Journal of Guidance, Control, and Dynamics 27, 218–228 (2004)
17. Mayne, D., Rawlings, J., Rao, C., Scokaert, P.: Constrained model predictive control: stability and optimality. Automatica 36, 789–814 (2000)

18. Olfati-Saber, R.: Global configuration stabilization for the vtol aircraft with strong input coupling. IEEE Trans. Automatica Control 47, 1949–1952 (2002)
19. Pan, Y., Wang, J.: Model predictive control of unknown nonlinear dynamical systems based on recurrent neural networks. IEEE Trans. Ind. Electron. 59, 3089–3101 (2012)
20. Parisini, T., Zoppoli, R.: A receding-horizon regulator for nonlinear systems and a neural approximation. Automatica 31, 1443–1451 (1995)
21. Piche, S., Rodsari, B., Johnson, D., Gerules, M.: Nonlinear model predictive control using neural networks. IEEE Control Syst. Mag. 20, 53–62 (2002)
22. Rugh, W., Shamma, J.: Research on gain scheduling. Automatica 36, 1401–1425 (2000)
23. Shamma, J.S., Athans, M.: Guaranteed properties of gain scheduled control for linear parameter-varying plants. Automatica 27, 559–564 (1991)
24. Xia, Y., Feng, G., Wang, J.: A novel neural network for solving nonlinear optimization problems with inequality constraints. IEEE Tran. Neural Networks 19, 1340–1353 (2008)
25. Yan, Z., Wang, J.: Model predictive control of nonlinear systems with unmodeled dynamics based on feedforward and recurrent neural networks. IEEE Trans. Ind. Informat. 8, 746–756 (2012)
26. Yan, Z., Wang, J.: Model predictive control of tracking of underactuated vessels based on recurrent neural networks. IEEE J. Ocean. Eng. 37, 717–726 (2012)
27. Yan, Z., Wang, J.: Robust model predictive control of nonlinear systems with unmodeled dynamics and bounded uncertainties based on neural networks. IEEE Tran. Neural Netw. 25, 457–469 (2014)
28. Yu, S., Böhm, C., Chen, H., Allgöwer, F.: Model predictive control of constrained lpv systems. International Journal of Control 85(6), 671–683 (2012)
29. Yu, Y., Arkun, Y.: Quasi-min-max MPC algorithms for LPV systems. Automatica 36, 527–540 (2000)
30. Zhang, L., Wang, C., Chen, L.: Stability and stabilization of a class of multimode linear discrete systems with polytopic uncertainties. IEEE Trans. Ind. Electron. 56, 3684–3692 (2009)

# Author Index